The *What PC?* Guide to your PC

ROB YOUNG

PRENTICE HALL
London New York Toronto Sydney Tokyo
Singapore Madrid Mexico City Munich Paris

First published 1990 by
Prentice Hall International
Campus 400, Maylands Avenue
Hemel Hempstead
Hertfordshire, HP2 7EZ
A division of
Simon & Schuster International Group

Typeset in $9\frac{1}{2}/12$ Bookman Light
by PPS, London Road, Amesbury, Wiltshire

Printed and bound in Great Britain by
T.J. International Ltd, Padstow, Cornwall

Library of Congress Cataloging-in-Publication Data

Young, Rob.
PCs in pieces / Rob Young.
p. cm.
Includes index.
1. Microcomputers—Popular works. 2. Internet (Computer network)—
—Popular works. I. Title.
TK7885.4.Y68 1996 96–48476
004.16—dc21 CIP

British Library Cataloguing in Publication Data

A catalogue record for this book is available from
the British Library

ISBN 0–13–617952–5

1 2 3 4 5 01 00 99 98 97

Trademarks

Contents

Chapter 5 Working with files 113

About this book

Welcome to *The What PC? Guide to your PC*, the all-in-one answer to all your PC questions!

Many people are having to deal with PCs from a standing start. Perhaps you've suddenly found yourself grappling with a PC at work, or your kids are using PCs at school and blinding you with technical gibberish. Maybe you want to work faster, organize your business or connect to the Internet.

In *The What PC? Guide to your PC* you'll find clear explanations and advice to help you decide what you need, buy with confidence, and start getting results from your PC. But instead of just leaving you to muddle through alone, *The What PC? Guide to your PC* will help you graduate from 'nervous novice' status by acting as a comprehensive reference whenever you want to buy new hardware and software, solve a problem, or become more expert at using Windows and MS-DOS.

How to use this book

Although you *can* read this book from cover to cover you probably won't want to, or indeed need to. For this reason, *The What PC? Guide to your PC* makes it easy to casually 'dip in' and find what you need, whether you're buying, learning, troubleshooting or looking for a few practical tips. You can use the contents pages or the index to locate what you need, or just flick through until you see something you'd like to know more about. Here's a thumbnail description of what you'll find in each chapter:

- **Chapter 1** looks at the PC itself, together with all its internal bits and pieces such as memory, disks and processor. What are they? What do they do to each other when they get together? What should you have in *your PC?*
- **Chapter 2** focuses on the external parts of a PC – mouse, monitor, keyboard – and other things you might want to add such as a printer, a modem or a soundcard. It tells you all you need to know about choosing these gadgets, connecting them to your computer and getting them working.
- **Chapter 3** gives tips on choosing the right PC for your needs, points to check before buying, and advice on making the purchase and setting up the computer.
- **Chapter 4** covers the basics of using a PC with Windows 3.1, Windows 3.11 or Windows 95: what you see on the screen, what it means and how you use it to do something useful.
- **Chapter 5** gives you all the details you'll need to work with files and folders (or directories) in Windows. Learn how to how to open, save, edit and print files, switch between programs, work with fonts and OLE, and understand file names, attributes and associations.
- **Chapter 6** examines the types of program you can use on your PC to accomplish different tasks, and the most popular titles in each category. With plenty of tips and clear advice on what to buy, you'll learn how to install and un-install software and start getting results from the applications you choose.
- **Chapter 7** takes a close look at the Internet and gives easy steps to getting connected in Windows 3.1 and Windows 95. Find out what software you need and where to get it, and learn how to send and receive e-mail, download files and browse the World Wide Web.
- **Chapter 8** delves into the world of MS-DOS. For anyone using Windows 3.1, 3.11 or 95 there are times when a little knowledge of MS-DOS is useful. But learning about DOS is pretty dull – it's far better to have a reference to dip into when you need it!
- **Chapter 9** provides a useful resource for all Windows 3.1 and 3.11 users. All the essential details are here, with plenty of tips to make it easier, faster or more fun.
- **Chapter 10** is the indispensable Windows 95 reference – another tip-filled chapter to help you master the day-to-day use of Windows 95 and get everything working the way you want it.

Finding the bottom line

If you're planning to buy a PC you'll find all the explanations you need to decipher the jargon used in computer advertisements. If you want to buy hardware or software for your PC you can find out what your options are, weigh up the pros and cons of different types of product and learn how they're used. All the detail you want is here!

Of course, you don't always want to read detailed explanations, so each chapter is split into sections, with each section further split into headings. If you come to a heading that looks a bit dull or unnecessarily technical, skip it! And if you want to cut to the chase, you'll find a *Buyers' Guide* at the end of many sections summarizing the features to look for (or avoid!) in a particular type of hardware or software, together with details of some of the most popular products.

Making contact

Most of the companies referred to in this book have their own sites on the Internet's World Wide Web. To find out more about the products mentioned (and even download copies of some of the software) point your browser at the addresses given on pp. 244–246. The UK edition of *The What PC? Guide to your PC* also includes an extensive directory of software and hardware companies, services, computer retailers and Internet Access Providers to bring all the information you'll ever need within easy reach.

Introduction

Consider the VCR. The Video Cassette Recorder was *the* gadget of the 1980s. Resistance was useless: sooner or later you just had to have one. And so began the ritual 'new toy' combination of button-pushing and swearing. In desperation, perhaps, you read the manual. Eventually you admitted defeat, and asked the nearest 8 year old for a clue. Within a week, you'd probably achieved the ultimate goal of taping the programme you hoped you were taping, and the rest was history.

The VCR is a type of computer. But, with apologies to anyone still struggling to use theirs, it's a pretty basic one – it handles just one task after all – so choosing a VCR is a relatively simple process of weighing up price, ease-of-use and appearance. There's no jargon involved, no add-on bits and pieces to buy, no need to read books about it before buying.

Choosing a PC is a whole different ball-game. The PC is capable of handling a vast number of tasks, but this capability isn't actually *built into* the machine. What your computer can do depends almost entirely on your choice of hardware and software, and each separate element comes complete with its own set of jargon and techno-speak. To make matters more confusing still, the computer is one of the few items you buy inside-out! All the internal organs of a computer are proudly listed in its advertisements to let you poke around and decide what you want in yours.

The important point to understand is that this is *good*! Although a little daunting at first, it's all this choice that makes the PC so much more versatile than the VCR. And it's the reason why the PC is able to earn its keep in almost any environment: multinational company, school, small business, child's bedroom, film or music studio.

At this stage, of course, the 'daunting' aspect is going to win every time, but don't be put off by all the acronyms, abbreviations and technical twaddle in the early sections of the book. You don't *have* to know how it all works to buy it or use it, and you certainly don't have to memorize it all!

Get in touch – we'd like to hear from you!

Your opinion counts

If you have any comments about this book – positive or negative, long or short – please send them in. We want to refine our books according to the needs of our readers, so do tell us if there is something that you would like to see in future editions of this book. Your input could well appear in print! We genuinely appreciate it when people take the time to contact us, so every month we give away a free Prentice Hall computer book for the most helpful and comprehensive comments.

Please feel free to email me personally with your comments:

feedback@prenhall.co.uk

Or you can write to me:

Jason Dunne
Prentice Hall
Campus 400
Maylands Avenue
Hemel Hempstead
Herts.
HP2 7EZ
United Kingdom

Please note that Prentice Hall cannot serve as a technical resource for questions about hardware or software problems.

We would also love to hear your ideas for new books, whether it is just for a book that you want to see in print or one you intend writing yourself. Our guide for new authors can be found in the back of this book.

Thanks for choosing Prentice Hall.

Jason Dunne
Acquisition Editor, Prentice Hall
jdunne@prenhall.co.uk

CHAPTER 1

Inside the PC

What is a PC?

What is a computer?

In its most basic terms, the computer is a device that accepts some form of input (you punch in a number, for example), processes it in some way (adds it to a number you'd punched in previously) and produces an output or result (gives you the answer to its piece of addition).

Obviously we're talking calculators here. The pocket calculator is a non-technical, non-frightening example, but it has all the basic attributes of the modern computer: it has buttons for input, a processor to do the calculations, a small amount of memory to let it remember one number while dealing with another, and a screen to display its output. The major difference is that the calculator knows only one trick, and it isn't likely to learn any new ones. In fact, the very first home computers way back in the mid-1970s were little more than glorified adding machines, but they had one extra vital ingredient: ambition!

JARGONBUSTER

Hardware

Hardware is a blanket term that describes all the electronic components of a computer: a piece of hardware could be anything from a mains plug to a monitor. Think of it this way: would it break if you dropped it from the top of a building? If it would, it's hardware. However, most computer stores would prefer you just to ask.

The Personal Computer

PC is simply an abbreviation of Personal Computer. This general term could be applied to any moderately small computer containing all the hardware and software it needs to 'compute' by itself. The idea behind a computer being 'personal' is that it should be cheap enough that each user should be able to have his or her own machine rather than sharing it with the entire office, and small enough that it fits on a desktop or sits on your lap.

JARGONBUSTER

Software

The general term that describes a coputer program (or a set of computer programs) that tells the computer to carry out particular processes according to the input you provide. Common software you're likely to need would be a word-processing program (to write letters and reports) and a spreadsheet program (to manipulate lists of numbers and keep track of accounts).

This general definition could encompass a vast range of computers and manufacturers including Apple Macintosh, Atari, Amiga and Acorn. In recent years however, the term has taken on a new *generic* meaning and now refers specifically to a computer that is **IBM Personal Computer** compatible.

Cloning around

The IBM Personal Computer arrived on the scene in 1981 as a groundbreaking product, but IBM were slow to appreciate just how popular a small, reasonably affordable computer would be. By the time they spotted its true potential, other companies had spotted it too and had begun making products similar enough to do the same job (known as **clones**), and making them better and cheaper than IBM. Seen as a business opportunity too good to miss, the market was soon filled with manufacturers producing better, cheaper, smaller computers based on IBM's original design, and the PC-compatible became the industry standard. The irony of the situation is that although IBM-PC compatibility is vital to the product we buy today, only a tiny proportion of these are actually *made* by IBM!

Enter Microsoft

The other vital aspect of the PC is its operating system. The original IBM-PC came with a Microsoft-produced operating system that IBM chose to call **PC-DOS**. (Like most computing acronyms, DOS is just as unexciting, standing for Disk Operating System.) Although the IBM-PC and PC-DOS got rather left behind, Microsoft had supplied the operating system under licence and were still free to supply it to all the clone manufacturers using their own name for it, *MS-DOS*. (Microsoft Disk Operating System. You probably guessed.) For a software program to be used on any of these PC clones, therefore, it had to be MS-DOS compatible. The end result of all this has been a lasting and a neatly circular one: PC manufacturers included MS-DOS for its widely-available software; software producers made their programs MS-DOS compatible for highest potential sales; Microsoft collected a steady income from licensing MS-DOS, enabling them to consolidate their position in both the operating system and software markets.

JARGONBUSTER

Operating system

An essential group of programs that the computer loads into its memory when you first switch it on. The operating system acts as a 'friendly face' of the computer to let you communicate with it easily and intuitively. It's also fundamental in controlling how the computer works behind the scenes. The term 'operating system' is often abbreviated to just 'OS'.

What's in the box?

As we said earlier, we buy PCs in pieces: *It's got to have one of these, and one of those, and I want a built-in thingummy and a couple of wossnames.* Nevertheless, any self-respecting computer store will put all this together for you, check that it works, and present you with a large cardboard box. Apart from a year's supply of polystyrene, what will that box contain?

There are five basic elements to a computer. These will vary in description depending on your choice of **Desktop** or **Notebook** machine (covered on the next few pages), and each element will be explained in greater detail later on, but here's a thumbnail view:

- *System unit.* This is the largest component, a case which houses the computer itself. In here, should you choose to look, you'll find the **motherboard**: this is a large circuit board containing the processor, memory chips and expansion slots. In the drive bays towards the front of the unit you should spot a **hard-disk drive** and a **floppy-disk drive**. Looking at the outside of the unit, the floppy-disk drive is a little more obvious, having a slot to insert the disk and a light to indicate when the drive is busy. You should also find a power switch, a reset switch and varying numbers of coloured lights (some manufacturers seem to be frustrated disc jockeys!). We'll be looking more closely at the contents of the system unit in the next few sections.

JARGONBUSTER

Drive bays

A drive bay is a slot in the front of the system unit where more disk drives can be installed. Drive bays are of two different sizes, 5.25 inch and 3.5 inch, to accept different-sized drives. CD-ROM drives are 5.25 inches wide, floppy-disk and tape drives are usually 3.5 inches. Most new PCs will offer *at least* three bays, one of which will already have a floppy-disk drive fitted.

- *Monitor.* The large item that looks a lot like a TV screen. In the computer's Input/Process/Output sequence, the monitor represents the main output device, letting you see the results of your input and the computer's processing. The monitor is connected to the system unit by two cables: one is a power cable drawing current from the system unit's power supply; the other connects to the display adapter (a circuit board situated in one of the expansion slots) from which the monitor receives its picture. We'll delve deeper into the issues of monitors and display adapters on p. 42.
- *Keyboard.*The keyboard is one of the two ubiquitous input devices that passes what you type into the system unit for processing by means of a

single cable. This cable also provides a tiny power supply to the keyboard. Turn to p. 55 for a more detailed view of the keyboard.

- *Mouse.* This is the second of the two input devices. Movement of the mouse around your desk controls the movement of a small arrow-shaped pointer on the monitor screen. By itself this doesn't accomplish much, but the mouse also has two or three buttons: clicking these buttons will make the computer do different things depending upon what you're 'pointing' at when you 'click'. More properly, the mouse should be referred to here as a *pointing device:* there's a variety of devices available that produce the same result, and the one you choose will depend upon personal taste and the sort of tasks you most use your computer for. We'll take a closer look at the mouse and other types of pointing device on p. 49.
- *Software.* Okay, this is a bit of a sly one. You might find a small amount of software in the box (most computer stores give away a few games or product samplers with a new computer which you can install or ignore as you wish) but the most important software should be already installed on the hard disk and ready to use. Fundamentally this should be an **operating system**, a collection of software programs that handle the vital task of interpreting your input and telling the rest of the system what to do to make you happy. Depending on the deal offered by the computer store, and/or the software that you specifically asked for, you might have other software packages included too. The store will almost always install the software itself and make sure it all runs correctly: if that wasn't done, the store would risk the expense of sending someone out to help you if you got into difficulties!

Of course, with each of these elements there are choices to be made when buying, and they usually come down to a balance between *what you like* and *what you need to do.* So we might as well round off this first look at the PC by addressing one of the basic choices you'll have to make: **Desktop** or **Notebook**?

The Desktop PC

The Desktop PC has long been the established standard, and it's probably what you picture when you think of a computer. As its name suggests, it's designed to sit on your desk and stay there. One big difference between this and the Notebook PC is size: the system unit has a mass of free space inside allowing extra components to be fitted that increase the power and flexibility of your machine. Once installed, these new accessories are instantly available every time you switch on your PC. Similarly, it's usually easy to replace *existing* components with newer, more powerful ones (known as **upgrading**) if the need arises.

Despite its name, the Desktop PC's system unit no longer needs to be on the desk. Traditionally, the unit sat behind your keyboard and you plonked the monitor on top of it. In response to demand, manufacturers started building these units so that they could be stood on their sides on the floor. A little re-jigging of layout has resulted in a system unit with a *tower* case: in a small room, this has the great advantage that you can stow the unit out of the way under your desk and still be able to pop a disk into its floppy-disk drive without too many physical contortions.

The second major difference between the Desktop and the Notebook is price. In contrast with many of the products we buy, in the world of PCs, *bigger is cheaper*! The technical difficulties involved in building all this power into a smaller box means that a Notebook PC is always more expensive than a Desktop with the same specifications.

The Notebook PC

The Notebook PC has been known by quite a variety of names over the years: to begin with it was called the *portable*, a term which required a slight stretch of the imagination when trying to carry one any distance. The portable gradually became smaller and lighter and today these early portables tend to be known as *luggables* for obvious reasons. Further downward shifts in scale have given us the *Laptop*, and now finally the *Notebook*, so-called because of its similarity in size to a sheet of A4 paper (apart from being about two inches thicker of course!).

To actually make a PC portable isn't easy. It has to have similar capabilities to the Desktop variety in a much smaller case which obviously involves removing a few components and making a number of others more compact. Nevertheless, the fundamentals are all there: the monitor is housed in the hinged lid which flips up to reveal the keyboard; the mouse is replaced by an integral trackball which requires less room to manoeuvre; the hard- and floppy-disk drives sit beneath the keyboard together with the slot-in rechargeable battery.

As with the Desktop PC, extra accessories can be added to the Notebook but, due to the constraints of size, they can't be fitted permanently – there's no space for them! The usual solution is the addition of slots in the side of the case into which these extras (in the form of credit-card sized devices called **PC Cards**) can be plugged when needed. Another constraint upon Notebook users is that upgrading internal components can be difficult, expensive and, in some cases, impossible, so it becomes all the more important to choose your machine carefully.

JARGONBUSTER

Upgrading

The act of replacing one or more pieces of hardware or software with more recent, and usually improved, versions. While upgrading hardware components is usually possible, bear in mind that it's always more costly than choosing the right equipment to begin with, and it might prove impossible to sell or trade-in the device you're replacing.

The incredible shrinking PC

In the design and production of all things electronic, there's an almost religious zest to follow a trend that's never applied to items like can-openers and cars: when you've made it work reliably and fast, make it smaller! As we've seen above, the portable computer has passed through several name changes and reductions in size over the last 15 years, and it's probably shrunk about as far as it can without surrendering its identity as a PC. But these guys don't give up easily – they've found a whole new challenge by turning the trend upside down!

The third type of PC is the **Palmtop** (sometimes called a 'Handheld'). Rather than being a scaled-down PC, this is best thought of as a scaled-up calculator. From its humble background in simple arithmetic, the pocket calculator passed through the 'scientific' stage and emerged as an 'electronic organizer' capable of storing and recalling a few phone numbers, logging appointments and beeping excitedly at odd intervals. Its most recent metamorphosis has shifted it into the PC market by adding a few new tricks to its repertoire such as word processing, accounting and databases. On more advanced models, extra hardware can be slotted into the side of the case and a cable can be attached to link your Palmtop to your Desktop for transferring files between the two.

We're not going to dwell on the Palmtop computer in this book: it still doesn't quite deserve its 'PC' tag, lacking the power, flexibility and ease-of-use of the Desktop or Notebook varieties. Indeed, very few Palmtops are actually IBM compatible. Also, because it's considerably cheaper and bought as a single 'take-it-or-leave-it' unit, the decision to buy is a far easier one to make. At present, the primary use of the Palmtop is as a scratch-pad for notes and ideas that occur while you're away from your Desktop.

Ins and outs of the PC

In the next few sections we'll delve deeper into the system unit to find out what all its internal gadgetry does, how the pieces connect to pass data around and process it, and what's going on behind the scenes as you work. The Notebook PC, being a fully integrated machine, doesn't have a system unit as such, but the same components are tucked away inside the case and doing an identical job to their Desktop counterparts.

JARGONBUSTER

Data

A sort of synonym for 'information'. While the computer is storing it or working with it, it's data – a meaningless stream of numbers to you and me. When some sense has been made of it all and it's presented on screen or paper, it's information.

Before we get involved in detailed explanations of the major components, let's first take a couple of pages to cast an eye over the system as a whole and see what it's doing with your data.

What's going on in there?

The basic principles of how the computer operates are quite straightforward – the PC works very much like you do:

- Your brain receives input from your ears, eyes and so on; the computer receives input from the keyboard and the mouse (and, perhaps, one or two other optional devices you've connected).
- You have a brain for working things out; the computer has a **processor**.
- You have various methods of outputting the results of your brainwork, such as writing or speaking; the computer might output its results to be displayed on the monitor, printed on paper, or saved onto a disk.
- As you try to think out a tricky problem, you keep as many of the details in your mind as you can; the computer has its own forms of **memory** to do a similar job.
- If a job comes in that suddenly requires your full attention, you make notes about the first job on a piece of paper so that you can come back to it later; the modern PC is able to empty its memory enough to handle a different task and then 'read' this same information back in when it wants to use it again.

- You probably have a filing cabinet or a drawer where you keep your important files and documents; the computer contains a **disk** for the same purpose.

The brains behind the operation

In the internal workings of the human being, nothing at all can happen without the active participation of the brain. The same is true of the computer, but the 'brain' in question is a small chip called a CPU (Central Processing Unit) or **processor**.

Because the processor plays a vital part in everything the computer does, it's constantly working behind the scenes and juggling a large number of tasks in blindingly quick succession. Exactly *how* fast it can handle each task is one of the main yardsticks we use in determining that subjective factor, the *power* of the computer. To a large extent, the faster your processor, the more powerful your PC.

Ins and outs

To continue the 'brain' analogy just a little longer, the processor sends data to most parts of the PC's 'body', and receives data back from most of them. But notice the use of the word *most* – not every part of the system will receive data, and not every part will send it. The computer is made up of three types of hardware component: input devices, output devices, and combined input/output devices.

- An **input** device *sends* data to the processor but doesn't need to receive anything in return: the mouse is a good example of an input-only device.
- An **output** device *receives* data from the processor and presents it to us in some way, an example of this being the monitor.
- An **input/output** device *exchanges* data back and forth with the processor. The archetypal input/output device is the hard disk: sometimes the processor will send data to the disk to be stored; at other times it will retrieve data from the disk to be used.

Bits and PCs

As you can tell from the brief outline above, there's a lot going on, and data is endlessly being passed around the system. But what is this data? What form does it take?

Computers work only with **binary numbers**. The binary system is a method of counting in base two which involves using combinations of the numbers 0 and 1, equating to 'off' and 'on'. On the surface this may seem limiting, but if the processor only has to distinguish between these two possible states it can therefore handle immense streams of these digits (generically known as *data*) in a very short space of time. Each of these 0s and 1s is called a **bit**, short for BInary digiT.

Because a single bit by itself can't convey much information, bits are grouped into sets of eight called **bytes**. A byte is far more meaningful, offering 256 different combinations of 0s and 1s, so a single byte can communicate numbers from 0 to 255. As a point of interest, one byte is equivalent to a single typed character.

Kilobytes and megabytes

Bits and bytes are terms used to count quantities of data, but they're pretty small measures and computers have to deal with much larger chunks of data. For example, a small word processor program with fairly limited features could be around 200 000 bytes in size. Because we're dealing with numbers of this order most of the time, two additional terms are used: the **kilobyte** (abbreviated to **K**) which equals 1024 bytes, and the **megabyte** (abbreviated to **Mb**) which equals 1024 kilobytes or 1 048 576 bytes. Another term being encountered more and more frequently as technology progresses is the **gigabyte** (**Gb**), equal to 1024 megabytes.

These terms are used most frequently when discussing the capacities of two particular types of computer hardware: **memory** and **hard disk**.

Memory and storage

The computer, as we know, deals with huge amounts of data. However, at any one time only a comparatively tiny amount is actually being processed, and a small amount is travelling between the various components. So where's all the rest of it?

By far the largest amount of data is *stored* ready for use whenever it's needed (which might be in a couple of minutes' time, or might be next year!) and the main storage medium is the **hard disk**. This is a magnetic disk inside the computer on which all your programs are kept, together with the documents you create when using those programs, and all the other software required to control the computer itself.

Programs and operating systems are getting bigger all the time (Windows 95, for example, will take an absolute minimum of 49 Mb of space on your hard disk), so the greater the capacity of the hard disk, the better.

Memory is a type of short-term storage, and the modern PC has several types of memory at its disposal. The most important of these is called **RAM** (Random Access Memory) which comes in the form of small modules on cards that slot into the computer's motherboard. Every program and document you use at any one time (including the operating system) is read from the hard disk and loaded into the computer's RAM. When the RAM gets full, the computer has to find alternative places to put some of this data temporarily. These alternatives do exist, but they can't send back the data as quickly as RAM when it's next needed, which results in the whole computer slowing down. The bottom line here is: there's no such thing as too much RAM!

Motherboard

A large circuit board inside the system unit on which most of the computer's major components are situated: the design of the board ensures that everything attached to it (including any devices you add later) will be able to communicate with everything else.

Files, programs and documents

Returning once again to the 'human body' analogy, data is the *blood* of the computer, being passed around its major organs all the time and keeping the whole thing working. Although all this data moves around as a stream of bits, it needs to be grouped and stored in a more organized way to let you find the data you need quickly and easily. These groups of related data are known generically as **files**, and a file will be one of two types: a **program** or a **document**.

- A **program** is a file that contains a specific set of instructions or commands to the computer itself. Some of these programs will be run automatically when your computer starts (or, indeed, while you're using it) to make the computer work as it should. These are part of the operating system. Other programs you will run yourself when you need to use them – a word-processing application when you want to write a letter, or a graphics application when you want to draw a picture. Because program files contain commands, and these commands have to be executed for anything to happen, program files are sometimes referred to as **executables**.

Application

An application is a type of program that is used to create something – a drawing, a table, a database, and so on – as distinct from a program that provides entertainment (such as a game) or lets you change system settings or dial a phone number. The word 'applications' is sometimes colloquially abbreviated to 'apps'.

- A **document** file is a good deal simpler: when you run your word-processing application and write a letter, this letter is being stored in short-term memory (RAM) while you're working on it. When it's finished and sitting on the screen in front of you, you can choose what to do with it. You can, if you want to, just print it out on paper ready to send to someone, close down the application and forget it – if you do this, the RAM will forget it too. Or you can *save* the letter as a file that you can look at and edit in the future; in effect, this means you're moving your letter from the short-term memory to the permanent store (the hard disk). Files that you create yourself in this way, containing meaningful information, are called 'documents'.

▶ *Take a look at p. 113 to find out more about how all the files are organized on your computer.*

On the buses

At this point, we've covered what the data is and what the major pieces of a computer do with it. We've also made more references to the human body than is advisable in polite company. The only thing we haven't covered is *how* the data gets from one component to another, and for this it's time to switch metaphors.

All these components are connected by a network of pathways called a **bus**, in the same way that towns and cities are connected by a network of roads. If you can travel from place to place on a motorway you're going to get there a lot faster than you would on a single-track country lane. The concept behind these pathways is that we want our data to be travelling down motorways as often as possible so that a larger amount of data can travel at a greater speed.

This isn't just greed or impatience: it has actually become necessary over recent years. As modern processors have become more powerful, hardware and software manufacturers have consistently taken advantage of these increases in power by building more and more features and enhancements into their products. This, of course, results in more data being pumped around the system. It's all very well to have components like processors that can cope with all this data quickly, but if the roads are too narrow for the data to *reach* these components fast enough, the result is a bottleneck that makes the whole idea of a fast processor pointless.

So the design of the bus, known as the **bus architecture**, is something people have spent sleepless nights worrying about (no, not normal people – computer designers), resulting in several different types. The original standard was **ISA** (Industry Standard Architecture) which spawned an extended design, **EISA**. A second standard, used only by IBM in its PS/2 computers, was **MCA** (Micro Channel Architecture). Both EISA and MCA could pump data around the system in 32-bit chunks (like a 32-lane motorway), which is twice as 'wide' as the original ISA, but these motorways had a speed limit of only 8 or 10 MHz (megahertz).

To speed things up, an additional bus called a **local bus** was added to the system. The local bus connects several of the primary components and brings them closer together, so the data they send and receive has a short drive down a relatively empty road. It also removes some of the traffic from the other road. Think of it as a bypass!

JARGONBUSTER

Peripherals

A general term for hardware devices that you might decide to add to your computer such as a CD-ROM drive, modem or soundcard. Peripherals are devices that add capabilities to your PC that it didn't have before.

The two local bus designs are **VESA** (or VL bus) and **PCI** (Peripheral Control Interface). PCI is the current standard, still giving the 32-bit pathway (although a 64-bit PCI is on its way) but pushing the maximum speed up to 33 MHz. A couple of major benefits to PCI over VESA are support for Plug & Play (see pp. 41 and 373) and suitability for use with SCSI devices (p. 31).

If all that seems complicated, just remember this: PCI is good!

The processor

What is the processor?

The processor is the *brain* of the computer, the chip that makes all the calculations and produces the results, so it's one of the most important parts of the machine despite its diminutive size (roughly 4 centimetres square). You'll sometimes see it referred to as a **microprocessor** or a **CPU** (for Central Processing Unit), but these names all refer to the same thing. The processor slots into the motherboard, usually by means of a ZIF socket to make for easy replacement if you ever want to. Along with the amount of memory and capacity of your hard disk, your choice of processor will make a big difference to your computing life.

JARGONBUSTER

ZIF socket

ZIF is an acronym for Zero Insertion Force and refers to a type of socket found in modern PCs that the processor slots into. It has a small lever which ejects the chip and then locks the new chip into position, removing the need to be brutal when trying to replace this delicate component.

Because of its essential nature, the type of processor included is used to describe the computer and distinguish it from other PCs: if you have a powerful computer, then that really means that you have a computer with a powerful processor.

What does it do?

Just like the human brain, the processor does a vast number of things. It obeys instructions one at a time, obeying them so fast that they all appear to be happening at the same time. In any given fraction of a second, the processor will take a look at the keyboard input socket to see if you typed anything, and at the mouse input to see if you moved or clicked the mouse; it might send more data to be displayed on the monitor, and read data from the computer's memory store or hard disk. If you have other devices attached to your computer such as a printer or a modem, it will be watching these for incoming data and/or sending data to them.

So, however calm and unflustered it all seems on the surface, the processor is actually going like crazy underneath! And it follows that whatever you do and whenever you do it, you're going to interrupt its well-organized routine. Just as the human brain is adept at swapping back and forth between different tasks, the processor uses the computer's memory chips (the RAM) to keep track of what it was doing before you interrupted.

If you've looked at advertisements for PCs, you've probably noticed that they prominently feature a line like one of these:

486DX4 100 MHz

Pentium 120 MHz

This line is one of the most important to check in any computer ad. The first part of each line (**486DX4** or **Pentium**) refers to the *type* of processor chip, the second refers to the chip's *speed* in megahertz. You might find the Pentium models occasionally abbreviated to just 'P' (as in P120 for the example above).

Playing the game

Processors have traditionally been given numeric names, and as technology marched forward and new processors appeared the numbers got higher. So the higher the number, the more recent (and, usually, better) the processor. When a new type of processor appears on the market, it starts a little chain of events in which its predecessor drops to second place and quickly becomes a lot cheaper, while the chip that *had* been in second place is relegated to third and soon vanishes from the market altogether.

Because a new chip seems to appear every 18 months or so, the PC market never quite gets the chance to settle into a groove before the whole cycle starts up again. For all the hardware and software manufacturers in the game, this is great news. They create newer, better, feature-packed products to take advantage of this new chip; computer users replace their old chip with the new one if they can, or buy a new computer if they can't, and gradually switch over to these new products to avoid being left behind. By the time the most reluctant buyer has caved in and shelled out, the major players have done very nicely and the game begins again.

This might seem like a slightly cynical view to take; after all, we *want* technology to progress, don't we? And, as the popular argument goes, no one is holding a gun to our heads to make us buy. Nevertheless, advances in processor technology determine the shape of the entire PC market, and once you've bought into it you're usually in for good, so it's well worth knowing the rules before you place a stake.

Processor types

The family of processors used in PCs is the 86 series, designed by Intel, although also available from other manufacturers. Since 1984 this family has passed through three generations, the 80286, 80386, and 80486, all commonly known by their last three digits. The next in the series, and the current standard, is called the **Pentium**. (Being unable to trademark a number, Intel found an alternative name for what would have been the 80586.) Similarly, the latest '80686' has been dubbed the **Pentium-Pro**. The 286 and 386 are now obsolete, being unable to meet the demands of modern operating systems and software, and the Pentium-Pro is still too new, unnecessarily high-powered for home and small office use, and too expensive to be a viable option, leaving you with a choice between the 486 and the Pentium.

If you opt for the 486, you'll find you're faced with a choice of 486SX, 486DX, 486DX2 and 486DX4. Rather than going into complicated explanations, let's keep it simple: the DX4 is the most powerful, so buy it! In terms of speed, a fast DX4 doesn't differ much from a low-to-mid-range Pentium.

TIP

By choosing a 486 you've taken the cheapest route into the PC market; choosing anything lower-powered than a 486DX4 will usually be a false economy in the long term.

Processor speeds

After the choice of processor comes the choice of **clock speed**, measured in megahertz (MHz); 1 MHz equals one million cycles per second, so these machines skip along pretty fast. It obviously follows that the higher the clock speed, the faster the computer and the more quickly your PC will respond to your input as you work. It also follows that you'll want to buy the fastest computer you can afford.

The 486DX4 is available at speeds of 66, 100 or 120 MHz; the Pentium comes in at speeds ranging from 66 to a blistering 200 MHz. (You might find yourself tempted by a 60 MHz Pentium, but this was regarded by many as a bit of a turkey and well worth avoiding.)

There's one last, weird point to consider on the subject of speed: due to the different designs of the 486 and Pentium processors, a 100 MHz Pentium will work faster than a 100 MHz 486. Weirder still, you might expect a 150 MHz Pentium to work about twice as fast as a 75 MHz Pentium. It doesn't. It does work *faster*, of course, just not *twice* as fast.

Does it matter?

When you read about different types of processor, different speeds and so on, does it really make much difference as long as you've *got* one?

Yes, unfortunately, it makes a lot of difference. Everything you ask your computer to do takes processor time – sometimes a little, sometimes a lot. For example, when you type a letter, the processor has to deal with the data coming in from your keyboard, and send more data off to your monitor to make it display the characters you're typing. It can do this apparently instantaneously without raising much of sweat. But playing a multimedia presentation, an arcade-type game or a video clip is a whole new proposition: to construct and display all these separate pictures fast enough that they appear to be moving takes a lot of power. If your processor isn't up to the task, the result will be very jerky and disjointed.

In addition, modern operating systems like Windows 95 are built to handle several tasks at the same time. Some of these tasks involve the operating system talking to the computer behind the scenes to keep everything running smoothly, and others will be things *you're* trying to do, such as printing one document while working on another. A less powerful processor will still handle all these tasks, but the difference in speed could mean that the computer won't let you get on with anything else until it's sorted itself out. This could be minutes in the worst cases, or it could be mere seconds, but it's *always* frustrating!

Turbo

Many modern PCs have a switch on the front marked **Turbo**. It's tempting to think that you've found a way to make your computer go even faster. In fact, it should be switched on all the time and it's a way to make it run slower! Because these new computers are so powerful, a few (*very* few) software programs that you might want to use just can't run at those speeds, so you can use the Turbo switch to slow down the processor. You might also find it a handy feature to have if you play games on your computer: if your little guy always gets blown up before you've had a chance to fire a shot, go for your button!

Buyers' guide: Processors

- If you possibly can, buy a computer with a Pentium processor. Some of the latest software requires a Pentium processor to run, and won't work on a 486. All software will run on a Pentium. Should you need to in the future, you can replace your Pentium chip with a Pentium-Pro. Upgrading a 486 will vary between costly and impossible.
- Choose the fastest processor you can afford: the individual 'jumps' from 75 to 90 and upwards give a noticeable improvement in performance.
- If you intend to do much work involving graphics, video, or digitally recorded sound, a fast processor (together with plenty of RAM) is absolutely vital.
- For maximum security and reliability, choose an **Intel**-manufactured chip. You can be sure that this is well tested and well supported. Other good chip-makers are **AMD** and **Cyrix**.
- If you buy a 486-based computer, ask if it's compatible with the **Pentium Overdrive** processor. If it is, you can upgrade the processor to Pentium-class later on if you want to.
- *Why buy a 486?* There are really only two reasons for buying a 486 as opposed to a Pentium: (a) this is your first computer and you'd rather buy something cheap to find out if you really need it; (b) you know exactly what software you want to run, you know it runs happily on a 486, and you intend to keep using only this software for a long time. This is good, sound economical planning provided you're really sure you won't get itchy for *new* software in a few months!
- *Why buy a Pentium-Pro?* You want a hugely powerful machine running the OS/2 or Windows NT operating systems, and you don't mind spending over the odds to get it. The Pentium-Pro is said to actually *slow down* Windows 95.

Memory

What is memory?

In a general sense, memory is a short-term holding place for data that is currently in use, or is about to be used, or has just been used. In fact, there are *several* holding places of different types that the PC uses in different situations, and they vary in speed and effectiveness. The most important of these is called **RAM**.

The first fundamental point about RAM is that the data it's holding can be grabbed *fast* as soon as it's needed. The second is that it's only a *temporary* holding place for data: when you turn off your computer, or close the document you were working on without saving it to the hard disk, the data is gone for good!

In the previous section we looked at the processor. What we didn't say was that the processor contains its own small memory store, known as the **cache**. This wasn't forgetfulness, it was simply that this store is just too small to be an issue: all the commands and data that aren't immediately being processed need to be kept somewhere else but within easy reach, and this is where the primary form of memory, RAM, comes into play.

RAM and chips

So we're back to acronyms again – RAM stands for Random Access Memory, which essentially means it's a type of memory that allows data to be stored (or *written*) in it, read from it, and removed from it to make way for other data. Like most elements of the computer, RAM comes on tiny components called **chips**: several of these chips are attached to a small circuit board which slots into the PC's main motherboard.

Are you ready for a few more acronyms? On most PCs, the circuit boards containing those little RAM chips are called **SIMMs**, or Single In-line Memory Modules. When RAM is what you need, SIMMs are what you get, and a single SIMM will contain anything from 4 to 32 Mb of RAM. This will be 'dynamic' RAM (or **DRAM**, pronounced 'dee-ram'), although it's usually just referred to as plain old RAM in the advertisements. Over the last year or so, there's been a move to a slightly different type of memory called **EDO RAM** (Enhanced Data Out) which gives a performance boost to a Pentium-based PC compared to the standard DRAM.

JARGONBUSTER

Access time

This is a term that applies to both memory and disks, and, in fact, anywhere that data might be situated. It refers to how long it takes to retrieve the required data from memory or disk. Cache memory is lightning fast, so it has a short access time; RAM's access time is about four times as long, but that's still immensely quick. Hard-disk access time is about 100 000 times that of RAM – very slow by comparison, but still a good deal faster than floppy-disk access.

RAM in use

All the data the computer needs is stored on the hard disk in files, but in the fast-moving world of the PC, the hard disk chugs along relatively slowly. So as soon as you run an application or open a file, it's dragged from the hard disk into RAM from where it can be accessed far more quickly when the processor is ready for it. The more RAM there is available, the greater the quantity of data that can be put there, and the better prepared the computer will be. If the *majority* of the data that's likely to be needed is waiting in the speedy RAM, the sluggish hard disk shouldn't need to be accessed very often and the computer will work faster.

At any given moment when you're using your computer, the operating system is running, probably one or more applications are running, and one or more documents is open in each of those applications. This means that at any given moment, all the required files for these applications and documents are theoretically residing in RAM. If they really are, that's great. It means that as you switch back and forth between applications or documents, the processor can quickly retrieve the data it needs and keep up with you.

However much RAM you have in your machine, if you keep loading more and more files into it, sooner or later it's going to get full. Fortunately, the computer is smart enough to see this coming; instead of just waiting for a 'RAM-jam' and then going into a dead sulk, it rearranges things to make sure it's always got room to manoeuvre. This involves identifying the data that isn't currently being used and moving some of it from RAM into a different type of memory – *virtual* memory – and this is where things start to get ugly!

Virtual memory

Virtual memory, as the name suggests, isn't 'real' memory; it's actually an area of the hard disk *pretending* to be RAM. The concept of virtual memory has its pros and cons: on the positive side the hard disk is huge, and the area used for virtual memory can be increased to fill all its remaining space, so there's little danger of running out! Unfortunately, the negative side wins: although this area is optimized for the job it's doing, it's still the hard disk and it still takes a whole lot longer to retrieve data from it than it does from RAM.

Once again, there's an obvious conclusion to be drawn from this which should probably be accompanied by an orchestra of cash registers: to prevent your computer writing and reading data to and from virtual memory too often, and thus keep it working as fast as possible, sell your granny and buy more RAM!

▶ *Virtual memory is covered in more depth on pp. 308 and 379.*

The cache machine

A *cache* (pronounced 'cash') is a type of memory designed to improve on the performance of 'ordinary' RAM. The cache holds recently used instructions and data, working on the premise that they may be needed again, and the processor always looks here first. As long as the cache is holding the piece of data the processor wants each time, it doesn't need to go looking in the main RAM for it. The Pentium processor contains its own 8 K cache, but modern PCs also have a larger *secondary cache*.

Cache memory is a slightly different type of RAM called 'static' RAM (or **SRAM**, pronounced 'ess-ram'). It's expensive, but it's at least four times as fast as DRAM and you don't have to agonize over whether you want it or how much you want: you *definitely* want it, and a Pentium-based PC should have a 256 K secondary cache built in. A few high-specification PCs even offer 512 K. If you're planning to buy a 486, however, inclusion of secondary cache isn't a foregone conclusion, so always ask!

JARGONBUSTER

Buffer

A 'buffer' is an area of RAM that stores the tiny amount of data you're currently working on, which is passing through on its way to or from the main RAM. The buffer is usually filled with data which can then be passed to wherever it's going in one chunk, a more economical method than passing continuous streams of single bits around.

What's ROM?

One last type of memory, coupled with one last acronym for this section! **ROM** stands for Read Only Memory, a type of memory from which the data can be *read*, but into which no *new* data can be stored. Unlike RAM, the data in ROM is stored permanently – when you turn off your computer, the data in the ROM chip will still be there.

All computers have ROM chips containing a set of vital instructions known as the **BIOS**. We'll look more closely at the BIOS on p. 33 but, as a very brief description, the BIOS tests the computer when you first switch it on and tells it to load the operating system. The BIOS relates to the computer in much the same way as the ignition key relates to the car.

Memory doublers

As we've established, RAM is a vital part of your computer and you'll want quite a lot of it to run modern operating systems and applications at a decent speed. But RAM costs money and, inexplicably, the SIMM is one of the only components to have held a steady price over the years, despite the fact that its volume of sales has rocketed. (An equally inexplicable fall has seen RAM prices plummet by about 50 per cent in recent months!)

Because RAM seems to be needed in increasingly large quantities, enterprising software companies have started producing so-called 'memory-doubling' software which, in theory at least, makes your computer work as if you had twice as much RAM installed.

The results of using RAM-doubling programs vary according to the situation, but there have been some amusing stories about a few outright failures: not only could they not provide you with any *extra* memory, they were *using* memory themselves while they were running – a net result of *less* memory! These programs were quite cheap, but if something doesn't work it's expensive at any price. This isn't to imply that *all* RAM-doubling software is useless; some will certainly be more effective than this. But why take the chance? If more RAM is what you need, buy more RAM – at least you *know* it works!

▶ *For the long and the short of PC memory (mainly the short of it!), turn to section **8.6**.*

Buyer's Guide: Memory

- The golden rule when it comes to RAM is: *you can't have too much!* If you're looking for a way to improve your machine's performance, more RAM is nearly always a good bet.
- When adding more RAM to your computer, check your manual carefully before buying SIMMs – many recent computers need SIMMs to be fitted in particular combinations. For example, if you have 8 Mb and you want more, you might find that you have to step straight up to 16 Mb. Similarly, if you have 16 Mb consisting of four 4 Mb SIMMs, your next step will probably involve *replacing* at least two of these with 8 Mb SIMMs.
- If you're buying a new computer, keep an eye out for **EDO RAM**, a type of enhanced RAM. It's not a major issue, but it might net you a 10 per cent

improvement on the standard RAM and the price difference between the two is relatively small.

- To ensure compatibility, and avoid embarrassing trips back to the computer tore, make sure you know the type, make and speed of your SIMMs when you want to add more memory to the system, and that you haven't already reached the maximum amount of RAM that can be fitted in your PC.
- When buying a new computer, check the specifications for mention of a **256 K cache** for additional speed. If you see **512 K cache**, that's twice as good! References to **pipelined burst mode** cache or **Triton chipset** will mean an even greater increase in performance and are a must for a Pentium.
- SIMMs can be damaged very easily and are especially at risk from static electricity, even in small amounts. Whenever you add more memory to your computer, make sure you hold the card only by its edges and always keep one hand on the metal case of the system unit to earth yourself (or wear the wrist-band often supplied free by memory retailers).

Hard disk and floppy disk

What is a disk?

To describe what disks are for, we shall return to that 'roads' metaphor again. Think of your files (operating system, applications and documents) as a car: when you want to *use* your car you take it out onto the road, and drive about between Processorville, RAM City and other nearby places; when you don't want to use it you *park* it somewhere. Once you've parked it, you can leave it there as long as you like. That might be just a minute or two, or it might be months or even years!

So the *disk* is a car park for your files, known generically as a 'mass storage medium', and there are two different types: the **hard disk**, and the **floppy disk** (sometimes referred to as a **diskette**). Of these two, the hard disk is by far the more important because it can hold much more data. Since the most significant consideration about any storage device is *how much* data you can store, hard disks are noted by their capacities in megabytes (Mb).

What's the difference?

Because both types of disk are capable of storing the same types of data they must have a lot in common. The data is stored magnetically, for example, and all the methods of organizing, storing and retrieving data are identical to both. Nevertheless, there are several differences between the two types, so let's look at these first:

- The hard disk is usually fixed permanently inside your PC's system unit, whereas a floppy disk comes housed in a small plastic case to protect it, and is slotted into the floppy-disk drive on front of the system unit when you need to use it.
- The hard disk in a modern PC commonly has a capacity of between 500 Mb and 2 Gb; the floppy disk has a capacity of either 720 K or 1.44 Mb (think *tiny* by comparison).
- They are used in different ways: due to the floppy disk's small capacity (and slower access times) it tends to be mostly used for transferring files from one computer to another, perhaps to give a file to a friend. The hard disk is used for general storage of all files – operating system, applications and documents – so that they're always available when you want them, without all the fuss of trying to find the right floppy disk and put it in the slot.
- Finally, the price! You'll buy floppy disks in tens or hundreds, but one hard disk is expense enough for most people.

What's hard, what's floppy?

You might have spotted a running thread in the names given to just about everything in the computer world: there's a distinct lack of imagination! The hard disk gained it's name by being made of metal. *Hey guys, this disk is kinda hard. What shall we call it?* And the floppy disk? Inside that plastic casing, the disk itself is made from a thin flexible sheet of plastic. Rigid it isn't.

▶ *There's another kind of drive found more and more often in new PCs: the CD-ROM drive. We'll take a look at this one on p. 63.*

Disk drives

No, this isn't anything to do with that 'driving' metaphor! The **drive** is the collective term for all the mechanical bits and pieces that hold these disks, make them rotate, and so on. Both hard-disk drive and floppy-disk drive have a light on the front of the system unit to show when the disk is being used. (The floppy-disk drive also has a button on the front to eject the disk from the slot when you've finished with it.) When talking or writing about drives, as a sort of economy measure, the terms 'hard-disk drive' and 'floppy-disk drive' tend to be shortened to just 'hard drive' and 'floppy drive'.

The primary part of the disk-drive mechanism is the **read/write head**. In the hard drive this is a small device that flies over the surface of the disk on a little cushion of air (never quite touching it, to avoid damage to either component) and reads data from it to send to RAM or receives data from RAM to be stored on the disk. In the floppy drive the disk and head are in contact but the results are the same.

How do disks work?

Let's think about another type of disk first, the long-play record. The sound signal on a record is laid down in one long groove which starts on the outside edge and spirals its way to the inside. Once you start the record playing, all the music on that side of the record will be played in the same order it was put there. In computing jargon this would be known as a *sequential access* device.

Whenever you save a new file onto a disk, the data is stored in sequence in a similar way: the read/write head searches for the first clear space and writes the data into it. The next file you save will be placed after it, and so on. But the disk drive is a *random access* device: when a particular file is needed it doesn't have to trawl through all the data on the disk until it gets to the right place – it knows exactly where to find it! The hard disk contains a small area which acts as a kind of 'address-book' for files, called the **FAT** ('File Allocation Table'). When the disk drive has to fetch a particular file, it looks at the FAT to see where the file lives and then goes straight to that address to get it.

Although disks are referred to as *storage* devices, files can be removed (*deleted*) from the disk if you no longer need them. And one of the great pastimes of computer owners is to take a look through the files on their huge hard disk, gaze in wonder at files they'd forgotten all about, and then delete them to regain some space. Although you can hit the *Delete* key on your keyboard and have the satisfaction of seeing the file disappear from the screen, it isn't actually removed from the *disk* just yet. Instead, the area of the disk that file was using is marked as now being 'free space': as you save more files, sooner or later this space will be reused, covering the old data. So if you delete a file by accident, and you're quick to act, it's usually possible to *un*-delete it.

Drive names – learn your ABC

Whenever you want to use a particular file, you have to tell the computer what it's called. Curiously, even though the data is stored on the disk itself, you tell the computer which *drive* to look at to find the file rather than which *disk*. In fact, this isn't as odd as it might seem.

In the early days of computing, hard disks were rare. Everyone had a floppy drive and they popped a disk into the drive to use the files it contained. A lot of people bought a *second* floppy drive in order to reduce the amount of time they spent inserting and removing disks. Over a period of time, they might collect hundreds of floppy disks and it would be unreasonable to expect the computer to know exactly what was on each one! So they just stuck a disk into one of the drives and told the computer which drive to look at.

Because the normal computer had one floppy drive, it came to be called **Drive A**. If a second floppy drive was added, it would be called **Drive B**. When the hard drive arrived on the scene, it was automatically assigned the name **Drive C**. These names have stuck, so on today's standard PC with its one floppy drive and one hard drive, these are called Drive A and Drive C respectively.

Hard drive size and type

When it comes to buying a hard drive (whether as part of a new computer or as an add-on *second* hard drive) there are two considerations: *type* and *size*. Size is easy – the bigger the better!

TIP

In your early days of computing you might look at a 500 Mb disk and think you'd never need anything that big; in fact, 500 Mb tends to be a *minimum* size for a hard disk these days and you might fill it pretty quickly. For example, install an operating system like Windows 95 and a suite of useful applications such as **Office 95** and you've filled 100–130 Mb already! You're sure to want other programs too, and you need space on the disk to save all the document files you create.

The type of disk really comes down to a choice of three: **IDE** (Integrated Drive Electronics), **EIDE** (Enhanced IDE) or **SCSI** (Small Computer Systems Interface).

Given the choice between IDE and EIDE, there really *isn't* a choice: buy EIDE! You might have noticed in advertisements that IDE drives are a little more expensive than EIDE which would tend to suggest they're better, but in fact IDE is an old standard and EIDE is infinitely superior! IDE will allow a maximum of two hard drives in your computer, neither of which can have a larger capacity than 528 Mb, with a top speed of about 1 Mb per second when reading and writing data. Opt for EIDE and you can connect up to four drives (which can be hard drives, CD-ROM drives or tape drives), hard disks can be several *gigabytes* in size, and the transfer rate will be about 7 Mb per second. Can't really argue with that, can you?

SCSI (pronounced 'skuzzy') hard drives tend to be bought as extra add-on drives rather than as standard devices built into a new computer. There are various types of SCSI device available, so we'll take a look at the SCSI standard on p. 31.

JARGONBUSTER

Disk compression

This is something we'll take a closer look at on p. 385. Briefly, it's a method of 'squashing' files so that they occupy less space on a disk. The benefit is that you can obviously then fit more data onto that disk, but there's usually a slight trade-off in the speed of access because a file has to be *uncompressed* before you can use it.

Floppy drive size and type

The original floppy disk was a very poorly protected affair that tended to get full of dust and spilt coffee and would suddenly refuse to work. This disk was 5.25 inches square and slotted into a 5.25-inch drive. For obvious reasons, this disk and its drive are all but obsolete.

Instead we now use the more recent 3.5-inch disk and drive, and this smaller disk has a plastic casing to protect it from your lunch. All the same, it's still very susceptible to dust and dirt and should always be kept in a closed box when not in use. In one corner of the disk there's a little plastic tab called the **Write-Protect Tab**: when this is moved upwards (so that you can see through the hole it was covering) the read/write head will be unable to write any new data onto the disk and, more importantly, unable to delete its existing data.

TIP

Insert floppy disks into the drive with the sliding metal cover going in first and the label side up. The disk is held steady in the drive with a spring mechanism so press it firmly until it clicks into position. Press the button to eject the disk.

The 3.5-inch disk comes in two flavours, **double density** and **high density**, referring to the capacities of the disks. The double-density disk has a total capacity of 720 K, the high-density a capacity of 1.44 Mb. The standard

3.5-inch floppy drive included as standard in all PCs can work happily with both disk capacities.

Disk formatting

Being small and cheap, floppy disks are commonly sold in packs of 10, 50, or 100, and the price varies according to the quantity you buy and whether you buy *branded* disks (made by a well-known manufacturer) or *unbranded* disks (manufacturer unknown). You might reasonably expect the more expensive branded disks to be of a superior quality, but it ain't necessarily so: despite all the claims and guarantees on the boxes, they don't actually seem to be any more reliable than the cheaper ones.

Whichever you buy, before you can use them they have to be **formatted**. In its 'out-of-the-box' state, the 3.5-inch blank floppy disk is a standard disk type that can be used by many different types of computer, and other electronic devices with disk drives. Different computers create their own format on a blank disk so that they can use it, and the PC can only use disks with a 'DOS format'.

It is actually possible to buy boxes of floppy disks ready-formatted for a PC to save you the trouble of doing it yourself. They cost a little more, but they're worth considering if you buy and use in bulk.

Getting the formatting process started is a simple job of putting the disk in the drive slot, choosing the operating system's Format command and telling it what capacity of disk it is. You then sit back and wait for about a minute while the drive makes odd 'chugging' noises. What it's doing at this point is to divide the disk into concentric circles called **tracks** or **cylinders**, split each track into separate little areas called **sectors**, and create the FAT (see above). As soon as it's finished, you can start writing data to the disk or, if you enjoyed the experience, format another one!

You can format a disk that you've already used and which still contains data if you want to, but be warned: formatting a disk erases it completely and (usually) irrevocably! Always make sure you've put the correct disk in the drive before you choose the Format command.

▶ *To format a floppy disk in Windows 3.1, turn to p. 285; to do the same in Windows 95, see p. 334.*

What a failure!

One last point about disks, hard and floppy: *disks fail!* One day you're cheerfully using files from a disk; the next, for no apparent reason, the computer tells you it can't find any data on it, or the disk is unreadable. Floppy disks are the more susceptible to this because they spend most of their time outside the computer where all kinds of muck and rubbish can find its way onto the disk surface. The hard disk, on the other hand, is in a sealed case fixed inside the system unit so it's much better protected. Nevertheless, hard disks fail too, and this is usually a much bigger blow than losing a floppy disk. If the worst does happen, there are specialist companies who can usually retrieve the data for you, but prevention is better than cure!

The sensible precaution is to make copies of any data you can't afford to lose. If the data is on a floppy disk, copy it to *another* floppy disk or to your hard disk. Regarding the data on your hard disk, the ideal scenario is that you'd have a **backup drive** (see p. 80) with sufficient capacity to hold copies of all your important files. The final option is to copy files from the hard disk to a set of floppy disks, but this can be a time-consuming and extremely boring job, and one that you'd have to do quite regularly as you create new files or make changes to existing ones.

Buyers' guide: Disk drives

- Go for a large hard disk. If you intend to run a Windows operating system you'll need a minimum capacity of 500 Mb, but a healthier size would be at least 800 Mb.
- Always go for an EIDE hard-disk drive rather than IDE; the benefits are massive and the price will be the same or perhaps lower. If neither term is mentioned, look for a data transfer speed of over 4 Mb per second.
- Popular hard-disk manufacturers are **Conner**, **Seagate** and **Western Digital**.
- If you expect to do a lot of work with floppy disks, consider adding a second floppy-disk drive to your system – it's one of the cheapest pieces of hardware you can buy for your PC.

Card and slots

At this point in proceedings, most of the items lurking in your system unit have been prodded and poked and forced to surrender their secrets. The intention of this book isn't to cover *every* tiny component, so we have to draw the line somewhere. For example, your computer has a power supply, but that's dull. It has a small loudspeaker so that it can go 'beep' every so often, but there's not much we can say about that without being rude.

You may well have other items inside the system unit, or you may add some new devices to it in the future, and you'll find these covered in Chapter 2. Many of these devices will either be in the form of a circuit board (or **card**) that slots into the system unit, or an external device (a separate device in its own case, such as a printer) that plugs into one of these cards. So let's take a quick look at these cards and connections in general terms.

The motherboard

The motherboard is the major circuit board inside the system unit to which most of the fixtures and fittings are attached. The processor and a great many smaller components sit directly on the motherboard, and units that look rather like racks of shelving are fixed to it. The circuits in the motherboard itself physically connect these items together. The bus runs between the processor and items that aren't directly connected to the motherboard (such as disk drives) to transfer data backwards and forwards between them.

Let's go back to those 'racks of shelving' again. Each 'shelf' is actually one long thin socket called a **slot**. Into these slots, smaller circuit boards called **cards** can be fitted. These may be SIMM cards to provide the PC with its vital memory, or they may be cards that add extra capabilities to the computer. This second type of card is generically referred to as an **expansion card** (because it expands the computer's range of functions), and the slots these cards plug into are called **expansion slots**.

Counting cards

If you were to remove the cover from your system-unit and squint into its murky depths, you should find at least one expansion card in there, the **display adapter**, which handles the transfer of data to your monitor. Other cards might give your computer audio capabilities (for playing CDs or using MIDI), or fax/modem capabilities (for sending faxes or connecting to the Internet).

The cards in these slots are connected to the rest of the system by a bus and, as we know, there are two types of bus: the old, slow ISA bus and the fast, new PCI or VESA local bus. The local bus is used to provide fast data-transmission to and from *some* of these slots rather than all of them. You'll have to check your own computer's specifications on this one, but many modern computers offer eight slots in total, with four each connected to local and ISA buses. Clearly the more slots that are available, the more internal add-on devices you'll be able to install.

When it comes to buying new expansion cards, you'll need to know which type of local bus standard your PC uses. VESA (also known as VL bus) was the first local bus standard to arrive, with PCI coming along more recently and offering more speed, power and features. Your computer's manual should tell you, but in general a 486-based PC will have VESA and a Pentium-based PC will have PCI.

TIP

You'll need to keep track of how many slots you've got and how many you've used: knowing it's a PCI card you need to buy is a good start; buying it and then finding out all your PCI slots are full is a rather poor finish!

SCSI cards

SCSI (pronounced 'skuzzy') provides a slightly different system for installing add-on hardware devices to your PC, but a very fast one. A SCSI adapter card is fitted to one of your local bus expansion slots, and then up to eight SCSI-compatible devices can be connected together in a chain linking back to the adapter. These are usually storage devices like hard drives and CD-ROM drives, but SCSI can control all sorts of devices. And if you want to add even more devices (or you experience compatibility problems with some of the devices), you can add a second SCSI controller!

Since SCSI devices are connected in a chain, there are two points to know about this system. First, each device in the chain must have its own ID number so the SCSI controller knows how to talk to one without talking to all. Second, the last device in the chain needs a switch called a **terminator** to tell the controller it's at the end.

Buyers' guide: Motherboard

- You won't get a vast amount of choice in this, but once you've selected which type and speed of processor you want, make sure the motherboard uses the latest standard of local bus design, PCI. Its speed is comparable with that of the VL bus, but PCI is more 'future-proof' and has the added benefit of supporting Plug & Play.
- With an eye to the future, check how many expansion slots are included. This may depend upon your choice of case size (desktop, tower, or mini-tower) but in general, more available slots is good news, more available PCI slots is better news!
- Find out what the top limit is for installing RAM. New Pentium-based PCs should allow you to fit 128 Mb. For normal everyday use with a modern operating system, you might want to expand to about 32 Mb later on, so make sure you're not restricted to anything less than this.
- If expansion looks like becoming an issue, try to think ahead: SCSI offers great expansion opportunities but you'll need at least one free PCI slot for the adapter(s). If your PCI slots are all full already, you'll have to remove one card to free-up a slot and replace that device with the SCSI equivalent.

Booting the computer

In previous sections we've looked at the major components found in the PC's system unit and what they're all getting up to behind the scenes. In this section we'll look at what happens when you boot your computer, and marvel at the wonders of that little ROM chip, the **BIOS**. This section suffers from a nasty little rash of acronyms, but don't be put off – the details themselves are quite painless.

A pair of boots

Right now you're probably thinking: *This is silly talk. Right?* It might seem that way, but in fact **booting** is a real computing term – it's a refreshingly interesting way of saying 'starting'. Booting is short for 'bootstrapping' which, in turn, is derived from 'pulling it up by its own bootstraps'. The 'bootstraps' in question refer to the **BIOS** (pronounced 'by-oss').

There are two possible types of boot: a *cold boot* and a *warm boot*. A cold boot means starting your computer from cold, the state you find it in when you start work every morning; a warm boot (also called 'reset') means *restarting* the computer after you've already had it running a while.

Because a particular (if rather odd) term is used, you might be thinking that *booting* the computer is something else you'll have to learn how to do. You won't – your job is just to operate the power switch, and the computer will handle all the spade work.

The BIOS

'BIOS' is an acronym for Basic Input/Output System. As the name suggests, the BIOS plays an important part in transferring your *input* (from the keyboard, for example) to the processor, and transferring the processor's *output* to the monitor and other devices. As far as this goes, it's comforting to know that *something* is doing that, but it's not very interesting and we won't dwell on it. However, before the BIOS embarks on this full-time job, it has a sort of paper-round to take care of first: it has to get your system working.

The BIOS is a set of small programs stored on a ROM chip (see p. 21) whose basic role is to tell your computer about itself. When you turn on your computer's power switch, the BIOS's programs spring into action and start a sequence known as the **POST** (Power-On Self Test). Until the PC knows it has a hard drive, a floppy drive, memory, a keyboard, and so on, and that they're all properly connected and working, it can't start to use them. The BIOS also takes a look at a small amount of data stored on a special type of RAM chip called the **CMOS**. Finally, it looks at your boot-disk to find your operating system and loads it. This whole routine, from switching on to being able to start work, should take no more than 30–60 seconds.

The CMOS

This is pronounced 'see-moss' and stands for Complementary Metal-Oxide Semiconductor. The CMOS is a special kind of RAM chip which doesn't quite follow the rules – when your computer is turned off, the data stays in the chip. The reason this needs to be a RAM chip is that you might one day need to alter its settings.

It's the CMOS that actually holds all the information about hard drives, floppy drives and so on that the BIOS uses, and these are obviously details that might change: for example, you might add a second floppy drive to your system, or swap your hard disk for one with a greater capacity. The new details need to be entered in the CMOS so that the BIOS can pass them on to the rest of the system which, in turn, will be able to make use of the devices.

You've probably seen an important point begin to emerge: if the details are *wrong*, or if they're missing entirely because the CMOS has failed, the computer can't 'see' these devices. So a sensible early move after taking delivery of a new computer is to look at the CMOS setup and note its settings on a piece of paper, especially those for the hard drive. This isn't essential, but it might save an enormous amount of hassle at some point in the future, and it's easy to do. When you first switch on your PC and the BIOS routine starts, you'll see a little message on the screen telling you to hit a certain key (usually *Del* or *Esc*) to enter the Setup. Just hit the required key on the keyboard, and follow the instructions on the screen that let you see the information you want. When you've finished, you'll usually be offered the choice of two different keys to exit and let the BIOS continue: one key will save any changes you made to the settings, the other won't. Try to choose the one that doesn't save the settings in case you changed something by accident (though it's unlikely you'd have done that without noticing).

Boot disk

Another useful setting in the CMOS concerns the **boot disk**. The boot disk is the disk that contains the operating system files; the BIOS take its cue from this setting when it's ready to start loading the operating system.

Modern operating systems tend to be quite large so you'd naturally expect the operating system to be on your hard drive. If you have just one hard-drive, as is standard, this means the BIOS will expect to find the operating system files on Drive C, the usual name for the primary or only hard disk. But if the hard disk were to fail for some reason, you'd be unable to use your PC at all until you replaced it or got it working.

For this reason, operating systems give you the option to make a **Startup disk** on a floppy disk. This obviously can't contain the whole operating system, but it contains enough of the basic files to get your computer started and let you communicate with the system. Because this is a floppy disk, and you'll usually have just one floppy drive, you would put this disk into Drive A before switching on the computer.

So the CMOS setting for the boot disk sequence should show Drive A and Drive C in that order. The BIOS will then look at Drive A first to see if you've inserted a floppy disk; if you have, it will read the files on that, neatly bypassing your faulty 'C' drive. If it doesn't find a floppy disk in the 'A' drive (which, most of the time, it shouldn't of course), it turns its attention to Drive C.

TIP

Whichever operating system you use, make sure you always have at least one startup floppy disk. And before you consign it to a box somewhere, make sure it works by rebooting the computer with that disk in the floppy drive. There's no point in having this disk if you don't know whether you can rely on it in times of crisis!

▶ *Instructions for creating a startup disk are given on p. 307 for Windows 3.1 and p. 378 for Windows 95.*

Reboot and restart

We've briefly mentioned that a *warm boot* means booting the computer again when it's already been running (i.e. it's already *warm*). There are actually two subtly different methods of doing this which tend to be known as 'rebooting' and 'restarting'.

Rebooting is exactly the same process as the cold boot: the BIOS runs the POST, looks at the CMOS and loads the operating system, just as if you'd turned off your computer and then turned it back on again. Most PCs have a button marked **Reset** on the front or rear of the system unit for doing this: using the computer's power-switch to switch off and on again puts unnecessary strain on the internal components which the Reset button avoids.

Restarting is slightly different in that it doesn't run the POST; the computer remembers the details of the devices that were found from when you cold-booted. Restarting is usually done by pressing a combination of keys on the keyboard, often *Ctrl+Alt+Del* at the same time. Keep in mind that when you reboot/restart the computer, the RAM is emptied. If you were working on a document and you didn't save it before restarting, you've lost it! In practice, however, it's hard to do this by accident: the program you were using knows you haven't saved the document and, if it can, it will ask if you'd like to do that first.

Why restart?

But why would you want to reboot/restart? Surely, once the system is up and running, you want to leave it that way and keep working? On a modern PC that's quite true, and restarting the computer should rarely be necessary: there are really just two occasions when you might have no choice.

The first of these is when you make some fundamental change to the system: this might be installing a new application, customizing some aspect of the operating system, or changing the settings for one of your hardware devices. In these instances, the computer sometimes needs to run through the startup routine again to make a few internal adjustments and perhaps read a few extra files into memory that enable it to do what you're asking.

The second occasion is when the system *crashes*. The most common cause of a system crash is badly behaved software; an application trying to use an area of the computer's RAM that's already been allocated to another application, for example. In the worst cases, these two applications get into conflict and bring the whole system to a grinding halt, and the only way out is to restart the computer. Modern operating systems like Windows 95 offer some protection against this kind of argument occurring, but it hasn't been entirely eradicated.

Buyers' guide: BIOS

- Don't start insisting you want a PC with a BIOS when you go to the computer store; they'll laugh in a polite and bemused kind of way and explain gently that it's got one.
- Make sure your BIOS is 'Plug & Play compatible' (this is explained on p. p. 41): this makes installing and configuring new hardware an automatic process rather than a long, irritating, hit-and-miss one.
- An energy-saving, or so-called 'green' BIOS is worthy of consideration. It keeps an eye on whether or not you're using the computer, and if you wander away to do something else the BIOS will put your PC to sleep after a pre-specified period and draw just enough power to keep the contents of the RAM intact.
- Two big names in BIOS manufacture are **Award** and **AMI** (pronounced 'am-ee').

CHAPTER 2

Hardware and peripherals

Installing new hardware

What is installation?

The installation of new hardware is actually two things tied up neatly in one word. The first and most obvious of these is that you have to physically *attach* the new device to the computer: with some devices this is the easy bit; with others it's more or less the *only* bit! How to attach the hardware will depend upon whether it's an **internal** or an **external** device. Once the device has been connected, you have to set it up properly to tell the computer what it is, where it is, and how to communicate with it.

Fitting a new device

Internal devices are usually plugged into the expansion slots described on p. 30; the exception to the rule is additional drives which slide into the drive bays at the front of the system unit and are bolted to restraining brackets to hold them in place. Expansion cards and their slots contain all the connections necessary to power the devices and pass data to them and from them. Drives, on the other hand, have to be connected manually. First of all they need to be connected to the computer's power supply, and there are usually several spare power connectors in the system unit for this purpose. Secondly, they have to be connected to the main bus in order to transfer data. You'll see a 4 cm wide grey ribbon inside the case (called the **interface**

cable) with several plastic connectors on it: one of these connectors needs to be attached to the new device. (If the new device is a CD-ROM drive you'll also have to connect its Audio Out cable to your soundcard's Audio In if you want to use it to play audio-CDs.)

External devices are very simple to connect: they usually have just one cable that has to be connected to a port (or socket) at the rear of the system unit to enable data-transfer. That, and a mains cable, is all there is to it!

TIP

Don't install more than one piece of hardware at a time. If you install several and your PC doesn't work properly next time you start it, you won't know which device caused the problem.

Serial and parallel ports

Well, that's *almost* all there is to it. You have to make sure you plug it into the *correct* socket, some of which are known as **ports**. Ports are similar to the sockets you'd find on just about anything, in the sense that you plug something into them, and they're usually labelled. The main difference is that the PC's sockets are configured in different ways to enable them to deal with different types of data doing different things at different speeds. There are two types of port:

- *Serial ports.* Your PC will have at least two serial ports, called **COM1** and **COM2** (short for 'Communications port'). The mouse should be connected to COM1, and the modem (if you have one) to COM2. Serial ports are still not standardized and you see both 9-pin and 25-pin connectors (you can tell which type you've got by counting the pins in the socket or the tiny holes in the plug). If your device and your computer use different types you can buy a very cheap adapter to get around the problem. Serial ports transmit and receive data in a one-bit *series*, the format needed to send data over a telephone line.
- *Parallel ports.* You'll usually have only one of these called **LPT1** (for Line Printer port), although some computers offer two or three. To the LPT port(s), unsurprisingly, you attach your printer(s). The connectors for parallel ports *are* standardized but few devices other than printers and scanners are ever connected to parallel ports. The parallel port sends data in 8-bit chunks, and is able to check that the printer is ready to receive more data.

Apart from the connections to power supply and monitor mentioned earlier in the book (which are usually very easy to spot), the other socket you'll find is the Keyboard socket (and this one really *is* called a 'socket'!).

Drivers

With almost any new hardware you install, you'll also have to install something called a **device driver** to go with it. This is a program that helps the PC to talk the same language as the new device, and it will usually be provided on a floppy disk bundled with the hardware itself.

Try to make sure you're always using the most recent drivers for all your hardware to get the best out of each device. These can usually be downloaded free of charge from a company's World Wide Web site or an online service (see Chapter 6), or you could just phone the company and pester them to send you a copy if you're sure an updated version exists!

How you install the driver will vary from one device to another, and indeed from one manufacturer to another, but in general there are two methods. The neatest of these is that the manufacturer supplies a small program on the floppy disk that will copy the driver onto your hard disk and make sure the computer knows where to find it when it needs it. The second method is less automated, but not particularly difficult: most operating systems have a reasonably friendly little collection of programs called a Control Panel, and one of these programs will let you carry out a similar routine in a step-by-step fashion.

Resources

With many types of hardware you add to your system, the question of **resource settings** will raise its ugly head, particularly with expansion cards. Resources are one of the most complicated areas of PCs you're likely to come up against, but you shouldn't have to deal with them too often unless you plan on buying new hardware every few weeks. (And if you do, they'll soon seem quite easy anyway!) Let's first try looking at this in simpler terms.

A car has resources; it has petrol, oil and water. Some of its components need petrol, some need oil, others need water. So car-makers *assign* these resources where they're needed: if a particular component needs petrol, for example, they make sure there's a hose connecting it to the petrol tank.

In a PC, there are also three typical resources that different components might need, which should be clearly listed in the device's manual: **I/O Port Address** (also known as Input/Output address or I/O range), **IRQ** (Interrupt Request Line) and **DMA** (Direct Memory Access). Here's a short description of each:

- *I/O Port address* – Identifies a particular area in memory that a single specific device can use.
- *IRQ* – Whenever a device is called upon to do something (for example, your soundcard needs to play a sound), it has to *interrupt* whatever the processor is doing at that time. So it sends a request for processor time (an *interrupt request*) down a line to the processor, and these lines are numbered. The lower the number assigned to a particular device, the higher its priority in the queue when the processor is busy.
- *DMA* – These are numbered channels rather like IRQs. A DMA channel is a direct line to the computer's memory, bypassing the processor. This gives an improvement in response times from the device, coupled with the fact that the processor is left alone to get on with other things in the meantime.

The most important aspect of these resources (which, sadly, doesn't remotely fit our car metaphor) is that these settings must be *unique* to each device. For example, if two devices are assigned IRQ2, one or both of them will be unable to work. This situation is known as a **hardware conflict**. Resolving a hardware conflict follows the same principles as the initial setting of resources.

Setting resource allocations

In a very similar way to that explained in 'Drivers' above, there are two methods of allocating resources to a newly installed device. If you're lucky (or you bought carefully), the device will come with a program on a floppy disk to help you out. This program will examine your entire system to see which resources are available (that is, haven't been assigned to another device) and tell you which ones you should choose. Most of the time this will be as simple as agreeing to the program's suggestions and letting it update the system for you, but occasionally you might need to change settings on the hardware itself (see 'Jumpers and DIP switches' below).

If you're unlucky, you might have to configure these resource settings yourself. This will involve looking at the resources already allocated to all the other devices attached to your computer and making notes of any available ones. You'll then need to check the manual for the new device to see which settings are suitable. For example, despite the fact that there are 15 IRQ lines, some devices (typically the cheaper ones) might be able to work with only two or three of them. If these two or three lines are already being used, you've got the added thrill of checking the manuals of *other* devices to see if you can swap the IRQs around and free-up one of the lines you need.

Jumpers and DIP switches

You might have one extra little delight in store when you're setting the resource allocations for a new expansion card. When you've found the available resources in the PC you need to make sure the card itself is set to work with those settings.

Most devices leave the factory set up in a particular way. In most cases, all will go smoothly and these default settings will also be available in your computer. But just occasionally you might find that where the device is set to use IRQ2, for example, your PC doesn't have IRQ2 free but you *can* use IRQ7. That will mean changing the IRQ setting on the card itself from 2 to 7.

The facility for changing the card's settings is usually given using either **jumpers** or **DIP switches** (Dual In-line Package), and whichever method is used by a particular card, there should be straightforward diagrams in the manual showing how to make the setting you need. Some older cards had neither jumpers nor DIP switches, so your only recourse was a bit of intimate poking with a soldering iron. Even the most technically minded PC users tended to lose their sense of humour quite quickly dealing with these.

Plug & Play

If you're considering buying your first PC, and you've struggled valiantly through the last few pages, you're probably wondering whether to spend your money on a new typewriter and a few bottles of correction fluid instead. But so far we've reckoned without Plug & Play.

Plug & Play is a recent standard that makes the installation of new devices automatic (apart from actually connecting them to the machine of course!). Quite simply, all you need to do is attach the device and boot the computer. As part of its usual job, the BIOS will have a look around the system and find the new card. After a few tests and a bit of conversation between the two, the BIOS will know what kind of device it is and instruct the operating system to set it up. The operating system has a list of all the best-known types, makes and models and their requirements and can almost always finish the job in just a few seconds. If, on the rare occasion, a device is found that isn't recognized, the operating system will ask you a few questions and talk you through the process painlessly.

Notebook add-ons

Notebook PCs obviously don't give quite the same problems as their Desktop counterparts. To begin with, there's no space inside to be able to slot anything in there. More importantly, being a recent technology, standards have quickly emerged and become accepted to make the connection of new devices a much less 'suck-it-and-see' experience than it is with Desktops.

There are basically three different ways to connect peripherals to your Notebook, but two of them could barely be called 'solutions'. The first option is to buy your new device in **PC Card** format which can be slotted into a PCMCIA socket in the side of your Notebook when you need to use it. The PCMCIA socket is the Notebook's approximate equivalent of the expansion slots found in Desktop PCs.

The second option is to buy the device as a separate item with its own power supply and plug it into a serial or parallel port to use it. This, of course, tends to make nonsense of the concept of portability! A third option is to buy a **docking station**. This is similar to a Desktop PC which, as you'd expect, sits on your desk and comes alive when you plug your Notebook into it.

Notebook batteries

The 'external device' you can't live without if you have a Notebook PC is the battery, or perhaps *batteries* if you'll be relying heavily on your machine. Notebook batteries are all removable and rechargeable, and come in three delicious flavours: nickel-cadmium (*NiCad*), nickel metal hydride (*NiMH*), or lithium.

The NiCad battery has been around the longest and is therefore the cheapest; in the middle sits the NiMH with a longer life, and a slightly higher price to go with it; and at the top end comes the lithium battery which can power your Notebook for longer than either of the others, but is also more expensive.

TIP

When buying a Notebook, always find out how long it takes to recharge the battery (some batteries will recharge fully in as little as two hours) and how many hours you can get from a fully-charged battery in normal use. Another good question to ask is whether you can continue to use the PC while the battery is recharging.

The monitor

Just as your choice of processor and quantity of RAM is of vital importance in the technical aspects of the PC, your choice of monitor is of vital practical and aesthetic significance. You'll probably be spending long hours gazing at it, so you need to be happy with the picture quality and controls, and you need to know it'll be able to do what you want from it. There are two separate items involved here: the monitor itself, which is quite easy to choose, and the display adapter.

Monitor size and clarity

These are the monitor's two most important attributes, and clarity is easy – how does it look? Make sure it doesn't flicker, and check for the 'pincushion' effect, a picture distortion caused by the curvature of the screen which sometimes makes straight lines appear to bend. Check out the controls too: make sure you can adjust brightness and contrast effectively, and fine-tune the vertical and horizontal size and position of the picture on the screen. Some monitors have on-screen controls, which is a neat approach but not worth paying a lot of extra money for as you probably won't alter the settings from one month to the next!

If you find a monitor at the right price and size with a poor picture, don't pass it over immediately - experiment with the controls. Some stores just connect it all up to show it off, but don't bother trying to make it look good.

Monitor size is fairly straightforward too: try to go for a 15-inch screen. The old standard was the 14-inch which was fine for working at a resolution of 640 × 480 dpi (dots per inch – see 'Resolution and colour depth' below), but rather cramped working at 800 × 600 dpi, a more commonly used resolution. Better still, but quite a lot more expensive, is the 17-inch screen ideally suited to desktop publishing (DTP) or spreadsheets where you need to see more information on the screen at once.

If you're buying a new PC the monitor will be part of the package and its size will usually be mentioned in advertisements. All the same, if the store is including a 14-inch monitor in the deal and you want a 15 or 17, they'll usually be delighted to relieve you of some extra cash!

Refresh rates and interlacing

The image you see on the monitor is constantly being redrawn line-by-line, which is how things like the mouse-pointer appear to move around. The number of times per second this happens is called the **refresh rate** and is measured in hertz (Hz). On a screen with a slow refresh rate (56–60 Hz) the image will seem to flicker, whereas a faster rate (around 80 Hz) will appear much smoother.

Interlacing is another culprit when it comes to flickering screens. An interlaced monitor draws alternate lines down the screen, then works its way back up drawing in the others (rather like lacing up a pair of boots). The non-interlaced monitor draws each line consecutively, resulting in smoother movement and a lot less screen-flicker.

Energy conservation

Monitors draw a large amount of power while they're working and, of course, they're *still* working when you've stopped to get a bite to eat. New energy-efficiency standards have started to arrive on the scene which effectively 'put your monitor to sleep' if the

PC hasn't received any input from you for some time, causing it to draw significantly less power. Pressing a key on the keyboard or moving the mouse will wake it up again. Common standards to look out for are **MPR-II** and **Energy Star**.

TIP

Most monitors have their own on/off switch which, of course, is a 'manual' energy-efficiency device! Turning off the monitor won't affect anything you're working on – it has the same effect on your data as closing your eyes!

Notebook displays

When dealing with Notebook PCs nothing is cheap, and the problems involved in constructing such a small, slim, integral monitor inflate the price more than anything else. There are three types of display found on Notebooks: the mono screen (black and white); the dual-scan passive-matrix screen (colour); and the active-matrix, or *TFT* screen (also colour). Of these, the mono screen is the cheapest by far and quite satisfactory if you're using MS-DOS rather than Windows, or if you're only using your Notebook for a bit of word-processing and so on. It's also the most economic of the three in the battery power it uses.

Either of the two colour screens are preferable for use with modern operating systems, and the TFT screen is the most recent (and expensive!) technology that gives results as good as the Desktop monitor screen, but both of these will deplete your Notebook's battery at a much faster rate than the mono screen.

The display adapter

In order to display anything at all, the monitor needs an expansion card called a **display adapter** to be installed in the PC's system unit. This card is actually known by a variety of different names. To start with, the word *adapter* is interchangeable with *controller, accelerator* and *card*. In addition, the word *display* may be substituted with *video* or *graphics*. It all helps to contribute to that wonderful buying experience. There are subtle differences between some of the fusions of these words, but the points to look for are colour depth, resolution and memory.

Video memory

Display adapters contain their own on-board RAM chips, which might be either the good old-fashioned DRAM (as used for the PC's main memory) or the Video RAM (**VRAM**). VRAM is slightly different from the ordinary DRAM in that data can be read from it and written to it at the same time, making it a good deal faster. It probably goes without saying that that makes it more expensive too! Windows RAM (**WRAM**) is another technological advance that adds to both speed and price.

The RAM chips receive data from the processor and store it to be displayed – the actual amount of RAM varying from one adapter to another. The more RAM you have on your adapter, the more you're going to have to pay for it of course, but the RAM has a major bearing on your available options when it comes to choosing screen resolution and colour depth:

- 256 K will display 16 colours at up to 800 × 600 dpi
- 512 K will display 16 colours at up to 1024 × 768 dpi, or 256 colours at up to 800 × 600 dpi
- 1 Mb will display 256 colours at up to 1024 × 786 dpi, or 16.7 million colours at 640 × 480 dpi
- 1.5 Mb will display 16.7 million colours at up to 800 × 600 dpi
- 2.5 Mb will display 16.7 million colours at up to 1024 × 768 dpi

You can probably see that there's a trade-off between large colour palettes and higher resolutions, and fast refresh rates make a difference too. Quite simply, each of these items requires processing time and memory, and there's going to be a limit to the amount of either that's available. So you might find that to work at an ultra-high resolution such as 1280 × 1024 dpi will restrict you to 256 colours, but if you reduce the resolution to 800 × 600 you can then display 64 000 colours. Always find out what the monitor and the display adapter are capable of, and make sure they can *both* handle the display modes you want to use.

Resolution and colour depth

The monitor screen is made up of thousands of tiny dots called **pixels** (short for 'picture elements' and sometimes further abbreviated to **pels**), and each of these pixels will be a particular colour. Taken as a whole, all these tiny different-coloured pixels form the images you see on the screen. When something appears to 'move' on the screen, what you're actually seeing is bunches of pixels changing colour very quickly.

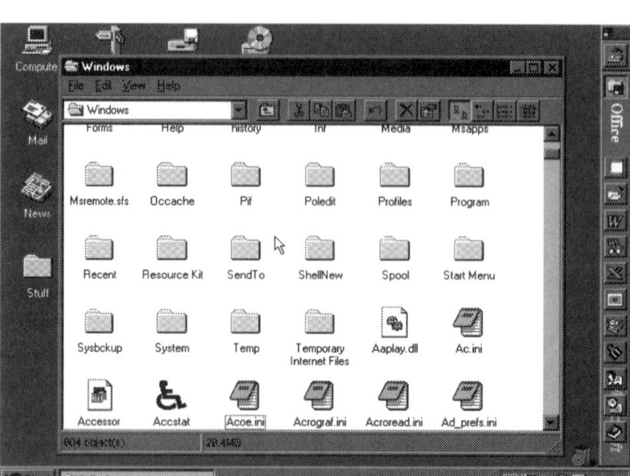

Figure 2.1 A monitor screen using resolution of 640 × 480 dpi.

Let's deal with the question of **colour depth** first. You can set your adapter to use colours from several sizes of 'colour-palette' – 16 colours, 256 colours, 64 K colours or 16.7 million colours. Clearly 16.7 million colours is going to be the most 'true-to-life', especially when viewing photographs and videos where natural colour produces some very fine gradations of hue. This means that every time a pixel changes colour, the processor has to select the correct colour for it from a choice of almost 17 million. You wouldn't want to be that processor, would you? On the other hand, if your adapter is set to display only 16 different colours, picking the right one is a much quicker and less labour-intensive task for the processor and thus beneficial to the rest of your system.

JARGONBUSTER

24-bit colour

Bits tend to crop up in advertisements and articles about colour depth, but don't be baffled:

- 4-bit colour means 16 colours
- 8-bit colour means 256 colours
- 16-bit colour means 64 000 colours (or *High colour*)
- 24-bit colour means 16.7 million colours (or *True colour*)

And so to **resolution**. We've already seen the common resolutions in the list above: 640 × 480 dpi, 800 × 600 dpi, and 1024 × 768 dpi (dpi stands for *dots per inch*, and comes back to those pixels again). On a low-resolution display, every square inch of the screen contains 640 pixels horizontally and 480 vertically (Figure 2.1). That's a lot of dots, all of which have to be assigned their own colour individually. Moving up to medium resolution (800 × 600) and high resolution (1024 × 768), that's a lot *more* dots for the processor to cope with (Figure 2.2).

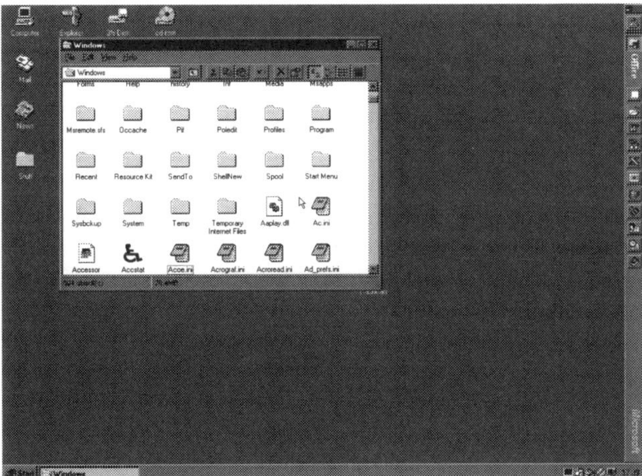

Figure 2.2 The same screen as Figure 2.1, this time at 1024 × 768 dpi.

The result of changing to a higher resolution is that everything will now appear smaller on the screen. And, of course, if everything takes up less space, you'll be able to show more information on the screen at one time.

TIP

The higher the resolution you use, and the more colours you're trying to display, the harder your processor has to work, which could have a noticeable impact on general performance. In reality, working at 800 × 600 dpi with 256 colours is a good trade-off between usability and performance for any adapter with 512 K or more of memory.

Screensavers

As a little light relief from all this technical stuff, now is a good time to introduce the screensaver. Screensavers are fun, but they serve a useful purpose: when you leave your computer and monitor on for long periods without using them, the image can literally 'burn' into the coating on the inside of the screen. This, needless to say, is bad news, leaving permanent ghost-images on your monitor. One answer is to turn off your monitor when you wander away for a while, but on some monitors that's not possible. A more enjoyable answer is the screensaver which kicks in after a predetermined time (similar to the energy-efficiency option mentioned earlier) and changes the image.

The old bog-standard screensaver would just fade the screen to black (which is too dark to burn the phosphor). More recent screensavers show moving images such as evolving patterns, cartoons and animations, or send on teams of little animals to start eating your icons, and some even include sound effects and music to accompany the on-screen lunacy. In fact, a lot of screensavers are better than TV!

All operating systems come with a few screensavers built in, and many more pop up on magazine cover-disks and the Internet, but some of the most popular savers come from Berkeley Systems' 'After Dark' series and are well worth checking out.

Buyers' guide: Monitors and video adapters

- As a sensible basic monitor specification, go for a 15-inch non-interlaced monitor that can handle a refresh rate of *at least* 72 Hz in the resolution you want to use (commonly 800 × 600 dpi with 256 colours).
- If your budget will stretch to it, consider buying a 17-inch monitor, particularly if you'll be using your computer for long periods and with a Windows operating system.
- Make sure both monitor and adapter are capable of handling the resolutions, colour depths and refresh rates you want to use before you buy either item. A 64-bit card is good; a 128-bit card is even better.
- If you're buying a Notebook PC (and you think TFT screens should be gold-plated for *that* price), check out as many machines with dual-scan colour screens as you can. Some are almost as good as TFTs; others tend to have very slow refresh rates and blur outrageously when screen objects 'move'.
- If someone offers you a **VGA** adapter, don't take it. VGA is an outdated mode that lets you display an extremely limited 16 colours at 640 × 480 dpi. The modern standard is **SVGA** (Super Video Graphics Array) which can handle the resolutions and palettes we've covered in this section.
- For all day-to-day uses, a display adapter with 2 Mb of VRAM is the average buy, capable of high resolutions and good colour depths. Regard 1 Mb of DRAM as the minimum. Popular display adapters are **Cirrus Logic**, Diamond Multimedia's **Stealth** series, and VideoLogic's **GrafixStar** series.
- If you intend to use your PC for video or true-colour photographs, get a card with VRAM or WRAM rather than DRAM fitted and aim for 4 Mb.
- Before buying, find out if you can add more memory to your card at a later stage.
- Most popular adapters are available for both PCI bus and VL bus systems, but make sure you specify the right one when you buy!

The mouse

Meet the mouse

The original type of input device for a PC was the keyboard, and that was fine for the purpose because most of the original operating systems and programs were text-based. The arrival of the graphical user interface (GUI) with its friendly buttons and icons required a more intuitive method of working, and the mouse became a ubiquitous feature of PCs, based largely upon a device called a **trackball** that was used in much earlier computer systems (and, in fact, still survives as a mouse alternative). Most mice plug into one of your PC's serial ports (COM1 is recommended) although a few use a smaller PS/2 port.

The mouse is a small plastic box sculpted to fit under your palm, with two or three buttons at the front and a cable (or tail!) leading to the PC's system unit. A ball in the base of the mouse enables it to roll around your desk, and sensors inside measure the direction and speed of travel. The movement of the mouse controls the movement of a small pointer on the monitor screen in a thoroughly intuitive way – move the mouse to the left and the pointer moves to the left, and so on.

The movement of the mouse just enables you to position the pointer wherever you want it; it doesn't actually *achieve* anything useful by itself. However, once the pointer is placed over an icon or button, pressing (or **clicking**) one of the mouse's buttons will perform some kind of action. Exactly *what* happens will depend upon the operating system, the object you're clicking on and a variety of other things, but various types of mouse-click might run a program, display more details about the object in question, or present you with a list of options (known as a **menu**) to choose from (Figure 2.3).

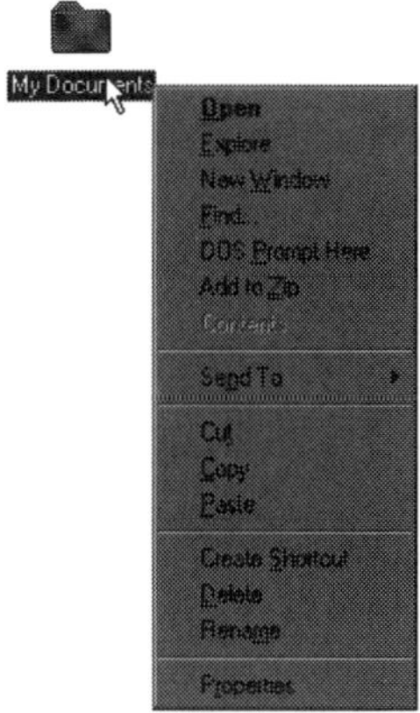

Figure 2.3 Clicking a mouse-button on this icon produces a menu of options. Moving the pointer onto one of these options and clicking again will select that option.

Never swing the mouse around by its tail, tempting though it is. And if it stops working, don't flush it down the toilet!

Clicks and double-clicks

You probably noticed the phrase casually thrown into the last paragraph, '*various types of mouse-click*', so it ought to be explained. The mouse usually has two buttons side by side, referred to as the primary button and the secondary button. For right-handed people the primary button is the left button, and is the button that tends to be most used. So any instruction to **click** on a particular object means that you should press the left button once. If you're to use the secondary button the instruction will be more explicit: **right-click**.

The other term you'll come across is the **double-click**. Once again, this tacitly refers to the left button, and involves clicking twice in quick succession. This is a technique that takes a bit of time to master, but, although there's usually a way to do the same thing using the keyboard, it's worth persevering since modern software is increasingly designed to be more mouse-oriented.

A few manufacturers, most notably **Logitech**, make a three-button mouse. The third button isn't actually supported by the PC, but the manufacturer includes a software program to get around this problem. That extra 'middle button' can usually be assigned a variety of tasks, and one of its favourite tricks is to take the place of a double-click.

Drag & Drop

The whole idea of a graphical user interface (GUI) is that you work with on-screen pictures that represent your files (known as **icons**) rather than long unfriendly lists of commands and file names, and much of the design of the GUI is based on the way people work in a normal office; for example, you can group particular collections of *files* together in a *folder* so that all the files relating to a certain subject can be found quickly.

This leads us to another mouse trick that goes hand-in-hand with clicking. In a normal office, if you're tidying up and you find a document in the wrong folder, you take it out and put it in the correct one. Drag & Drop is a mouse procedure that does the same thing: you click once on the itinerant document and, while continuing to hold down the button, move (or *drag*) the mouse across the screen to the other folder. When the pointer is over the folder, release the mouse button and the document is *dropped* into that folder.

The performing mouse

The on-screen pointer offers an unparalleled chance to make computing fun – after all, as long as you can point at objects with it, it's doing its job – so you can choose what shape you want your pointer to be. Of course, this has its practical advantages too: if you're working on a Notebook screen or on a Desktop screen at a high resolution where everything appears much smaller, it can be handy to use a larger pointer to make it more easily visible. But pointers come in all sorts of shapes and sizes, as Figure 2.4 shows.

This customization extends further than just the plain old 'arrow' pointer. At different times, when the computer is doing different things, the pointer will automatically change shape: when the computer is completing a task and can't accept any input from you until it's finished, the pointer commonly turns into an hourglass to indicate that you've got to wait; if the computer is working hard and might respond a little slower than usual for a short time, a smaller hourglass might appear *beside* the pointer. At other times the pointer will magically transform itself into a shape that should make the job you're doing easier, and you can usually choose between a whole range of shapes for each.

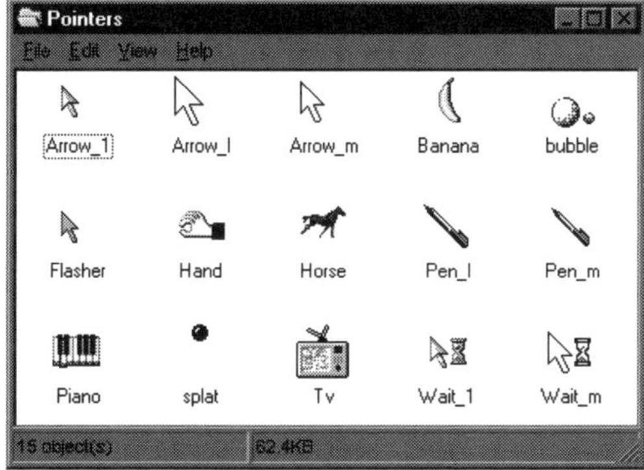

Figure 2.4 A few of the pointer options offered by Windows 95.

Another amusing option is the *animated* pointer, which might be a pointer that 'throbs' or changes colour, or something as *un*-pointer-like as a galloping horse! Animated pointers obviously take a little more processing power to produce, so they're something of a luxury, and your monitor and display adapter must be up to the task, but they're well within the capabilities of the average PC setup.

JARGONBUSTER

Cursors

A cursor is actually a small, flashing, vertical line that was used on older text-based computers to indicate 'where you were' in the document – the next character you typed would appear at the cursor position. In recent times, the word *cursor* has come to be used as a synonym for *pointer* (for example, we often talk about 'animated cursors'), and this vertical line, still used in word-processing applications, has become known as a *text cursor* to distinguish it from other pointer shapes.

The mouse's other talents

Apart from its tricks with pointer shapes, the humble rodent has a few other talents which can help to make it easier to use in particular situations. Depending on the operating system you use (and the software, if any, supplied with your mouse), you might find your options are even greater, but here's a few of the common ones:

- *Mouse trails.* As the pointer moves around the screen, it leaves a trail of 'ghost pointers' in its wake to make it easier to spot on a Notebook or high-resolution screen.
- *Acceleration.* Another useful option for the high-resolution screen. A mouse that seems to rocket from one side of the screen to the other at 640 × 480 dpi will seem barely able to crawl at 1024 × 768. The mouse-accelerator gives the little guy a kick-start so that it travels further on the screen in relation to your hand movement.
- *Button swapping.* For left-handed users it's more comfortable to use the button on the right as the primary button, and this facility allows you to switch. What it doesn't do, unfortunately, is to change the shape of the mouse itself and, of course, many mice are designed for right-handed people. Quite often the best you can expect is a completely symmetrical mouse which is uniformly uncomfortable for everybody!

The trackball

The trackball is like an upside-down mouse, with the ball on top. The design of trackballs can vary from the mundane to the eccentric, and the buttons can end up just about anywhere, but trackballs all have one thing in common: they're stationary. Instead of moving the whole device around your desk, your hand rests on it and moves the ball in its socket; one benefit of this approach is that no arm movement is required.

Most Notebook PCs have their own small version of the trackball built into the case, and usually positioned just below the spacebar of the keyboard for operation with either thumb. For fans of the rodent, it's usually possible to plug a mouse into your Notebook, but you'll need to find a reasonably flat surface to use it effectively.

The light pen

This is a slightly unusual sort of device that seems to surface from time to time, fail entirely to catch on, and then vanish again. It looks a lot like a normal writing pen with an added cable to connect it to the computer, and it lets you 'draw' on the monitor screen. A tiny sensor in the tip of the pen detects when a particular row of pixels on the screen is refreshed (see 'Refresh rates and interlacing' on p. 43) and sends that information back to the computer which can then work out where the pen is. Buttons on the side of the pen are used to click and double-click.

The light pen is a device the PC isn't used to working with, so an expansion card has to be installed that can deal with it, unlike the other types of pointing device that can plug straight into one of the PC's serial ports. On the positive side, because the light pen is an expansion device, you can still have a mouse or trackball connected as well.

One of the primary uses for the light pen is in artwork and graphics (an area to which the mouse isn't well suited) since you can hold it up to the screen and use it like a pen on paper. And therein lies the cause of its lack of success: the discomfort of holding your arm up for long periods soon makes you want your rodent back!

The graphics tablet

The tablet is a more popular alternative to the light pen. It features a touch-sensitive square pad that sits on your desk, and the movement of the on-screen pointer is controlled by the movement of your finger or an attached stylus over the pad's surface. Clicking may be carried out by tapping the pad, using buttons on the tablet's case, or a combination of the two. The larger-sized tablets give about the best input method for graphic design and artwork applications.

The joystick

Okay, this isn't a pointing device in quite the same way as the mouse. The joystick is a device known and loved by computer-game fans and ignored by everybody else, but it has essentially the same features: a handgrip for controlling the movements of objects on the screen, and a variety of buttons and triggers for wiping out all alien life-forms.

Game-play isn't a subject we're going to dwell on too much, so while we're here it's worth pointing out a few basic pros and cons. On the positive side, there's a huge number of games available for the PC, and the better ones (when you're lucky or informed enough to find them) can be every bit as good as their arcade counterparts. On the negative side, games more than anything test your PC to the limits with their need for speed, good graphics support, a soundcard and CD-ROM drive.

Buyers' guide: Pointing devices

- The most important consideration for *any* pointing device is comfort: Does it fit snugly into your hand? Can you reach the buttons easily? Does it move well?

- A close second is how responsive the device is in movement and click. Always test a mouse before buying (unless it's cheap enough to take a chance on), and especially make sure your fingers can't stray onto the wrong button by mistake.

- **Logitech** is one of the biggest names in the mouse and trackball sector of the market with a good range of products (including a cordless radio-controlled mouse). **Microsoft** produce their own very popular two-button mouse named, after much research, Microsoft Mouse. Both manufacturers include software which can optionally be installed to add some of the facilities mentioned in this section.

- Light pens and tablets are few and far between. The tablet is almost certainly the better bet, but make sure its active area is large enough to give you precise control over the pointer's position.

- Check whether the mouse of your dreams plugs into a COM (serial) port or a PS/2 port before you buy it. The serial port is more usual, and some will use either. Plug a serial mouse into COM1 – if you plug it into a different serial port the PC will waste time searching COM1 for it every time you boot the computer.

The keyboard

Meet the keyboard

The computer keyboard is remarkably similar to its typewriter counterpart, despite the much wider range of actions called for by a PC. For example, the same QWERTY layout is used, the *Tab, Shift* and *Caps Lock* keys survive, and there's even the equivalent of a carriage return lever called the *Return* key.

JARGONBUSTER

QWERTY keyboard

The standard UK keyboard layout, named after the first six keys found on the top row. The QWERTY system was originally designed as a counterintuitive layout to slow down typists who were reaching such great speeds that the typewriter keys kept getting stuck in a bunch. Obviously this can't happen on a computer keyboard, but by now we're all too used to it to change!

Because this *is* a computer keyboard a few extra keys have been added, so let's take a look at them one by one (Figure 2.5):

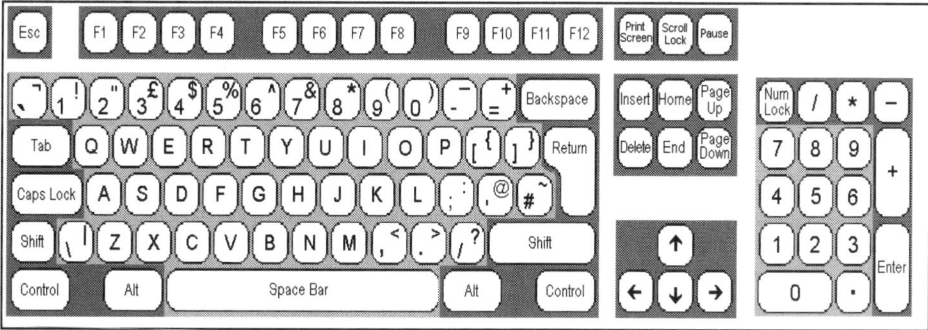

Figure 2.5 The standard 102-key computer keyboard.

- *Function keys.* A row of keys usually located at the top of the keyboard numbered F1, F2, and so on. Different operating systems and programs assign different commands to some of these keys, usually serving as alternatives to clicking an option with the mouse. A whole new set of functions may also become available if the function keys are used in combination with *Alt* or *Ctrl.*

- *ALT key.* The *Alt* (short for 'Alternate') key works rather like the *Shift* key, in that it's used in combination with other keys to produce a result. These key-combinations are used mostly to select options from menus, once again as an alternative to using the mouse. The *Alt* key can also give access to another range of characters (as the *Shift* key does) when used in combination with the number keys on the numeric keypad.
- *CTRL key.* The *Ctrl* (short for 'Control') key is also used in combination with other keys, frequently to choose menu-options in place of a mouse-click.
- *Arrow keys.* These are four keys for Up/Down/Left/Right which are chiefly used either for moving the cursor around a block of text or for navigating through lists or groups of icons.
- *Page Up/Page Down keys.* Because modern operating systems display each document in its own 'window' (a box on the screen), it may not be possible to view the whole of a long document at once. The *Page* keys provide one method of moving up and down the document a screenful at a time, rather like rolling a piece of paper backwards and forwards through a typewriter.
- *Home/End keys.* These provide a quick method of moving the cursor to the beginning or end of a line, or to the top or bottom of a long document or window.
- *Del.* Short for 'Delete', and not surprisingly used to erase the files or section of text you select in advance. In a word processor, it deletes the character immediately to the right of the current cursor position.
- *Backspace.* In a word processor, this deletes the character immediately to the left of the current cursor position, moving the cursor back one step in the process.
- *Esc.* Short for 'Escape', this key is commonly used to back out of something you've started and would rather not finish – a sort of Cancel button.
- *Print Screen.* Not the most useful thing to have a dedicated key for; this key 'photographs' the entire contents of the screen and stores it away so that you can . . . well, you'll probably think of something! Actually, in MS-DOS, it *does* have a practical use – it sends the contents of the screen straight off to the printer.
- *Numeric keypad.* A group of keys on the right of the keyboard. This group contains copies of the numerical and arithmetical keys on a calculator (together with *Enter* which does the same as *Return*). These keys actually have dual-functionality: with the key marked *Num Lock* turned on they function as calculator keys; with *Num Lock* off they double as an extra set of *Home/End/Page/Arrow* keys.

For Windows 95 users, there are also keyboards available that include three extra keys to give keyboard shortcuts to some of Windows 95's new features.

Key combinations

Key combinations almost always carry out commands that you could access with the mouse just as easily, but there are certain situations where the keyboard wins. For example, if you're typing a long document in a word processor and you want to enter a few words in bold type, it's easier just to enter the correct combination of keys without breaking the flow than to stop and reach for the mouse.

Key combinations are usually noted as *Ctrl + B* or *Alt + F4, R*. The first of these means to press the *Ctrl* key and keep holding it while you press the *B*. The second means press and hold *Alt* while you press *F4*, then press *R* after you've let these go.

Keyboard ergonomics

With business and industry moving increasingly to computers, and the computers being able to handle most of their needs, many people are spending their entire working day sitting at their PCs. As a result, some of the latest technical terms to hit computing are distinctly medical – RSI (Repetitive Strain Injury), upper-limb disorder, carpal-tunnel syndrome, and so on – and these have given PC manufacturers something new to think about: **ergonomics**, an attention to designing equipment that's comfortable to use for long periods and less likely to result in stress, illness or litigation.

Many manufacturers are producing ergonomically designed equipment, usually with radically different ideas about exactly what form it should take, but in the area of keyboards there seems to be some agreement. The most common features are wrist-supports, a layout that slopes upwards towards the back, and a central split which divides the keys into two clear left-hand/right-hand groups. The split-keyboard feature has great ergonomic benefits, and it's quite easy to become accustomed to for a touch-typist, but the two-finger typist will probably be reduced to using just one, and be thwarted still further by the slight angling-apart of the halves in most designs.

Keyboard tricks

In contrast with the mouse, there generally isn't much that can be altered about what the keyboard does or how it does it, and most keyboards don't have additional software to provide extra functions. The standard options you'll find built into the operating system are the ability to change the **repeat delay** and **repeat speed** (how long you have to hold a key before it repeats, and how fast it will repeat), and facilities for remapping the keys so that you can type in a different language (adding language-specific letters such as ß and á, and punctuation marks like ¿ and «).

The Windows 95 operating system also offers a set of **Accessibility Options** that includes a helpful bleep from the PC's speaker whenever you hit the *Caps Lock* key (a polite way of saying *You've done it again, you fool!*), the option to control the on-screen pointer using the arrow keys instead of the mouse, and the choice of entering key-combinations one key at a time rather than holding down two or three keys at once.

Buyers' guide: Keyboards

- Keyboards are almost always bundled in a new computer package with no option to choose a different one, but fortunately they're cheap enough that buying a replacement shouldn't be too much of a drain on your resources (with the exception of the ergonomic keyboards, some of which are ten times the price of the standard design!).
- The main factors to consider are key spacing and responsiveness. The *sound* of a keyboard can make a difference too – most users like to hear a slight click as they press a key, but some keyboards give a very plastic, rattly noise which can grate on your nerves after short time.
- If you buy a replacement keyboard, check the socket size at the back of your system unit first: most keyboards will plug into a standard-sized keyboard socket, but others require a smaller PS/2 socket. And *never* plug in a keyboard while your PC is switched on!
- Ergonomic or not, a keyboard is often more comfortable to use if you can lift the back of it and tilt it slightly towards you. Most keyboards have recessed legs for this purpose, but it's best to check before you buy.
- With a Notebook PC the keyboard is built into the unit, so swapping it for another isn't an option. For this reason, making sure you like the feel and response of the keyboard is far more important than it is for a Desktop PC.

The printer

Along with the monitor, the printer is one of the PC's main output devices; if you want to see the results of your labours on paper, a printer is what you need. Although it's an optional add-on device, and almost always bought as an entirely separate deal from the packaged PC, the question usually isn't *Do I need one?* but *What shall I get?*

There are only three common types of printer so you wouldn't expect the choice to be too tough, but the decision is complicated further by issues of resolution, colour or mono, speed, output quality, and how much it costs to use. Generally speaking, most users opt for the inkjet printer, and with so little to choose between mono and colour in terms of price it makes sense to go for a colour model. But, as with most of the hardware and software covered in this book, keep in mind the most vital question: *What do I want to use it for?*

Dot-matrix printers

The dot-matrix printer has been around the longest, and is therefore the cheapest type of printer you can buy for your PC. The dot matrix works a little like a typewriter in that the characters are produced by 'stamping' the ink onto the paper, but the method used is slightly different: the print mechanism consists of a set of pins, and pins are pressed against the ink ribbon in particular combinations to produce the shapes of particular characters. So the most important aspect of the printer is how many pins it uses, the options being 9 pin or 24 pin. Using a 9-pin printer, the individual dots that make up each character will be larger and more noticeable, whereas the 24-pin variety will use smaller, less individually noticeable dots and produce a better quality (though still far from impressive) result.

A dot-matrix printer is a sensible buy only if quality of presentation isn't such an issue as just being able to print. As this is the only type of printer to work by forcibly stamping the characters onto the paper, it can also be used for NCR stationery. A colour dot-matrix printer is usually fine for producing small blocks of a certain colour, or typing the title of a document in blue for example, but if you wanted to print coloured graphics and photographs you wouldn't be at all happy with the result.

JARGONBUSTER

CPS (characters per second)

Printer advertisements often quote a print speed in **cps**, indicating how many characters will be printed each second. As a comparison between different models it can be valuable, but the speed itself will depend upon the size and type of font you're using (see p. 150).

Mono inkjets

Inkjet printers tend to be the most popular, giving a good laser-quality output at a reasonable speed, and prices have plummeted for mono (black print) inkjets as the colour variety have become more popular. The inkjet printer works by squirting ink through tiny nozzles onto the paper, and the number of nozzles is what determines the printer's *resolution*. Just like screen resolution covered on p. 46, printer resolution is measured in dots per inch (dpi), and the *larger* the number of dots, the sharper the printed result. The minimum is usually 360 dots, but many reasonably priced inkjets can manage 720 dpi.

Most mono inkjets can print on paper of any quality, but the cost to watch out for is in the ink itself. In some cases the ink reservoir can be replaced very cheaply; in others you'll have to buy a new ink cartridge which can start to get expensive if you do a lot of printing. You might be able to economize by buying ink refills and refilling the same cartridge when it runs out, but this isn't as cheap as you might expect a simple bottle of ink and a plastic syringe to be.

Pages per minute

This is one to watch for the unwary: many inkjet printers quote a speed in 'pages per minute' which shouldn't be taken too literally. It's generally assumed that only one-third of a page's area will need to be printed, but any use of graphics or densely packed text could more than double this area, and will mean the page takes longer to print.

Colour inkjets

The price-difference between the mono and colour inkjets has become narrower recently, so this is a much more affordable option. Colour printing works by mixing cyan, magenta and yellow inks to produce the different colours, but how it does this can vary and (of course) it affects the price.

The cheapest type is the **colour-capable**, which can use only one cartridge at a time. For text-only printing, you'd use the cartridge containing the black ink; for printing of coloured pictures and graphs you'd swap to the colour cartridge containing the cyan, magenta and yellow each in its own chamber. The drawback with this type of system is that pages using a mixture of black text and coloured graphics would have to use the colour cartridge, and the black text will be created by mixing the three colours together. Not only does this use up your coloured inks faster, it also produces a rather more washed-out black (known as a 'compound' black).

The next step up is the device that really can call itself a colour printer, using a single four-colour cartridge (the fourth colour being black). This obviously means that pages combining text and graphics will be better presented as the text can be a true black, but there's still a drawback: because most of your printing will probably be text-only, usually in black, the black ink in the cartridge will run out before the three colours. You could easily find yourself replacing cartridges that still contain a lot of ink. The colour-capable is a better choice at this cheaper end of the inkjet market.

Moving up another step, we come to the two-cartridge printer. One cartridge contains the black ink, the other contains the three colours. Clearly this is a much better system to have, since you get all the benefits of colour printing and black text without the drawback of the four-colour cartridge. At the top of the heap comes the four-cartridge printer, using a separate cartridge for each colour. Technically this should produce the same quality as having two cartridges, but since this system is only used in top-of-the-range printers you might find the quality to be even better. You have the added expense of four cartridges that need replacing, but of course *nothing* needs to be replaced until it's empty!

JARGONBUSTER

Bleeding and saturation

These refer to two ways ink tends to misbehave on cheaper papers. 'Bleeding' means that the colours tend to run slightly while still wet so that one colour overlaps another; 'saturation' means that the ink passes through the paper and is clearly visible on the other side.

A few 720 dpi colour inkjets (using two or four separate cartridges) are very affordable and tempting, but check the paper requirements before buying. All inkjets can print onto ordinary paper, but many colour inkjets only produce their best results on specially coated paper that prevents bleeding and saturation, and enhances the colours. This paper can cost a good deal more than the standard photocopier paper you might use for printing text.

TIP

When you're trying to perfect the graphics and layout of a colour page, you can cut costs if you avoid using the coated paper until you're ready to print the 'finished article'.

Laser printers

The laser printer has traditionally been a large, expensive beast not often seen outside its native habitat, the professional office. Nowadays the price of a moderate laser printer is similar to that of an inkjet, making it eminently suited to the small office/home office (SoHo) market where quality results and fast output are just as important.

Lasers printers definitely are fast, and the 'pages-per-minute' measurement for a laser printer *can* be trusted, with 6 pages per minute being a good score at the cheaper end of the spectrum. The main point to check is their internal memory – laser printers have built-in RAM chips to relieve the pressure on the PC's own resources, and this can easily vary from a paltry 128 K to a far more respectable 2 Mb. In most (though not all) cases, you can fit more RAM if you need it, but it's a shame to be needing it before you start! There are good, cheap laser printers around that can print at a very nice 600 dpi, but this resolution requires 8 Mb of RAM. If your PC has more than 8 Mb you're okay, but if a sizeable amount of the required 8 Mb is in the printer itself your computer should find the going much easier.

Buyers' guide: Printers

- Whatever type of printer you choose, and especially in the case of colour inkjets, make sure you get a sample of its output to judge the quality for yourself.
- If you go for a *colour-capable* inkjet, get a sample of output using a mixture of colour graphics and black text to check the quality of the compound black.
- Go for the highest resolution you can afford, particularly for printing graphics – 600 or 720 dpi is a massive improvement on 360 dpi.
- Some printers have built-in paper feeds that can hold around 100 sheets. For long print jobs this means you won't have to stand by the printer feeding in a new sheet of paper every minute or so!
- Check the cost of consumables – cartridges and refills for inkjets, toner for laser printers – they all ultimately add to the cost of the printer. Both colour inkjets and laser printers need special types of coated paper which cost more than plain copy paper.
- Make sure you buy a printer-cable; they're not usually included with a new printer.
- If you have a Notebook PC you can buy a portable inkjet printer to carry with it, running off its own NiCad or NiMH battery with enough power for 200–300 pages. But bear in mind that the more 'portable' devices you add, the more likely you are to need a wheelbarrow to take them anywhere. You might find it easier just to wait and connect your (slightly cheaper) desktop printer when you get back to your desk.
- The big names in printers are **Canon**, **Epson** and **Hewlett-Packard**. All three produce a range of inkjets and lasers that covers most price ranges while offering maximum compatibility and security.

The CD-ROM drive

What is a CD-ROM?

CD-ROM is an abbreviation of Compact Disk Read Only Memory. The CD in question is a 4.7-inch diameter silver disk identical to any audio CD. The 'ROM' tag means that data can be read from the disk, but you can't *write* any new data to it. The concept of the CD-ROM is rather like that of the floppy disk – a removable storage medium for files. But while the floppy disk can usually hold only 1.44 Mb, the CD-ROM can hold almost 700 Mb!

Why do I need one?

Because of its size and its immense capacity, the compact disk has allowed all sorts of data to become easily and cheaply available to computer users. For example, some of the most popular software titles on CD-ROM are encyclopaedias: imagine how many floppy disks it would take to store an entire encyclopaedia! Not only that, but if you wanted to *use* the encyclopaedia you'd have to feed all these disks one by one into your floppy drive and copy all the data onto hard disk so that the PC could find what it wanted. Games, video and multimedia titles all contain huge amounts of data that can realistically be supplied only on CD-ROM.

JARGONBUSTER

Digital audio

A method of converting sound into a sequence of binary numbers (1s and 0s) as they're recorded. Because these numbers can't spontaneously change into *other* numbers, the quality of the sound can't deteriorate. In addition, because you're dealing with numbers, the audio data you've recorded can be edited in any number of ways without suffering any ill effects.

If games and multimedia aren't really your thing, there's another great reason to buy a CD-ROM drive: modern operating systems and software programs are getting bigger and bigger too! It isn't unusual to buy a new program and open the box to find 20 or more floppy disks waiting to be installed. Of course, you normally have to install the software just once but it becomes a much easier and quicker process if you can slip a single CD-ROM into its drive and watch it all happen automatically.

Which drive?

The key consideration about a CD-ROM drive is its speed. The current standard is the quad-speed drive, which is beginning to give way to the newer and faster six-speed drives. A faster drive is clearly preferable, but makes its mark most noticeably in playback of video and digital audio and for some of the 'fast'n'furious' action games. For simply installing and running CD-ROM-based applications, a quad-speed drive will certainly do the job adequately. There's no real gain to be had in buying the latest eight-speed drives: although the disk turns faster you won't get at its data any quicker in most cases.

CD-ROM interfaces

A CD-ROM drive needs an interface card to be able to communicate with the rest of the system. If you use a SCSI drive, the interface is built into the SCSI card already plugged into one of your expansion slots. If you don't, there are two options: one is to buy a drive with an expansion card and install it in a free slot; the other (more sensible) option is to buy a soundcard at the same time. Soundcards contain built-in CD-ROM interfaces, and the soundcard itself has more practical value than a dedicated CD-ROM interface, bearing in mind that either one will be occupying a valuable expansion slot!

JARGONBUSTER

Interface

An interface is a rather vague term for something that allows communication with the rest of the system. It may be the serial port your mouse connects to, or the socket and circuitry on a soundcard that lets you connect a CD-ROM drive to it. Or it could be a software interface: what you see on the screen after your operating system or a particular application has loaded is referred to as its *interface* because it lets *you* communicate with the system.

The catch with this method is that, until recently, nobody had agreed upon a standard interface for the CD-ROM, so some soundcard manufacturers built in interfaces for **Panasonic** drives while others included **Sony** or **Mitsumi** interfaces. Lately the generic IDE interface is beginning to emerge as standard, but it's still vital to make sure your choice of soundcard and CD-ROM drive follow *compatible* standards.

Multimedia kits

Luckily, a solution has arrived in the shape of the **Multimedia kit**. This usually comprises a CD-ROM drive, soundcard and stereo speakers and has the huge benefit that the devices are guaranteed to work happily together (not forgetting the fact that the instructions should explain all the connections that are necessary to make this happen!). Multimedia kits can vary quite considerably, particularly in the quality of the soundcard and speakers. Soundcards are the subject of the next section, but for the remaining devices try to go for speakers with a high output and a minimum quad-speed CD-ROM drive.

JARGONBUSTER

Multimedia

A method of presenting information using a combination of sound, video, animation, graphics and text, but the term is getting wider all the time as new media such as television are being added to the PC's capabilities. 'Multimedia kit' is actually something of a misnomer – the kit will usually include CD-ROM, soundcard and speakers, but it won't include an MPEG card to improve video playback, or a microphone to let you record sound.

Software control

As the CD-ROM drive has become a standard feature of computers, operating systems have adapted to make it easier to control. Obviously there's no getting away from the need to insert the disk in the drive, but it's usually possible to open and close the tray with a couple of mouse-clicks.

TIP

If a CD gets stuck in the drive and the tray won't eject, find a paper clip and straighten it out, insert it into the tiny hole in the front of the drive unit and push. The tray will slowly slide out. If the tray won't close by pushing the button after you've removed the offending CD, push it gently back into the unit and restart your PC as soon as you can to let the drive reset itself.

The CD-ROM drive can also play audio CDs as well as handling the more usual types of computer data; most drives have a headphone socket and volume control but you'll get better (and more comfortable) results from having a soundcard and stereo speakers. The software joins in here as well: Windows 3.1 allows you to play audio CDs with its **Media Player** program; Windows 95 has gone a step further and added a dedicated **CD Player** program.

Another little Windows 95 trick is **Autoplay**. As soon as you insert a CD in the drive, the system takes a look at it. If it's an audio disk, Windows runs the CD Player program and starts playing it. If it's a disk containing data, Windows searches the disk for a program called **Autorun** which it again runs automatically. The Autorun program may be a multimedia presentation that introduces the contents of the disk in a friendlier format than just a plain list of files, or it may start your CD-based game automatically.

TIP

When you install your new CD-ROM drive into a free drive bay, remember that the tray slides outwards when opened. If you position it in the lowest bay you might have to move your keyboard every time you want to put a disk in! Similarly, if you have a tower case and keep it on your desk, can you reach that topmost bay when you're sitting down?

▶ *For more on **Media Player** and **CD Player**, turn to pp. 367 and 369.*

Other CD-ROM options

There are two other options worthy of a brief mention, both of which are recent additions to the peripherals market. The first of these is the multi-disk **autochanger**, a cartridge that can usually hold four CDs at once. If there are particular disks you use frequently, a drive with an autochanger can save some of that irritating disk-swapping. The other new arrival on the scene is the **recordable CD** drive, which makes it possible to *write* data to compact disk as well as read it. Tempting though this sounds, recordable CD drives are still at the overpriced stage, so this is probably one of those items to avoid putting on the shopping-list for another year or two!

▶ *If you're tempted by the idea of recordable CD, take a look at p. 80 to find out about backup and archives drives.*

Buyers' guide: CD-ROM drives

- Don't buy anything slower than a quad-speed drive, whether as a single purchase or as part of a multimedia kit. Six-speed drives will give better performance, particularly when reading motion video and arcade-style games. Don't buy an eight-speed – a new high-density drive called **DVD-ROM** will appear soon that will better justify the extra expense.
- Remember that a CD-ROM drive needs an interface card which will occupy one of your expansion slots. Consider buying a soundcard with a built-in interface matching your chosen drive at the same time, or an all-in-one multimedia kit.
- Make sure you've got a spare 5.25-inch drive bay in your system unit before buying!
- One of the biggest names to look out for is **Panasonic**, producing quad- to eight-speed drives and PCMCIA versions for Notebooks. Other popular brands are **Sony** and **Mitsumi**.
- If you use (or intend to use) Windows 95, look out for a drive or multimedia kit that supports Plug & Play.

The soundcard

What is a soundcard?

The soundcard is an expansion card that adds sound capabilities to your PC, letting you hear the soundtracks of games and videos, play audio CDs (as long as you have a CD-ROM drive), and create and play your own musical extravaganzas using MIDI or digitally recorded sound.

MIDI

MIDI is an acronym for Musical Instrument Digital Interface, a method of passing data between electronic musical instruments and computers. Notes you play on one instrument can be sent into another to be played at the same time, or sent to a computer to be recorded and edited (taking out the *wrong* notes perhaps!).

In Windows operating systems the soundcard adds another little luxury to your computing life: you can assign different sound effects to so-called **system events**. If you've used a computer before, you'll have heard the indignant bleep from the speaker in the system unit when you do something you shouldn't. If you have a soundcard, you can replace that irritating sound with a short music clip, or a cough, or whatever you like. Indeed, you can assign different sounds to be played every time you run a particular application, click on a menu option, and so on.

Because soundcards have this wide range of uses there's a variety of products available with different features and specifications, suited to different uses, and at different prices. All these features serve to make it more complicated to choose a card, but they're really just the icing on the cake. There are two basic specifications to look out for: the number of bits used to produce the sound, and the method of synthesis used. Let's take the 'bits' issue first.

Digital audio

The soundcard's primary job is to handle digital audio, both in recording it and in playing it back. When recording, the card listens to the sound thousands of times every second and converts what it hears each time into a series of numbers. The frequency with which it does this is known as the **sample rate**. The more of these little 'snippets' of sound the card manages to capture and convert to numbers (i.e. the higher the sample rate) the more accurate its recording will be. But the big issue here is *which numbers* are used in the conversion: an 8-bit card can use numbers up to 255 to encode the sound; a 16-bit card can use numbers up to 65 535 which results in a more accurate, clean sound with a lot less background noise. Because of the huge amount of data they contain, audio files are very large and better sound quality means a larger file still.

► *See pp. 141 and 214 for more on digital audio. Windows includes a program called Sound Recorder for recording and playing digital audio files, covered on p. 368.*

Sound synthesis

The soundcard's second job is in handling sound synthesis. The soundcard is told what notes to play and when, and what sounds to use for different notes, and it creates these sounds itself using one of two methods: **FM synthesis** or **Wavetable synthesis**.

FM (Frequency Modulation, sometimes known as OPL3) is found on cheaper soundcards and is essentially useful only for non-musical uses, and some of the older game software that relies more on bangs, beeps and squawks than background music and credible sound effects. Its methods of imitating musical instruments result in sounds that are all slightly different from each other, but couldn't be mistaken for real instruments however much you'd had to drink!

Wavetable (or OPL4) synthesis is the standard, and most common form (although most wavetable cards have built-in support for FM synthesis too). Rather than trying to *mimic* the sound of a real instrument, wavetable synthesis uses a stored, digitally recorded sample of the instrument itself. This will obviously give a more realistic result than FM, but each card from each manufacturer will have its own collection of sounds, and which you prefer will usually be a question of personal taste.

In most wavetable cards the sounds are stored in a ROM chip, making each sound instantly available. In some, however, the sounds are stored on your hard disk and you have to choose which to use and load them into the card's internal RAM ready for use, which is a good deal slower. Some of the better cards have facilities to add your own sounds, and you may be able to add more memory just as you can with the PC itself.

The standard soundcard is the **SoundBlaster** series, made by Creative Labs. This has grabbed such a firm hold on the sound capabilities of the PC that most other cards (and almost *all* games) boast SoundBlaster (SB) compatibility. If you buy a card from a different manufacturer, SB and/or SB Pro compatibility will ensure that the card works with any software you have that uses sound.

The soundcard and MIDI

When it comes to playing audio CDs or sampled sounds, the method of sound synthesis used by the card doesn't matter: all the data that makes up the sound you hear is on the CD or in the sample file on your hard disk and the soundcard decodes and plays it. A **MIDI** file, on the other hand, just contains simple instructions that tell the soundcard which sounds to use and which notes to play on each sound at a particular time – the sounds themselves being in the soundcard's ROM or RAM chips rather than stored in the MIDI file. So a typical four-minute MIDI file might be only 50 K in size, compared to a good-quality digital recording of the same music which would weigh in at roughly 40 Mb!

Due to the vast difference in data sizes, MIDI is often used to play the musical soundtracks of games, but its primary use is in being able to create your own pieces of music without needing a recording studio and a full orchestra. The standard to look out for in a soundcard is called **General MIDI** (GM) which offers a range of 128 sounds including orchestral instruments, a drumkit and sound effects; 16 different sounds can be played at once. The only variable you're likely to come across (apart from the quality of the sounds, as mentioned above) is the number of **voices** the card can produce. Each note the card has to play requires one voice. If a card has 24 voices (the minimum requirement for GM compatibility) it can therefore play 24 notes at once, but these get used quicker than you'd imagine! Some cards offer 32 voices which is useful extra headroom to have if you plan on using the MIDI capabilities to a great extent. The card should also include reverb and chorus effects (and maybe a few more) that can be applied to the sounds to give them a more professional shine.

▶ *Turn to p. 215 for more on MIDI.*

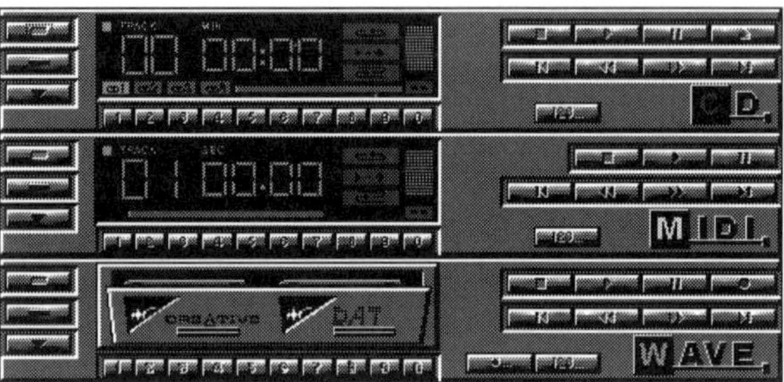

Figure 2.6 Comprehensive player software from Creative Labs' SoundBlaster AWE32.

Soundcard software

As well as the vital features of the hardware itself, many soundcards aim to get your vote by including software with the device. Most cards will give you an on-screen mixing desk to let you adjust the volume of input (for recording), and separate volume controls for playing compact disks, MIDI files and sampled sound ('wave') files. Another popular software utility is 'playback' software, often designed to look like a home stereo unit (see Figure 2.6). Above this, the package can get quite exotic: you might have an application that lets you create and edit your own digital recordings; another that lets you create play-lists of MIDI files; another that can read out a text file in a synthesized voice. Tempting as these can be, bear in mind that this type of software can usually be found cheaply any time you want it, but if you're not happy with the soundcard itself you've got to buy a new one!

Soundcard resources

The soundcard plugs into a standard ISA expansion slot in your motherboard, so there are none of the complications of having to choose the correct local bus type. You do need to make sure your card has a suitable interface built in if you want to connect your CD-ROM drive to it. If you buy the soundcard as part of a **multimedia kit** (see p. 65), both CD-ROM and soundcard will be compatible. If you haven't yet bought a CD-ROM drive, try to get a soundcard with an IDE interface for maximum choice later on.

The card will need to have a range of system resources allocated to it: I/O address for the soundcard itself (usually 220 H), another I/O address for MIDI compatibility (usually 330 H), IRQ (usually interrupt 5) and DMA (usually channels 1 and 5). Most cards will be supplied with a software program that identifies and sets these resources; if you're using Windows 95, look out for a soundcard labelled as Plug & Play-compatible to make the job even easier (see p. 41).

Once the card is slotted into place, its sockets should be accessible at the back of your PC so that you can plug in speakers and headphones. You might also have inputs for a MIDI instrument and a joystick. If you have a Line Out socket, you can connect this to your hi-fi's amplifier. Speaker systems are available from many manufacturers and the more expensive systems can rival hi-fi performance for musical use; the cheaper systems are better suited to playing system sound effects and voice communications.

Buyers' guide: Soundcards

- Whichever make of soundcard you buy, make sure it has SoundBlaster (SB) or SoundBlaster Pro compatibility, or preferably both, together with MIDI support.
- For any use in which the sound quality matters, buy a **16-bit** or **32-bit** wavetable soundcard. For serious musical use, the more memory included on the card the better: a common figure for onboard memory is 512 K, but 1 Mb is a more useful minimum. It's useful to be able to add more memory if you need to – find out what the limit is.
- Make sure the card quotes **General MIDI** compatibility and has a minimum of 24 voices.
- If you use your PC for games, avoid cards that don't store their sounds in ROM. In order to work, these cards require extra files to be loaded into the computer's memory which may prevent your game from running.
- Two of the most popular types of card are the **Creative Labs' SoundBlaster AWE32** and the **Advanced Gravis Ultrasound**. The first of these is the more suitable for games, but both are good for other audio uses including MIDI and digital audio recording/playback.
- Don't forget you'll need to connect speakers or headphones to hear any of the results of your soundcard's labours!
- If you already have a CD-ROM drive and you want to use the soundcard as its interface to replace your dedicated CD-ROM interface, make sure your soundcard has either an IDE CD-ROM interface built in, or an interface that matches your make of CD-ROM drive.

- If you have a soundcard already but it doesn't have wavetable support, a few manufacturers sell wavetable upgrade boards (often termed **daughterboards**) that you can add to your system to save the expense of buying a whole new soundcard.

- Watch out for the vague words *16-bit soundcard* in advertisements and specifications: if the musical quality of the device is important to you, make sure that the device uses wavetable synthesis and is a known-brand product.

The modem

What is a modem?

Remember that lack of imagination in naming computer devices mentioned a while back? The name 'modem' features this same lack of imagination, but this time cunningly disguised. What the modem does is to *MODulate* and *DEModulate* a signal – take a handful of initial letters and stir well.

To be more precise, the modem takes data in the computer's native digital language, binary code, and *modulates* it to an analog sound wave that can be transmitted over telephone lines. When the signal reaches the modem at the other end, the data is *demodulated* back to its original binary form. The data itself could be anything at all: fax, e-mail, a picture, an application, even a whole operating system!

Why do I need one?

The sudden popularity of the **Internet** and the sudden rush to buy modems is more than coincidental; we'll look more closely at the Internet in Chapter 7, but if surfing the 'Net sounds like your thing, you'll need to join the queue at the modem checkout. Other uses include the capability of sending and receiving faxes from your computer instead of having a separate fax machine, and dialling the phone from your computer to save the exertion of all that button pushing. Modems with voicemail ability will let you use your computer as an answer-phone, storing incoming messages to hard disk (provided you leave your computer running when you're away from your desk or out of the office). Voicemail systems will need a soundcard to be installed in your PC for recording and playback of messages (see p. 67), although a few systems include a fairly basic soundcard in the package.

Internal or external?

There are two types of modem to choose from: *internal* and *external*. The internal modem is a card that slots into an ISA expansion slot in your motherboard, while the external modem is a separate box that plugs into one of your PC's serial ports (usually COM2). Both types have their pros and cons:

- The external modem has the benefit of lights on the front panel that let you see when a connection is made and when data is passing into or out of the computer. It plugs easily into the back of your PC. If your computer tends to be on for long periods, the external modem has the benefit that it can be turned off. Without the advantage of flashing lights, it has been known for the internal-modem users to remain unwittingly connected, running up online charges long after they thought they had disconnected. On the negative side, an external modem means another power socket needed.
- The internal modem has the advantage that it doesn't need a separate power supply, but it does need resources to be allocated like any other expansion card, with the same potential for conflicts.

So quite a good case can be made for the external modem, but there's another issue which involves a chip called the UART, the chip which controls the serial port: your PC may use a UART chip numbered 8250 or it may use the more modern 16550 chip. To get the best out of a fast *external* modem (28 800 bps – explained below – and higher) you'll need to connect it to a port with a 16550 UART – most recent computers have these as standard. If yours doesn't, you can buy a cheap high-speed serial port card with this later chip installed and use that in place of your normal serial port. Internal modems skirt this issue very neatly by having a compatible chip built in.

You can find out which type of chip your PC uses. Run Microsoft's **Msd.exe** program in MS-DOS, press 'C' to look at the COM Ports details and look at the entry beside 'UART Chip Used'.

If you're looking for another benefit to the internal modem, they tend to be a little cheaper than their external counterparts, and most manufacturers produce the same modem in both forms. Whichever type you opt for you'll need a telephone line to plug it into, and a phone socket within reach of your PC.

Keep your modem at least a few feet away from any fluorescent lights – they can cause interference, lost data and even dropped connections if they're too close.

Modem speed

Modem speeds are measured in **bps**, or *bits per second*, referring to the amount of data they can transmit and receive in this period of time (you might see 'bps' replaced with **baud**, but the meaning is the same). The two common speeds for modems are **14 400 bps** (14.4 Kbps) and **28 800 bps** (28.8 Kbps), but faster **33 600 bps** (33.6 Kbps) modems have recently made an appearance. You'll also find these referred to somewhat cryptically as V32bis, V34 and V34-plus respectively. It isn't worth buying anything slower than a 14.4 Kbps modem, and for small-scale use, such as sending and receiving faxes and e-mail, this is quite adequate. For Internet connections one of the two faster modems should quickly pay for itself in lower telephone charges.

JARGONBUSTER

Download

The action of copying a file on one distant computer (perhaps on the other side of the world) across a network of computers and telephone lines to your own computer. The opposite term is 'upload' – copying a file from your own PC to a remote computer.

An important point to remember is that a fast modem doesn't necessarily mean you'll be whizzing around the Internet faster than people with 14.4 or 9.6 Kbps modems. You've probably heard the term 'the superhighway' used in reference to the Internet; like any highway, there's a lot of people all trying to get to the same place, and things can get jammed solid. When this happens and the person with the slow modem is anxiously watching his screen for some sign of data coming down the line again, the person with the fast modem is doing just the same. All the same, when everything's running smoothly a 28.8 modem is streets ahead of the 14.4.

TIP

Make the most of your modem. Because data is compressed, make sure it's being sent from your PC to your modem at least twice as fast as your modem's rated speed. Find the settings for the COM port your modem is connected to and change the port speed to 38 400 for a 14.4 Kbps model and 57 600 for a 28.8 Kbps model.

Talking modem-speak

More than most devices the modem has an ocean of terms you'll have to navigate sooner or later. The first of these is the **AT Command Set** used by Hayes modems and adopted by most others as a common standard (these devices being known as 'Hayes-compatible'). The 'AT' simply stands for 'Attention', and the command-set contains a list of modem commands that begin with these two letters. ATDT tells the modem to tone-dial the following number; ATDP to pulse-dial the following number; ATH is the code to hang up; ATM is the code to turn off (mute) the modem's internal speaker. Nevertheless, even if a modem boasts Hayes-compatibility, it may not respond to *every* AT command, so some delving into the manual will inevitably be needed.

A common set of questions you might be asked when trying to make a connection refers to **Data Bits**, **Parity** and **Stop Bits**. Without going too deeply into their meanings, settings of 8, None, and 1 respectively (often written **8N1**) should suit almost all connections. If you find one that this doesn't work with, try 7, Even, and 1 (**7E1**) instead. You may also be asked which file-transfer protocol you want to use. If it's there, choose **Zmodem**; if not, choose **Ymodem**. If you're asked about Terminal Emulation, **VT100** is the most common setting.

If you have **Call Waiting** on your modem's telephone line, make sure you turn it off before making a modem connection. An incoming call at the wrong moment could disconnect you mere seconds before that 5 Mb download would have been complete! You can usually enter a command in your modem setup to turn off Call Waiting automatically before dialling and turn it back on when you disconnect.

Easy faxing

Almost all modems have fax capabilities, and most are bundled with some form of fax software to help you organize, print and store incoming and outgoing faxes, usually coupled with a database for phone numbers. There are several benefits to faxing from the PC: you'll have a lot less paper to file away; there's no need to print the document ready to send, just click the mouse a couple of times and it's on its way. Most importantly, perhaps, you don't need a large, expensive fax machine squatting on your desk.

The main disadvantage of computer-based faxing is that you need to have your computer and modem switched on, and your fax software running, to receive a fax. In a reasonably busy office that shouldn't be too much of a problem, but if you don't expect to receive many faxes it's easier just to ask people to telephone before trying to send a fax so that you can get prepared.

Buyers' guide: Modems

- Decide whether you want an internal or an external modem. If you want the internal variety, check you've got a free ISA slot for it.
- Make sure the modem you choose has fax capabilities if you want to fax to and from your PC. Most importantly, make sure your modem can *receive* faxes as well as send them – unusual as it sounds, it's not a foregone conclusion.
- In the modems market, **Hayes** is one of the biggest names, but hot on their heels are **US Robotics** with cheaper, very popular devices.
- If you see a mention of **Flash ROM** in a modem advertisement, this is good news. It means that the instructions stored in the modem's internal ROM can be updated by installing new software from the manufacturer, either from floppy disk or by downloading it from the Internet. This is infinitely preferable to replacing the modem at a later date!

The scanner

What is a scanner?

The scanner is an input device that works in a similar way to a photocopier. When you photocopy a sheet of paper, its contents are photographed and copied to another piece of paper; when you *scan* a sheet of paper, its contents are photographed in a similar way, but copied into your computer. From here you can edit the scan in various ways and store it on disk.

Why do I need one?

One of the major uses of a scanner is as a paper-replacement: if your office is swimming in paper and your filing cabinet is full, scan some of this paper into your computer and keep it on hard disk instead. Any time you need a paper copy again, just print it as you do with any other document. Scanning can also be handy for grabbing pictures or a company logo that you want to include in your own documents, and typewritten or printed text that you want to edit in a word processor (as long as you have OCR software – see below). Finally, a scanner makes a very cheap alternative to a photocopier – just scan the page you want and then print it! Some scanners make this even easier by allowing you to scan directly to the printer without needing to save first.

Handheld, page or flatbed?

The scanner comes in three flavours, **handheld**, **page** and **flatbed**, and as usual heach of these has its own strengths and weaknesses.

The **handheld scanner** is a small device that you roll over the document to be scanned. Its main benefits are its compact size and low price, but its size also has to count as its greatest disadvantage: a large document can't be scanned in one 'pass' down the page, so you have to make several passes which the software should then stitch together to form the complete page. Because you have to actually drag the scanner yourself, most have a warning light and/or bleeper to tell you if you're dragging too fast for the scanner to read the document. You've also got the problem of dragging smoothly at a single speed and in a straight line which takes a little time to master, but this method of working does allow you to scan pages from books and magazines that you couldn't pass through a page scanner without first tearing them up!

The **page scanner** is a larger desktop device that looks and works rather like a printer: feed in a sheet of paper to be scanned and it handles the rest automatically. The benefits are an improvement in quality over the handheld type, and the ability to scan larger sheets without needing to stitch the images together. The disadvantage is that only single sheets can be scanned, although there are two or three excellent page scanners on the market which allow the scanning head to be detached and used like a handheld, giving the best of both worlds.

The **flatbed scanner** is the top-of-the-range model: the page, book or photograph is placed face down on its surface and the image is scanned at the push of a button. The only disadvantages are the expense and the amount of desk space required, but when added together they tend to make this the device for the professional.

Colours and dots

After deciding which type of scanner you need, you've got some other selections to make. The first of these is **colour depth**: some scanners provide 24-bit colour (16.7 million colours, often known as 'true' colour); others offer 256 grey scales, producing a result very similar to a so-called 'black and white' photograph in which colours in the original are replaced with one of 256 shades of grey varying from white to black. Scanners with 32 grey scales can be found, but they're not significantly cheaper than the 256 grey scale models.

TIP

st of your scanning work will be done with the intention of printing, remember that a colour scan will still print in grey scale on a non-colour printer. If you plan on buying a colour printer in the future, a colour scanner may be worth while; if you don't, go for the cheaper grey-scale scanner.

Your next selection is for **resolution**, measured in *dpi* (dots per inch), which follows exactly the same principles as the monitor and printer. The higher the resolution of your scanner, the more accurate the results. Most scanners can handle a resolution of at least 300 dpi, and a great many handheld and page scanners offer 400 dpi. Some scanners (particularly handhelds) achieve these resolutions by using a method called **interpolation**, which actually scans at a lower resolution and fills in the missing pixels by looking at those around them and choosing a good colour average.

TIP

If your printer has a resolution of 300 dpi, paying extra for a 600 dpi scanner is money wasted unless you've also got a new printer on your shopping list.

A point to bear in mind is that scanning at high resolutions or in true-colour will add to the size of the file and create a large amount of data for the computer to deal with. A Pentium PC with 8 Mb RAM might still take quite a time to stitch together two pieces of a 400 dpi true-colour full-page scan for example. This isn't to say don't do it – just don't scan at a high resolution or in true colour if you don't need to, and consider adding more RAM to help your computer shunt some of this data around while it's working with it.

Scanner software

Most scanners, particularly the page and flatbed types, include comprehensive software for organizing and managing scans, and choosing whether to send the scan straight to a printer, straight to hard disk or to a particular application to be edited. One useful specific inclusion to watch out for is **OCR** software. OCR stands for Optical Character Recognition – when you scan printed text, the OCR software can recognize the individual characters and recreate them in a word processor ready to be edited like any other text-based file. The potential 'curse of the wobbly hand' means that handheld scanners are best avoided for OCR work but the results are pretty consistent in the other types, with the occasional exception of multi-column text (as in newspapers) which confuses some OCR software.

The TWAIN driver

Yes, honestly, there is such a thing! And it gets better – this is a computing acronym with a sense of humour. TWAIN stands for Tool Without An Interesting Name. TWAIN is a standard supported by most (but definitely not all) scanners which lets you scan directly into a variety of applications such as word processors, graphics and drawing packages, and DTP software. Once again, not all *applications* support TWAIN either, and the options provided by different drivers can vary, but in general it's worth looking out for a scanner with TWAIN compatibility.

JARGONBUSTER

DTP

An acronym for Desktop Publishing, a type of software that allows you to incorporate and manipulate text and graphics in a single document to create brochures, flyers, newsletters and so on. Many recent word-processing packages can handle similar types of document, but DTP is designed expressly for the job and includes tools that make it easier to create a professional page layout. See section p. 191 for more on DTP.

Scanner connections

The scanner is a curious beast in its methods of connecting to your PC – just about anything goes! Some devices connect to a serial (COM) port, others to a parallel (LPT) port, and still others require an ISA interface card to be installed and connect to that. The majority plug into an LPT port, so if you have only one parallel port make sure that any scanner that plugs into it has a built-in printer port so that you can still scan directly to the printer.

Buyers' guide: Scanners

- Before buying a scanner, consider carefully what you want to use it for and how often you'll use it. For large amounts of work, go for a page scanner with a built-in sheet-feeder so that you can put in a bundle of pages and leave it to get on with it. For heavy OCR work any grey-scale scanner that includes good OCR software will do fine, and resolution doesn't make much difference. Hand scanners are worth considering for small amounts of scanning: OCR may be unreliable and the stitching process for large pages may take a while, but for scanning smaller areas the handheld will usually be good enough.

- If you opt for a handheld, choose one with the widest scanning head you can (normally about 4.5 inches) – the wider the head, the fewer the number of passes needed to scan in a wide document.
- To get the best results from scanning photographs and artwork, go for a flatbed scanner.
- TWAIN-compatibility is well worth having to help integrate the scanner with your everyday applications, but is not a necessity. The scanner is one of the few devices with which the quality of its bundled software can add considerably to its ease of use and capabilities.
- For maximum flexibility, take a look at page-scanners which double as handhelds, such as the **Logitech PageScan Color** and the **Primax Colour Mobile**.
- Other scanner manufacturers worth a look are **Hewlett-Packard** and **Epson**.

The backup drive

Backups and archives

As we've mentioned previously, both hard disks and (especially) floppy disks are known to be fallible so it's sensible to keep copies of any files you can't afford to lose on a different disk: these copies are known as **backups**. One common scenario is to copy vital files from your hard disk to a floppy disk, but you may have lots of files you wouldn't want to lose which might call for a huge stack of floppies and most of a day to do the job.

Archives work in a slightly different way: many PC hard disks get filled up with large files that are rarely used – multimedia PCs are especially prone to this. Graphics, sound and video files might be occupying vast areas of your hard disk which could be put to better use storing documents or more applications. *Archiving* these files means clearing them out to a different disk so they're available when you need them (albeit with slower access times than from the hard disk) but not getting in your way.

What is a backup drive?

A backup drive is a mass-storage drive, separate from your hard disk, used chiefly for backups and archives. In effect it's like having a second hard disk in your computer to which you regularly copy the entire contents of the first. Indeed you could actually install a second hard drive for the purpose, but one of the reasons for having backups is to guard against losing your data in the event of theft or fire – in either situation, that second hard disk has gone the way of the first! The only sure method is to backup the data to a removable device, similar to having an ultra-high-capacity floppy disk, and that's the kind of storage provided by backup drives.

Although many types and makes of drive advertise themselves as being 'backup drives', some really don't have the capacity or flexibility to make the claim a valid one, and are better suited to simple archive uses.

Archive drives

The recordable CD is a good example of a drive that can be useful for archiving purposes but quite hopeless for backups. The prime reason is that once a CD has had data recorded onto it, the data can be read, but it can't be erased or replaced. You could build up a collection of home-recorded CDs containing your multimedia files, but regular daily or weekly backups of your entire hard disk would take at least one disk each. And what can you do with 52 CDs full of last year's data?

One of the most popular archive-drive types is Iomega's **Zip** series, which is available as either an external device or an internal one that installs into a 3.5-inch drive bay. Its primary benefit over the tape drives used for backups is its random-access capabilities: you can search for a particular file on a Zip disk just as you would on a hard or floppy disk. It uses 100 Mb disks which provide good storage capacity for files you want to archive. You could conceivably use it as a full backup device, but a half-full 1 Gb hard disk would need five of these disks.

Backup drives

The most common backup drives use magnetic tape, as opposed to disk, a similar concept to the cassette recorder. Although tape can be just as fallible a medium as the floppy disk, the advantages of tape storage outweigh the disadvantages: each tape can hold up to 750 Mb of data, and the software included with the drive can backup the full system without needing you to hold its hand or feed it new tapes (as long as all the data will fit onto a single tape). A recent tape standard, **Travan**, is supported by most tape-drives and should help to push tape prices even lower.

TIP

Because magnetic tape is recognized as being a less than perfect medium, the software bundled with tape drives includes a **Verify** procedure that checks the recently stored data against the original. It might double the start-to-finish time of the procedure, but it's a good idea to select this option, particularly if you reuse the same tape over and over (as you'd normally expect to).

With tape drives and high-capacity tapes cheaply available, it's tempting to use these devices as archive storage. The main point to be aware of is that tape drives are sequential-access devices: if you want to use a file whose name begins with 'K', for example, the drive has to wind through A to J before it can find it.

Another type of backup drive, less commonly used, is the **optical** disk drive. These provide a more reliable storage medium than tape, but the units are a lot more expensive and the disks themselves, megabyte for megabyte, cost roughly double the price of tape storage.

Fixtures and fittings

Like modems, tape-backup drives may be internal or external. Almost all internal tape drives are supplied as a 3.5-inch unit in a removable 5.25-inch case, which means they can slot into whichever size of drive bay you prefer (or whichever you have free). Connecting the drive to the rest of the system involves attaching a power lead from the PC's main power supply, and connecting its data ribbon-cable to that of the floppy-drive in a similar way to installing a CD-ROM drive (see p. 37).

External drives plug into your printer port (a parallel port which will usually be LPT1), and your printer can then be plugged into a 'through' port built into the drive. The external unit has the usual disadvantage that it needs its own power supply. Unusually, though, it has two advantages: it's easy to 'install', and it often works faster than its internal counterpart!

The Travan tape standard

Finally, watch out for the quoted capacities of the Travan standard – a supposed 400 Mb uncompressed, 800 Mb compressed. Before the tape can be used it has to be formatted, and the formatting process uses over 20 Mb of space on the tape. This leaves roughly a 375 Mb capacity which can in theory hold 750 Mb of data by compressing all the files it stores. However, this assumed compression ratio of 2 : 1 is extremely optimistic – some types of data compress a lot better than others. Nevertheless, standardization is a good thing: even if you can only store 500 Mb per tape, the tapes are cheap, getting cheaper, and more readily available than non-standardized formats.

Buyers' guide: Backup drives

- Make sure you have a drive bay free before buying an internal drive. If you're down to your last bay, make sure the drive really can fit in that size bay.
- If you like the idea of expanding your system to include SCSI devices, the backup drive is a good place to start – several SCSI drives come packaged with a SCSI interface card which saves you the trouble (and some of the expense) of buying one separately.
- Make sure your tape drive (also known as a **tape streamer**) supports the Travan standard before buying.
- Popular tape-drive manufacturers, all of whom support Travan, are **Connor**, **Hewlett-Packard's Colorado** series and **Iomega**. If you must have a CD recorder, check out **Plasmon Data**'s CDR4240, currently the best (and, oddly, the cheapest) on the market.

PC Cards

What is a PC Card?

PC Card is a more recent name for PCMCIA cards (short for Personal Computer Memory Card International Association). Notebook computers have PCMCIA slots into which these credit-card sized devices can be slotted when needed. A PC Card might be a hard drive, CD-ROM drive, modem, extra memory – almost anything you can buy for your Desktop computer can be bought in PC Card form. The main difference (if you ignore the high cost of these cards) is that only one or two of these cards can be plugged in at any time, but cards are just beginning to appear that combine several accessories into one device, so the full multimedia card equipped with sound, CD-ROM and video capabilities might be just around the corner!

Slot machine

PCMCIA slots come in two different sizes: the Type II slot which takes smaller cards such as RAM and modems, and the Type III slot for larger accessories like hard disks. The usual Notebook specification now includes two Type II slots mounted one above the other, allowing two small cards or one large one to be inserted.

The size and weight of these cards makes them easy to carry around in a pocket or briefcase, but the prices are considerably higher than those for comparable full-sized devices. For Notebook users on a budget, one option is to buy the smallest full-size device you can get your hands on and connect it to the Notebook's serial or parallel port when you need it, but of course you'll need access to a mains supply and you're now carrying a larger piece of kit plus two cables instead of one small card.

TIP

When a PC Card is connected to your Notebook it's still drawing battery power whether you're using it or not. Make sure you remove any cards after use.

Cards on the Desktop

PC Cards aren't limited to Notebook PCs – you can buy a PCMCIA interface card for your Desktop machine and use PC Cards with that too. Clearly this isn't the kind of expansion-option that the typical Desktop user will regard as a must-have: why pay twice the going rate for a modem that keeps getting lost among your other office clutter? For the confirmed Notebook user, on the other hand, it might be a worthwhile investment. If most of your work is done on the Notebook and you keep a Desktop machine for occasional use, a PCMCIA interface will let you use the accessories you've already bought rather than having to equip the Desktop with similar full-size devices.

Buyers' guide: PC cards

- If you use Windows 95 make sure the card you intend to buy includes compatible-device drivers. To many PC Card manufacturers, the arrival of Windows 95 seemed to come as a surprise, and some still haven't included support. Windows 95 drivers will provide valuable features, including the ability to 'hot-swap' cards (unplug one and plug in another without restarting the computer).
- When buying larger card devices such as CD-ROM drives, make sure the cable between the card and the drive itself is long enough: a short cable might mean you have to balance both Notebook and drive on your lap at the same time.

Quickfire peripherals

The PC has been around long enough that an endless array of gadgets and small, expensive plastic things has found its way into the stores. Here's a few of the presents you might want to buy for your computer.

- *Mouse mat.* A rubber pad with a cloth covering that makes a better surface than a desktop for smooth mouse control. These come in all sorts of shapes, designs and colours – some have a built-in wrist support (another little extra you can also buy separately!), or a tray for holding pens and other office bits and bobs.
- *Mouse house.* A rodent residence designed to keep the little guy dust-free while you're not using him. There are several million cheaper ways of doing this, but none is quite as cute.
- *Microphone.* A multimedia accessory. Plug a microphone into your soundcard (it has a microphone input socket) and record voice messages or sing along with your favourite CD.
- *Keyboard cover.* A fitted cover for your keyboard that keeps the crumbs and coffee out but still lets you tap away.
- *Computer covers.* Separate plastic dust covers are available for monitor, system unit and keyboard to keep them clean and dust-free while you're not using the PC. The monitor cover is an especially sensible buy.
- *Copy holder.* A plastic arm that attaches to the side of your monitor with a clip to hold papers you need to refer to while working. A cheap and very useful accessory.
- *Anti-glare filter.* A thin mesh that fits over the front of your monitor and cuts reflections from nearby lights and windows to prevent eye strain. These filters can also increase your privacy by making the screen contents difficult to see from an angle.
- *Network Interface Card (NIC).* An expansion card required if you want to connect your PC to a LAN (Local Area Network). A LAN may be a group of computers in your office or building, or you may have two home PCs and want to access files, applications, printers and other hardware connected to one computer while using the other.

CHAPTER 3

Buying a PC

First thoughts

In the preceding chapters we've dealt with the major widgets and gadgets and bodily functions of the PC and by now you should have a good idea of what everything does, and how and why. The time now comes to put it all together in a single unit that can do everything you want from it – in other words, it's decision time!

In theory, you should choose a PC according to the software you want to use – after all, it's the software that makes the PC a useful tool. For example, if you just need to run an integrated package like **Microsoft Works** or one large application at a time like **Lotus WordPro**, you could get by with a 486DX2 with 4 Mb RAM. While it's obviously sensible to make sure that you choose a PC specification that can cope with your choice of software, however, it's hard to be sure that that's *all* you'll want to use the PC for in a year's time. Many people running Pentium PCs will be using the same single application a lot of the time, but they've got the security of knowing they can get a lot more out of it when they need to.

So the single most important piece of advice to keep in mind as you decide what to buy is *Think ahead!* This applies just as much to one-off pieces of hardware as to the PC itself.

▶ *If you're unsure about what software you need, turn to Chapter 6 for a close look at some of the popular types and titles.*

Buying a Desktop PC

The Desktop machine is by far the cheapest route to take both in terms of initial cost and in the price of add-on hardware. All the same, a high-specification PC is still a major purchase so you don't want to get it wrong. Table 3.1 shows the specifications of four example computers, ranging from a minimum specification to a high-spec machine, with a few explanatory notes beneath. These specifications are included for guidance only – to save on initial costs, you can add extra RAM, a CD-ROM drive, soundcard and so on later if you need to. Pay particular attention to processor, monitor and hard-disk capacity. These are elements that are expensive or (sometimes) complicated to either upgrade or replace later.

Table 3.1 Average Desktop PC specifications

	Minimum	**Low**	**Standard**	**High**
Processor type	486DX2	486DX4	Pentium	Pentium
Processor speed	66	120	120	200
Cache memory	128 K	256 K	256 K Pipeline-burst	512 K Pipeline-burst
RAM	4 Mb	8 Mb	16 Mb EDO	32 Mb EDO
Hard disk	500 Mb	850 Mb	1 Gb	2 Gb
Floppy-disk drive	1	1	1	1
Tape backup drive	—	—	—	1
Monitor size	14 inch	14 inch	15 inch	17 inch
Display adapter	1 Mb DRAM	1 Mb DRAM	2 Mb VRAM	4 Mb VRAM
CD-ROM drive	—	Quad speed	Six speed	Six speed
Soundcard	—	—	16-bit wavetable	16-bit wavetable
Stereo speakers	—	—	15 W	70 W
Modem	—	—	—	28.8 Kbps

Notes to table
Minimum. If you hunt around, you might find a PC with a lower specification, but this is the minimum worth buying. This machine will run MS-DOS and Windows 3.1 operating systems comfortably, although rather slowly with some Windows applications. This isn't a sufficiently powerful machine to run Windows 95 and be happy with the results.
Low. A far more practical base for running Windows 3.1 at a satisfactory speed. Windows 95 will run on this, though an extra 4 or 8 Mb RAM will make it gallop rather than trot.
Standard. This is an ideal specification for someone intending to use Windows 95, and do a bit of dabbling in multimedia and/or games, with plenty of storage space for applications and documents (applications that run under Windows 95 are usually larger than those that run under Windows 3.1). Very few PC users want to do *just* word processing or *just* graphics, and this specification has enough power to make most uses possible.
High. A powerful machine, though certainly not the highest specification you'll come across. If you insist on having the best, or you're sure you really need a powerful machine, this is for you. Otherwise, stick with the *Standard* and add, or upgrade to, the power you need over a period of time. With prices falling, if you add these extra items over the course of a year you'll probably save money!

Points to check

- Make sure the machine you buy has cache memory – preferably at least 256 K.
- Try to buy a machine with PCI local bus rather than VESA (VL bus).
- Decide whether you want a desktop, mini-tower or full-tower case.
- Make sure you have enough free drive-bays to install a CD-ROM drive (if you don't already have one) and at least one other type of drive.
- Make sure you have easy access to RAM card slots without having to remove any of the PC's innards first, and make sure you can install *at least* 32 Mb total.
- Check you have enough free expansion slots for any extra cards you might add later.
- Find out if you can upgrade the processor later if you need to.

Buying a multimedia PC

Both the *Standard* and *High* specifications listed above would qualify as multimedia PCs, but the term is very loosely defined. For example, you can get a PCTV expansion card that lets you watch TV on your computer, and while this falls into the 'multimedia' category you'd normally have to say you specifically want one and pay extra for it.

There is some guidance on multimedia specifications in the form of the **MPC3** standard. This is the latest specification following (as you might have guessed) MPC1 and MPC2. Any PC that meets the standard is entitled to display the MPC logo, but there's nothing on the logo that tells you *which* of the three it met, so it's quite a pointless exercise! The specification for MPC3 is given in Table 3.2.

Table 3.2 Specification for MPC3

Processor	Pentium 75 MHz
Hard Disk	540 Mb
RAM	8 Mb
CD-ROM	Quad speed
Soundcard	16-bit wavetable with MIDI playback
Speakers	Optional (3 W per channel recommended)
Graphics/Video playback	352 × 288 video image at 25 frames per second with 32 768 colours and an MPEG card

Clearly the details in Table 3.2 should be regarded as a *minimum* standard and they're all quite low. For good multimedia, go for a faster Pentium, 16 Mb RAM and a six-speed CD-ROM drive.

The most important aspect of a multimedia PC is video playback, since the other hardware is becoming standard in almost *any* PC. An ordinary display adapter will play back **.avi** videos in a small window. For good quality, full-screen full motion video you need an **MPEG** expansion card. Beware of PCs advertising *software* MPEG – although software exists that can playback

MPEG video, it may not be full screen and it usually won't have the quality of true hardware support.

Buying a Notebook PC

Although buying *any* PC should never be done lightly, buying a Notebook takes even more care than buying a Desktop since its components are either much more expensive or totally impossible to replace. PC Cards give you the ability to add extra RAM or a hard disk but they fill a slot you could be using for something else if the PC itself were better equipped.

The four specifications in Table 3.3 assume that you need to use your Notebook for exactly the same tasks for which you'd use a Desktop PC – in other words, as a complete mobile computer.

Table 3.3 Average Notebook PC specifications

	Minimum	**Low**	**Standard**	**High**
Processor type	486DX2	486DX4	Pentium	Pentium
Processor speed	66	75	75	100
RAM	4 Mb	4 Mb	8 Mb	16 Mb
Cache memory	—	128 K	256 K	256 K
Hard disk	260 Mb	350 Mb	540 Mb	850 Mb
Floppy-disk drive	—	1	1	1
Screen	9.5-inch Mono	10.1-inch Mono	10.5-inch Dual-Scan Colour	11.3-inch TFT Colour
Max. screen resolution	640 × 480	640 × 480	640 × 480	800 × 600
PCMCIA slots	1 × Type II	1 × Type II, 1 × Type III	2 × Type II or 1 × Type III	2 × Type II or 1 × Type III
CD-ROM drive	—	—	—	Quad speed
Soundcard	—	—	—	16-bit
Stereo speakers	—	—	—	Yes

Notes to table

Minimum. This is a suitable machine for running MS-DOS and its associated applications. It would be possible to run Windows 3.1 but the mono screen doesn't make it the most pleasant experience, and the small hard disk doesn't leave much room to install applications and save documents once MS-DOS and Windows 3.1 have grabbed their share.

Low. A more usable specification for MS-DOS and Windows 3.1. A larger hard disk would be handy if you want to install a number of applications and the mono screen is better suited to DOS use. With another 4 Mb RAM added, Windows 95 becomes a possibility if speed isn't a concern.

Standard. A good middle-of-the-road specification: all the basics are here to run either of the Windows operating systems. The two Type II PCMCIA slots (doubling as a single Type III slot) give all the flexibility you need to add extra devices. The dual-scan colour screen makes Windows much easier to work with, and gives good results with just about anything except full-motion video.

High. This is a model with multimedia elements which sacrifices its floppy-drive to make way for an internal CD-ROM drive, soundcard, and built-in speakers (although sound quality is usually terrible!). Once again, you can find better-specified Notebooks than this; the icing on the cake would be another 8 Mb RAM, a P120 processor and a 1.2 Gb hard disk. Note that the CD-ROM drive and floppy drive are usually interchangeable so you'll have to *carry* the one you're not using.

Points to check

- Make sure you're comfortable with the keyboard and pointing-device.
- Check the battery life for normal use and its recharge time.
- An 800 × 600 display will usually let you see more information on the screen at any time, but make sure you can read text clearly enough at this resolution. Some 800 × 600 dual-scan displays have a very poor image quality.
- Find out what the limit is on adding RAM.

Built-in obsolescence

The favourite line of the computer salesperson is the often-heard *Sorry guv, it's obsolete,* which usually leads into a mouth-watering description of the latest computer/device/operating system/application designed to part you from your cash. Sooner or later you'll reach a point where you want to buy the latest device or operating system for your computer only to be told that your tired old machine can't cope with it. In some cases, you may be able to upgrade your PC sufficiently to *make* it cope, but at this point the writing's on the wall. (To some extent, the 486-based PC has reached this point already.)

Hence the importance of focusing on why you need a PC. If there's a particular range of things you need a PC for, and you buy the correct computer, peripherals, operating system and software to do the job, you are, theoretically at least, future-proof! This same computer can still be doing these same things in the same way in 10 years' time. So if you choose carefully, your computer will only become obsolete when *you* decide you want to replace it.

Warranties

All new computers should come with at least a one-year warranty as standard. Many packages (as well as one-off peripheral purchases) give you the chance to extend the warranty to three or more years in return for cash. Don't be tempted! There are two reasons why the standard one-year warranty is enough: first and foremost, if a component is going to curl up and die, it's usually going to do it long before the first year is up; second, if it fails after the first year, prices will have fallen still further and you'll probably be able to replace the part yourself for a lot less than the price of the extra cover!

Support is often more useful than a warranty. Ask if there's a telephone support-line you can call – it's more likely that you'll need help distinguishing between the ISA and PCI slots, for example, than it is that you'll need the PC taken away to be fixed.

Software bundles

Most computer packages include a range of software, most of which has already been installed when you take delivery (with the exception of games and multimedia titles intended to be run from CD-ROM). This bundle of software will include an operating system (see below), together with a range of office applications such as a word processor, spreadsheet and PIM (Personal Information Manager), perhaps a few games, and so on. This bundle of software will look very tempting (it's supposed to) and, being free, amazingly good value.

The first point to remember is: *Nothing is free!* This software is included in the price you pay and the best you could say is that it's cheap. Being cheap isn't a crime of course, and one of the most popular integrated office applications, **Microsoft Works**, costs very little even if you buy it at full price. If this is included in the bundle, it's probably worth considering – you're sure to need these types of application at least occasionally, whatever the primary use of your PC will be. A full office suite like **Microsoft Office** or **Lotus SmartSuite** can seem a very attractive proposition, but they're large and powerful applications with many more features than the average user is ever likely to need and might just find unwieldy for day-to-day working.

This highlights the second point: Do you really need this software? Hopefully you'll have a good idea of what you'll be using your PC to do; if this software isn't what you had in mind, you may be able to find a similar computer with no bundled software at a cheaper price, and use the saving to buy the software you want.

Finally, if this software is going to be pre-installed, make sure you'll be provided with the manuals to go with it, and the installation disk(s) in case you ever need to re-install the software yourself, preferably on CD-ROM if you have a CD-ROM drive.

► *Turn to p. 204 for details of the major office suites and integrated applications, including **Microsoft Works**.*

Operating systems

In Chapters 8 to 10 we'll be looking at the primary operating systems used on the PC, Microsoft's **MS-DOS**, **Windows 3.1** and **Windows 95**. The most recent, and most feature-packed, of these is Windows 95 which is pre-installed in most new computers with sufficiently high specifications. Most Notebooks and 486s, and a few Pentiums, come with MS-DOS and Windows 3.1 installed instead. Few people actually *use* DOS these days, but Windows 3.1 needs DOS to be installed, and acts as a kind of mask over DOS's head to make it more attractive to the user. A third choice of operating system is IBM's **OS/2 Warp**.

There are two points to consider when choosing an operating system: *Is it enjoyable, easy and fast to use?* and *Is there plenty of software available for it?* The answer, for both versions of Windows, is a simple 'Yes' to both questions. The earlier of the two versions, 3.1, has been on the market for roughly three years, and has found a place on the vast majority of PCs around the world, so huge amounts of software have been written for it. The follow-up, Windows 95, will run almost all the software written for 3.1 without a hitch, and has its own endless stream of new software titles arriving on the market.

When it comes to IBM's OS/2 Warp, the answer to the first question is 'Yes' once again. It has a similar look and feel to Windows 3.1, and the same ease of use, coupled with the power and stability of Windows 95. The big difference is that OS/2 failed to capture the PC-user's imagination in the same way that Windows did and, by comparison, has a tiny user-base. As a result, there is comparatively little OS/2 software available, and some areas of computing, such as MIDI, have no professional-quality software at all. OS/2 Warp can run DOS programs, however, and the OS/2 Warp 'Fullpack' version can run most Windows 3.1 software with only a few minor limitations.

One of these operating systems should be included with your new PC and pre-installed for you; installing an operating system is rarely regarded as a fun experience, especially for a newcomer to computing, so you really don't want to install it yourself. Make sure the operating system's manuals and installation disks are included, and (if you have a CD-ROM drive) get the CD-ROM version rather than the floppy-disk version if you can.

Buying tips

Apart from choosing the PC itself and any other peripherals and software you want, a few other points need attention when buying. Here's a list of the more important ones that apply equally to both whole computer systems and single add-on devices:

- For extra security, try to pay by credit card.
- Always check what the final price will be, including extra peripherals or software you asked to be added, tax and delivery, and get it in writing.
- When you place an order, tell the vendor what you want to use the computer for. This will give you extra leverage if the PC doesn't prove fit for the task.
- Find out what your options are for refund or replacement if you're unhappy with your purchase. Make sure you get written confirmation of these terms.
- If you order by telephone, keep records of who you spoke to and when, and make notes on what was offered and at what price. Follow up with a fax or letter detailing the order, agreed terms and price. If a delivery date was given and is vital, include the words 'Time is of the essence'. This is a legal term that gives you the right to cancel the order if delivery isn't made by the quoted date.
- When you sign for the delivery, add the words 'Goods not inspected' before your signature.
- When you receive the goods, set everything up and check it carefully. Make sure you inform the vendor immediately if something is missing or not working – if you leave it too long, you may find it more difficult to justify a refund or replacement.
- Keep all the cartons and packaging in case you need to return the system or send it for repair sometime in the future.
- Keep *all* the paperwork that came with the computer in one place.
- Don't fill in any warranty or registration cards for hardware or software until you know it's complete and it works.

Setup and use

Siting the PC

Where you site your Desktop PC takes some careful thought. You'll need to be within easy reach of power-sockets (and a phone socket if you have a modem), and have enough desk space to make external devices such as keyboard, mouse and printer accessible. Remember that monitors take up a lot of space – if necessary, pull your desk out from the wall a little way so that you can move the monitor further back. Also, make sure the monitor is situated and angled in such a way that it can't reflect sunlight or a lightbulb into your eyes.

The system unit is the other bulky device that needs to be found a home. You'll need to leave at least six inches of fresh air behind it, partly because of the cables that have to be plugged in, but primarily to ensure that its internal components don't overheat. Desktop cases are intended to be placed behind your keyboard with the monitor placed on top of them, though you may prefer to place it elsewhere. Small tower-cases are usually placed on the desk beside your monitor; larger tower-cases are intended to be placed on the floor under your desk. Remember you'll need to reach the floppy-disk or CD-ROM drives, and avoid putting the case anywhere it can be jolted or kicked: if this happens while the hard drive is working, it can cause serious damage to both disk and read/write head which will usually mean loss of data and a replacement drive.

Make sure none of the connected cables is stretched taut between devices, and keep all the spaghetti at the back as tangle-free as you can. Take special care to secure all this cabling in some way so that no one can drag it off the desk by getting their feet caught up in it! Lastly, choose somewhere comfortable: your monitor should be in front of you, and at eye level without the need to stretch or slump; you'll need room to rest your hands in front of the keyboard; you'll need space on your desk for a mouse mat, and plenty of elbow room to move the mouse.

Protection

Two simple pieces of advice here. First of all, fit a **surge protector** to prevent power surges and spikes damaging your PC while it's switched on, and make sure you plug all peripheral devices into it too. Second, unplug the whole system from the mains whenever you're not using it to avoid damage from lightning. For the same reason, if you have a modem, unplug the cable connection to the telephone socket.

Turning on, turning off

The most important rule to remember in turning your PC on and off is: *Try not to do it!* In general, try to turn your computer off only when you won't be using it again for several hours. The surge of power into the unit each time you start up, and the change in temperature of the internal components, can shorten their life-span if it happens unnecessarily often. Turning the PC off and immediately back on again should only be done in desperate circumstances and you should pause for at least 30 seconds in between. Whenever a restart is necessary, use the **Reset** switch on the system unit to do it (see p. 35).

Whenever you switch on your system, there's a routine that should be followed to ensure that everything is powered-up in the correct order and avoid damage to components and devices. Your PC's manual should give precise details, but the usual routine is to switch on the system unit, then the monitor, then any peripherals. When you've finished for the day, follow the same steps in reverse.

► *If you use a Windows operating system, there's a routine that should be followed to shut down Windows before switching off the PC.* *Turn to p. 272 for the Windows 3.1 details, and to p. 318 for Windows 95.*

CHAPTER 4

Using a Windows PC

The operating system

What is an operating system?

As we've seen, components such as a processor, RAM and hard disk are vital to the computer, and extras such as printers and modems are useful to have. But by themselves they're no more than expensive ornaments cluttering up your desk! To justify all the money you've spent, something else is required that tells these components what to do and when to do it, and this is the role of a set of files collectively known as the **operating system** (often abbreviated to 'OS'). The operating system lies between the hardware elements of the PC and its software applications, enabling one to work with the other.

When you start your computer, one of the jobs of the BIOS is to load operating system files into RAM. Some of these files are used just to get the system running and then unloaded; others remain in memory to *keep* the system running until you switch off; the rest will be loaded if and when they're needed. The operating system files fall into two categories:

- *The kernel.* The kernel is the group of files that manage all the legwork that goes on behind the scenes; the stuff that, most of the time, you shouldn't be aware of.
- *The shell.* The shell is the friendly face of the operating system that determines how things look on the screen and how you tell the computer what you want to do.

Although the shell might involve a sizeable group of small programs and data files, these are subsidiary to the main shell program. In MS-DOS this is **Command.com**; in Windows 3.1 it's **Program Manager** (Progman.exe); and in Windows 95 it's **Explorer** (Explorer.exe). The shell may be in one of two formats: older operating systems such as MS-DOS used a *command-line user interface* into which commands had to be typed to make anything happen – not remotely intuitive, and not easy to use until you'd learnt all the commands and how they fitted together. It was the arrival of the more recent *graphical user interface* (GUI, pronounced 'gooey') which made computers as popular as they are today: almost everything you need to do or use is represented by a picture, a button, or a list of simple options.

Accessories and utilities

As well as the basic software needed to make your PC function, modern operating systems include a collection of extra accessories and utilities so that you can begin doing something useful with your computer right from the start. Indeed, the quantity and quality of software included might make it unnecessary to buy more sophisticated applications in some cases.

JARGONBUSTER

Utility

A utility is a software program that helps you carry out basic 'housekeeping' tasks to do with the system itself rather than to create or use a file. Typical utilities might compress your hard disk to gain more space, or let you select a group of files to be regularly copied to a backup drive.

▶ *Accessories are covered starting on p. 296 for Windows 3.1 and p. 362 for Windows 95.*

Multitasking

Multitasking – a feature of modern GUI operating systems – lets you handle several tasks at the same time. Its main use is in switching between running applications, perhaps to copy information between them, or to refer to one while working in the other. You might have several programs running at the same time but the one you're currently using will be given maximum processor time; this is called the **foreground** (or *active*) application, and the others are **background** (or *inactive*) applications. Any time you want to switch to one of the background programs you type a key combination on the keyboard or use the mouse to click a button on the screen and the program you need to use will move to the foreground and grab the processor's attention.

In contrast, older operating systems like MS-DOS are *single tasking* – only one application can run at any time. To work with a different application means first shutting down the one you're using.

User interfaces

The command-line interface

The command-line interface, as used by MS-DOS, tends to be regarded as an unfriendly looking interface by newcomers to the PC: there's no colourful screen, nothing to click a mouse button at; in fact there's nothing at all but a plain black screen and a few characters that usually reads **C:\\>**, with a cursor flashing expectantly beside them. These characters are known as the **command prompt** and they are, quite simply, prompting you to enter a command. Until you do, nothing will happen.

The command-line interface (Figure 4.1) is text-based, so all your communications with the computer have to be entered from the keyboard, using a set of recognized commands. Provided you can type, there's no real problem there, but to use a command-line interface at reasonable speed takes practice and patience. To begin with, you have to learn the commands and their *syntax* (the precise way they should be laid out). In addition, you might type a long and complicated command, and press the *Enter* key on the keyboard to make the computer carry out your instructions, only to be told that the command you entered isn't valid. All it takes is one wrong character, or perhaps a missing space, and the computer doesn't know what you mean. But, rather than just being able to make the necessary alteration to the command, you have to type the whole thing again. This is where the patience is required!

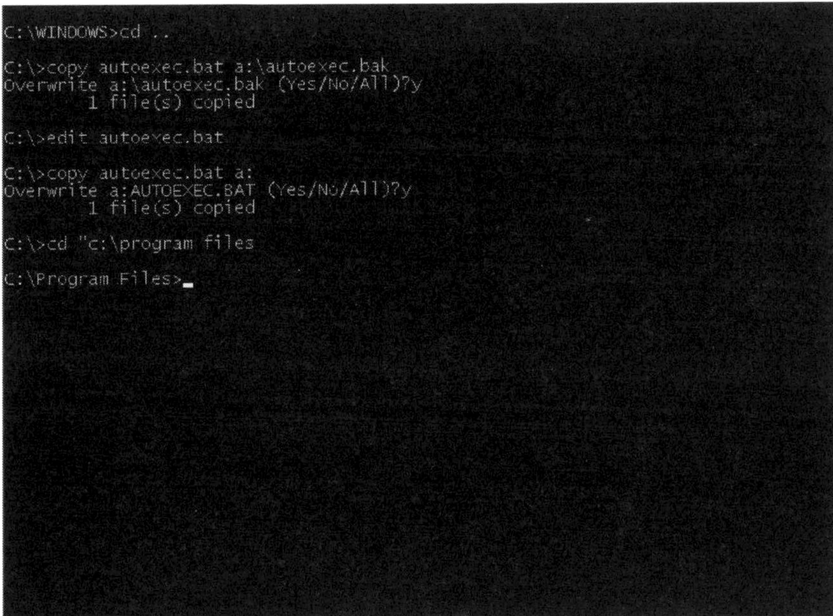

Figure 4.1 The MS-DOS command-line interface.

The commands themselves vary in complexity. The command **cls** clears the screen of text apart from the command prompt. That's an easy one. Other commands need extra information (known as **parameters**) and offer extra options about how the command should run (known as **switches**).

As an example, to format a floppy disk you'd use the **format** command, but the command requires a parameter that tells the PC which drive the disk is in and a switch that says what the capacity of the disk is, so the whole command line might be **format a: /f:720**. In plain English this means 'Format the disk that's in Drive A, which has a capacity of 720 K', but the tricky thing to remember is that the switch specifying the capacity is **/f:** which is hardly intuitive.

▶ *Turn to Chapter 8 for more information about DOS commands and syntax.*

Nowadays, knowledge of MS-DOS and the command-line interface tends to be unnecessary most of the time. Some long-time PC users are experienced in its workings, have a range of software designed for DOS and they're quite happy to stick with it rather than move to Windows, buy a whole new set of software, and learn how to use it. The command-line interface still exists within the Windows operating systems (though it's rather better hidden in Windows 95), but most of the time you'll be unaware of its existence unless you choose to use it.

The graphical user interface

The graphical user interface (GUI), as used by the Windows operating systems, uses a metaphor of a desktop to give a more intuitive, pictorial method of working. The idea is that just as your desk might be covered in objects that you pick up and use, so the objects in your computer (applications, documents, printer, modem, and so on) should be presented as pictures on the screen that you can 'pick up' (click with the mouse) and use in a similar way.

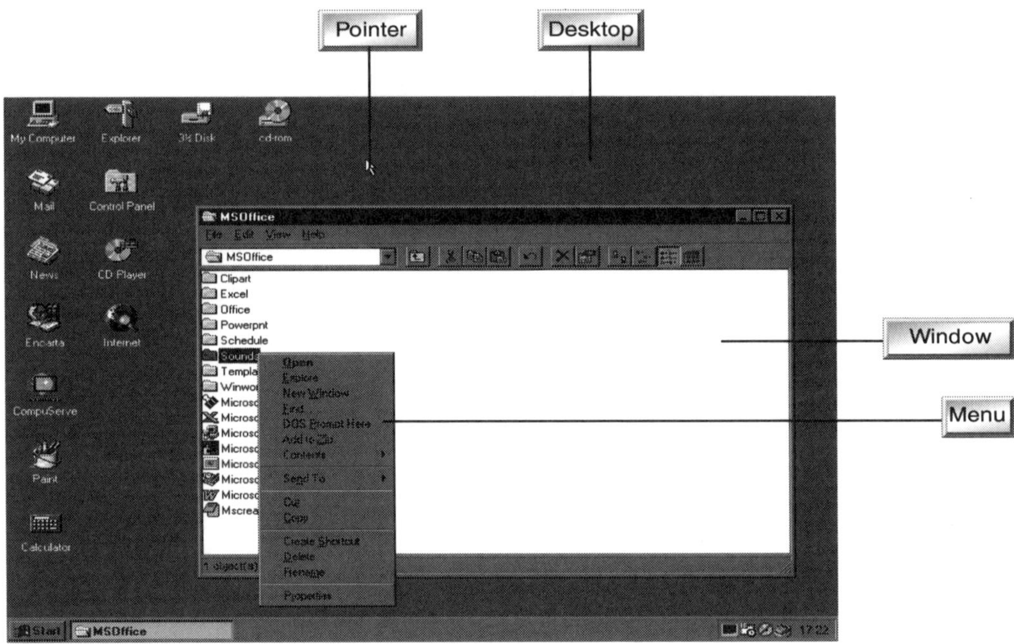

Figure 4.2 The Windows 95 desktop and the four elements that make it a WIMP.

Windows is a **WIMP**. That's not as derogatory as it sounds; WIMP stands for Windows, Icons, Menus, Pointer, the four main elements of a graphical interface shown in Figure 4.2. Some of these items we've looked at already, so we'll just recap briefly: an **icon** is a small picture that represents a resource such as an application, a document, a disk drive or a printer; a **menu** is a list of options that you can choose from (just like a menu in a restaurant); the **pointer** is the arrow that moves around the screen controlled by the mouse and allows you to select an icon or menu-option by clicking a mouse button.

The fundamental element of the graphic interface is the **window** (hence the name of the 'Windows' operating systems). A window is a box on the desktop which displays a document or application, or groups of icons representing the files on your hard disk. You might have several windows open at the same time and switch between them when you need to. For example, in one window you might have your word processor running to type a sales report; another window could contain your spreadsheet application so that you can refer to your sales figures; a third window might display icons for all the spreadsheet documents you've created this year so that you can select which month's figures you need to look at.

In this example, the word-processor window would usually be in the foreground so that all your keyboard input would be entered into the report you're typing. The other two windows would be, quite literally, in the background: the word-processor window is covering them up like the top sheet on a stack of papers, perhaps leaving just a corner or an edge visible. When you switch to the spreadsheet window, this will move to the foreground (the top of the stack) instead, and the word-processor window will disappear behind it. The fact that you can no longer *see* this window doesn't mean it's not there, or that the report you were typing into it has been lost – you can switch it back to the foreground whenever you want to. Or you can place the windows side by side on the screen so that you can refer to one as you type into the other.

What is a window?

Over the next few sections we'll take a look at the constituent parts of a GUI and what they do, and examine some of the features and issues you'll encounter working with files and programs. Both of the major operating systems, Windows 3.1 and Windows 95, follow the same general principles, but they differ to varying degrees in their appearance, layout and methods of use. In this part of the book, however, we'll just concentrate on the basic 'how it all works' aspects of the PC, in which the two operating systems are almost identical, and leave the specific details of each to Chapters 9 and 10.

Let's start by looking at the most important part of a graphical interface, the **window**. This is one area in which the two operating systems differ slightly in appearance, so the same window-elements are labelled for both in Figures 4.3 and 4.4, and described below.

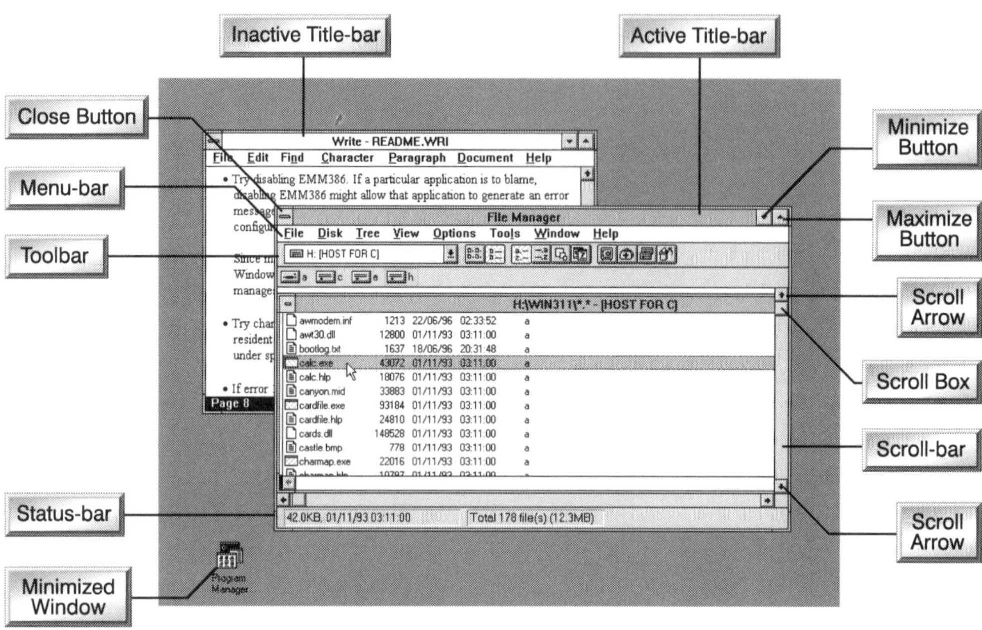

Figure 4.3 Window elements in Windows 3.1.

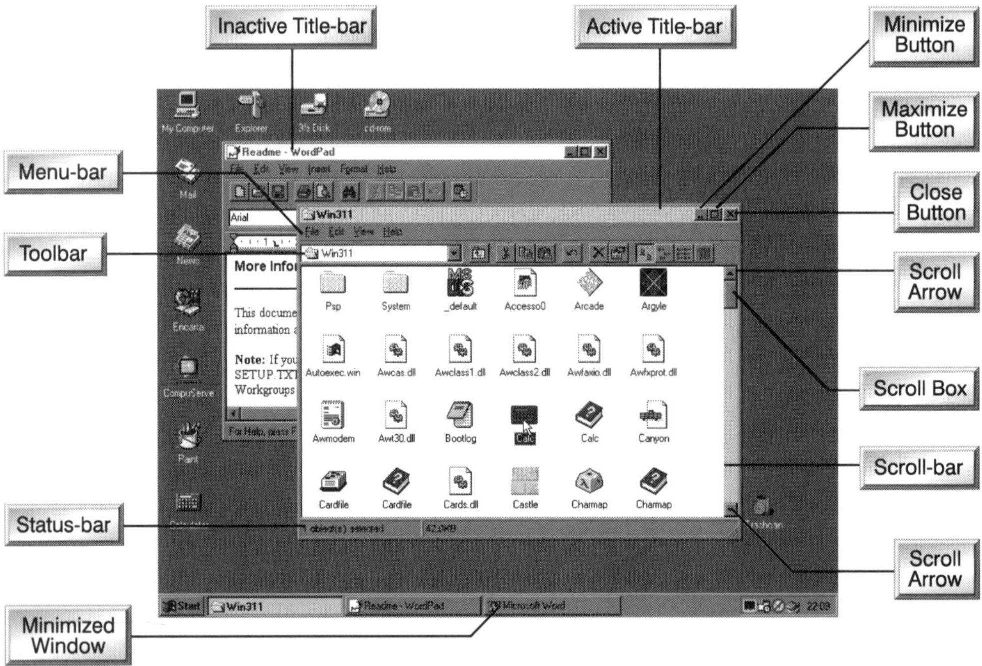

Figure 4.4 Window elements in Windows 95.

The title-bar

The title-bar is a horizontal strip across the top of every window which displays the name of the application, or the name of the document you're working on, or both. As you can see in Figures 4.3 and 4.4, the title-bars are two different colours: the window in the foreground will have a title-bar of one colour to indicate that it's the *active* window; any windows in the background will have title-bars of a second colour (usually a comparatively dull one such as white or grey) to indicate that they're *inactive*.

Only one window can be active at any time, but you can have as many inactive windows open as you want to, limited only by your PC's memory. In Figures 4.3 and 4.4, enough of the inactive window can be seen that you could switch to it (make it the active window) by just moving the pointer over it and clicking. The title-bar can also be used if you want to *move* a window: just click the left mouse button on the title-bar and drag the window to where you want it before releasing the button.

Title-bar buttons

Just as every window has a title-bar, on every title-bar you'll find this set of three buttons for **Minimize, Maximize** and **Close**.

Clicking on the **Close** button (or *double-clicking* it in Windows 3.1) will, unsurprisingly, close the window. If the window contained a document you'd created or made changes to and hadn't yet saved to disk, another small window called a **dialog** will open to warn you that the changes will be lost if you don't save and give you the opportunity to do so.

If you prefer to work from the keyboard, holding *Alt* and pressing *F4* will close a window in exactly the same way as clicking the **Close** button.

Clicking on the **Minimize** button will remove the window from the screen and replace it with an icon at the bottom of the screen. This doesn't affect the document you were working on however, and you can bring the window back by just clicking its icon (or double-clicking it in Windows 3.1).

Clicking the **Maximize** button will make the window expand to fill the entire screen, letting you see more of the document you're working on. Once again, any inactive windows will be hidden from view but are still running, and you can bring one of them to the front by holding down the *Alt* key and pressing *Tab* repeatedly until you see the title of the window you want.

The **Maximize** button has a little quirk in its design: once a window has been maximized and it fills the screen, the maximize button is no longer of use – the window can't get any bigger! So the maximize button changes to a **Restore** button, with a different picture on it. Clicking this button will return the window to its previous size and position on the screen, and the Restore button becomes a Maximize button again.

▶ *You'll also find the* ***Control Menu*** *on the left of the title-bar, explained on p. 111. Turn to p. 108 for more on dialog boxes.*

The menu-bar

The menu-bar is a feature of most (though not all) windows. It's a narrow horizontal strip below the title-bar containing a row of words such as **File**, **Edit**, **View** and **Help.** Each of these words is the name of a menu: clicking on the word **File**, for example, will cause a drop-down menu to open that contains options such as **New** (to start creating a new document), **Open** (to open an existing document), and **Save** (to save the document you're working on to disk).

▶ *Turn to p. 110 for more information about menus and the menu-bar.*

The toolbar

Once again, not all windows have a toolbar, and for those that do you can often choose whether to display it or not. The toolbar contains a row of buttons that you click with the mouse, usually providing an alternative method of reaching some of the more useful options from the menus.

TIP

In many windows, when you click on a **toolbar** button its function is briefly displayed in the **status-bar**. If you click and hold down the button you can read what it does – the action isn't carried out until you actually *release* the button. If you decide you don't want to do it after all, just move the pointer away from the toolbar before releasing the mouse button.

Some of the more powerful applications even provide a range of toolbars for different uses. You might have a text-formatting toolbar containing buttons to underline, double space and enlarge text; a drawing toolbar with buttons to select various tools, colours and shapes; and so on. Of course, if all these toolbars were displayed at once there wouldn't be much space left in the window to see the document you're working on, so these toolbars can be turned on and off as needed.

The status-bar

The status-bar is yet another element that some windows have and others don't, and this can usually be turned on or off like the toolbar. The role of the status-bar is to provide you with information. If you're looking at the contents of a particular folder the status-bar might tell you how many files are in the folder and their total size; if you're working on a document in a word processor, the status-bar might tell you which page you're currently looking at.

▶ *Folders are explained on pp. 113–116.*

The scroll-bar

The scroll-bar is a vertical strip along the right-hand side of a window which contains a small square called a **scroll box** and buttons at either end called **scroll arrows**. The function of these items is to indicate your position in a document and let you move around it. For example, if you're working on a 20-page report in your word processor, you'd only see about half a page at a time on your screen. As the report gets longer, the scroll box gradually shrinks to indicate that you're seeing a smaller and smaller percentage of the document on the screen. The position of the box on the scroll-bar indicates your current position in the document – you can use the pointer to drag the scroll box upwards and downwards to jump to different parts of the document.

You can also move around a document by clicking on the scroll-bar itself, above or below the scroll box, to jump upwards or downwards respectively.

The scroll arrow buttons let you move the document upwards and downwards in a similar, but more controlled, manner. Clicking a button once will move the document up or down by one line in a word processor; keeping the button depressed will scroll the document up or down, just like winding a long sheet of paper through a typewriter.

In some windows there will be a scroll-bar running horizontally across the bottom of the screen, indicating that the information you're working with (such as a large picture) extends past the sides of the window and you have to move the scroll box left or right to bring it into view.

Multiple document interfaces

A handy feature found in some applications is the multiple document interface (MDI) which allows several documents to be open in the same application at once. Each document is given its own window *inside* the application's own window, and you can arrange these document windows to be side by side, one above the other, or in a 'stack' so that only the top window is visible. Just as only one *application* at a time can be active, in a MDI only one *document* at a time can be active, indicated by the colour of its title-bar.

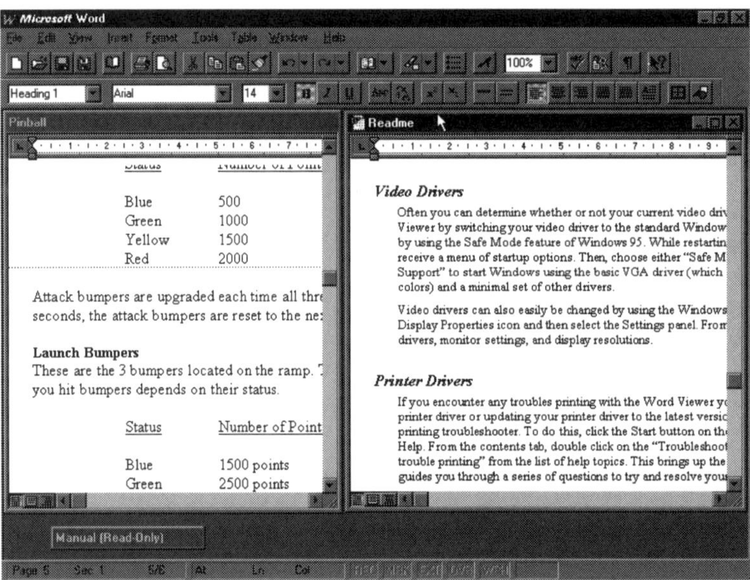

Figure 4.5 Microsoft Word's multiple document interface.

In Figure 4.5, the document window on the right is active, so any keys you type on the keyboard, and any options you select from the toolbar or menus, will be applied to this document. The active document window is the only one to have maximize, minimize and close buttons: the close button will close the document (prompting you to save it if necessary); the maximize button will make the document window expand to fill the whole application window; the minimize button will reduce the document to a rectangular icon at the bottom of the application window.

To switch from one open document to another you can click the mouse in the window you want to work in to make it active (if you can see it), or hold *Ctrl* and press *F6*, or click on the **Window** menu and choose from the list of open documents. And just as you can close an application window from the keyboard by using the keystroke *Alt+F4*, you can close the active document window in a MDI by pressing *Ctrl+F4*. You can also close a document by clicking its window's **Close** button, or by choosing **Close** from the **File** menu.

Utility windows

So far we've been concentrating on just one type of window, but it's probably the type you'll work with most. It's distinguishing feature is its large expanse of white space into which you type or draw, or in which the contents of a particular drive or folder are displayed. But windows vary in appearance depending upon what function they serve: for example, as we'll see in the next section, a window might appear that just says **Are you sure?** – it doesn't need this white space, nor menus and scroll-bars, it just needs two buttons marked **OK** and **Cancel**.

Figure 4.6 The Media Player utility.

Figure 4.6 shows **Media Player**, a utility included with both versions of Windows that plays MIDI, digital-audio and video files. It doesn't let you create anything, so it has no need of a large 'document area' which makes it a much smaller window. Although at first it seems quite different, it has a lot in common with our application windows: there's a toolbar and a status-bar side by side at the bottom; the scroll-bar runs through the middle, with the scroll box becoming a moving pointer, indicating how much time has elapsed in the file it's playing; and the title-bar and menu-bar are still there.

Dialog boxes

Prompts and informative dialogs

A dialog box is a window that gives you information about a task the operating system is carrying out, provides you with a warning or prompt when you do something you might regret later, or asks you for information.

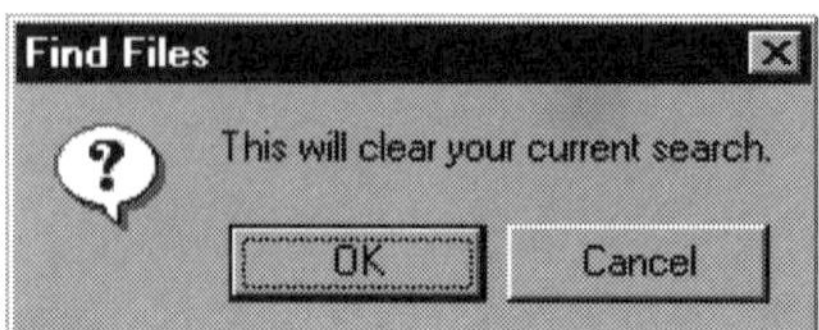

Figure 4.7 A prompt dialog.

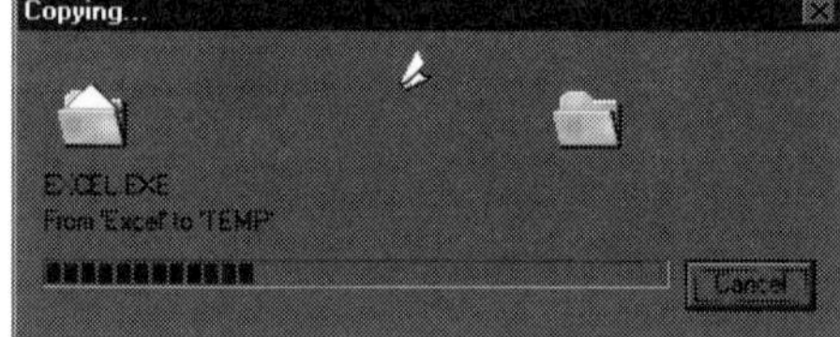

Figure 4.8 A progress dialog.

As dialogs go, the prompt and the progress dialog shown in Figures 4.7 and 4.8 are quite straightforward. The **prompt dialog** warns you of the consequences of an action you tried to carry out – if you're happy to carry on and do it you click the **OK** button; if you'd rather not, click on **Cancel**. This dialog won't go away until you choose one or the other. A slightly different type of prompt may ask you a question, and give you three buttons for **Yes**, **No** and **Cancel**.

The **progress dialog** is indicating how far the system has got in copying a file from one place to another. When the copy process has finished this dialog will disappear automatically, but until it does you can cancel the operation by clicking its single button.

All dialog boxes have a *default* button, indicated by a dark outline (like the **OK** button in Figure 4.7). If you want to select the option indicated by the default button, you can just press the *Enter* or *Return* key on your keyboard instead of moving the pointer to the button and clicking.

Selection dialogs

The more involved type of dialog box is the one that asks you for information. In some cases the information required might just be the name of a file that you type into a space and then click an **OK** button, or, as in Figure 4.9, there may be a range of options that you can choose from, or several pieces of information that you need to enter, with another little group of graphic objects.

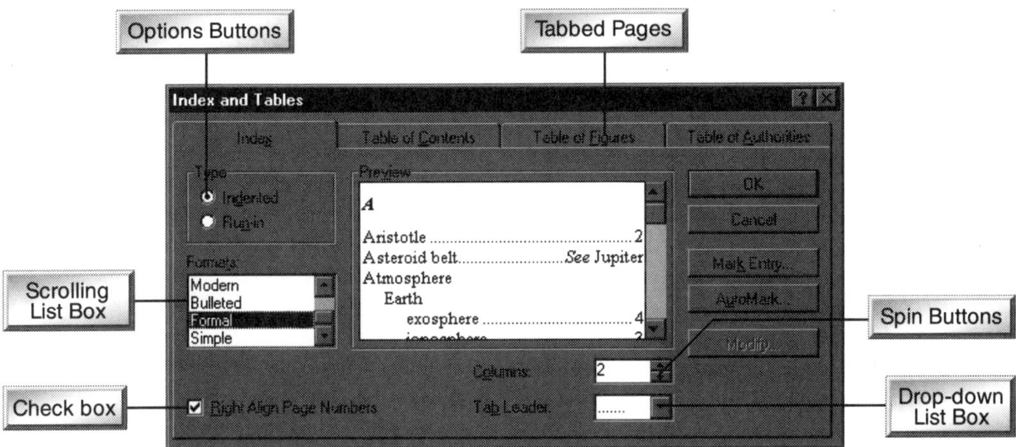

Figure 4.9 The common methods of making choices in dialog boxes.

- *Scrolling list box.* A small box that looks like a miniature document window. It contains a list of options that may be longer than the box can display, so the scroll-bar to its right is used to bring the remaining options into view. You select an option by clicking its name, and the option will be highlighted to confirm your choice. Only one option can be chosen from the list.
- *Drop-down list box.* This works like the scrolling variety, but in its normal state only one option can be seen. If you click the arrow button beside it, the box will drop downwards displaying a list of options. When you click on an option, the list will vanish, and the option you have chosen will be displayed in the box.
- *Option buttons.* These occur in groups of two or more, and they let you choose a single option. The selected option has a black dot on its button; if you click on a different option the dot will move to that button instead.
- *Check box.* These are straightforward selection boxes, and you can choose as many of these as you need to. To select an option, click on the box and a check mark will appear; if you want to de-select the option, click it again to remove the check mark.
- *Spin buttons.* A pair of up/down arrow buttons that increase or decrease the value in the box by 1 each time you click one, or you can hold a button down to spin rapidly through the values. These are not the most user-friendly of buttons, and it's often easier to click once inside the box, use the *Delete* or *Backspace* key to erase the value, and just type in a new one.

- *Tabbed pages.* This is a Windows 95-only feature. In modern powerful applications, there are often lots of functions that you can customize to suit your methods of working. All these options together could easily fill the entire screen and wouldn't be pleasant to work with, so instead they're organized into groups, with each group on a separate 'page', and each page having its own tab. Clicking on one of these named tabs will bring the corresponding page to the front. (From the keyboard, hold *Ctrl* and press *Tab* repeatedly to move from page to page.)

In addition to these objects, and the ubiquitous **OK** and **Cancel** buttons, there are several other buttons on the page whose labels end with an ellipsis (. . .). An ellipsis beside a command or option means that by selecting it you won't be committing yourself to anything just yet, but you'll be presented with another selection dialog.

Menus

Menu names

As we've seen on p. 104, the menu-bar is a feature found in most types of window, consisting of a row of words such as **File**, **View** and **Help**. Each of these words is the name of a different menu; clicking on a word will display the menu from which you can then choose the option you want with another click.

If you're a confirmed keyboard user, you can open menus by holding down the *Alt* key and pressing the underlined letter – for example, *Alt+F* to open the **File** menu. When the menu is displayed there are two methods of selecting items on it: either use the arrow keys to move to the option you want and then press *Enter*, or just press the option's underlined letter (for example, press '**O**' for **Open**).

The menu names that appear on the menu-bar depend on the type of window and the sort of information being displayed. In a paint program, for example, you might have a menu called **Image** that you wouldn't expect to find on a word processor's menu-bar. Similarly, many application windows have a menu named **Tools**, but the *options* contained in these menus will differ because different applications have their own sets of tools to suit their purposes.

When you're reading about a piece of software, you might come across something like **File/New**. This means to open the **File** menu and select the **New** command. It might be something longer such as **View / Options / File**

Types which would mean to open the **View** menu, select the **Options** command and then select whatever you can see that says **File Types** on it – it might be another menu, a button, or a tabbed-page, but it isn't usually hard to find!

Any time you select a menu and then realize you don't want to select an option from it, either press *Esc* or click the mouse somewhere outside the menu – it'll go away again! Pressing *Esc* will also banish most dialogs, acting as a substitute for clicking the **Cancel** button.

Why the ellipsis?

Many of the options you see on these menus end with an ellipsis, such as **Find....** The ellipsis indicates that selecting this option won't carry out a command, but will open a dialog box to let you provide more information. In this example, 'Find' by itself is clearly meaningless until you tell the software what you want to search for.

Keyboard shortcuts

Beside some menu commands you'll see keyboard references such as *Ctrl+O* next to **Open** and *Ctrl+P* next to **Print**. This is another aspect of Windows trying to be helpful, reminding you that you can access these options by using their key combinations instead of using mouse and menus. Many of these same options will also feature as buttons on the toolbar, so most of the frequently used functions can be reached easily in several different ways.

The control menu

The control menu is reached from a small icon in the extreme top-left corner of most windows, and duplicates window controls we've seen already: the **Maximize**, **Minimize**, **Restore** and **Close** buttons. In Windows 95, the control menu's icon changes according to what information or application the window contains; in Windows 3.1 the icon will always look the same (Figure 4.10).

Figure 4.10 The control menu icons in Windows 3.1 (left) and Windows 95.

In both operating systems, clicking this icon once will display the control menu, and double-clicking it will close the window. But because the options on this menu duplicate the functions of buttons, it isn't of much interest to mouse fanatics; its main value is to the committed keyboard user. The key combination to open the menu is *Alt+Spacebar*, which you can then follow with *X* for **Maximise**; *N* for **Minimize**; *R* for **Restore**; or *C* for **Close**. In a multiple document interface (MDI) you can open the control menu for the active *document* window using *Alt+* – (minus sign).

▶ *Skip back to p. 103 for information on these control-menu options.*

CHAPTER 5

Working with files

Folders and subfolders

When you take delivery of your new computer, switch it on, and watch Windows load, you'll be expecting to find a large number of files on your hard disk, especially if the PC came bundled with extra software titles that were pre-installed for you. But how are all these files organized?

Organizing files

The way files are organized goes back to that metaphor of the office desk. In most offices there's a vast amount of paperwork, and if it was all bundled together and left in a pile you'd never be able to find what you wanted. Instead, you sort all these pieces of paper into smaller collections of *related* documents, place them in labelled folders and put the folders into a filing cabinet in alphabetical order. In this way, when you need to look at a certain document, knowing what it's about will help you figure out which folder you put it into, and the folder itself should be easy to find.

In the computer the concept is exactly the same. The 'filing cabinet' is a program called **File Manager** in Windows 3.1 or **Explorer** in Windows 95. When you run one of these programs a window will open, split vertically into two sections known as *panes* (well, it's a window, isn't it?). In the left-hand pane is a list of identical yellow icons, each of which has a name beside it: these are the 'folders'. In fact, in Windows 95, they *are* called **folders**; in MS-DOS and Windows 3.1 they're called **directories**, but they work in just the same way. For clarity we'll continue to refer to them as folders.

Opening folders

Just as in an office, if you want to see what's inside a folder you have to *open* it. There are several methods of doing this, and which you use will often depend on the context and your preferred methods of working. In general, you can see the contents of a folder by clicking or double-clicking on its icon. The right-hand pane of the window will change to show what's in the folder, and the name of the folder you're looking at will be displayed in the window's title-bar. If the folder you opened contains other folders, you can open these in the same way.

The folder tree

In both Windows 3.1's *File Manager* and Windows 95's *Explorer*, the left pane shows the **folder tree**, and this is the whole basis of file organization. Your hard disk is usually Drive C, and this is regarded as being one big folder called **C:**. When **Windows** was installed, it put a few files into this main folder, and created a new folder inside **C:** which it called **Windows**. Into this folder it put a bunch of files, and created a few more folders inside **Windows**, one of which was called **System**.

Now let's examine this *tree* idea. Once again it's based on a metaphor. Picture a large tree with plenty of branches, normal in every respect but one: it's upside-down! This tree is your hard disk, and at the top of this tree you find its root. The root is that main folder called **C:** (and it's often referred to as the **root folder** or **root directory**). As you move down from the root you'll come to a branch, called Windows. If you move along this branch, you'll find several other branches attached to it, one of which is called System.

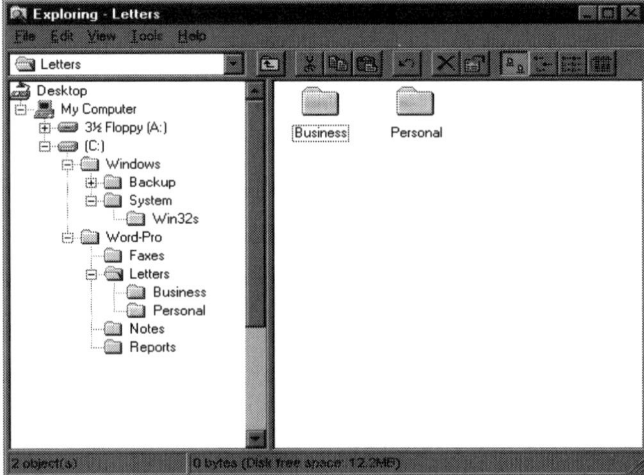

Figure 5.1 The left pane shows the folder tree in Windows 95's **Explorer**.

Now let's go back to the root again. Apart from having a branch called Windows, it might have many more branches growing out of it, and each of those might have several more branches growing out of them. To organize your files, you can create your own branches wherever you want to. For example, you might create new a folder in C:\ called Word-Pro and keep all the documents you created with your word processor inside it. Or you might want to go a stage further and create folders *inside* Word-Pro called Letters, Faxes, Reports, and Notes. You could organize still further by creating folders inside Letters called Personal and Business (see Figure 5.1).

Subfolders and parent folders

There are a couple more terms used to describe the whereabouts of folders within this tree. If a folder is *inside* another folder, it's said to be a **subfolder**, so the System folder is a subfolder of the Windows folder, and the Windows folder is a subfolder of the root folder. If you picture the same relationship in reverse, the Windows folder is the System folder's **parent**.

Paths

Because of this tree structure, you might have to open folders several levels deep to find a particular file. For example, if you wanted to look at a file inside the System folder, you'd open File Manager or Explorer to display the main C:\ folder, open the Windows folder you found inside it, and then open the System folder you found inside that. In other words, you have to follow a certain route through the folders to find the file you need, and the computer does it just the same way, calling it a **path**.

A path is simply a list of the folders the computer will need to open, each separated by a backslash (\). So to specify a file in the System folder called **Readme.txt**, you'd type:

C:\Windows\System\Readme.txt

Other drives on your system work in exactly the same way. Your floppy-disk drive is usually called Drive A, so (as long as there's a disk in the drive) the computer sees it as one big root-folder called **A:**. If you had a file called **Readme.txt** on this floppy disk, its path would be:

A:\Readme.txt

As usual, you can create new folders and subfolders in **A:**, and use the same method to direct the computer to the locations of particular files on a floppy disk.

Despite the way they're noted here, the names of drives, folders and files are not case-sensitive – for instance, you could type **a:\readme.txt** or **A:\REaDmE.tXT** and the operating system would understand. The colon and backslashes are essential though.

Creating folders

You can create new folders in the main root folder or any other folder you choose. Windows 3.1's **File Manager** has an option on its **File** menu labelled **Create Directory**; Windows 95's **Explorer** has an option labelled **New** which leads to a menu of new items that you can create, including folders. The new folder will be created inside the folder whose contents are currently being displayed, but if you create it in the wrong one by accident you can use the pointer to drag it to where you wanted it.

► *For more on Windows 95's 'New' menu, turn to p. 345.*

Before you can use a new folder, it has to be given a name. The rules for naming folders are very similar to those for naming files, discussed in the next section. In MS-DOS and Windows 3.1, a folder name can consist of up to eight characters, although you can increase this to eleven by inserting a dot after the eighth. Characters such as **?\+,;=[]** and spaces cannot be used, and names will always be displayed in upper-case characters (although Windows 3.1's File Manager will let you view them as all lower-case if you prefer).

Windows 95 offers far more flexibility in its naming-rules, allowing folder names to be up to 255 characters in length, and permitting the use of spaces and mixed upper- and lower-case characters.

Files and file names

What is a file?

Every program and document you work with or create consists of a set of data stored on a disk in a **file**. Each of these sets of data is given a name so that you (and the computer) can find it whenever it's needed, and files will vary in size according to how much data they contain. For example, if you run your word processor and create a file that just consists of somebody's name and address, the file might contain only 5 K of data; the file containing the word processor itself might be about 2 Mb in size (roughly 400 times as much data!).

As well as having a name, every file also has a location, known as its **path** (see p. 115). Whenever you want to use a particular file the computer needs to know its full path in order to find it; that is, which disk drive it has to look at, and which folders it will have to open to get to the file.

Naming files

Any time you create a new file, you choose a name for it and select which folder you want to save it in, but a folder can't contain more than one file of a particular name. For example, if a folder already contains a file called **Letter.doc** and you try to save a newly created file into the same folder using the same name, you'll be asked if you want to replace the original **Letter.doc** with this new one, or cancel the operation. You could get around this by choosing a different name, such as **Letter2.doc**, or, if you're really determined to use this name, you could save the new file into a different folder.

You can have multiple files in the same folder with the same file name provided the extension for each is different. For example, a folder could contain **Letter.doc**, **Letter.txt** and **Letter.pdf** quite happily.

As you can see from the file names in the previous paragraph, and others mentioned in earlier sections, files are named in a particular way: a few characters, a dot, and three more characters. The characters to the left of the dot are known as the **file name**, the three to its right are the **extension**.

The file name

MS-DOS and Windows 3.1 use a system of **short file names** (also known as **MS-DOS names**): the maximum name-length is eight characters, and certain characters such as spaces, and **?\+"*.,;=<>|[]** can't be used. Short file names can be quite restrictive: if you write a letter to Sandy you could call it **Sandylet**, which isn't too bad. The problem comes when Sandy replies, and you're morally compelled to write back – should it be **Sandylt2**, **Sndylet2**, or what? One way out is to use carefully organized folders so that all letters are saved into a folder called **Letters** and can be called **Sandy1**, **Sandy2** and so on. (The other workaround, of course, is to limit your circle of friends to people with four-letter names!)

Windows 95 uses a system of **long file names**: the maximum name-length is 255 characters, and the name can include mixed upper- and lower-case characters and a few extra symbols. The symbols you can't use are **\ / : * ?** " < > | but you can use one or more dots in the name itself. Handy though these long file names are, if you actually tried to give a file a 255-character name, you'd hardly ever be able to see this whole name because Windows just hasn't got room to display it! A more sensible length is about 25 characters, but this still gives you plenty of scope to choose a descriptive and easily recognizable name, such as **Letter to Sandy #2**.

File extensions

File extensions are not strictly necessary, but they do serve a useful purpose – certainly a far more useful one than having *no* extension would serve. In MS-DOS and Windows 3.1 an extension can be one, two or (most often) three characters; in Windows 95 it can be longer, but three characters is still the norm.

The function of the extension is to identify what *type* of file it is, and the three characters used are often an abbreviation of a longer word. For example, the extension **.txt** is an abbreviation of text-file; **.bmp** is an abbreviation of bitmap file (a type of graphics format); **.wav** is an abbreviation of wave sound (a digital audio file). It's within the realms of possibility that you might have three files called 'Bird' on your hard disk: **Bird.txt**, an essay about birds; **Bird.bmp**, a picture of a bird; and **Bird.wav**, a recording of birdsong. If it wasn't for extensions, you wouldn't know which was which and, more importantly, the application that you used to create the picture-file wouldn't be able to open the text or the wave files. So when you look at the extension you know which application you need to run in order to open the file.

TIP

A useful extension to commit to memory is **.exe**. This stands for *executable* and indicates that the file is a program rather than a file you've created yourself. For example, the Windows 3.1 paint program is called **Paintbrush**, and the file containing this program is called **Pbrush.exe**.

Extensions go a little further than this, though. Let's take word-processor applications as an example. The word processor does a particular job – it lets you type in text, format it and lay it out as you want it, and save it as a file. So you wouldn't expect a word processor to be able to open a sound or video file, for example. But one word processor won't necessarily be able to open a file created by a *different* word processor either. Although all word processors do a similar job, the *way* they do it differs. So the file you save, apart from containing the text you typed, will contain data specific to that particular word processor which another wouldn't be able to work with.

To get around this, word processors have their own *proprietary* extensions so that you can tell which application was used to create a file: Windows 3.1's Write program uses the extension **.wri**; Lotus WordPro uses **.lwp**; Microsoft Word uses **.doc**. The idea carries through to *all* types of application in exactly the same way to ensure that you can always tell which application to run when you want to work with a particular file.

So file extensions are useful things, and there's nothing to be gained by not adding an extension to the file name even though it's possible. But extensions have another use that makes them indispensable...

Associations and icons

One way to open a file is to run the program that created it, go to its **File** menu, choose the **Open** command and then hunt through your folders for the file you want and click it. It works (and we'll explain it in detail on p. 125), but it's a slow way of doing things, so file extensions provide another handy feature – *associations*.

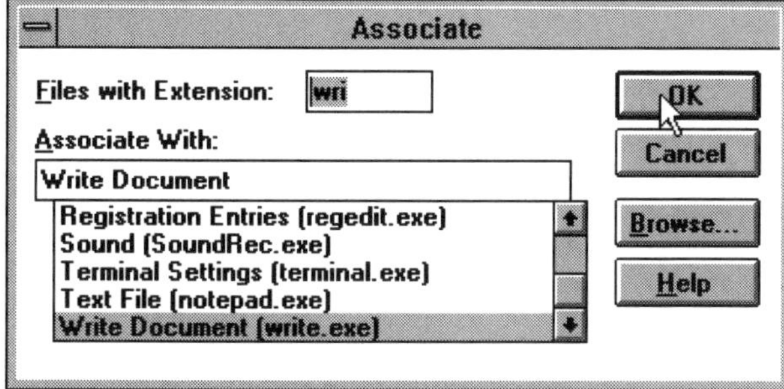

Figure 5.2 Windows 3.1's **Associate** dialog.

Windows 3.1's file associations

In Windows 3.1 the concept is very straightforward: you can associate a particular *extension* with a particular *program*. For example, the **.wri** extension is associated with Windows 3.1's **Write** program (as shown in Figure 5.2), so if you want to open a file called **Readme.wri** all you have to do is double-click on its icon or name. Windows sees that this file has a **.wri** extension, runs **Write** and opens this file in one simple operation. (For the keyboard-oriented, you can use the arrow buttons to move to the file you want, and then press *Enter* or *Return* to open it.)

As usual in a GUI, files in Windows 3.1 are represented by **icons**. The icons don't provide much information, but there's enough to work with. Apart from the folder icons mentioned on p. 113, when you run **File Manager** you'll see three other types of icon: the first two look like pages from a book, but one is blank and the other has 'writing' on it.

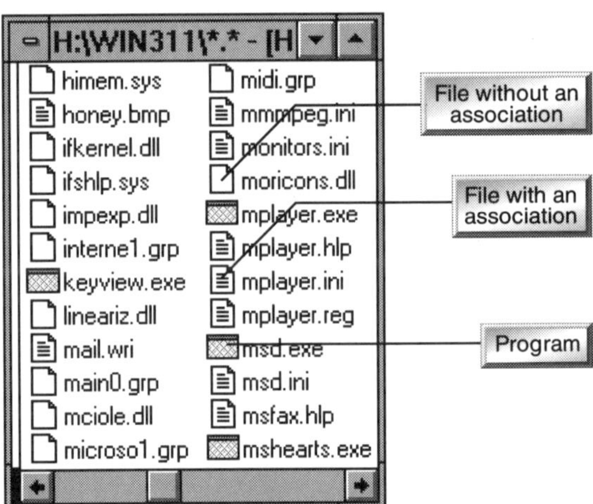

Figure 5.3 File icons in Windows 3.1's **File Manager**.

The blank-page icon indicates that this file has an extension that hasn't been associated with any program, so if you double-click it nothing will happen (a file with *no* extension will have this icon too). The written-page icon means that the file's extension *has* been associated with a program. (In Figure 5.3 you can see a file called **Mail.wri** which has the written-page icon, indicating that the **.wri** extension has been associated with a program.) The third icon is a blue-and-grey box which indicates that the file is a program or application: if you double-click this the program will run. (A fourth icon you might see consists of the same page-icon with a red exclamation mark. This denotes that the file has its **System** or **Hidden** attribute set, explained on p. 145, but these files will be visible in File Manager only if you've checked the **Show Hidden/System Files** option.)

Windows 95's file types

Windows 95 uses a similar system for exactly the same purpose, but complicates it slightly. The thinking seems to have been that you might have several different file extensions that you'd like to associate with the same program. As an example, the Media Player utility can play MIDI files, wave files, videos, animations and so on, which accounts for the extensions **.mid**, **.wav**, **.avi**, **.ani** and a few others. Instead of associating each of these extensions with Media Player separately, Windows 95 groups all these extensions together as one *type* called Media Clips, and then associates this *type* of file with Media Player. (Windows 95 refers to this as *registering* a file type in a few dialogs, and as *adding* one in others, but we'll stick with *associating* for clarity.)

This may not sound a whole lot different to the Windows 3.1 method and, as long as you're happy for all these files to open in Media Player, it doesn't make a lot of difference. The difficulty comes if you buy a new piece of software for playing animations, for example, and you want to change the association for **.ani** files so that they open in this new program instead. In Windows 3.1 this is a job you can do in 30 seconds; Windows 95 makes it uncharacteristically difficult – first you have to delete the Media Clips type, then you create a replacement that includes only **.mid**, **.wav** and **.avi** files, and finally create a separate new file type for **.ani** files.

▶ *Turn to p. 342 for more on creating, using and surviving file types.*

Windows 95's icons

In Windows 3.1 it's easy enough to tell that a particular extension has an association, but there's no quick way of finding out *which program* it's been associated with (other than by double-clicking it and seeing what opens!). In Windows 95 every program has its own individual icon, so when you run **Explorer** and have a look at the files on your system, instead of those identical blue-and-grey icons you see a variety of more colourful little pictures. But it doesn't end there – when a file type is associated with a program, all the files of this type are given an icon matching that of the program, so you can see at glance which file will open in which application.

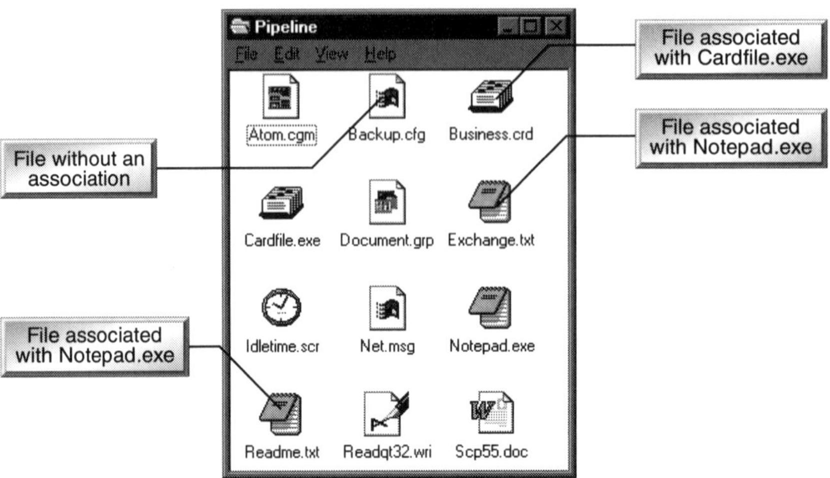

Figure 5.4 File icons in Windows 95's Explorer.

Figure 5.4 shows a collection of icons representing programs (with the **.exe** extension) and other types of file. There are two files here with the extension **.txt** which belong to a file type associated with **Notepad.exe**, and they therefore have Notepad's icon. In the same way, if you were to double-click the file called **Business.crd**, the program **Cardfile.exe** would be run with this file opened in it.

There are also a couple of files shown here whose icon contains the 'flying-window' logo. This icon indicates that files with this extension don't belong to any file type, so if you double-click one of these there's no associated program to run. Instead, as an improvement on Windows 3.1, a dialog box called **Open With** will appear to let you choose from a list of programs (see p. 348).

▶ *For more on opening files by double-clicking their icons, see 'Multiple instances' on p. 148.*

Creating and deleting files

Creating files

To be able to create a new file, you have to run the application that works with the type of information you want to use in the document. So the first decision to be made is what sort of document you want: for a text-based report or letter you need to run your word-processing software; for a drawing or picture you'll need your paint program; to enter and manipulate sets of numbers you'll run your spreadsheet application. In almost all cases this is all there is to it! When the window opens containing the application you selected, it will start with a 'clean sheet of paper' so to speak – a large white space into which you can begin typing your letter or drawing your picture, or a grid of boxes to begin entering your numbers into.

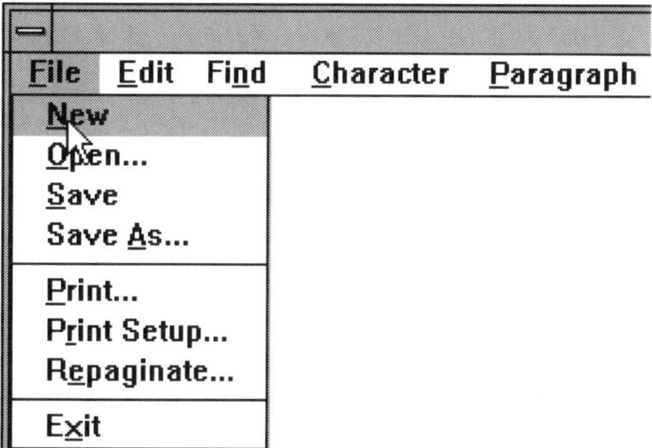

Figure 5.5 The **New** option found on the **File** menu in both Windows 3.1 and Windows 95.

Of course, the application you need to use may already be running. You might have just finished working on a report in your word processor and now want to type a letter. In this case, you just click on the application's **File** menu (or press *Alt* + *F*) and click on the word **New** (or press *N*) as shown in Figure 5.5. At this point, one of two things will happen. *Either*:

- in an application with a multiple document interface (see p. 106), a new document window will open, covering your other document's window, with the usual 'clean sheet'. (You can check that the other document is still there by clicking on the **Window** menu. Towards the bottom of the menu you'll see the names of two documents, one of which will probably be *Untitled* or *Document 1* – the same name as shown in the new document-window's title-bar. You can switch to the other document by clicking its name.)

Or:

- if the application doesn't have a multiple document interface, the previous document will be wiped from the screen to make way for the new one. If you hadn't saved the previous document since making changes to it, you'll first be prompted to do so – if you don't save it, these changes will be permanently lost (see p. 127).

Deleting files

Deleting a file is a very simple process, handled from File Manager in Windows 3.1 or Explorer in Windows 95. Just click once on the file to select it and press the *Delete* key. A confirmation dialog similar to the one in Figure 5.6 will appear to check you really mean it (although you can suppress these confirmation prompts if you want to). Deleting a file doesn't immediately remove its contents from disk. Instead, the disk sectors used by the file are marked as being reusable, so that sooner or later another file will be saved over the top. This therefore means that you can usually *undelete* a file if you have to and if you're quick off the mark, and Windows 3.1 includes an Undelete utility for this purpose.

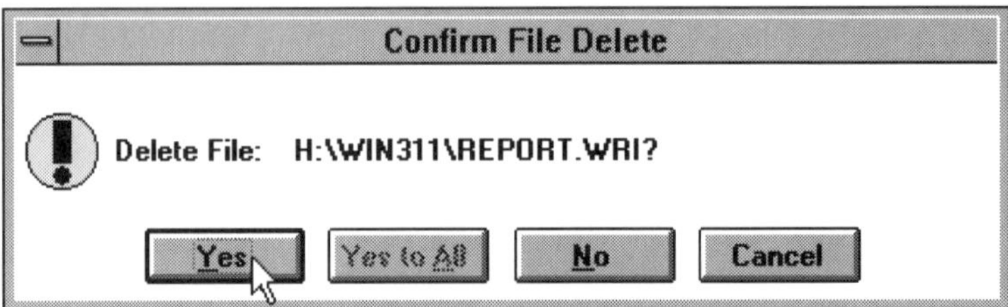

Figure 5.6 Windows 3.1's delete-confirmation dialog.

Windows 95 has a slightly different method of dealing with deletions which addresses the potential problem of trashing the wrong file by mistake. Whenever you delete a file, it simply gets moved to a holding place called the **Recycle Bin**. Continuing the traditional 'office' metaphor, you can throw anything you don't want into the bin, but until the bin is emptied you can rummage around and retrieve items you need. We'll take a closer look at the Bin on p. 335.

Deleting folders is done in precisely the same way, but when you delete a folder you're also deleting its entire contents including files, any subfolders it contains, and any files in those subfolders. Folders can't be undeleted – you just create a new one with the same name in the same location if you need to.

Opening a file

On p. 120 we've seen one quick way to open a file – just double-click its icon. This method has the time-saving benefit of opening both application and file in one manoeuvre. It's a handy method to use when you want to open the file in the application it's associated with (which won't necessarily be the case), and as long as that application isn't already running. So although it's a neat way to open a file, it isn't the *only* way. But before we look at the others, let's grapple with a more fundamental question.

What is opening?

When you look at your files in File Manager or Explorer, the names and icons you see just indicate that these various sets of data exist on disk – you can't see the data itself. To be able to view the *contents* of a file you have to *open* it in a program. This can be seen as two separate operations: first you have to start (or *run*) the program that can work with the type of data in your file; second, you have to load (or *open*) the file itself into that program, which will display the file's contents in its window in a form that you can work with. The program and the file must be compatible with each other. A paint program can't open a database file, for example, and a database program can't open a graphics file.

Open from the file menu

One of the most common methods of opening a file in an application that's already running is to use the **Open...** option found on the application's **File** menu (shown in Figure 5.5). The ellipsis added to this option indicates that it leads to a dialog box in which you'll tell the application which file you want to open and where it's located (known as its **path** – see p. 115).

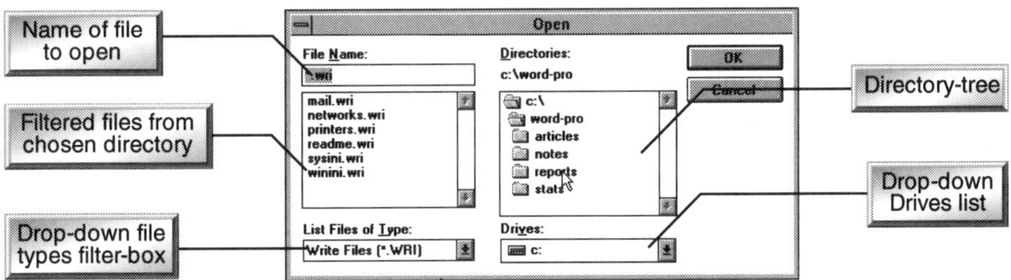

Figure 5.7 The **Open** dialog in Windows 3.1.

Let's assume that we're using Windows 3.1's **Write** program (as in Figure 5.7) and we want to open a file called **C:\Word-Pro\Reports\Sales.wri.** One way to open the file is to type this path into the upper-left box labelled **File Name** and then click on **OK**. Most Windows users avoid typing paths (usually because they can't remember them), hence the other boxes in the dialog, aimed chiefly at mouse users. The method is the same to open any file, so let's run through it step by step.

1. In the box labelled **List Files of Type**, check that **.wri** files are shown. **Write**, like many applications, is able to work with several types of file. This box acts as a filter to show only the type of file you're looking for. If **.wri** files aren't shown, click the arrow to the right of the box and click its entry in the list that drops down.
2. In the box labelled **Drives** make sure drive **C:** is shown. If it isn't, click the arrow beside the box to see a list of the drives on your system and click on **C:**.
3. In the box above it, labelled **Directories** (the Windows 3.1 word for 'folders') double-click on **C:**. The **C:** folder will open showing all its subfolders. Use the scroll box to find the **Word-Pro** folder and double-click it; this will open in the same way to show its subfolders. Double-click on the **Reports** folder.
4. In the large box on the left you'll see a list of files found in the **Reports** folder. Which files are shown in the list depends on the setting of the filter box we used in step 1, so in this case only files with the **.wri** extension will be shown even though the folder may contain files with other extensions too. One of these files should be **Sales.wri** (you might have to use the scroll box to bring it into view).
5. Finally, either click once on **Sales.wri** (which will display its name in the **File Name** box) and click **OK**, or double-click **Sales.wri**.

▶ *Windows 95 has a rather more sophisticated* ***Open*** *dialog which allows you to carry out complete file-management tasks as well as opening files. We'll take a closer look at these features on p. 343.*

When you open a file, the results will be similar to those of creating a new file explained on p. 123: if the application has a multiple document interface (MDI), the file will be opened in a new document window; if not, you'll be prompted to save an edited file as soon as you select the **Open...** option and the file you open will take the window of the one you were working on.

Recent files

Many programs include a list of recently used files on their **File** menus, as a quick method of working with a small group of files on a regular basis. Every time you open a file using one of the standard methods, it's placed at the top of the list. To reopen one of these recent files you just have to click on the **File** menu followed by the file you want. Some programs also give you the option to choose how many files should be shown in this list: the maximum number will usually be between four and eight.

Open using Drag & Drop

Another method of opening files in an application that's already running is to use **Drag & Drop** (see section **2.3**). In Windows 3.1, this means that you need to be able to see the icon of the file you want to open, and at least a small part of the top of the application's window, so some window arranging might be needed beforehand. Then just click on the file's icon and drag it to the application's window. Providing the application allows this method of opening files, you'll see a small box containing a cross added to the pointer when the file can be dropped. The file will open in the same way as mentioned above.

TIP

Try to drop the file on the application's title-bar/menu-bar area. In some applications, dropping the file into the document window will create an **embedded** file in the original document instead of opening your new one. (Linked and embedded objects are covered on pp. 156–160.)

Windows 95 allows the Drag & Drop approach to be used, but makes it a little easier by means of the **Taskbar**. See 'Copying or moving files and Folders' on p. 329.

▶ *You may have another* ***Open*** *option at your disposal which can be useful if an application doesn't have a MDI. Turn to the 'Multiple instances' heading on p. 148.*

Saving a file

When you look at an application's **File** menu (shown in Figure 5.5) you'll see there are two similar options: **Save** and **Save As....** Both of these save your file, but they do it in slightly different ways so we'll take them one at a time. But first let's clarify *why* a file should be saved and what it entails.

What is saving?

When you have an application running and you open a file in it, that file is loaded into RAM. If you just take a look at the file and then close it again it's cleared out of RAM but it's still on the disk it came from. If, on the other hand, you start editing the file these changes are stored in the PC's various forms of short-term memory, so if you then close the file these changes are cleared out of memory along with the rest of the file, and the file on your disk remains unchanged. (This is worth remembering if you make changes to a file and feel you've made it worse – you can just close it, and reopen it!)

To keep the changes you've made to the file you have to store them on disk. The *save* process takes the whole edited file and writes it onto the disk, usually (but not necessarily) overwriting the original version with the new edited version. Saving a file doesn't close it – you can (and should!) save a file regularly as you work on it.

Save

The **Save** entry on the **File** menu is a command (as opposed to **Save As...** which, as the ellipsis shows, leads to a dialog), but it works in two slightly different ways depending upon the file you want to save. If you opened an existing file to work on and you now want to save it, selecting **Save** will write it to the same location on the same disk using the same name; in other words, overwriting the original with this updated file. (In many applications, you can save a file by using the key combination *Ctrl* + *S*.)

If you created a *new* file, as on p. 122, selecting **Save** will lead to the same dialog as **Save As...** (see below). This is because the file you're trying to save doesn't yet have a name or a location to be saved to, so the computer can't do the job until you've supplied the information it needs to do it.

TIP

The **Save** and **Save As...** dialogs, together with any other menu options you select, will apply only to the *active* document window in a MDI. If you have several document windows open, each document you work on must be saved separately.

Save As ...

The **Save As...** option is used when you want to specify a name and location for the file you're saving. Its primary use is for saving a newly created file that doesn't yet possess these details – in this situation, either of the two 'Save' options will lead to the **Save As...** dialog. Its secondary use is for saving an existing file to a different location, or with a different name, or both. For example, you might have a file on your hard disk that needs to be altered slightly and then given to someone else. So you open it, edit it, and use **Save As...** to save it to floppy disk instead of hard disk by selecting the corresponding drive (usually **A:**) from the **Drives** drop-down box. Alternatively, you may have opened and edited a file and can't decide whether you want to commit yourself to the changes you've made: in this case, you could save it back to the same location but type a different name into the **File Name** box so that you've still got the original. In other words, the **Save As...** option gives you the chance to *save* the file *as* something different from the file you opened.

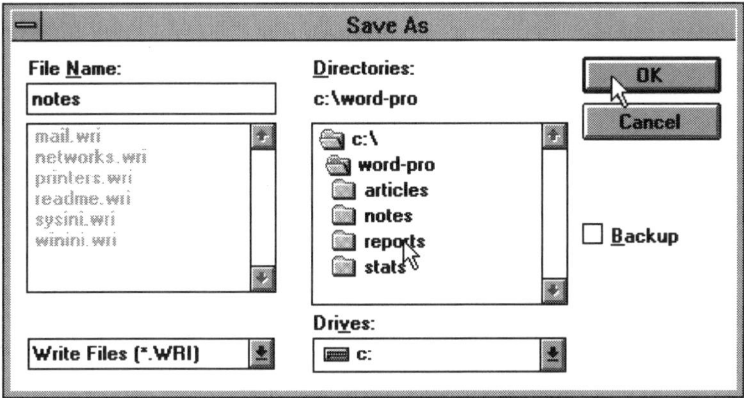

Figure 5.8 The **Save As...** dialog in Windows 3.1.

Each element of the **Save As...** dialog works in exactly the same way as it does in the **Open** dialog. In the **File Name** box you can type the full path and name you'd like to assign to the file, or you can use the **Drives** and **Directories/Folders** boxes to display the target drive and folder. If you use this second method you need only type a file name in the **File Name** box.

In Figure 5.8 the name 'Notes' has been chosen for the file; the box in the bottom-left of the window indicates that this file will have the extension **.wri** automatically tagged onto it, as the default extension for this application. However, Write – like many other applications – can save files in several different formats; to use one of those instead, you can select it from this drop-down list in the usual way and the corresponding extension will be added to the file instead of **.wri**.

If you needed to, you could save the file in one format, then click **Save As...** again and save it with a *different* format and extension, thereby having two copies of the file on disk in different formats.

▶ *File formats are explained on pp. 138–142.*

Replacing files

You can also use the **Save As...** dialog to replace another file with the one you're saving. For example, you might already have a file called **Notes.wri** that you want to replace with this newly created one. In the same way as above, navigate to the folder containing **Notes.wri** and you'll see its name among the list of files. Click on its name and click **OK** (or just *double*-click its name). A prompt will appear, like the one in Figure 5.9, asking if you're sure you want to replace the file. Click on **Yes** if you are sure, or **No** to return to the **Save As...** dialog and choose a different name.

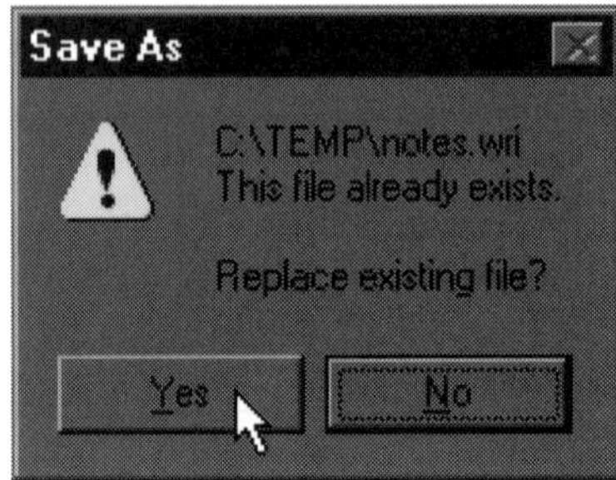

Figure 5.9 The prompt dialog that prevents you accidentally overwriting a file.

Making a backup

Some applications have a facility to create an automatic backup every time you save a file. Instead of the original file being overwritten, it's given a slightly different name (often by changing its extension to **.bak**) ensuring that you've always got two generations of the file on disk. This is a facility worth making use of, but it's usually switched off by default so you have to find the option and select it. In some applications it's in the form of a check box on the **Save As...** menu (see Figure 5.8); in others you'll find it on the **Options** menu, or on the **Options** dialog selected from the **View** menu.

▶ *In keeping with its **Open** dialog, Windows 95 also has an enhanced **Save As...** dialog – see p. 343.*

Printing a file

Along with opening, saving and creating files, printing them is something you'll be doing very frequently (if you've got a printer!). **Print** options and commands are listed on the **File** menu and are fairly standard from one application to another, so we'll take a look at each of the entries you're likely to come across.

Print...

The **Print** option is often followed by an ellipsis indicating that it leads to a dialog rather than printing immediately. To print a single copy of the document on the default (or only) printer, click on **OK** or press *Return* when this dialog appears. Provided your printer is switched on and has paper, the document will print.

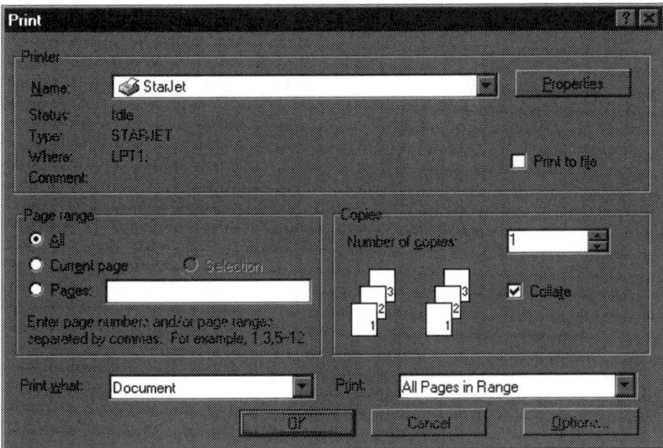

Figure 5.10 A **Print** dialog from Windows 95.

The **Print** dialog itself can vary from one application to another, and between Windows 3.1 and 95, but you'll find many of the same options there somewhere. The default printer will be shown together with the port it's connected to (usually LPT1) – if you have more than one printer you can select which you want to use from a drop-down list box. A box with spin-buttons will show the number of copies to print, defaulting to one, and there will usually be some method of specifying a range of pages to print if you don't want to print the whole document.

If there's a **Print** button on the application's toolbar, you can click this to bypass the **Print** dialog. Selecting this option will print one copy of the document on the default printer without stopping to ask questions.

Print Setup...

The **Print Setup** dialog, found in Windows 3.1 applications, is where you make choices relating to your printer itself, such as which printer to use, paper orientation (landscape or portrait), paper size, and print quality (draft or high quality). In Windows 95, some of these options are found on the **Print** dialog itself, and others will be reached by clicking the **Properties** button on the **Print** dialog.

Page Setup...

A dialog commonly found in Windows 95, although the same options will be found in other dialogs in Windows 3.1. Typical options here are paper size and orientation, and the sizes of margins. The settings you choose will usually be reflected in the layout of the document on screen – for example, if you increase the sizes of the margins in a word-processor document, the margin size will be increased by similar amounts on screen to give you an impression of how the document will appear when printed. This is an example of WYSIWYG at work (see below).

Print Preview

Of the various print-related entries on the **File** menu, this is the only one that doesn't have the ellipsis. Selecting this option displays the whole of the page you're working on shrunk to fit on the screen to let you check the overall appearance and layout of the page before printing. In some applications you may have an option to view two or more pages side by side, which involves shrinking them still further. Clicking somewhere on the page will usually allow you to zoom in and out on a particular area of the page, and you can usually cycle through a multi-page document using the *PageUp/PageDown* keys.

Quick printing

You don't necessarily have to be running an application to be able to print a file. Both File Manager and Explorer have a **Print** option on their **File** menus – just click once on the file you want to print and choose **File/Print**. In some cases the application will open briefly as it processes the command; in others you'll just see a dialog of the 'Preparing to print' variety, with a **Cancel** button in case you change your mind. For this to work under Windows 3.1 the file you choose must have an association – it's the associated application that handles the print process. In Windows 95 the equivalent is true – the file must belong to a registered file *type* – but **Print** must also be listed as an action for files of this type. File types and their actions are explained on pp. 345–348.

Print spooling

Print *spooling* involves sending the stream of data from the application to hard disk where it's stored in a temporary file, instead of sending the data directly from application to printer. From here the data is passed (spooled) to the printer when the printer is ready for it and the temporary file is automatically deleted when the print job is done. Print spooling is an important part of Windows' **multitasking** abilities (see p. 97) that frees up the application more quickly for you to continue working.

WYSIWYG

The acronym to end all acronyms: 'What You See Is What You Get' (pronounced 'wizzy-wig'). WYSIWYG is one of the huge benefits of using a graphical interface: what you see on the screen will be a reasonably precise representation of what you'll get on paper when you print. This means that a document created using a desktop publishing (DTP) application, using a variety of pictures and diagrams, incorporating different text fonts and sizes, carefully laid out to look effective on screen, should look identical when printed. The WYSIWYG concept holds true in all GUI-based applications whether you're working with text, graphics, or a mixture of the two, although some applications are better at it than others, giving rise to the extended acronym WYSIWYGMOL: 'What You See Is What You Get, More Or Less.'

Editing a file

One of the main reasons for opening a file is to add to it or change it in some way – in other words, *edit it*. Since any application that allows you to create and save a document will also allow you to edit it, the **Edit** menu is as much a fixture on the menu-bar as the **File** menu. In fact, most of the *other* menus you'll find are also geared towards making the editing easier, but their names, and the entries they contain, will vary widely from one application to another depending upon the type of information you're working with (for example, a database application has no need of a menu called 'Sound Effects'!). The **Edit** menu has its own variations too of course, but there are a few entries here that turn up in almost every application.

Cut, Copy, Paste

These three commands form a group of the most useful editing tools you'll come across, enabling you to move or copy large chunks of a document around instead of needing to repeat work you've done once already.

These commands work with something called the **clipboard**, a temporary storage place provided by Windows that any application can access whenever it needs to. The clipboard can hold any kind of data you select – a picture, a block of text, a snippet of sound or video, or even a whole document. (The various ways of selecting the data to be edited are explained in 'Selection methods' below.)

- The **Cut** command works rather like the *Delete* key on the keyboard: the item you selected will vanish from the screen in the same way, but it will be placed on the clipboard rather than disappearing forever.
- The **Copy** command 'photographs' the item you selected and stores a copy of it on the clipboard. The original text, picture or document isn't affected.
- The **Paste** command places the item currently on the clipboard into your document. In a word processor, spreadsheet or other text-based application the pasted item will be placed at the position indicated by the flashing cursor (known as the **insertion point**); in a graphics-based application the pasted item will usually appear surrounded by a dotted-box attached to the pointer – just move the pointer until the item is where you want it to be, and click.

TIP

The Cut, Copy and Paste commands can be accessed from the keyboard using the keystrokes *Ctrl* + *X*, *Ctrl* + *C* and *Ctrl* + *V* respectively. You'll be using these commands a lot (particularly in Windows 95 to sort your files and folders) so it's well worth remembering the keystrokes even if you're more of a mouse lover.

The **Clipboard** can hold only one item at a time, so if you cut a section of text, and then cut another one it will replace the first. Also, since there's only one clipboard, if you copy something with one application, then switch to another application and copy something else, the first copy will be replaced on the clipboard. However, once something has been placed on the clipboard (using either **Cut** or **Copy**) it can be **Pasted** as many times, and to as many different places, as you want it.

▶ *Both Windows 3.1 and Windows 95 include a small program called* ***Clipboard Viewer*** *(or an enhanced version called* ***Clipbook Viewer****) that lets you see and work with the clipboard's contents –* *turn to p. 301.*

Undo

As the name suggests, this is the command you head for when you do something you didn't mean to. It could be something as minor as typing a wrong letter in a word processor (although the *Backspace* key would take care of this more easily), or something as major as accidentally deleting a paragraph or part of a picture – selecting **Undo** reverts to the original, as if it never happened.

Some applications have several levels of undo. Windows 95's **Paint** program, for example, will let you undo your last three actions by selecting **Undo** three times. (An 'action' refers to the period of time between clicking a mouse button in the drawing area and releasing it again; in this time you might have made just a single dot or you might have drawn a large and intricate freehand shape.)

TIP

In most applications, you can undo your last action by pressing *Ctrl + Z* instead of sending your mouse off to the menu-bar.

Find and Replace

These are options found in text-based applications such as word processors, spreadsheets, databases and so on (the word *Find* being replaced with *Search* in the apparently less-optimistic Windows 3.1). Find and Replace are actually two separate dialogs, but they work in a similar way. **Find** allows you to search a document for all occurrences of a particular word or phrase that you type into its box; when an occurrence is found you can stop and make a change to it or search for the next. A **Match Case** check box lets you narrow down your search to occurrences using the same combination of upper- and lower-case characters you entered. Checking a second box marked **Find Whole Words Only** ensures that the search ignores longer words containing the letters you specified – for example, if you wanted to search for occurrences of the word **rant**, checking this box would prevent the word **currant** being found.

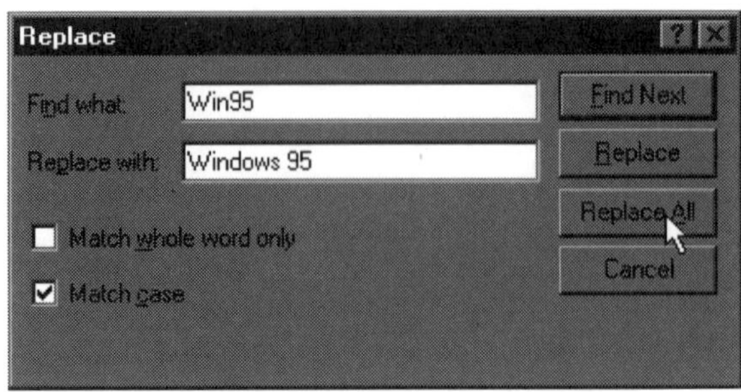

Figure 5.11 A **Replace** dialog in Windows 95.

In the **Replace** dialog (Figure 5.11), you type a word or phrase (or just a single character) to search for and a second entry to replace it with. Clicking the **Replace All** button will automate the process, and a final dialog will tell you how many occurrences were replaced. If you prefer, you can step through the document from one occurrence to the next clicking the **Replace** button to replace the text that was found or the **Find Next** button to ignore it and move to the next occurrence.

Select All

This is another option found more often in text-based, rather than graphics-based, applications. Choosing this option (or using its keystroke *Ctrl + A*) will highlight the contents of the entire document in preparation for some kind of global editing action. There are few occasions when this might be useful: one of these is so that you can 'Copy' the document to the clipboard ready to 'Paste' into a different document or application; another is so that you can apply a formatting command to the whole document such as changing the font or text size.

Selection methods

Whenever you want to carry out some editing action on a part of a document you first have to *select* that part, otherwise the action might have no effect at all, or, worse still, it might affect the whole document! There are various selection methods, and which to use will depend on the type of document you're working on and how much of it you need to select.

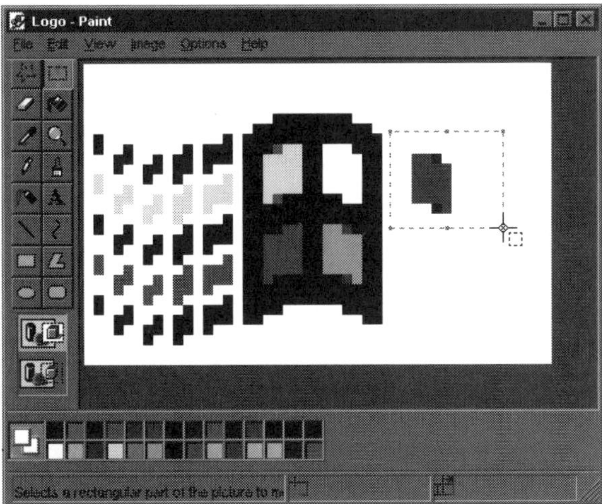

Figure 5.12 Using the selection tool in Paint or Paintbrush.

In a graphics application such as Windows 95's Paint or Windows 3.1's Paintbrush, a 'selection tool' called Scissors or Pick is used to mark the area you want to select. After choosing this tool, click the mouse button at one corner of the required area and drag diagonally – a dotted box will expand as you do so (see Figure 5.12). When the required area is outlined by this box, release the mouse button and choose the editing action you want.

A similar method is used to select multiple cells in a spreadsheet or table: click in one cell and drag the mouse vertically, horizontally or diagonally to highlight the cells you want to work with. Another method (which is also used to select multiple files in File Manager or Explorer) is to press and hold *Ctrl* and click in each of the required cells. In this way you can select cells scattered throughout the document rather than having to select a block of adjoining cells.

UK	NZ/Au	Total
34	22	56
6	10	16
21	14	35
18	6	24
30	8	38
13	2	15
4	2	6
6	4	10
19	2	21
32	30	62
21	7	[illegible]
44	7	51
6	3	9
8	3	11
26	2	28

Figure 5.13 Dragging to highlight cells in a spreadsheet.

When working with text there are several possible methods you can use, one of which is the good old favourite, dragging. Move the pointer to the left of the first word you want to select, and simply click and drag along the line or diagonally down the page until you've highlighted all you want. Here's a quickfire list of other methods (some of which are limited to Microsoft applications):

- To select characters one by one using the keyboard, hold *Shift* and use the left or right arrow keys to highlight consecutive characters.
- To select a single word, double-click it with the mouse.
- To select words one by one using the keyboard, hold *Ctrl* + *Shift* and use the left or right arrow keys to highlight consecutive words.
- To select a whole line from the keyboard, move the cursor (*insertion point*) to the beginning of the line and press *Shift* + *End*.
- To select a whole line (as an alternative method for some Microsoft word processors) move the text-pointer to the extreme left of the line: when it turns into a right-slanted arrow, click once.
- To select a whole paragraph, triple-click it with the mouse. This is a Microsoft trick, used only in software designed for Windows 95, requiring a whole new nimbleness from the mouse-button finger!
- To select a whole paragraph (another alternative Microsoft method) move the text-pointer to the extreme left of the paragraph: when it turns into a right-slanted arrow, double-click.
- To select all text between the insertion point and the end of the document, press *Ctrl* + *Shift* + *End*.
- To select all text between the insertion point and the beginning of the document, press *Ctrl* + *Shift* + *Home*.
- To select the whole document (a Microsoft alternative to the **Select All** menu option), move the text-pointer to the extreme left margin once again: when it turns into a right-slanted arrow, triple-click.

File formats

What are file formats?

As we've seen in earlier sections, if you use a particular application to create a file, you know that same application will be able to open it again. Another application may not, even though it might be able to create a file that looks very similar. This is because different applications save the data in your file in different ways, known as the **file format**.

To ensure that you're able to identify which file belongs to which application, a proprietary extension is added to the file name when you save it, and files without that extension are filtered out of the dialog when you select the application's **Open...** option. But many applications are able to open a variety of file formats, and you can change the filter (shown in Figure 5.7) to show files conforming to one of these formats, or indeed select the **All Files** filter and try to open *any* file at all.

Proprietary formats

There are two separate issues involved in determining whether an application can open a file:

- *Type of file.* If you run your word processor and try to open a digital-audio file in it you're going to be out of luck: even if you'd changed the extension of this file to one the word processor is used to working with, it won't be able to load the data. If you try to open a text-based file created by a *different* word processor, you at least stand a chance because a word processor knows how to handle text...
- *File format.* ...but will your word processor be able to read the *other* data in the file, such as font types and sizes, paragraph formatting, tab spacing, bullet points, and so on? To you they appear as just a part of the text; to the application they're a complex set of codes, specific to the application that created the file, which have to be interpreted.

To this end, many applications support the file formats created by the same company's *other* products – for example, Microsoft Word can open files created by the Microsoft Works word processor – to enable their customers to upgrade to more sophisticated applications and still open their existing files. They sometimes even support the file formats of their competitors' software for similar reasons. This support comes in the form of conversion files that effectively *translate* the codes used by this file format into the codes used by the application. When you choose the **Open...** command in Word and select a Works file to open, Word consults the corresponding conversion file and starts translating; an application that doesn't have the necessary conversion file has no means of understanding the data.

Universal formats

Apart from these proprietary formats used by applications, there is a variety of universal formats used for a range of file types. The concept behind universal formats is that it should be possible to share information with other computer users regardless of which particular applications they favour. In fact, as computers are being used more and more in communications and networking, there are proprietary formats which are *becoming* universal by virtue of being first on the scene in a particular field, so software-producers working in that field have to include support for the format in order to tempt customers. The following sections give a brief description of some of the main universal file formats you'll come across, together with their corresponding extensions.

Text formats

- *ASCII.* Pronounced 'ass-key'. A plain-text format that consists of 96 standard keyboard characters and 32 control codes such as carriage return and tab. File sizes are typically small since there's nothing to save but these characters and codes, each being 7 bits long. ASCII files are also known as **text files** and usually have the extension **.txt**. These files can be opened in, and created by, any word processor.
- *Rich-text format.* A format that allows a 'richer' variety of text-formatting options to be used including choice of font type, colour and size; bold, italic and underline; and paragraph formatting such as centred or right-aligned text. These files have the extension **.rtf** and almost all word processors can work with them. File sizes are usually much larger than the same file saved in a proprietary word-processor format would be. Rich-text format is supported by Windows 95's **WordPad**.
- *Adobe Acrobat.* A word-processor format of Adobe Systems Incorporated. It is commonly used to distribute text files via the Internet and online services. Acrobat files can be read only with Adobe's own **Acrobat Reader** software, but this is available free from Adobe's World Wide Web site (see p. 244). Acrobat files have the extension **.pdf** which stands for 'Portable Document Format', derived from the fact that all the fonts (typefaces) used in a document are embedded in the file so you needn't have the correct fonts on your system to be able to view the document exactly as it was created.
- *Microsoft Word.* Another proprietary word-processor format becoming popular as a distribution medium. Word files have the extension **.doc** and are compatible with **WordPad** (included with Windows 95) and **Word** itself. Reader software called **Word Viewer** is available from Microsoft's web site (see p. 244).

▶ *Turn to p. 301 for more details on Notepad, and to p. 364 for WordPad.*

Graphics formats

- *Bitmap.* A file format that stores an image pixel-by-pixel and in a variety of compressed forms. A common form of compression involves replacing blocks of identically coloured pixels with the computer equivalent of ditto marks, although other variations are used, each identified by its own extension. The most common forms are **.bmp** and **.pcx** (used by Windows' Paint and Paintbrush); **.gif** (GIF – also known as CompuServe Image Format); **.jpg** (JPEG); and **.tif** (TIFF) which is the common file format used in desktop publishing. The amount of compression used on an image file can often be selected when saving, but heavily compressed files will usually result in a loss of quality. Different types of image will result in a smaller file depending upon which method of compression is used. For example, a simple picture that uses large blocks of identical colours will compress to a relatively small file in **.bmp** format, whereas a scanned photograph will barely compress at all in this format since many adjacent pixels will be slightly different colours, meaning that the data for almost every pixel must be saved. Photographs are best saved in JPEG or GIF format for a balance between file size and quality.

▶ *For more on Paintbrush and Paint, see pp. 298 and 366 respectively.*

TIP

When saving a bitmap file, experiment with all the formats at your disposal to see which creates the smallest file for your image with the least reduction in quality. You'll soon start to get a feel for which format to use for a particular image.

- *Vector graphics* (also known as *Line art*). A method that stores drawings as a set of commands to draw particular shapes, lines and arcs together with their positions and sizes, resulting in an image that can be *scaled* (enlarged or reduced without affecting the quality of the picture). Common types are Windows Metafile (**.wmf**); Computer Graphics Metafile (**.cgm**); and Encapsulated PostScript (**.eps**). The latter can also store bitmap images, but is supported by relatively few applications. The Windows Metafile is the most common format, although two slightly different types exist which are not always both supported in an application.

▶ *Turn to p. 186 for details of applications that create bitmap and vector graphics image files.*

Sound formats

- *Wave sound.* The primary file format for digital audio is the **.wav** file, used by Windows to provide its system sound effects (see pp. 288 and 354) and supported by **Sound Recorder** and **Media Player** which are included with both versions of Windows. Wave files vary in size according to the sample rate used to record them, and the method used to compress and decompress the sound data (known as a **codec**). A top-quality (CD-quality) sound file will occupy roughly 10 Mb of disk space for every minute of audio recorded.

- *MIDI file*. A file format denoted by the extension **.mid** used with computers and other types of dedicated musical hardware. The MIDI file contains simple commands to tell an electronic device which notes to play and when, so file sizes are usually small. Almost any MIDI-sequencing software will recognize **.mid** files, together with many 'player' programs such as Windows' **Media Player**.

▶ *Turn to pp. 68–70 snf 214–216 for more on digital audio and MIDI.*

Video formats

- *MPEG* (pronounced 'emm-peg'). The primary universal video format with the extension **.mpg**, providing excellent compression of video to make for smaller files, but being very processor-intensive. MPEG videos can be played using software programs designed for the job, but for best quality and full-screen playback a dedicated MPEG expansion card is required to supplement the processor.
- *Video for Windows*. A common Windows video format with the extension **.avi** supported by **Media Player**. Playback of this video format is handled by software so **.avi** videos generally play well only in a small window.

▶ *For more on video turn to p. 217.*

Properties and attributes

All the folders and files on your disks have their own **Properties sheet**, a type of dialog box that contains details about the item such as what it is, where it is, and when it was created and/or changed. Properties sheets also contain four switchable settings for an item, known as its **Attributes**. All these details are stored in an area on a disk called the File Allocation Table (**FAT**). The FAT is the basis of the PC's filing system that enables files to be found on a disk when they're needed.

Opening the properties sheet

In Windows 3.1 files, folders and shortcuts are shown as icons in Program Manager and File Manager, and each of these will have its own properties sheet. In Windows 95, files, folders, shortcuts and drives all have properties sheets, and their icons can be found in My Computer, Explorer, or on the Desktop. There are several methods of opening an item's properties sheet, most of which are common to both Windows 3.1 and Windows 95:

- Select the item by clicking it once or navigating to it using the keyboard arrow keys, then choose **Properties** from the **File** menu.
- Select the item in the same way and press *Alt + Enter.*
- Hold *Alt* and double-click on the item.
- In Windows 95 only, right-click on the item and choose **Properties** from the context menu that appears.

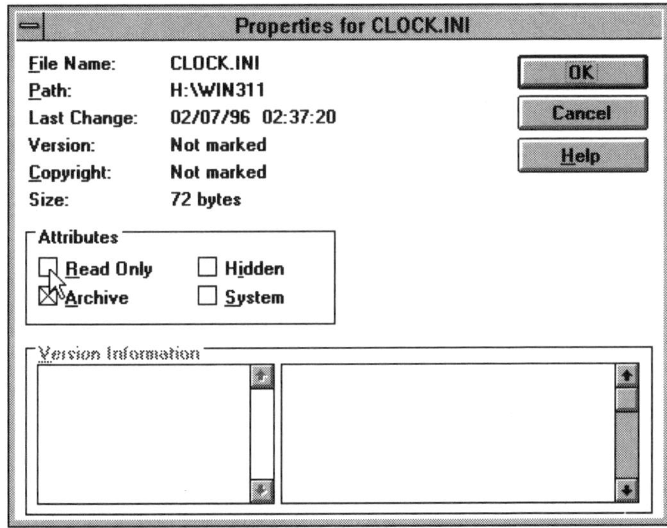

Figure 5.14 The standard properties sheet in Windows 3.1.

Windows 3.1's properties sheets

Windows 3.1 has one type of properties sheet for files and another for folders. The file's sheet is shown in Figure 5.14 and displays the file name and extension, the path to the folder containing the file, and the date and time of the last change that was made to the file. A file may have been changed as a result of your editing and re-saving it, or, in the case of system files, by the operating system itself. The size of the file is displayed in bytes. The boxes at the bottom of the sheet will display details of version number, producer and copyright of program files: these version numbers can be a handy thing to check to find out if you're using the latest version of the software.

The properties sheet for folders is much simpler, containing just the folder's name, path, and date and time of last change (which is, in fact, the folder's creation date).

Windows 95's properties sheets

The properties sheets for Windows 95 are rather different (Figure 5.15): in addition to the basic information about size and creation date, the information displayed can vary dramatically according to the type of item selected, and the sheet often consists of several tabbed pages leading to even more information. For example, a drive's properties sheet will have tabbed pages detailing its capacity, its remaining free space, and when the disk was last scanned for errors and backed-up. The properties sheet for a sound or video file will have extra pages giving details of file format, running time, and copyright details, together with a preview page from which you can play the file. The file name will be shown as you're used to seeing it (i.e. as a long file name) and also by its MS-DOS name (see p. 348 for more on the pros and cons of Windows 95's file naming).

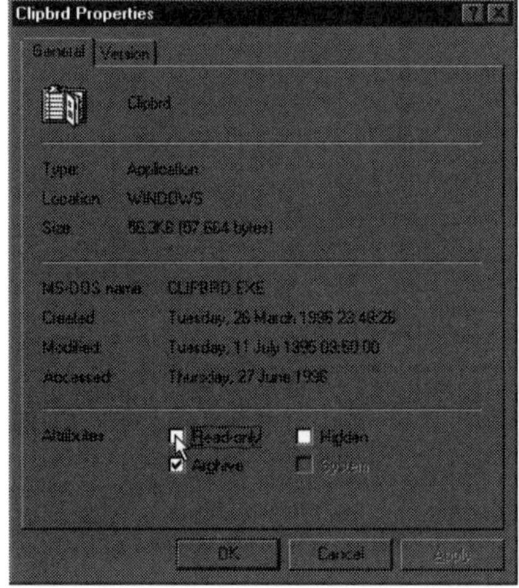

Figure 5.15 The first page of a typical properties sheet in Windows 95.

The Windows 95 properties sheet for a folder is far more useful than its Windows 3.1 counterpart: in addition to folder name, MS-DOS name, Location, and Creation date, there are two very useful entries: *Size* and *Contains*. The **Contains** entry details how many files and subfolders are within this folder; the **Size** entry gives the total size of these contents in K or Mb and in bytes.

Using attributes

There are four entries in the Attributes section of the properties sheet – **Read Only**, **Hidden**, **Archive** and **System** (see Figure 5.15) – and these settings are selected by checking the appropriate box.

- *Read Only*. If this option is checked, you'll be able to open the file (*read* it) but you won't be able to write any data to it. If you try to save a read-only file you'll be prompted to save it under another name or to another location. This makes it impossible to accidentally overwrite a file you want to keep. You can, however, delete a read-only file in File Manager or Explorer. File Manager makes it tougher by always pointing out that you're deleting a read-only file (or one with the **System** or **Hidden** attribute set); Explorer will never mention it if you've turned off the delete confirmation option for **Recycle Bin** (see p. 335).
- *Hidden*. Selecting this option for a file or a folder will remove its icon from File Manager and Explorer, effectively hiding it. This works as a form of security: for hidden items, the only way to access them is to select them by name and path from the Run command. In both versions of Windows, certain vital system files are hidden by default to prevent accidental deletion – it's security *from* you as well as *for* you! But both versions of Windows also have an option that puts hidden items back on view again: in Windows 3.1's File Manager, go to **View/By File Type...** and check the box marked **Show Hidden/System Files**; in Windows 95's Explorer, go to **View/Options/View** and click the option button marked **Show All Files**.
- *Archive*. Checking the Archive option determines whether certain backup programs will backup this file. If this option is checked, a single *bit* of data called the 'archive bit' will be added to the FAT when this file is edited and re-saved. When the backup procedure is next run, the existence of this archive bit tells the program that this file has been changed and therefore needs to be backed-up; after doing so, the program resets the archive bit.
- *System*. A check in this box indicates that the file is a part of the operating system and shouldn't be modified or deleted. On Windows 95 properties sheets this option will be greyed-out (unavailable) whether or not the box is checked. In Windows 3.1 you can uncheck this box if you want to, but there's little point in doing so – its only function is to inform you of the file's importance.

In Windows 3.1, files with either the System or Hidden attribute set, or both, are given a special icon containing a red exclamation mark (if you opted to view this type of file, as noted above) to make it even more difficult to delete them by accident. In Windows 95 there's no special icon. This, coupled with the lack of delete-confirmation prompts, means it's vital to check the properties sheet of any file you're unsure about before deleting it.

TIP

There are many important files that don't have a System or Hidden attribute. Avoid deleting any file from your hard disk's root folder (usually C:\), your Windows folder or any of its subfolders unless you know exactly what it is and why you're deleting it!

Working with software

Software is a generic name for computer programs – files that contains sets of instructions or data enabling a computer to carry out a particular task. Operating systems, along with applications, come under the software heading.

What is an application?

An application is a program (or, sometimes, a *set* of programs) that you can use to create a new file or to edit an existing file. Some applications will let you create pictures and graphics, some will let you enter, edit and format text, others will let you record and edit digital sound, create animations, enter and manipulate lists of numbers, and so on. Applications are sometimes referred to by the general term **productivity software** because they enable you to *produce* something.

There are a few other names that also crop up from time to time:

- *Utilities*. Programs that enable you to customize or make adjustments to the way your computer works. A utility might let you compress your hard disk to gain more space, set your computer's clock, change the speed or shape of your mouse pointer, and so on. Programs that let you view a file but not edit it, or play back a video or a CD, also tend to be referred to as utilities.

- *Applets.* An applet is a small program that can't run by itself, but is used as an add-on to an application to provide extra functions. For example, Microsoft Works provides an applet called **WordArt** that can be used when you run the Works word processor to create weird and wonderful text effects.
- *Accessories.* An accessory is a small program thrown in for good measure, often with an operating system or a piece of hardware. It's usually a much-simplified application or utility with a few useful functions, but without the sophistication of a program you'd pay money for. An accessory may also be a small program with a very narrow, specific function, such as a digital clock that sits on your desktop, or a counter that measures how many miles your mouse walks every day.

Of course, all these are just general labels applied to different types of software for convenience: with familiarity, the use of these terms is becoming more vague and interchangeable. The word *program* is a blanket term that covers all these types, and other indefinable software such as games, so you could talk about 'a word processing program', 'a word-processing application' or 'word-processing software'.

Fully featured

This is a term used to describe any software program (applications included) that offers all or most of the functions and options you're likely to need when you're doing a particular type of work – a program for the advanced user or professional in that field. Another phrase used with a similar meaning is *high level.*

Running a program

How a program is run will often depend on the type of program it is and the circumstances in which it's used. The primary methods of running applications have been mentioned earlier in the book, but we'll gather the various methods together here with a brief description of each, in ascending order of importance:

- *By another program.* Software exists that allows you to enter the details of a program and set up a schedule of times that this program should run. The scheduling software usually runs at startup (see below) and remains in the background watching the clock; when the specified time arrives, it runs the required program. This is chiefly used to schedule system utilities that scan your hard disk for errors or recompress your files, usually at a time you'll be away from your PC, but you can schedule any type of program you like.

- *On startup.* Both Windows 3.1 and Windows 95 have a **StartUp** group into which programs can be placed so that they start automatically as soon as the operating system has loaded. These are usually programs that you run constantly behind the scenes, such as a program that monitors your hard-disk space and beeps at you when you're getting low. If there are particular programs that you use every time you switch on your computer, it makes sense to include these here too, saving you the (admittedly minor) task of locating and running them manually.
- *Using the 'Run' command.* Both versions of Windows have a **Run** command which works in a similar way to the MS-DOS command line. An application can be run by typing its full path and name into this box and pressing *Enter* or clicking **OK**. The Run command is covered on p. 278 for Windows 3.1 and p. 322 on p. 120 for Windows 95.
- *By association.* As covered in section **5.3**, when you double-click a file associated with a particular program, the program will run automatically and this file will be loaded into it.
- *By shortcut.* Both Windows 3.1 and (especially) Windows 95 make use of shortcuts, and these are the primary method of running programs. A shortcut is an icon that sits on (or is within easy reach of) your desktop and acts as a 'pointer' to the program. When you double-click the icon, the path to the program it represents is passed to the operating system which finds and runs it. You can also assign different key combinations to each icon (known as **hotkeys**) so that pressing a certain combination will run the corresponding program.

▶ *Shortcuts are covered in more detail for Windows 3.1 on pp. 274–278, and for Windows 95 on pp. 337–342.*

Multiple instances

The MDI, explained on p. 106, can be extremely handy if you need to open two files in the same application at the same time, perhaps for reference purposes or to copy information from one to the other. But of course there are sure to be times when you want to do this and the application in question doesn't support multiple document windows, so you find yourself forever closing one file, opening a second to refer to, then closing it and reopening the first. In many cases, there's an easier way.

Many programs allow multiple instances to be run: that is, you can run two 'copies' of the program at the same time as if they were two different programs, and have a different file open in each. To open the second (or third, or fourth...) instance of a program you can double-click an associated file or the program's icon or shortcut, but its hotkey can only be used to open the first instance.

Figure 5.16 The *Alt* + *Tab* panel in Windows 95.

Task switching

In the normal use of a Windows operating system you'll almost certainly be making the most of multitasking – running several programs at the same time and switching between them to do different things. You can switch tasks in several ways:

- *Alt* + *Tab*. Press and hold the *Alt* key and then press *Tab* repeatedly until the icon for the program you want to switch to is shown on the pop-up panel, then release both keys. (*Alt* + *Tab* cycles only through program windows' icons – dialog windows don't feature in the list.)

If you're using *Alt* + *Tab* to cycle through iconized programs and you suddenly decide you want to just forget it and stay where you are, press *Esc* without letting go of *Alt* – the icon dialog will vanish and leave you in your original window.

- *Alt* + *Esc*. Press and hold Alt and press *Esc* repeatedly. This cycles through the actual windows themselves (rather than icons for them) bringing each to the foreground in turn. Release both keys when the window you want comes to the surface. (*Alt* + *Esc* does include dialog windows in its cycle, but doesn't include minimized windows.)

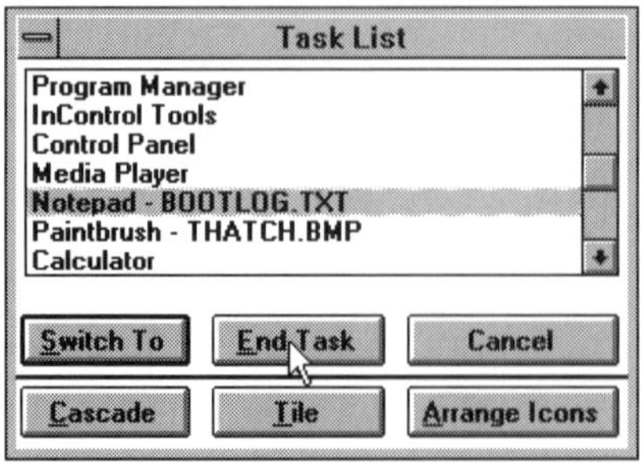

Figure 5.17 The task list in Windows 3.1 ...

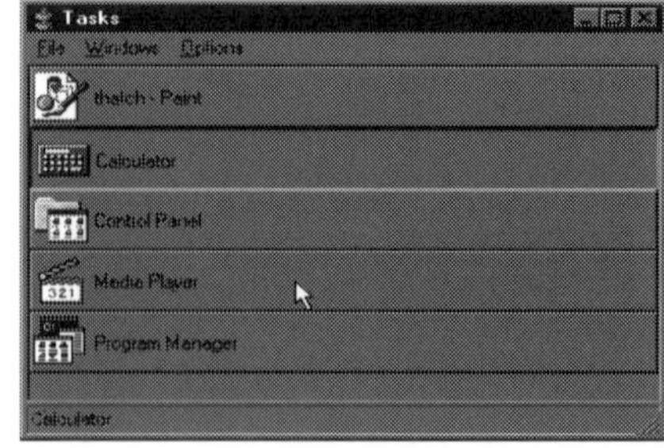

Figure 5.18 ...and in Windows 95.

- *Ctrl + Esc.* In Windows 3.1 only, this calls up a little program called **Taskman.exe** (shown in Figure 5.17) which displays a list of running applications. Just click the name you want and then click **Switch To**. Clicking on **End Task** will close the chosen program. (Windows 95 has a modernized version of Taskman, shown in Figure 5.18, but without a hotkey to run it. The inclusion of the **Taskbar** on the Windows 95 desktop tends to make Taskman unnecessary, but this little chap has many useful features packed into its menus.)

Fonts and font files

Fonts are sets of instructions that tell an operating system how to display text on the screen and how to print it, each font being a separate file (or, sometimes, two or more files) on your hard disk. The typical Windows-based PC has several different types of font installed which are used for different purposes, the most important of which, to the user, is the ability to use different typefaces, styles and text effects in a document.

Raster fonts

Raster fonts are bitmapped fonts, making them the font equivalent of the bitmap image-format we looked at on p. 140. Because each character you type is created as a single bitmap image, these fonts don't scale easily. Doubling the size of a raster font will usually be successful, but increasing its size by one-third will often make the characters jagged and difficult to read. Windows is supplied with several raster fonts, such as Symbol, MS Serif and MS Sans Serif, each of which consists of three files with the extension **.fon**.

Vector fonts

As raster fonts are similar to the bitmapped graphics image, vector fonts work in the same way as vector graphics – instead of containing an image of each character, vector fonts contain information about the shapes, lines and relative measurements that make up each character. As a result, these fonts can be successfully scaled, stretched, skewed and mangled. Windows is supplied with several vector fonts including Script and Roman which are also **.fon** files.

TrueType fonts

These are the primary day-to-day-use fonts for Windows users, developed by Microsoft. TrueType fonts can be scaled easily, can be manipulated in various ways, and provide reliable WYSIWYG results (see p. 133). TrueType fonts are originally supplied as a single file with the extension **.ttf**. When installed in Windows 3.1, each of these files spawns a second file with the same file name but a **.fot** extension which contains a few extra instructions to help Windows recreate the correct type style. In Windows 95 the **.ttf** file contains all the data required. Both versions of Windows are supplied with several TrueType fonts including Arial (a sans-serif font), Time New Roman (a serif font) and WingDings (a collection of useful or unusual symbols and signs).

JARGONBUSTER

Serif and sans-serif fonts

In a serif font the characters have small hooks or ornaments (called *serifs*) which add a slightly informal flourish; this sort of font is commonly used for block text. Sans-serif fonts don't have these ornamental additions and are mostly used in headings.

Installing fonts

In both Windows 3.1 and Windows 95, fonts are installed from the **Control Panel**. Double-click the icon labelled **Fonts** and you'll see your currently installed fonts as shown in Figures 5.19 and 5.20. Windows 3.1 presents these as a simple list of font-names; Windows 95 groups all its fonts together in a single folder using icons with a **TT** motif to indicate TrueType fonts and an **A** to indicate raster and vector fonts, and opens this folder when you double-click the Control Panel icon.

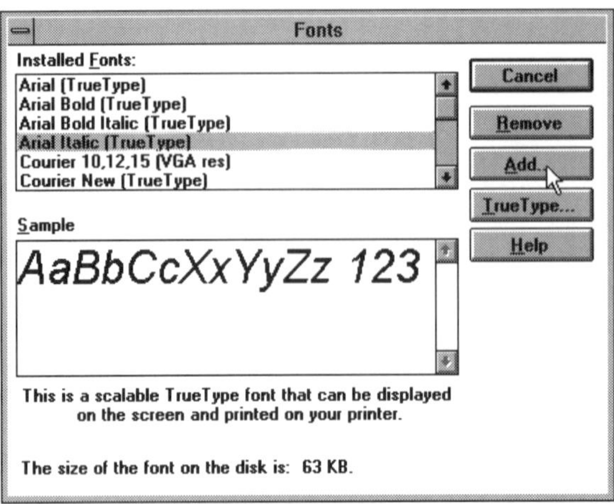

Figure 5.19 The **Fonts** dialog in Windows 3.1.

In Windows 3.1, clicking the **Add** button will lead to the installation dialog; in Windows 95 this dialog is reached by selecting **File/Install New Font...** . The installation dialog allows you to navigate through your folder-tree to find the drive or folder containing the fonts you want to add. When you locate this folder, Windows will display the names of the fonts it finds. To install all of them, click the **Select All** button and **OK**. If you only want to install a few, hold *Ctrl* and click the names of the ones you want. When you're done, click **OK** and the selected fonts will be installed.

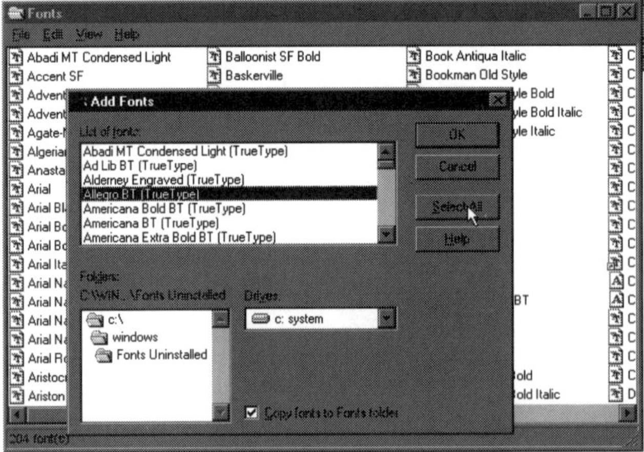

Figure 5.20 The **Install New Font** dialog and Fonts folder in Windows 95.

Both dialogs have a similar check box: **Copy fonts to Fonts folder** (in Windows 95), and **Copy fonts to Windows directory** (in Windows 3.1). These options mean the same thing in both cases, except that the two versions of Windows install their font files to different folders. The choice to make is whether you want to use these fonts from where they're currently situated (a floppy disk, a network drive or a different folder on your hard disk) or to copy the files to these locations. In Windows 3.1 it's preferable to check the option and thus keep all your font files together. Note that if you choose to keep the files on a floppy disk you'll only be able to use these fonts when this disk is in the drive.

TIP

In Windows 3.1 all the fonts you install have to be loaded into memory each time Windows starts. The more fonts you have, the more sluggish things will become, so try to stick with around 50. In Windows 95 fonts don't need to be loaded into memory so you can have as many as you want, although trying to locate the ones you need in an application from a list of 500 could be a bit of a headache!

In Windows 95 it's a good idea *not* to copy the files to your **Fonts** folder. In fact, a useful way of working is to actually *move* all your font files to a new folder, and then reinstall them all with this option left *unchecked*. Windows 95 then creates *shortcuts* to the files in the Fonts folder.

▶ *The Control Panel is explored in greater detail in sections beginning p. 286 for Windows 3.1 and p. 349 for Windows 95.*

Removing fonts

Removing fonts is approached in a similar way to installing them. Begin by double-clicking the **Fonts** icon in **Control Panel** and you'll see your list of installed fonts in Windows 3.1, or your Fonts folder in Windows 95. To remove fonts in Windows 3.1, hold *Ctrl* and click on all the font names you want to remove, and then click the **Remove** button. This will delete the **.fot** files, but leave the **.ttf** files in place so that they can be reinstalled in the future.

In Windows 95 fonts are removed in much the same way: hold *Ctrl* and click on each font icon you want to remove and then press the *Delete* key. The result is somewhat different though – this actually *deletes* the fonts! If you don't have another copy of the **.ttf** files somewhere else you won't be able to reinstall them later. However, if you follow the suggestion made above, you're only deleting *shortcuts* to the font files; the originals are still safely in your other folder.

In Windows 95, avoid deleting any fonts you didn't install yourself. Windows requires a particular bundle of fonts to draw its dialogs, buttons, labels and so on. If any of these are missing, Windows 95 will try to use something else but it might look very odd indeed, and the result could be almost unusable! If you're not sure about a particular font, make a copy of the **.ttf** or **.fon** file in a different folder or on a floppy disk before deleting it so that you can put it back if you need to.

▶ *Windows 95 has a handy font-related utility called Fontview, covered on p. 372.*

Where do fonts come from?

Apart from the few fonts included with Windows, you can pick up new ones from a variety of different sources. To begin with, many computer stores sell packs of hundreds or even thousands of TrueType fonts on floppy disk or CD-ROM. In addition, many software titles you install add a few more to your collection. Online services such as **CompuServe** and **America Online** (AOL) also have huge numbers of fonts, and programs you can use to create your own.

Using fonts

Many word-processing, spreadsheet, database and presentation applications have a toolbar like the one in Figure 5.21 containing the primary text-formatting options. From this bar you can select a font from the drop-down list box, choose the size of the font (measured in *points*) from another list box, and pick styles and effects (see Figure 5.22) such as bold, italic, underlined and coloured text in any combination from buttons that can be toggled on and off. In some high-level applications, there may be extra buttons on the toolbar or a **Format** menu offering even more text-formatting options.

Figure 5.21 The standard format toolbar.

These controls are very simple to use: if you're typing a document in a word processor and you know the next portion of text you want to enter should be Times New Roman, 12 point, and bold, just select the font and point size from the two drop-down lists, click the **B** button, and start typing. To type a word in 'normal' print (i.e. not bold), click the **B** button again to turn it off.

JARGONBUSTER

Point size

Points are the units of height measurement for fonts, in which 72 points equals one inch. (This would often be abbreviated to 72 pt.) Body-text, the typographer's name for standard paragraph text, is usually 11 pt or 12 pt.

You can also edit text you've already typed in just the same way. Let's say you want to underline a section of text: first select the portion of text you want, using any of the methods covered on pp. 136–138, then click the **U** button. You can change the font or point-size (or both) for selected text by choosing from the drop-down list boxes.

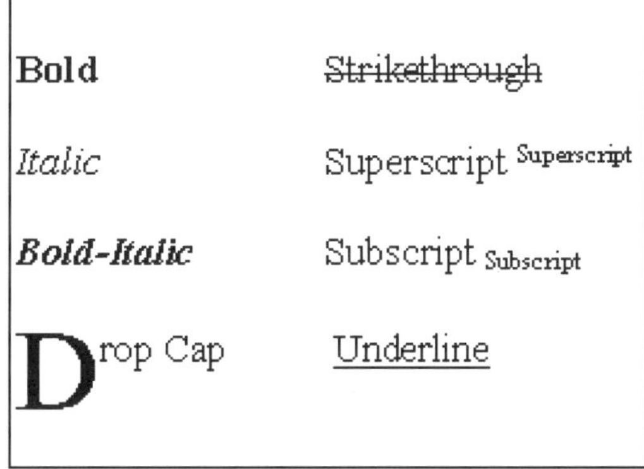

Figure 5.22 Some of the common, and not-so-common, text-formatting features you can use with TrueType fonts.

Object linking and embedding

What is OLE?

As we saw on p. 134, part of a document you're working on can be **Cut** or **Copied** to the Windows clipboard. Once there, it can be **Pasted** into another position in the same document, or you can paste it into a document in a different application. You've probably imagined this as copying a couple of paragraphs of text in one word processor, and then pasting them into another word processor, and this is certainly something you can do easily. But you can also place a completely *different* type of data, such as a sound-clip or a picture, into a word-processor document just as easily using **Object Linking and Embedding** (OLE).

Using OLE

To explain how OLE works, let's take a straightforward example. You're running your word processor and typing a newsletter about sailing that you intend to print when it's finished, and you remember you've got a bitmap image file of a boat on your hard disk that would finish the whole thing off nicely. You go to the **Insert** menu and choose the **Object...** option followed by **Create From File**. You then click the **Browse** button to search your folders for the image file and double-click it. You're now back to the **Create From File** dialog where you have the option to **Link To File** and to **Display As Icon** (see Figure 5.23) but you ignore both and just click **OK**. The image file then appears in your document at the insertion point. What you have now is a *compound document* — a document that contains two different types of data.

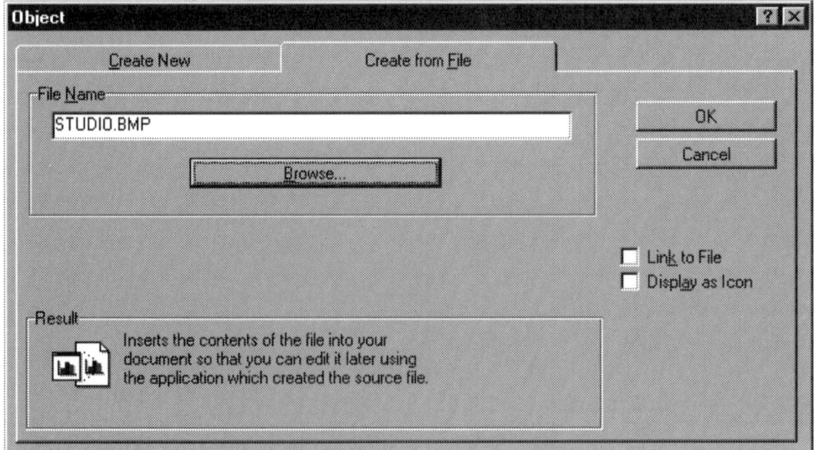

Figure 5.23 Inserting an object from an existing file.

The file you've just inserted is referred to as an *object* because, as far as your word processor is concerned, it doesn't know what it is and it can't work with it. It could be a sound file, video, spreadsheet or any one of many types of file – it will still be referred to anonymously as an object. And this is an *embedded* object because you didn't select the **Link To File** option that would have made it a *linked* object. 'Embedded' means that this image is now an entirely separate entity from the image file on your hard disk – you can edit this image in any way you like without affecting the file it came from. Because it's a separate entity, you can also save this compound document onto a floppy disk and give the disk to someone else who has the same word processor and when he or she opens the file the image will still be there. That's the good news. The bad news about embedding is that when you save your document it's going to be a much larger file than it would have been without the image.

Now let's assume you *did* select the **Link To File** option. The image you see in your document is now a *linked* object. That means it's a sort of shortcut to the image file on your disk that contains directions telling the software which file to display here. The good news in this case is that the document you save will still be quite small – the few directions contained in a linked object add almost nothing to the document's size. The bad news is that if you give this document to a friend, the image will not be visible – the file it's pointing to is still miles away on your hard disk! Links tend to be used when you intend to keep the resulting document for your own use. As long as you don't move or delete the image file, you'll continue to see the image in this word-pro document every time you open it. With an embedded image the result is that you're wasting disk space on *two* copies of the image – one in the document and one in the original file – unless you choose to delete the original image file.

Editing linked objects

Another difference between linked and embedded objects is in the way they can be edited. Because the linked object is just a pointer to a file on your hard disk, if you want to change how the image looks in your document you've got to edit the original file. When you do this, the changes you make will also be reflected in the document version.

In fact, however, this is usually viewed the other way round. Let's change the scenario slightly. You use a spreadsheet application to log the results of boating races and you want your monthly word-processed newsletter to include this chart. You could do it the slow way, filling in the spreadsheet, and then typing the same information into your word-pro document. Or you could create a link to the spreadsheet chart in your word-pro document. This way, typing the new information into the spreadsheet will automatically update what you see in the word-pro document.

Linking objects is often referred to as **Dynamic Data Exchange** (DDE), the word 'dynamic' reflecting the way the information is automatically updated. You can create DDE links to as many documents as you want to from the same original file and they'll all be updated in the same way.

Editing embedded objects

To edit an embedded object, all you have to do is double-click it. The embedded image also contains a small amount of extra information that points to an application capable of working with this image (such as **Paint** in Windows 95). So when you double-click the image this application runs and loads the image ready for you to edit.

There are two ways it might do this. In OLE version 1.0 (used by Windows 3.1) the application will open in its own window as applications usually do. When you've finished editing the image, click on the **File** menu. This will contain different commands from those you'd normally see. One of these is **Update**; if you click this option, the image will be updated in your word-pro document. You can switch to the document to have a look at the result, then switch back to the image and continue editing. When you're done, select the option that begins **Exit and Return to** (and is followed by the name of your document). You'll be asked if you want to update the image, so click **Yes**.

In OLE 2.0 (used by Windows 95), the application that opens will actually steal control of your word processor! This is known as **in-place editing** – you'll still see your word-processor's title-bar, and the text in your document, but the image application will replace the toolbars and menus with its own so that you can edit the image. When you're done, just click the mouse somewhere *outside* the image and everything will revert back to normal.

This raises just one qualification about an earlier point: you can send a document with an embedded object to someone else, and although that person will be able to see it, he or she will only be able to edit it if the correct application is available on that person's computer to work with this type of file. Taking our image example, most image formats are universal so there probably wouldn't be a problem; but in the second example, spreadsheet-file formats tend to be proprietary so your colleague would need to have the same spreadsheet application as you.

Create New

There was a brief mention, near the beginning of this section, of selecting a **Create From File** option and that's what we've been concentrating on – using existing files in compound documents. The other option you could have selected at this point is **Create New**. If you do that, you'll be presented with a list of all the possible types of file you can create (the contents of the list depending upon which applications are installed on your PC). When you choose the type of file you want to create, the corresponding application will open and you can start creating. The way the application opens, and the methods of updating and/or returning to your document, are exactly the same as covered in 'Editing embedded objects' above.

Paste Special

So far we've only talked about placing whole files in documents, but you can easily place part of a file into a document using the Windows clipboard. Copy some data to the clipboard in the usual way (see p. 134) and then switch to the application and document you want to insert it into. On the application's **Edit** menu click on **Paste Special...** and you'll see a list of formats in which the data on the clipboard could be pasted, as shown in Figure 5.24. Choose the format you want to use – the one at the top of the list will usually be the format of the original document – then decide whether to **Paste** (embed) the data or **Paste Link** (create a DDE link to this portion of the file).

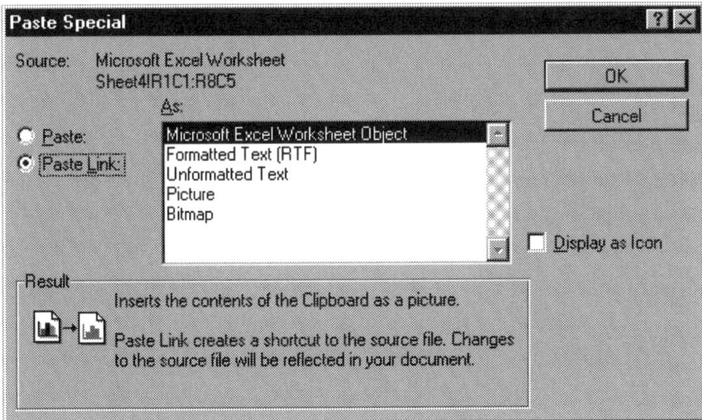

Figure 5.24 Linking or embedding information using **Paste Special**.

Embed using Drag & Drop

You can also embed objects using our two buddies, Drag & Drop. These may be whole files from File Manager or Explorer, or parts of a document selected and then dragged from another application. Simply arrange the two windows so that you can see both clearly, and drag from one to the other. When the mouse pointer gains an additional cross-shaped icon you can drop the file.

A bit of terminology

We've managed to avoid most of the jargon associated with OLE, but, for completeness, here it is:

- *OLE Server.* The application that opens when you double-click an embedded file to edit it, or choose to **Create New**. This application provides a *service* to the application containing the compound document. Also known as the *source application.*
- *OLE Client.* The application containing the compound document.
- *Container.* Another name for the compound document itself – it *contains* another object. Also termed the *host* document.
- *Source document.* The file that is being embedded or linked into a document.

For object linking to work, both the client and the server must support either DDE or OLE (or both), and for embedding both must support OLE.

CHAPTER 6

Software and multimedia

Choosing software

It could be argued that of all the separate 'pieces of computer' you've got to think about when buying, software should be right at the top of the list. After all, you know *why* you want a computer, so you know what you want to use it for, and you'll need software to use it for anything at all! In theory, at least, your choice of software should determine your choice of operating system, and the two together should point you towards the hardware, processing power and memory you'll need.

Although that's how we tend to make other sizeable purchases, it rarely works out that way with PCs. We pick up certain specific information and hang onto it for dear life – *I must have a Pentium*, and *It's got to be Windows 95* – and the all-important reason for buying the PC in the first place often becomes a last-minute *Oh yes, I need a word processor.* It's a fact of computer-buying life, but it's one to watch out for: a single graphics application, for example, might be nearly half the price of your PC, but you may never use more than a quarter of its features. Conversely you might find you have to replace software soon after buying it because it can't do what you need.

The aim of the following sections is to provide a basic introduction to some of the common types of software – what they do, how they do it, what's available and what's popular. Most of the software titles covered here are available both in 32-bit versions for Windows 95 and in 16-bit versions for Windows 3.1. If you've already decided which of these operating systems you'll use (or you're already using it!), make sure you buy the most recent version that's compatible with your operating system.

Points to check

Before we look at specific software types and the individual choices they present, here's a few general points to consider before buying:

Will it do what you need it to do?

The fundamental question that could save you both money and aggravation. Check this one carefully by reading reviews and comparing features with other applications. Try to get an in-store demonstration and a few minutes to explore it on your own.

Will it do more than you need it to do?

Given the alternative, it's better to buy something that does *more* than you need, but the heavy-weight professional applications can swallow chunks of system resources, and you might find the plethora of toolbars and menus distracting.

Will Windows' own accessories do the job?

Another case for some experimentation. These add-on accessories aren't intended to rival full-blown applications, but if your word-processing requirements are limited to short letters, memos and faxes, **Write** or **WordPad** could handle them for you comfortably.

Will file formats be compatible with your colleagues' applications?

For business users this can be an important consideration. If you need to pass the files you create to a colleague, make sure you can save files in a format compatible with your colleague's software. If you already use a particular application on your office PC, it makes sense to buy the same for your home or portable.

Can a different type of application do this job?

Modern word processors such as **Microsoft Word** and **Lotus WordPro** have built-in drawing tools that could easily make a separate drawing package redundant. A good spreadsheet application can make a very capable database. Draw up a list of the things you need to do with your PC and see how far you can reduce the number of separate applications required.

Check the upgrade path!

If you bought an application and you now need something more powerful, find out if you qualify for an upgrade price rather than having to buy the full product. In many cases, if you have a competitor's product installed, or a 'light-weight' version of the product you want, you can save 35–50 per cent by buying the upgrade version. (But beware – this version checks your hard disk to make sure you weren't kidding before it goes very far!) These upgrade prices apply even if the original software was supplied 'free' with your PC.

Consider office suites and integrated applications

If you need two or more heavy-duty applications, such as a word processor and a spreadsheet, you'll probably save money by buying one of these packages (covered on p. 204) *and* get two or three more applications thrown in for good measure.

Check that it will run on your PC

Take a look at the back or side panel of the software pack for the specifications needed to run the software, and remember that these are *minimum* requirements.

Buy the CD-ROM version

If you have a CD-ROM drive and the software is available on CD-ROM, this is a better buy than a bundle of floppy disks. Installation will be much faster and easier, and you might get a few extras that couldn't be squeezed onto a reasonable number of floppies.

Software versions

Software changes as fast as the hardware it's designed to work with, so software producers add version numbers to the names of their products to help you ensure you're buying the latest version, or the version that works with your operating system. A new product will be called version **1.0**; minor changes will lead to versions **1.1**, **1.2** and so on. When a major change in design takes place they'll call it version **2.0**. Very often the minor changes are the result of finding bugs (unexpected errors) in the previous release and putting them right.

Installing and uninstalling software

Installing software

Installation of software means making sure that all the files needed to run the program can be found by the computer when needed. This usually involves placing the files in particular folders on your hard disk, but a few programs are small and simple enough that you can run them from a floppy disk with no formal installation required. Other types of software, such as games or multimedia titles, may be several hundred megabytes in size and supplied on CD-ROM; copying this lot to your hard disk would be pretty impractical, so installation involves copying a few small files to your hard disk and leaving the rest where they are.

The most straightforward type of 'installation' simply involves copying a few files around manually. For example, a small program supplied on a floppy disk, or downloaded from the Internet, may just need you to create a new folder on your hard disk and copy the program files into it.

TIP

Don't install more than one application at a time. If you install five in one session and your PC goes into a sulk next time you start it, it'll be no fun at all trying to track down the culprit. Install one, reboot your computer, and check that everything's okay before installing the next.

Automated installation

The more common type of installation, particularly with today's large applications, involves a semi-automated *installation procedure*. The software is supplied on a CD-ROM, or a set of floppy disks, and the installation is handled by a program often called **Install.exe** or **Setup.exe** which you'll find on the CD-ROM or the first of the floppies. Running this program will lead you through the procedure step by step, asking you questions. This may vary in complexity: some software will just ask if you're sure you want to install and then start copying the files to your hard disk when you say 'Yes'. Other programs will give you an opportunity to choose which drive and folder you want the software installed into.

TIP

Before installing new software, close down any programs that are running. The installation procedure often needs to alter some of your existing files, and if they're in use by another program it won't be able to do this, which could botch the installation.

Larger software packages such as operating systems and top-level applications often require a lot of disk space and include a collection of optional files, so they usually prompt you to choose between a **Minimal** installation (leaving out most of the optional utilities and accessories to conserve disk space), a **Typical** installation (including the options most users will need), or a **Custom** installation. The Custom installation allows you to choose which elements of the software you want to install, usually giving a brief description of each one and keeping a running tally of the disk space required as you check off the items you want.

For all but the computing novice, it's worth taking the Custom option and choosing which elements you want installed. But whether you do this or not, you can run the Setup program again in the future and add or remove elements easily.

The necessary files will then be copied to various folders on your hard disk, and changes may be made to your system files so that the computer is made aware of this new software's arrival and the whereabouts of its files. In some cases you'll have to restart your PC after installation so that the computer can read these updated system files into memory. You may also be asked if you'd like icons to be added to your program groups: if you agree to this, you can delete the icons at any time if you want to; if you turn down the offer, you can still add the icons manually whenever you like.

▶ *Program groups provide a quick way of running programs by placing icons for them within easy reach of your desktop, thus saving you the hassle of searching through File Manager or Explorer for a particular program. Windows 3.1 keeps these icons in the Program Manager (see p. 273); Windows 95 uses the Start Menu (p. 319).*

Uninstalling software

Uninstalling software means removing it (and, in theory at least, all *traces* of it) from your computer. The method of doing this will usually reflect the method of installation: if you created a new folder and copied the files into it yourself, uninstallation is as simple as deleting the files you copied and deleting the folder. If you created an icon for the program on your desktop or elsewhere, you'll need to delete that too.

Most software that has it's own installation program, as described above, usually has an automated method of uninstallation too. This may involve running the **Setup** program again and clicking a button marked **Uninstall**, or you may find an uninstall program in the folder the software was installed into. This program should remove any files that were copied to your hard disk as a part of the installation, and reverse any changes made to your system files (again requiring you to restart the computer). It may or may not remove the icons it added to your program groups, and it usually won't delete any folders it created. This last point is actually good news: you might have saved files of your own into these folders which you wouldn't want to lose. Deleting a folder deletes its entire contents including any subfolders, and any files in those subfolders.

▶ *Windows 95 has its own built-in method of handling uninstallation of software that works in a similar way, provided the software in question was designed to take advantage of it.* *Turn to p. 363 for information.*

Word processors

In its simplest form, the word processor is the computer equivalent of a typewriter. When the program opens you'll see a wide expanse of white space in the middle, which is your 'paper', and you can start typing immediately. A flashing vertical line (known as the **cursor** or the **insertion point**) indicates where you are in the document – and this line will always appear immediately at the right of any text you type. You can move the insertion point to anywhere in the document using the arrow keys, or by clicking the left mouse button. Whenever the mouse is positioned over the 'paper', it turns into a shape called an **I-beam** (see Figure 6.1) to help you position the insertion point more easily between two adjacent characters than the ordinary pointer would allow.

Another important difference about a word processor is that you don't need to press the keyboard's carriage-return key (*Return* or *Enter*) when you reach the end of a line. Instead, the text *wraps* automatically onto the next line, and these keys are used only when you want to start a new paragraph or insert blank lines.

JARGONBUSTER

Text editor

A text editor (such as Windows' **Notepad**) is like a word processor with no flashy features, used to create plain text (ASCII) files that have no font styles, formatting or layout detail. Text editors work with files with a **.txt** extension and are useful for creating short notes, memos and so on, being quick and easy to use. In effect, *all* word processors are text editors – any word processor will be able to open and save files in this format.

Finally, of course, a word processor doesn't commit you to anything you've typed. You can make all the spelling mistakes you want to and sort them out later; if you change your mind about the order of the paragraphs you can use Cut and Paste to rearrange them. Most importantly, you can use a huge range of features to **format** the document, including fonts, tabs and paragraph alignment, line spacing, and text-colours. A top-level application will also include options to create graphs and tables, add logos and graphics, create boxes around text and so on.

► *For details about fonts and character formatting in word processors, turn to on p. 154. Common editing facilities found in word processors such as Cut/Copy/Paste, Find and Replace, together with the methods of selecting sections of text, are explained on p. 133.*

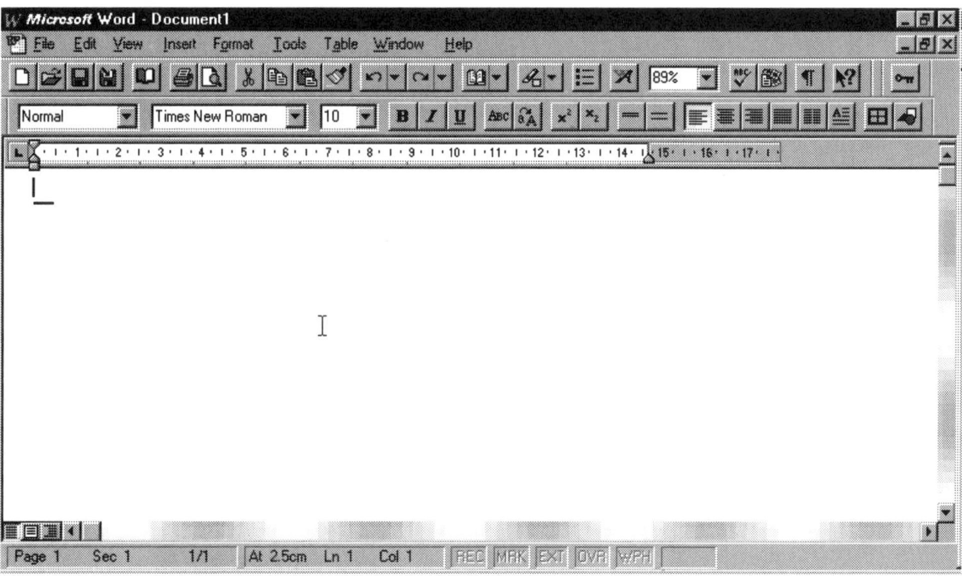

Figure 6.1 **Microsoft Word** ready for work, with the cursor in the corner of the document window and the I-beam in the centre.

Moving around

As you type text into your word processor and your document gets longer, the text scrolls upwards and gradually disappears off the top of the screen as if you'd threaded an everlasting roll of paper into your typewriter. The text is still there, of course, and you can move backwards and forwards through the document to view or edit your work any time you like. Here are some of the methods you can use:

- Use the arrow keys to move around one character or line at a time, or in conjunction with *Ctrl* to move back and forth one word at a time.
- Use the *PageUp/PageDown* keys to move up and down one screen at a time. A 'screen' will be smaller than a complete printed page.
- Use the *Home* and *End* keys to move to the beginning or end of a line, or together with *Ctrl* to move to the top or bottom of the document.
- Use the scroll-bar on the right of the screen, and click the mouse at the position you want the insertion point to appear.

JARGONBUSTER

Headers and footers

Small margins at the top and bottom of each page in a document that might contain the name of the document, or chapter titles. You would normally enter these once, perhaps with different entries for odd- and even-numbered pages, and they'll be automatically added to every page when you print the document. Page numbers can be inserted in the same way and the software will keep them updated as you add and delete text.

Margins and alignment

One of the fundamental needs in document formatting is the ability to set page margins. When you first start your word processor, the margins will be preset to defaults, but these are easily changed and the changes are saved together with the document. Margins are usually set from a **Page Setup...** entry on the **File** menu, and contain boxes for Top, Bottom, Left and Right into which you type a size for each margin in centimetres. You can usually type in a size for the header and footer too, and some top-level applications let you specify different inside and outside margins for documents that are to be bound, such as books and reports.

As well as changing the settings for the whole document, you can set margins for individual paragraphs. With the insertion point placed somewhere within the paragraph you want to change, open the **Paragraph** dialog which is usually found on the **Format** menu. Here are a few of the options you might find, and what they mean:

- *Indent.* This is the distance in centimetres that the selected paragraph (or its first line) should be moved from the left and right margins.
- *Spacing.* This changes the spacing between paragraphs. You'll have simple options like **double-spaced**, and you might also be able to specify exact spacing in **points**.

To make sure your document layout looks okay before printing, choose **Print Preview** from the **File** menu to view one (or possibly more than one) full page on the screen.

- *Left aligned.* This is the usual alignment option, in which each line of text will follow the line of the left margin and be ragged at the right. (Instead of opening the **Paragraph** dialog, you can often just use the hotkey *Ctrl+L*.)
- *Right aligned.* Text will follow the line of the right margin and be ragged at the left (used only for effect, usually for single lines, dates and addresses). The usual hotkey combination is *Ctrl+R*.
- *Justified.* Each line of the paragraph will be forced to follow both the left and right margins to give a completely 'square' look; spaces are added between words to make the lines the correct length. Justified text can be difficult to read and is now used just in short bursts for effect. You can usually press *Ctrl+J* for this one.
- *Centred.* This places the paragraph centrally between the left and right margins, and is used mostly for headings or unusual effects. The common hotkey is *Ctrl+E*.

Widows and orphans

Many word processors have an option to prevent widows and orphans in their paragraph-formatting dialogs. A *widow* is the last line of a paragraph printed by itself at the top of a new page; an *orphan* is the first line of a paragraph printed at the bottom of a page.

Spellchecker and thesaurus

These are two common features built into word processors more and more often, but it pays to check the box before buying – although users regard them as essentials, some software producers still don't! The **thesaurus** is a doddle to use: any time you're stuck for a word, type a word with a similar meaning, then start it up and see what suggestions are listed. If nothing appears that's quite right, look up one of the suggestions to see some synonyms for that. When you find what you want, you should have a **Replace** button that will enter it into your document for you.

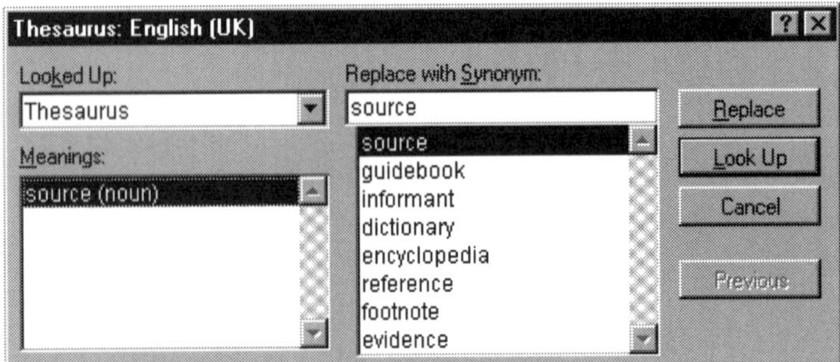

Figure 6.2 Ever needed a synonym for **thesaurus**?

Much as you'd expect, the **spellchecker** checks your spelling by looking through the document and prompting you when it finds a word not listed in its own dictionary. You can take the spellchecker's suggested word, edit the word yourself or add the word to your own **user dictionary** which the spellchecker uses in tandem with its own. The effectiveness of a spellchecker depends largely on the size of its dictionary, but it's important to make sure it can distinguish between American English and UK English. Some spellcheckers come with a bundle of foreign language dictionaries which might be useful.

When you start using a new word processor, create a document containing your name and address, and those of friends and colleagues, lists of technical terms and jargon you use regularly and so on, and then run it through the spellchecker to add these to the user dictionary. It makes the spellchecking of documents a much quicker process when you're trying to get some work done!

Mail merge

The mail merge options included in most mid- to high-end word processors can be a huge time-saver for business users, letting you create personalized mailshots automatically by merging customer details from a database, spreadsheet or personal organizer into a letter. The routine involves typing a standard sales-pitch letter, but instead of typing the recipient's name at the beginning you type something like *Dear «Title», «Surname»*, where the bracketed entries are the names of **fields** in the database. (This type of document is known as a **form letter**, and the fields are usually entered by clicking a button and choosing the field name from a list.) You then simply select the database you want to use and direct the word processor to **merge** the two items. The field references in the letter are replaced with the contents of those fields from the database, producing letters that look as if you've personally typed every single one!

► *Turn to p. 181 for more on setting up databases of client details.*

Extra features

Here, in brief, are a few of the clever features found in the top-end word processors:

- *Styles.* Type and format a heading, for example, choosing a particular font, size, colour, alignment and so on, and assign it a style name such as *Chapter.* You can then select any other text you type and apply this style to it with a single click rather than carrying out all that formatting each time.
- *Columns.* Split your page into multiple vertical columns, newspaper style.
- *Drawing tools.* Switch on the drawing toolbar and add pictures, logos and designs to your document without needing a separate draw or paint program.
- *Frames.* Traditionally the domain of desktop publishing, you can place text or drawings into frames and drag them wherever you want them in the document, force text to flow neatly around them or even place them *behind* the text like a watermark.
- *Autocorrect.* Automatic correction of words you commonly misspell. Enter your incorrect spellings into a list together with their correct spellings and the application will keep watch for these as you type and correct them automatically.
- *Group support.* If you work on documents in a team, your colleagues can enter their own corrections and annotations without removing the original information, letting you choose whether to incorporate their suggestions or not.

- *Indexing.* Automatic creation of indexes, tables of contents and cross-references which can be updated with a mouse-click or two as the document's contents change.

Buyers' guide: Word processors

- Top of the heap in the word processor world are **Microsoft Word** (the long-time best-seller) and **Lotus WordPro** (formally called Ami Pro). Either of these will require a minimum 8 Mb RAM to run under Windows 95. To use them in conjunction with other applications, 16 Mb is a more realistic minimum. Sitting well behind these two in the popularity stakes, though still with adequate features, is **Corel WordPerfect**.

- If you want to use Mail Merge, make sure the word processor can handle it, and check which formats it supports for importing records to be merged. You don't want to find yourself in the position of retyping your whole database into a different program if you can avoid it!

- Before buying a word processor, take a look at pp. 204–209 – you might be able to save money by buying an all-in-one office suite or integrated application.

Spreadsheets

The primary use of the spreadsheet program is to enter lists of numbers and perform calculations on them. For example, you might use a spreadsheet to log sales of a product, budget your money, manage your tax accounts, or chart the progress of your favourite football team. Once the numbers are entered, the spreadsheet can perform anything from simple addition of figures to a complicated statistical analysis of a selection of these numbers – the kind of stuff that would take hours with a calculator and years off your life!

However, spreadsheets are more than just number-manipulators – you can view these figures as colourful charts and graphs and import them into word-processed reports or presentations (see Figure 6.3), and create finished documents such as invoices, receipts and timesheets. In fact, you don't have to use numbers at all – the spreadsheet's **Find** and **Replace** facilities mean that you can use it as a database for any text-based information you want to keep track of too.

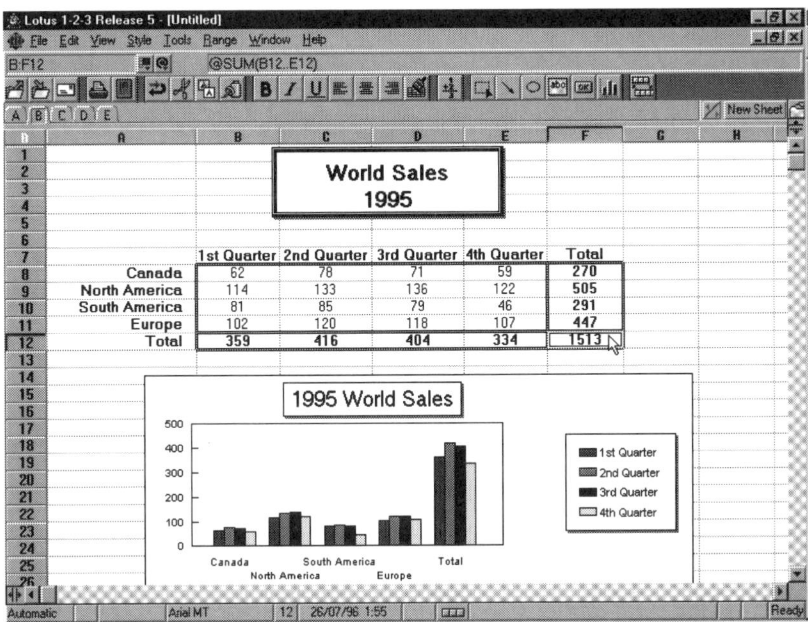

Figure 6.3 Figures and chart in **Lotus 1-2-3**.

Columns, rows and cells

On first opening a spreadsheet you're presented with a large grid of boxes; each of these boxes is a **cell**, and it's into these you'll enter text, figures and formulas. Each cell has its own **address** consisting of a column-letter and a row-number. For example, the cell in the top-left corner of a worksheet is called **A1**.

JARGONBUSTER

Worksheet

A spreadsheet application usually lets you create lots of sheets all in the same file, each of which is called a **worksheet**. You'll see tabs across the top or bottom of the window marked *Sheet 1*, *Sheet 2* and so on. Click on a tab to switch to it, or double-click to give it a more informative name. For example, you might keep your year's accounts in a single file with separate worksheets named *January*, *February*. . .

When you start up the spreadsheet application you'll see a thick box around cell A1 – this is the **cell selector** and lets you see where you are on the sheet (rather like the flashing text cursor in a word processor). You can move to a different cell using the keyboard's arrow keys or by clicking a cell with the mouse. If the cell you select contains an entry, this entry will be displayed in the formula-bar just above the column-headers, shown in Figure 6.4. Here's a quickfire list of things you should know about spreadsheets:

Figure 6.4 The all-important formula-bar.

- To enter text in an empty cell, move the selector to it using the arrow keys or by clicking it, and start typing. When you're done, you can press *Enter* to confirm, or click the ✓ button on the formula-bar, or move to a different cell.
- To delete an entry in a cell, click the cell and then press the *Delete* key.
- To cancel an entry you've typed wrongly, click the × button on the formula-bar. You can then either type in something different or press *Enter* to finish and leave the cell blank.
- To change an entry in a cell, just click it. If it contains data you entered yourself you can replace the data by typing something new – there's no need to delete the original data first. If the cell contains the result of a calculation, the function or formula you used will be displayed in the formula-bar and you can edit it there.
- You can select a whole column for editing by clicking its letter button, or a row by clicking its number button.
- Select a group of cells by clicking in one cell and dragging to highlight the cells you want to work with.
- Select cells scattered around the sheet by holding *Ctrl and clicking on each cell you need.*
- You can use Cut, Copy and Paste to move or copy the contents of cells from one part of the worksheet to another, or to a different worksheet. You can also paste (*embed*) them into a different type of document such as a word-processor report, or link them using DDE.
- If you see the entry ***** in a cell, it indicates that the cell isn't wide enough to hold the contents. Move the pointer to the right-hand side of the column button and drag it slightly to the right to widen the column.
- The usual way to begin creating a spreadsheet is to enter a list of names or labels in column A and along row 1 (making the columns wider if necessary) and then to enter all your data in the appropriate cells. Finally,

enter the formulas to make the necessary calculations, and add any formatting you want to make the whole thing look good. Check the results of formula cells carefully to make sure they're doing what you want before you start to rely on their output – it's easy to miss out a data cell you meant to include or enter the wrong symbol by mistake.

Formulas

Getting all the data into the spreadsheet (and making sure you've typed it correctly!) is a good start, but it's still just lists of numbers – nothing clever there, you could do that in a word processor. The 'clever' comes in the form of instructions entered into a cell that tell the application what you want to know about particular sets of figures. These instructions are known as **formulas** and consist of cell addresses and the standard mathematical symbols + (add), – (subtract), * (multiply) and / (divide). A formula will always start with the = (equals) sign to indicate to the software that you're entering is a formula rather than more data.

As an example, let's say you've entered a pair of numbers into cells A1 and A2 and you want to add them together. Click in A3, type

=A1+A2

and press *Enter*. The answer will appear in cell A3. Any time you click on A3 the formula you entered will be displayed in the formula-bar, but A3 itself will continue to show the result of the calculation. If you now change the number in A1 and press *Enter*, the total shown in A3 will immediately update – the application doesn't care which actual numbers are in the cells, it just knows it's got to add them together.

Instead of typing the cell addresses into the formula, you can just click the cell you want each time. (You've still got to type the mathematical symbols though!)

Make sure you enter the separate calculations into a formula in the order you want the application to perform them. For example, **=A1*B1+D4** would multiply A1 and B1 and then add D4 to the total, whereas **=A1*(B1+D4)** would multiply A1 by the sum of B1 and D4. You can use as many parenthesized entries in a formula as you like.

Functions

Although all formulas involve typing to some degree, there are ways to minimize the amount of keyboard bashing you've got to do. Typing =**A1**+**A2**, as in the example above, isn't too painful, but what if you had entries stretching down to A38? All those numbers, all those + signs! For this reason, applications include **functions**, predefined formulas that make the whole thing a lot quicker. Some of the most-used functions will be represented as buttons on the toolbar; other more exotic functions will be selected from a dialog such as **Microsoft Excel**'s 'Function Wizard'.

The most commonly used function is **SUM**, which adds together the contents of cells making it unnecessary to enter + signs. You can use the SUM function by typing =**SUM** in an empty cell or by clicking the toolbar button marked Σ and then selecting the cells you want to add together. Here are a few examples:

- To add together A1 to A38, type =**sum(a1:a38)** and press *Enter*. You must enter the parentheses, and make sure you don't enter any spaces. Sets of sequential cells like this are referred to as a **range**. A range can cover multiple columns and rows – for example, the range **(a1:c16)** would cover A1 to A16, B1 to B16 and C1 to C16, a total of 48 cells. To select this range, you'd click in A1 and drag the pointer diagonally to C16.

Save yourself the *Shift* key hassle of typing in the separating colon – you can usually use a dot instead and the software will understand what you mean and convert it to a colon for you automatically.

- Another way to total A1 to A38 with no typing at all is to click the Σ button, click in cell A1 and drag the pointer down to A38 to highlight all these cells (although A1 will remain un-highlighted) then press *Enter*.
- To total cells scattered all over your spreadsheet, such as A3, C19, B7 and D11, click the Σ button, hold *Ctrl* and click each of these cells. After clicking the last one you want to select, release *Ctrl* and press *Enter*.
- To total the entire contents of a row or column, click the Σ button then click on the header button for that row or column. Once again, you can select multiple headers in this way if you hold *Ctrl* as you click each one.

If you total an entire row or column by clicking the header button, make sure the cell into which you're entering the formula isn't in the *same* row or column: it'll try to add itself to the calculation and end up going around in circles (known as a **circular reference**).

A Spreadsheet example

Figure 6.5 shows the quarterly income generated by two sales teams, and the expenses incurred by each team over the year. Rows 8 to 11 contain some of the calculations you might want to make from data such as this. Let's look at the formulas and functions you'd enter to arrive at these results.

D11 =SUM(B8:C8)

	A	B	C	D
1		Sales Team 1	Sales Team 2	
2	1st Quarter Income	50,000	62,000	
3	2nd Quarter Income	45,000	75,000	
4	3rd Quarter Income	65,000	40,000	
5	4th Quarter Income	30,000	37,000	
6	Expenses	28,000	36,000	
7				
8	Total Income	190,000	214,000	
9	Total less Expenses	162,000	178,000	
10	Average per Quarter	47,500	53,500	
11	Total Company Income			404,000
12				

Figure 6.5 Typical spreadsheet data and calculations.

- To calculate the *Total Income* for Team 1 in B8, use the function =**sum(b2:b8)**. The total income for Team 2 in C8 would be calculated with =**sum(c2:c8)**.
- Calculate the *Total less Expenses* for Team 1 in B9 using the formula =**b8**–**b6**. To do the same for Team 2 in C9, you'd type =**c8**–**c6**.
- You could calculate the *Average Sales per Quarter* of Team 1 (cell B10) with the formula =**(b2+b3+b4+b5)/4**, but you should have a function that does this more easily: type =**average(b2:b5)**. For Team 2 in C10, enter =**average(c2:c5)**.
- The *Total Company Income* in D11 is calculated with the function =**sum(b8:c8)**.

Defining ranges

Entering SUM functions in the example above is quite easy – there are only two sales teams and the data is broken down into quarters. But imagine what the spreadsheet would look like if you had 30 teams and you were tracking their performance weekly – 30 columns by 52 rows of data! To set up calculations based upon each team's performance in particular months would involve a lot of careful typing or mouse-dragging to enter the correct ranges.

To make it easier and quicker to work with large amounts of data, spreadsheet applications allow you to assign a name to a bunch of cells you've selected in advance (look for the **Name** entry on the **Insert** or **Range** menu). For example, you might select the cells relating to Team 1's sales in March and assign them the name **T1Mar**. You can then type this name into your formulas and functions rather than having to work with individual cells.

For this to be useful you need to keep the names short – it's supposed to be a timesaver after all! – and these names might not be easy to understand next time you look at your spreadsheet. Consider using a separate worksheet as a reference by typing in the names you've defined and an explanation of what data they refer to.

Spreadsheet formatting

Although the spreadsheets you create are obviously supposed to be functional, spreadsheet applications include formatting facilities to make them look more attractive than just a plain grid of black text. In fact, formatting *adds* to a worksheet's functionality – for example, if all the cells containing the results of calculations are in bold type, or have a coloured border around them, you can find the information that matters a lot faster. You'll find all the formatting options in dialogs reached from a **Format** or **Style** menu, but some of the more common features will usually be gathered together as buttons on a toolbar.

Let's start with a quickfire list of the cell-formatting options you can use. These are applied to the selected cell or cells. To increase the font size of several cells, for example, there's no need to format each cell individually – just drag over the range with the pointer, or click all the cells you want to change while holding *Ctrl*.

- *Text formatting.* You'll have similar text-formatting options to those found in a word processor. You can change the font and size, underline text, or add effects such as bold, italic or colour. In addition, you can often rotate text by 90°, or place the characters vertically in a column.
- *Cell shading.* You can change the background colour of selected cells from the default white to one of a range of more interesting colours. This can be handy for distinguishing different types of data – in a sales-related sheet, for example, you could use a different background colour for cells relating to each of the four quarters.
- *Borders.* You can insert lines of various colours and styles around a cell or a group of cells. Each of the four edges of a cell can be a different colour.
- *Text boxes.* It's usually possible to create a text box into which you can type a heading for the worksheet and move it wherever you want it on the sheet. In this way you could create forms such as invoices with separate text boxes for your company name, company address, client details and so on.
- *Graphics.* You can usually insert graphics files into spreadsheets and position them where you want them, perhaps to add your company's logo to the top of a form.

Apart from the standard cell-formatting features, you may have other options that can be applied to the whole sheet:

- You can remove the column and row header buttons from the sheet, as well as the dotted gridlines.

TIP

The column and row header buttons and gridlines are included just for guidance – whether you choose to 'hide' them or not, they won't be printed when you send your worksheet off to the printer. This is a good reason for putting borders around blocks of cells.

- You might be able to place a background image on the worksheet, rather like the patterns and wallpapers you can add to the Windows desktop.
- Top-level spreadsheet applications offer a range of preset styles that include cell shading, borders, text colours and formatting which you can apply to your worksheet once you've finished adding all the data and formulas you need.
- Most applications include preset templates such as invoices, purchase orders and budgets. All you need do is insert personal or company details and add your data.

Charts and graphs

For sheer accuracy, numbers do it every time. But sometimes you don't really want to examine figures in a spreadsheet no matter how accurate they are. Particularly in the case of business presentations or printed reports, it's often far more meaningful to illustrate the point you're making with a chart than to provide reams of figures. A well-chosen chart can convey the information that matters with little more than a glance.

To this end, spreadsheet applications build in features that can create charts and graphs from your worksheet (or a selected portion of it) quickly and simply. Select the cells you want included in the chart, click the dedicated button on the toolbar, drag the pointer diagonally over an empty section of the worksheet to create a box for the chart and that's about all there is to it. In **Microsoft Excel** the **ChartWizard** will appear and offer you simple choices about style and layout. In **Lotus 1-2-3** you can double-click the chart to bring up the customization dialog.

As long as the chart remains on the worksheet (or linked to the file via a DDE link), any changes to the data within the cells will be reflected by the chart. In the same way, as the values in the cells increase, the chart will automatically increase its scale so that none can 'go off the end'.

▶ *For more on linking or embedding spreadsheet data in a word-processor document using DDE or OLE see pp. 156–160.*

Buyers' guide: Spreadsheets

- The undoubted king of spreadsheets, in terms of popularity and user-base, is **Microsoft Excel**, which has become the spreadsheet standard in corporate computing. Although most users will barely scratch the surface of its capabilities, it's as easy to work with as many 'lighter' applications. Its two competitors are **Lotus 1-2-3** and Corel's **Quattro Pro**, which can't match Excel's market share but still offer similar features and power.
- Regard 8 Mb RAM as the minimum to run one of these applications alone, and 16 Mb if you hope to run another application such as a database or word processor alongside it. For heavy-duty use (large, formula-filled sheets) a fast Pentium or DX4 processor is an advantage, and a 17-inch monitor will let you see more information.
- Excel, 1-2-3 and Quattro Pro are all bundled in office suites **Microsoft Office**, **Lotus SmartSuite** and **Corel Office Professional** respectively (see p. 204). If you need two or more office-quality applications, it's worth considering the suite.

> All three companies mentioned here include a spreadsheet in their integrated (Works) applications that can satisfy all your number-crunching and formatting requirements without terrifying you with complex options you feel you're supposed to be using.

Database managers

As the name suggests, a **database manager** is a program that lets you create, store and retrieve information. However, database managers come in a variety of flavours suited to different levels of use. For example, the Windows 3.1 **Cardfile** is a database manager of a sort: you can enter information on cards, save collections of cards as a single file, and use search facilities to locate the piece of information you want. However, Cardfile is limited by the size of its cards and the ways in which you can use and sort the information once it's entered.

An application that dares to call itself a database manager will let you place large amounts of information on each 'card', view the information in a variety of ways, and conduct searches for all the entries that meet your criteria. Databases work with information in three different ways:

- *Freeform databases*. Data can be entered anywhere, in any order rather like a jumble of papers on a desk. When you search for particular information, the whole database will be searched for any instances of the word or number you requested.
- *Flat-file databases*. This is the standard type of database. Information is entered in an organized way, using **field names**. As a result, you can also *retrieve* the information in an organized way.
- *Relational databases*. The relational database still uses fields to sort particular types of information, but the application can work with multiple databases and can answer queries spanning all these databases. Many relational database managers are **programmable** – if you understand the language you can build your own database applications tailor-made for specific information and uses.

Files, records and fields

There are three separate elements to a database:

- *Fields*. A field is a single piece of information such as someone's first name, or phone number. A field consists of a **field name** such as *Address* and a blank box into which you'd type the corresponding information.

- *Records.* A record is like a single card in a Rolodex or Cardfile with multiple fields, perhaps containing all the relevant information about a single person.
- *Files.* A file is a collection of records in the same way that a spreadsheet file can contain multiple tabbed worksheets.

Constructing a form

There are two distinct steps to creating a database. The first is to create a form that contains all the fields you need on each record, such as names, addresses, phone numbers and so on (Figure 6.6). In many recent applications you can choose from a range of preset templates designed for different uses such as employee records, music and video collections, mailing lists, recipes, and all kinds of exotica. You can then alter the field names if you need to, add and remove fields, and the first part of the job is done.

TIP

Split your records into as many fields as possible to make searching for information easier. For example, if you create three separate fields for day/month/year of birth it'll be easy to find details of anyone born in 1964. If you want to use your database for mail merges, make sure you've split the information into the fields you'll need to enter in the form letter. For example, if you want your letters to begin *Dear Mr Wilson* or *Dear Mrs Jones*, you'll need separate fields for title and surname.

If your database application doesn't offer preset templates, or you can't find one that works for you, you can create your own by starting from a blank sheet and adding fields to it. As you add a new field name, you'll see a box appear beside it into which you'll later type the relevant information – in most programs you'll have to specify how many characters you should be able to enter in each field.

Microsoft Works

File Edit View Insert Format Tools Window Help

Times New Roman 10

5.2cm 11.4cm

CONTACTS.WDB

Business Contacts

- **Date Entered:** 8-10-94
- **Mr/Mrs/Ms:** Mr
- **First Name:** Andrew — **Last Name:** Sparks
- **Job Title:** Director
- **Business Name:** Sparks International
- **Address Line 1:** 819-823 Main Road
- **Address Line 2:**
- **City:** WARE — **County:** Herts
- **Postal Code:** TA2 7PA — **Country:** England
- **Phone 1:** 225859 x462 — **Phone 2:**
- **Fax:** 225860
- **Hours Available:** 8:30am - 5pm — **Last Contacted:** 4-2-95
- **Meeting Date:**
- **Other Contact:** — **Contact Phone:**

Record 1

Press ALT for commands; type text followed by : to create field. Pg1 1 1/1

Figure 6.6 A simple database record in Microsoft's integrated Works application.

You can move the fields around the sheet by dragging them to create a sensible and attractive layout, and apply various types of colour and style formatting to personalize the database. In many applications you can import pictures (perhaps to include photographs of your employees on their records), and add simple selection buttons for either/or fields such as Male/Female or CD/Tape.

JARGONBUSTER

Protection

Databases often use two types of protection (neither of which is designed to stop them having lots of *little* databases, in case you were wondering!). **Form protection** prevents you accidentally mucking up field names and layout you've carefully entered; **data protection** keeps the information safe that you've entered into the fields. Turning on one of these forms of protection is known as **locking** the form or data, and it's well worth doing even though you'll have to unlock the data every time you want to enter something new.

▶ *For more on using a database and word processor in combination to create mail merges, turn to p. 171.*

Creating records

The second step in creating a database is to actually enter the information into your fields and build up a set of records. When you've typed information into one field, press *Tab* to move to the next, and so on until you've completed the first record. You can then click a button on the toolbar to add a new record and start filling the blanks in that. In most applications, the status-bar at the bottom of the window will keep you informed about how many records you've created, and usually has buttons to let you step forwards and backwards from one record to the next, or jump to the first or last (Figure 6.7).

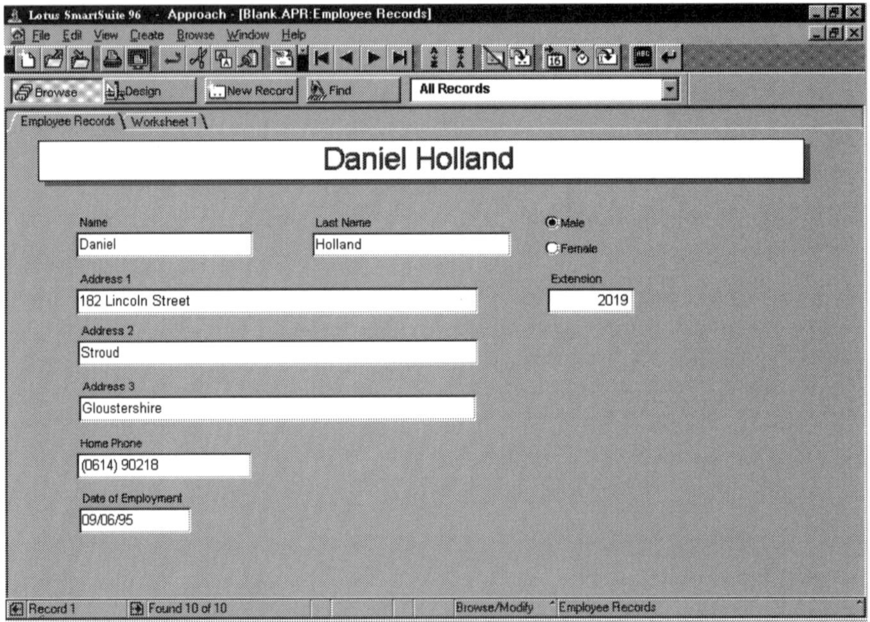

Figure 6.7 A single record in **Lotus Approach**.

Sorting records

When you add new records to a database they remain in the order you entered them, so as you browse through the records using the buttons on the status-bar you won't see any particular order to them. In some low-end applications the only way of organizing records in alphabetical order is to actually *insert* them alphabetically. However, mid- to high-end applications make this a lot easier by providing comprehensive sorting options: simply choose a field name to sort by and the software will juggle your records around for you.

Most database managers can also present the records in a 'list view' that looks and functions very like a spreadsheet, with each field having its own column and each record being in its own row. This can be useful for viewing and comparing a large number of records at once or making quick changes to the same field on every record.

Running queries

One of the most common things you want to do with a database is to look at one particular record. Select the **Find** option from a menu or toolbar and you'll see a blank copy of your form layout. Type details into as many of the fields as necessary to locate the record you want. For example, if you want to see the record of an employee called John you'd type **John** in the *First Name* field; if you have several employees called John you'd fill in the *Last Name* field as well.

The database manager really comes into its own when you need to perform more complicated searches (known as **queries**). Instead of typing fixed entries into the fields you can use a variety of wildcards and symbols to find records that meet a number of criteria. The common wildcards ? and * can be used to replace single or multiple characters respectively (so entering **J*** in the *First Name* field would find the record of anyone called John, James, Jim or Jan; entering **J??** would find Jim or Jan). The other symbols you have available will vary according to the application you're using, but here are a few of the common ones:

- **<75** Finds records with any value lower than 75 in this field.
- **>=100** Finds records with values greater than or equal to 100 in this field.
- **75...100** Finds records with any value between 75 and 100 in this field.
- **Jim,Jan** Finds any records with Jim or Jan in this field
- **Jim&Jan** Finds any records with both Jim and Jan in this field.

▶ *For more on wildcards, turn to p. 260.*

Buyers' guide: Databases

- At the top of the tree are the programmables, the list headed by **Borland Paradox** and **Microsoft Access**. Both combine power with ease of use, but unless you really need a professional-level application you'll be paying extra for features you're unlikely to use. **Access** is bundled with the more expensive Microsoft suite, **Office Professional**, but missing from the Standard edition.
- Both **Lotus Approach** and **Claris FileMaker Pro** offer similar features to the big guns, with hoards of templates and preset applications at a lower price. Both are relational. **Approach** is included as part of **Lotus SmartSuite** (see section p. 206).
- Each of the major integrated Works applications includes a basic flat-file database suitable for the casual or less demanding user. Simple preset templates are included but querying and sorting features are usually limited.
- Do you need a database at all? If you have a spreadsheet application you can create a great-looking, and totally searchable, database on a worksheet. If flashy presentation doesn't matter, you could even create a free-form database by typing details into a word-processor document and using the **Find** and **Find Next** features to find what you want.

Paint and draw programs

When it comes to adding artwork to text-based documents, or creating stand-alone graphics, there's very little you *can't* do on a PC. In this field of computing, more than most others, the variety of software available is immense and the features you'll find cover most points between 'incredibly basic' and 'full multimedia capabilities'. But this is also an area in which the computer can do little to automate the creation process – an expensive graphics package won't make an artist of you if there's no raw material there to start with, it'll just give you more to learn about while you're struggling! So, as a gesture of support to the artistically challenged, before we examine paint and draw programs themselves, let's take a look at another way you can add attention-grabbing graphics to your documents.

Clip art

One of the main funds of graphics is the **clip art** collection. Clip art is a term used for pictures created by somebody else and sold (or given away!) in collections, and many office suites and integrated applications come with their own library of clip art (sometimes termed a *gallery* in a burst of self-indulgence). The clips are usually grouped into categories such as Travel, Buildings, People, Sport and so on (Figure 6.8), to make it easier to find what you want among the hundreds or even thousands of pictures in the collection, and there's usually a bunch of utilitarian signs and symbols such as maps of the world, road signs, backgrounds, decorative borders, etc.

Clip art is notorious for varying in quality from bright, professional-looking drawings to ugly, smudgy black-and-white efforts. Make sure you're getting a quality collection before you part with hard cash – remember they put some of their best stuff on the back of the box, so if you don't like that, it's odds-on that you'll hate the rest!

How you work with clip art will depend how it's organized: most of the many collections available on CD-ROM will have a viewer program included which loads the clips in the category you choose. When you've selected a clip, just use **Copy** (*Ctrl+C*) to copy it to the clipboard and **Paste** (*Ctrl+V*) to paste it into your document. Applications such as Microsoft Office and Microsoft Works come with their own clip art collection and viewer to which you can add your own images to keep all your graphics files catalogued.

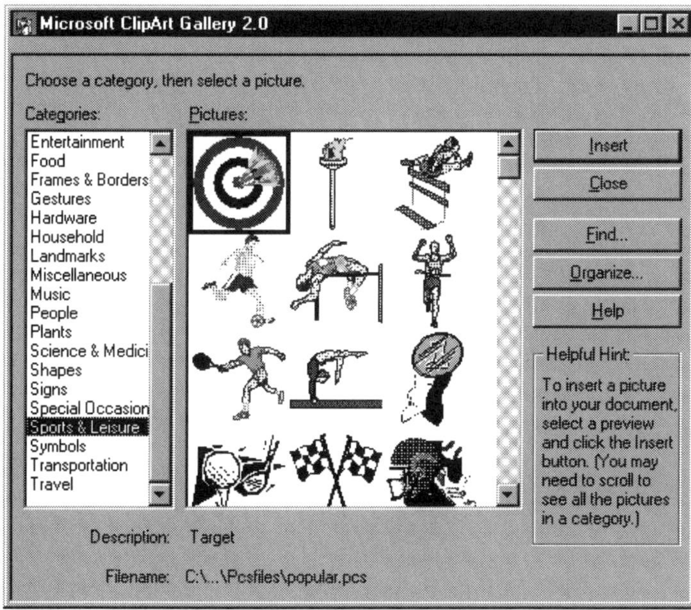

Figure 6.8 Cataloguing and inserting clip art with **Microsoft ClipArt Gallery**.

Paint programs

The Windows operating systems give you either **Paint** or **Paintbrush**, both examples of paint programs. A paint program is the simplest example of do-it-yourself graphics software, often lacking in power and features but easy to use. Because you're working with individual pixels and applying colour to them, the result will be saved as a bitmap, usually in Windows Bitmap (**.bmp**) format or PC Paintbrush (**.pcx**) format, although some paint programs can load and save the GIF and JPEG formats commonly used on the Internet and the TIFF format used in professional publishing and DTP. Remember that bitmap images can't be resized successfully other than in orders of two.

TIP

Although you can add text to your creations in paint programs, the text size will not necessarily be identical to the same TrueType font used in a word processor because the program has to convert the text to a bitmap. For the same reason, once the text is there it's just another part of the picture and can't be edited – the best you can do is delete and retype it.

▶ *If you want to know more about Windows'* ***Paintbrush*** *and* ***Paint****, skip ahead to pp. 298 and 366 respectively. For more details on the graphics formats mentioned here, take a look at p. 140.*

Draw programs

The **draw program**, even at its most basic, offers far more flexibility than the paint program. Draw programs can load, create and save vector graphics formats which are a great deal easier and more forgiving to work with. Each element of the picture is a separate shape, such as a circle, square or freehand outline which can then be filled with colour. So far this isn't much different from the paint program, but the clincher is that each of these shapes remains an individual object! You can click on any of these objects and drag it somewhere else, rotate it, or change its shape, without affecting any other part of the picture. The result of this object-oriented approach is that you can build complex pictures from the ground up by layering one object over another

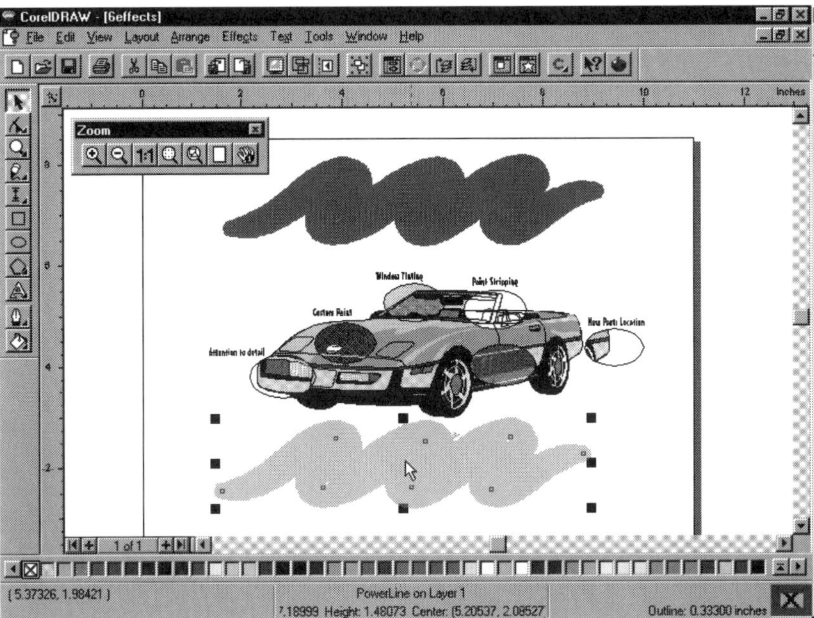

Figure 6.9 The popular and powerful **CorelDRAW**.

Because draw programs work with vector graphics formats, any object in the picture can be resized using the **grab-handles** that appear when you click the object (see Figure 6.9). Here are a few of the features you'll find in a draw program:

- *Gradient fills.* Instead of filling a shape with a solid colour, select a starting colour, a finishing colour and a direction and the first colour will gradually fade into the second.
- *Send forwards/backwards.* Because pictures are created by layering smaller sections, it's sometimes necessary to move items in front of or behind other items. These options are usually coupled with *Send To Back* and *Bring To Front.*
- *Grids and snapping.* To help in precise drawing you can add a grid overlay to the 'canvas'. Snapping is a useful option to ensure that objects (especially squares) are perfectly aligned with each other by forcing them to jump onto the nearest gridline as if magnetized.
- *Full text-editing.* Because these are not bitmapped graphics, text can be entered and edited freely as if in a word processor. Some draw programs even go so far as to include proofing tools for text such as a spellchecker and thesaurus!
- *Object grouping or linking.* You can create groups of two or more objects in a drawing that will respond as a single object when cut, copied, moved or resized. This is usually done using a selection tool to draw a dotted box

around the objects you want to select, but another option is often to hold *Shift* and click each object separately.

- *Scanner support.* Although most scanners come with their own software, many draw programs have scanner support and will allow you to work with scanned photos and images. You may also have a range of filter-options that let you apply weird treatments such as embossing or posterizing an image, or converting it to sepia-tones or a charcoal drawing.

▶ *Go back to p. 76 and reread the information on scanners. To make graphics work easier you might want to consider using a tablet instead of a mouse – return to p. 53 for details.*

WordArt

One final oddity in the field of graphics is **WordArt**, which lets you do weird things to perfectly innocent text while it's looking the other way. WordArt is a Microsoft applet that comes bundled with both Office and Works, although **Serif TypePlus** has similar capabilities as a stand-alone program that saves its results in Windows Metafile (**.wmf**) format.

You can insert a piece of WordArt into a document in any OLE-compliant application by selecting **Insert/Object** and choosing **Microsoft WordArt** from the list. A new toolbar will appear together with a small text box. Type your chosen text into the box and then start getting creative. From the drop-down lists you can choose a font and size, and apply one of various shapes to the text. Toolbar buttons let you add outlines and shadows to the characters, stretch or compress them, tilt or swivel them, and add coloured or patterned fills.

▶ *There's another popular type of graphics software known as Presentation Graphics, in which graphic elements are often mixed with text and multimedia clips – see p. 197.*

Buyers' guide: Paint and draw programs

- The market-leader in draw programs is **CorelDRAW**, though to refer to it simply as a draw program is a bit unfair. In addition to its drawing facilities, CorelDRAW can handle 3D image rendering, 3D animation, multimedia presentations, frame-by-frame video (**.avi**) editing, and includes sound and animation clips together with a 25 000-strong clip art library. If you're serious about computer graphics, this package is worth its serious price tag.
- At the cheaper end of the market are **GSP Designworks**, **Serif DrawPlus**, and the modestly titled but fuller-featured **Corel Graphics Pack**.

- If you want better graphics capabilities than Windows' Paint or Paintbrush, you might consider **Microsoft Office** or **Works**. Office applications have drawing facilities built in; Works comes with an OLE-server applet called **Microsoft Draw** that can create, edit and import vector graphics.
- Two other integrated Works packages, **ClarisWorks** and Corel's **PerfectWorks** both include surprisingly capable paint *and* draw applications.
- A popular and comprehensive paint program is JASC's **Paint Shop Pro**, a shareware application which supports a variety of bitmap and vector graphics formats and offers a fine array of filters, tools and editing possibilities.
- Microsoft's only foray into the dedicated graphics-application arena has been **Fine Artist**, an excellent children's paint program with extras such as sounds and cartoons.
- To create and work with images of any format and enjoy gratifying results you'll need a display that can handle at least 256 colours, but if you're working with photographs or you want to create photo-realistic artwork you'll need a 64 K or 16.7 million colour display (16-bit and 24-bit colour respectively). For intensive work with large graphics, 16 Mb RAM should be regarded as a minimum.

Desktop publishing

Desktop publishing packages (or DTP in geek-speak) are the applications that bring you newspapers, magazines, books, brochures, flyers and so on, the common link being an amalgamation of text and graphics in the same document. The main curiosity of DTP software is that text-editing and image-editing facilities are usually poor. This isn't as paradoxical as it seems; rather than aiming to replace the word processor and paint/draw program, DTP's role is to act as a receptacle for previously composed text and graphics, and to provide the necessary tools for final formatting and layout to construct a finished document.

Getting started

The first move is to write your text. This can be done in a simple text editor such as **Notepad**, but make sure you turn on the Word Wrap option – if you don't, you'll be tempted to insert carriage returns at the end of a line to keep from scrolling too far across the screen, and these will appear as separate paragraphs in the DTP document.

Preferably, use a more advanced word processor with a spellchecker so you can be sure the text is correct before you copy it to the DTP page, but save it in plain text (**.txt**) format.

Story

Text you import into a DTP document is referred to as a **story**, and a document can contain as many different stories as you want, just like a newspaper or magazine.

If you need to create graphics (other than basic lines, rectangles and circles), do these too but make sure you save them in a format your DTP program can open.

Working with text

The big difference between DTP programs and basic word processors is that text and graphics are placed in **frames**, rectangular dotted-line boxes. Text requires a text frame, pictures need a graphics frame. The tools for drawing these frames are frequently used so you'll normally find buttons for them on the toolbar.

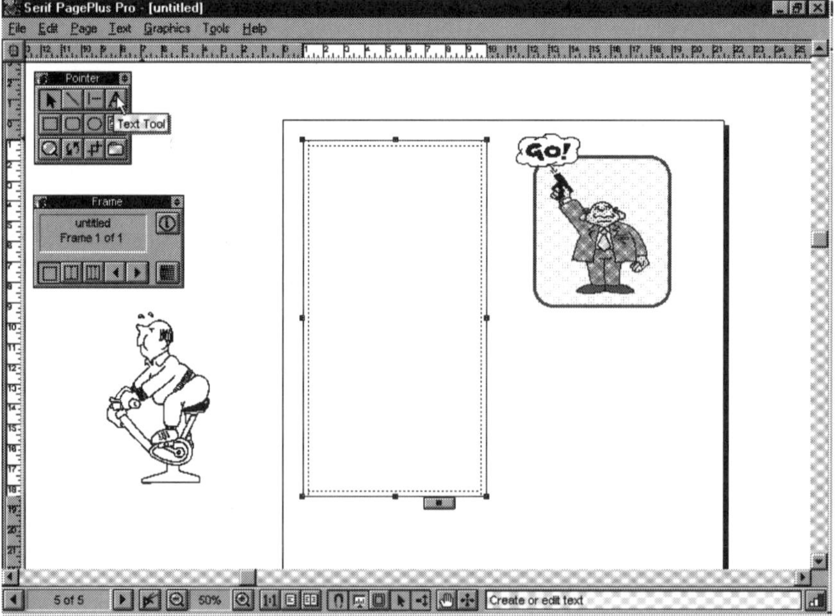

Figure 6.10 A text frame waiting for text, and a graphic waiting on the paste-up board.

To import your text, create a text frame like the one shown in Figure 6.10. You can create a single-column frame or choose to split the frame into two or more columns across the page and the text will flow from one to the next automatically. Then select the **Import Text** command and find and double-click the text file you created. If your frame isn't large enough to hold all the text, move the pointer onto one of the grab-handles and stretch it.

If you're importing an especially long story, create a number of text frames and link them together using the **Link** option. When frames are 'linked', the software knows it can use these frames for that story and will automatically *flow* the text from one frame to the next. If you have only one small frame and a very long story, it'll seem that most of your text has vanished until you create another frame!

As it appears in your document, the text looks rather dull (and in full-page mode it looks tiny too). The next step is to zoom in so that you can read the text comfortably and to start formatting. The formatting options are similar to those found in any word processor – fonts, sizes, colours, bold, italic, and so on – but there are fewer shortcuts to selecting text. Although it's possible to type *all* your text directly into the document, it's this lack of flexibility that makes the import method preferable. In some DTP applications, you can double-click a block of text and format it in a fairly normal-looking window instead.

Paste-up board

When you look at your DTP document in full-page view, the space you see around the document is known as the **paste-up board**. You can use this space to store imported stories and graphics to help you keep track of what you want to add, and drag them into the document itself when you're ready for them. In the same way, you can drag sections *out* of the document and onto the paste-up board if you want to do a rethink on layout.

Working with graphics

In a similar way to importing text, you'll usually have an **Import Picture** option on the **File** menu for bringing in graphics. First you'll have to create a graphics frame for the image: in some applications the imported image will expand or contract to fit the size of the frame and will seem distorted until you resize it; in others the box will be automatically resized to fit the image.

Make sure you *link* all the images you import into your DTP document rather than *embedding* them to prevent the file becoming too big. Most programs should have an option to automatically link any image you import that's over a certain size.

The idea of having separate text and graphics frames is a good one: you can move a graphics frame onto a text frame and (in most applications) the text will shift out of the way automatically and skirt around it, as in Figure 6.11. This is known as **text wrapping**; in some cases the application will handle it automatically, but in others you'll have to make the settings yourself for each graphic separately. You can usually choose whether the text surrounding the picture should form a square edge to it or follow its contours, and you may have extra options to let you choose how much space there should be between text and picture.

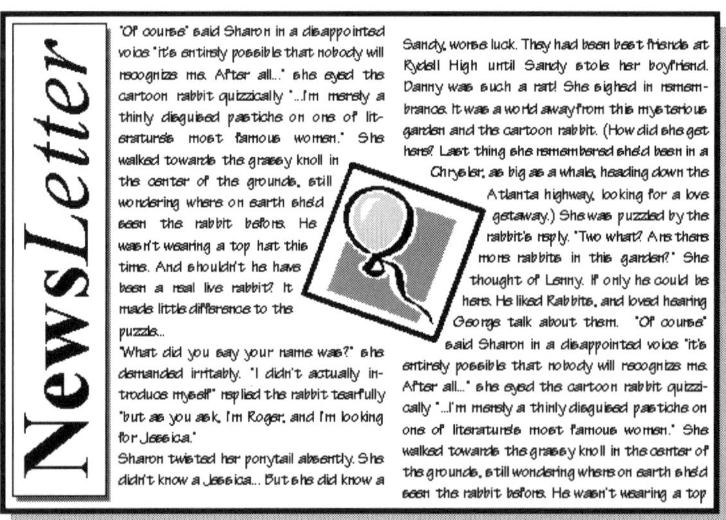

NewsLetter

"Of course" said Sharon in a disappointed voice "it's entirely possible that nobody will recognize me. After all..." she eyed the cartoon rabbit quizzically "...I'm merely a thinly disguised pastiche on one of literature's most famous women." She walked towards the grassy knoll in the center of the grounds, still wondering where on earth she'd seen the rabbit before. He wasn't wearing a top hat this time. And shouldn't he have been a real live rabbit? It made little difference to the puzzle...

"What did you say your name was?" she demanded irritably. "I didn't actually introduce myself" replied the rabbit tearfully "but as you ask, I'm Roger, and I'm looking for Jessica."

Sharon twisted her ponytail absently. She didn't know a Jessica... But she did know a Sandy, worse luck. They had been best friends at Rydell High until Sandy stole her boyfriend. Danny was such a rat! She sighed in remembrance. It was a world away from this mysterious garden and the cartoon rabbit. (How did she get here? Last thing she remembered she'd been in a Chrysler, as big as a whale, heading down the Atlanta highway, looking for a love getaway.) She was puzzled by the rabbit's reply. "Two what? Are there more rabbits in this garden?" She thought of Lenny. If only he could be here. He liked Rabbits, and loved hearing George talk about them. "Of course" said Sharon in a disappointed voice "it's entirely possible that nobody will recognize me. After all..." she eyed the cartoon rabbit quizzically "...I'm merely a thinly disguised pastiche on one of literature's most famous women." She walked towards the grassy knoll in the center of the grounds, still wondering where on earth she'd seen the rabbit before. He wasn't wearing a top

Figure 6.11 Some of the formatting options available, including text wrapping and drop shadows.

Drawing tools are usually basic, but you'll have the full range of colours to work with (including 'Clear' to make text or a graphic object transparent) and a few DTP applications support the Pantone colour chart for precise colour matching.

DTP hints

When laying out your document it's important to keep your eye on the ball. Although you can do all kinds of clever stuff with rotated text, coloured boxes and frame outlines, text wrapping and so on, a page overloaded with interesting effects becomes very difficult to read. In other words, less is more! That being said, here are a few tips and effects you can use:

- Place headlines or pictures in a box with a thin black outline and add a **drop shadow** to it by placing a grey rectangle underneath it shifted slightly downwards and to the right or left. This has the effect of pushing the text box towards the reader.
- Add shadows to text by making a copy of the text frame, changing the colour of the copied text and placing this behind the original but slightly off-centre.
- Place a small amount of justified text inside a circle (created using the circle-tool) and use text wrapping to wrap it to the inside edges of the circle. You can heighten the effect by making the circle and its border clear so that all you can see is the text itself.
- Choose your fonts carefully and try to stick with a maximum of four in a document. A serif font such as Times New Roman makes an easy-to-read body-text typeface; headlines often work well with sans-serif fonts such as Arial, but a more fancy font adds an informal air if it doesn't appear too often on the page.
- In brochures intended to sell a product, rotate pictures of the product a few degrees (between 6° and 10° should do it) rather than keeping them square on the page to make them look friendlier and more appealing. Use the Crop tool to remove any large expanses of distracting background, and use a paint or draw program to improve photographs (by adding the clear blue sky always found in holiday brochures, for example).
- If you want each page to follow a similar layout (for example, four columns with your company logo at the top), you can create a **master page** with each item in position which will be used as a template for each document page to save you repeating all the same moves for each page.

JARGONBUSTER

Leading and kerning

Two typesetting terms that pop up a lot in DTP. **Kerning** is adjusting the space between two characters. This is often used in headlines to tidy up irregular-looking spacing, but you can use it to great effect to give a headline or subhead a much tighter look. **Leading** (pronounced 'ledding') is the vertical distance between lines of type (measured in points).

▶ *For more on serif and sans-serif fonts, turn to p. 151.*

DTP vs word processor

Modern top-end word processors are becoming more like DTP programs all the time: you can flow text into columns, create drawings, import graphics, place pictures or text into frames and put the frames anywhere on the page, and much more. So why not just use a word processor instead?

In fact, there's no reason why you shouldn't. If you've already got an application like **Microsoft Word** or **Lotus WordPro** that includes drawing tools and frames, you can create remarkably sophisticated documents by placing everything into frames and moving these where you want them. Here's a few of the major differences and additions you'll find in a dedicated DTP program – if these don't matter to you, and you've got a good word processor already, stick with it.

- *Grouping.* Once you've placed multiple frames, pictures and objects where you want them and juggled around with the *Send To Back* and *Bring To Front* commands to layer everything correctly, you can group these items together as one to ensure you can't move one frame accidentally and ruin all your careful work. Word processors treat frames and drawing objects as separate items.
- *Snapping.* Precise alignment of frames is made simple with **snapping**, which forces the edges of a frame to jump to the nearest gridlines. You may even be able to type in exact coordinates and sizes for each frame.
- *Stacking.* You can stack as many frames and objects as you like one on top of the other regardless of their contents. A word processor will give you little choice about how different items can be stacked and which will remain visible.
- *Crop and rotate.* DTP programs allow you to crop pictures – chop out unnecessarily large areas of background and so on – and to rotate frames a degree at a time. (Watch out for programs that allow rotation only in huge 90° increments!)

Buyers' guide: Desktop publishing

- At the professional end of the market, you'll find **Quark Xpress** on most publishers' computers. (These computers are usually Apple-Macs, but Xpress actually runs faster on a PC of comparable specifications!) Slightly cheaper is **Adobe PageMaker**.

- There's a huge price difference between the best and the rest: in the more affordable price bracket are **Microsoft Publisher**, and the amazingly full-featured **Serif PagePlus**. The **Serif Publishing Suite** bundles PagePlus with DrawPlus and TypePlus (mentioned in the previous section) as a self-contained graphics and DTP package and is well worth a look.

- Successful DTP is harder to achieve on a standard 15-inch monitor. As you use the scroll-bars to see different parts of the page, you have to wait for the software to locate and draw each page element. If DTP is your thing, regard a 17-inch monitor as the minimum and a 20-inch monitor as a safer bet.

- As with any graphics-related application, the more RAM you have the better. You could find the going a bit slow with less than 16 Mb under Windows 95.

Presentation graphics

Presentations are not far removed from the desktop publishing documents we looked at in the previous section. The same combination of text and graphics is there, but presentations are primarily meant to be shown on screen rather than printed on paper so visual impact takes priority. Text tends to be in the form of headings, subheadings and bulleted lists or very short paragraphs. The name *presentations* gives a clue to the main purpose of this software: any time you have to get up in front of a bunch of people and announce a marketing strategy, explain a business plan or introduce a new product, you can create a new presentation that includes all the charts, graphs and pictures you need to show in the correct order.

Presentations are multiple-page files, with all the pages usually following a similar colour scheme and style. The pages are called **slides** and the finished presentation is often referred to as a **slide show**. You can print out all the slides on paper as **handouts** for your audience, or convert them to transparencies for overhead projectors or 35-mm slides for slide projectors.

Getting started

There are several ways to start work on a new presentation. You could start with a completely blank sheet, but unless you're both artistic *and* patient this isn't a favourite option. Method two is quite the reverse: programs such as **Microsoft PowerPoint** include whole presentations designed for particular uses (such as 'Communicating Bad News', with a mournful black background). All the slides you need are prepared and arranged in an order that should get the point across clearly. Just select the one that fits, read the tips and explanations on each slide and then replace them with your own personal text.

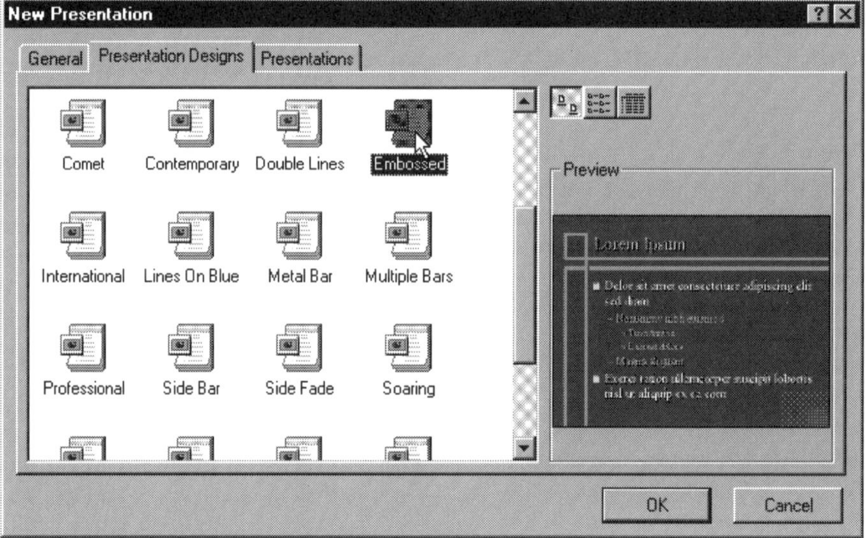

Figure 6.12 Choosing a style template for your presentation.

The third, and usual, way to begin is by choosing a style template for the presentation from those included with the program. There are usually plenty to choose from and most applications include a preview window like the one shown in Figure 6.12. If you later decide you don't like the choice you made here, you can apply a different style to your slides with just a couple of clicks.

TIP

Although the finished slide show will often be shown full screen, it's usual to work with a smaller representation of each slide (roughly 50 or 60 per cent) so that you can see the complete layout and still reach all the application's editing tools. At any time you can test a single slide, or all the slides you've added so far, to make sure the layout looks okay.

Once you've selected a style for the presentation, you'll usually see another dialog asking you to choose a layout for the first slide. Every time you want to add another slide to the presentation the same dialog will appear. The first slide would normally be a title slide, but other options might contain mixtures of charts, tables, bulleted lists, clip art and so on. You can also choose a blank slide that follows the selected style but has no layout detail.

Adding text and graphics

If you pick a slide with a predefined layout, you'll see several boxes that say 'Click here to add a title' or 'Click here to insert clip art', and it really is as simple as that! Just click and type in the text you want, or choose a piece of clip art from the library when it appears, and then move onto the next slide.

Although you'll rarely see a slide that says 'Click here to add a movie' you can add almost any type of file you wish. Presentation programs support OLE and DDE, so if you want to add an **.avi** video, a wave sound or a MIDI file you can do so. In some programs you can choose that the file plays as soon as its slide is displayed; in others you'll have to click or double-click its icon to play it.

Many presentation tools are similar to those you'd find in a DTP application: if you want to add more text to a slide just create a text box and start typing; if you want to add simple shapes and drawings you can do so.

▶ *Clip-art libraries are explained on p. 186.*

Adding effects

Any item on a slide is referred to as an **object**, whether it's a text box, drawing, chart or clip art. Each of these objects can have its own animation settings. First, you can choose which objects should be on the slide when it first appears, which should arrive later, and in which order they should arrive. These are known as **build** settings (because you're gradually building the slide) and one of the most fun aspects of builds is choosing *how* the objects should arrive. For example, you might choose to have each item in a bulleted list sliding onto the screen separately one after the other, accompanied by the sound of screeching tyres. Or you could choose to build the slide's title by making the letters appear one at a time to the sound of a typewriter.

If you want to add *different* effects to each line of a bulleted list, you'll have to place each line in a separate text box. Otherwise the effect you choose will apply to the whole list.

In programs designed for creating business presentations, your build choices will be limited. For example, you won't usually be able to specify a delay in seconds before an object appears, or choose how long it will take to fully appear. Similarly, you won't be able to specify how long it should stay on the screen and how long it should take to disappear. However, you'll usually be able to choose that the next object doesn't appear until you click the mouse.

Preparing the slide show

Once you've created all the slides you need for your presentation, the final step is to turn them into a working presentation. If you used a preset 'fill-in-the-blanks' presentation most of this work has been done for you. You might even have been so well prepared that you created the slides in the correct order, but there's still a couple of things you might need to do.

You'll usually be able to switch to a different view that shows thumbnails (tiny pictures) of each slide, similar to the one shown in Figure 6.13. To rearrange the order in which they'll be shown, just click on one and drag it to where you want it in the list. This is also the place where you'll fine-tune the running of the show. You can choose how long each slide should remain on the screen or opt to change slides with a mouse click (Figure 6.14), and choose **transitions** for each slide – special effects such as fades, wipes and dissolves – that determine how each slide should replace the previous one.

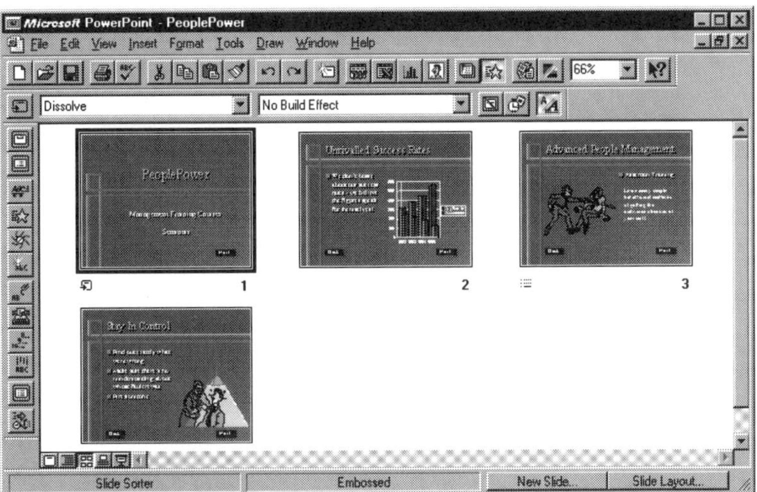

Figure 6.13 Fine tuning the slide show from the thumbnails view.

Business presentation packages also have pages for speakers' notes to help you plan the entire presentation as you go. With the notes printed out, you can run the slide show to time how long you need for each slide and have these timings automatically entered.

Running the show

One of the useful features of slide-show creation is that you can plan contingency actions: however carefully you think you've skirted it, some bright spark is sure to ask the question you didn't want to answer. Business presentation programs allow you to *hide* slides (that is, leave them out of the slide show) and bring them in only if you need to. By the same token, someone is sure to ask a question about something you dealt with four slides back, so it helps to be able to return to that slide.

TIP

Most presentations programs allow you to *export* your slide show as a complete file with a built-in viewer program that someone else can use on any PC. If you use this option, don't forget to *embed* all graphics and multimedia files you include in the show – if you *link* them they won't be included in the exported file!

To make this possible, business presentation programs have a small control-bar (either permanently displayed or optional) that allows you to pause the slide show, move to the next or previous slide, or choose a slide from the list. You may have other options such as drawing on the screen as if it were a chalkboard, and adding notes about points raised during your presentation. If your presentation is supposed to be completely self-contained you can choose to hide the pointer. This can be useful for presentations intended to run continuously and without supervision, perhaps on a PC sitting in the entrance hall of a trade fair.

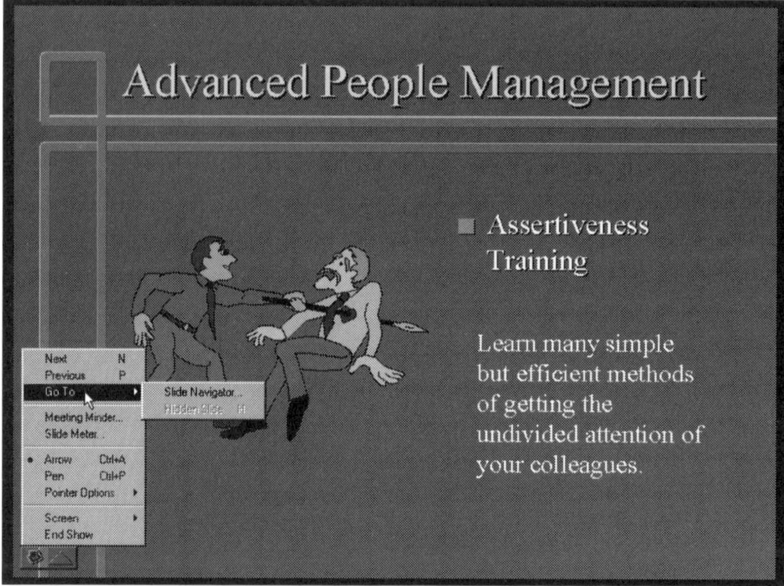

Figure 6.14 Using the mouse to control a business presentation.

Multimedia authoring

A separate, and rather more expensive, branch of presentation software is the *multimedia* presentation program, and the process is grandly referred to as **multimedia authoring**. Most of the creation methods are identical to those covered above, but the slide shows created are not intended for business presentations so there's rarely any support for speakers' notes, rehearsals and so on. Here's a quickfire list of just a few extras you *will* find in a full-featured multimedia presentation program:

- *Full multimedia support.* Not only can you add sound, MIDI and video files to these slides, you can choose exactly when they play and for how long.

- *Button controls.* You can add clickable buttons to slides that might give you a choice of slides to view next, play a multimedia clip, run a program, or reveal some other object not yet visible on the page. A single button might even start several of these actions at the same time. In some programs a button doesn't even have to *look* like a button – you could use a piece of clip art instead, or nominate several different areas of a large graphic to act as buttons.
- *Advanced builds.* Any object on the slide can have its own builds. You can choose exactly when the build begins and ends, and you can *unbuild* a slide by removing objects after a specified time using different effects.
- *Timeline.* The timeline is a common fine-tuning tool. Each object on the slide has its own line on the page calibrated in seconds according to the length of time the selected slide will remain on the screen. By placing markers at different points along the line you can choose exactly when an object's build should start and end (or when a media clip should play) and when the object should begin to disappear. Instead of having to specify an order for the different objects to appear, you can ensure that particular things will happen at exactly the same time.

Multimedia presentations are commonly used on magazine cover-mounted CDs to let you see the contents of the CD and install software with a single click. Just starting to appear, though with limited popularity so far, are CD-ROM-based magazines that use multimedia presentations instead of paper and you can click buttons instead of turning pages.

In the same way as business presentation packages, you can export these files as stand-alone programs so the possibilities for use are endless: if you're a musician or an artist you could mail out multimedia résumés; if you're selling software you could create interactive demos or tutorials for your program; if you're running an exhibition you could create an interactive map of each floor of the building to help people find their way around.

Buyers' guide: Presentations and multimedia authoring

- In the business presentations sphere, **Lotus Freelance** and **Microsoft PowerPoint** have got it well sewn up between them, both being well featured, reasonably priced and bundled with their respective Office suites. Both offer good quality preset-presentations and templates together with ease of use. Both applications can also publish slides directly to the World Wide Web in HTML format (see pp. 229–230).

- Multimedia authoring packages can cost as much as a full multimedia notebook PC with all the trimmings. King of the heap here is Macromedia's

Authorware, aimed at professional users. At the SoHo (Small office/Home office) end of things, the top choice is Gold Disk's accurately named **Astound**, followed by Digital Workshop's **Illuminatus**, which suffers slightly from the lack of a timeline in its current version.

- 8 Mb will cover a business presentation program running under Windows 95, but think in terms of 16 Mb minimum to run a multimedia authoring program. More RAM will ensure sharper builds and transitions, and help to ensure that actions intended to occur at the same time (such as a transition, a sound clip and an animation) really *do* happen together.

Office suites and Works applications

After reading the last few sections you might have built up a list of two or three or more types of software you want. If so, this is a good time to pause and look at another option – the integrated application or office suite. Instead of buying a bundle of separate software titles, you might be able to buy a single package that contains everything you need at a significantly lower price.

- *Office suites.* Often recognizable by the use of the word 'Office' somewhere in their names, these are collections of fully-featured applications, all of which are also available separately. The main selling point of Office suites is that the total package costs a lot less than you'd spend buying each item individually, but a few extras are thrown in for good measure. Office suites have added features that help you organize your work, share information between the different programs, and start or switch between each application easily.
- *Works applications.* These packages are known as **integrated applications** and include the word 'Works' in their names. Works software consists of a single all-in-one application that fulfils the same role as an Office suite in a smaller, cheaper package with fewer features. They are primarily aimed at non-professional users.

Office suite pros and cons

The main plus-point in buying an Office suite is price: if you need two or more professional-level applications you'll probably save money by buying the suite and gain another couple of applications and a few handy extras into the bargain. The second benefit is that each application will be carefully integrated – throughout the suite, the menus and toolbars follow a common layout to make the learning easier. This integration also helps you work with several applications at once. For example, you can quickly import names and addresses from the database into the word processor to create a mail-merge, or copy a chart from the spreadsheet into a business presentation.

On the negative side, Office suites are huge beasts: a typical installation might take 40–100 Mb of hard-disk space, and the power of these applications requires a lot more resources than a Works package. If you only need one top-level application (such as a good word processor) and you can make do with simpler spreadsheet and database features, there's no point in wasting money and hard-disk space on the full suite.

Works applications pros and cons

There are several simple reasons for the popularity of Works software: the package is compact, light on disk space and resource requirements, easy to use and gives great-looking results. Like the Office suites, each element is tightly integrated with all the others and uses common tools and menus. Although a Works package is a single application, it has a multiple document interface (MDI) so it's easy to have a database open in one window and a spreadsheet in another to compare or copy information between them. Finally, of course, the price: integrated applications are between one-quarter and one-third of the price of an Office suite.

If you buy the Works software and later decide you need the Office suite, you should be able to buy the **upgrade** version rather than pay full price, so you're usually not risking any money by picking the smaller of the two to learn with.

There's not much to be said against Works packages – because they're cheap it's not really a disaster if you decide you need something more powerful six months later. Indeed, you may decide you just need a more powerful word processor and go buy one, but continue to use the other elements of the Works application.

Which Office suite?

The two big players in the Office suites league are **Microsoft Office** and **Lotus SmartSuite**. Here's a closer look at what each contains:

Figure 6.15 The **Microsoft Office** shortcut-bar.

Microsoft Office

This is the top-selling Office suite, which is probably why most of its constituent applications also hold the top spot. **Office** comes in two flavours, *Standard* and *Professional*. Both contain **Word** (word processor), **Excel** (spreadsheet), **PowerPoint** (business presentations) and **Schedule+** (personal organizer). The Professional version also includes **Access** (relational, programmable database). These can be accessed from the **shortcut-bar** (shown in Figure 6.15) which docks at one side of the Windows desktop and works just like Windows 95's task-bar. You can add your own shortcuts to any program or folder as buttons on the bar. Another addition is **Binder**, which lets you group collections of related documents together in one file and switch between them in a single window. All the applications are powerful but easy to use. The weak link in the current version is the clunky Schedule+, due to be replaced in **Office 97**. You'll need 40–50 Mb disk space to install the Standard version, and 16 Mb RAM to work with two or more Office applications at the same time with reasonable speed.

Figure 6.16 Lotus SmartSuite's SmartCenter bar with drop-down 'drawers'.

Lotus SmartSuite

SmartSuite beats Microsoft Office on price, and comes in one all-in version. Applications consist of **WordPro** (word processor), **1-2-3** (spreadsheet), **Freelance** (business presentations), **Organizer** (personal organizer) and **Approach** (relational, programmable database). SmartSuite has a similar shortcut-bar (Figure 6.16) to that used by Office, which follows a file-cabinet metaphor: various 'drawers' open to display shortcuts to applications, shortcuts to documents, help-file icons, an address book and a calendar. Another quick-start option is **SuiteStart** which places icons for each application in Windows 95's Tray. A clever little extra is **ScreenCam** which can record everything you do on screen, play it back and save it as a file, making a useful tool for demonstrations and tutorials. Be prepared to sacrifice over 100 Mb of disk space when you install SmartSuite, and consider more than 16 Mb RAM – you may still find it runs rather slowly with 24 Mb.

Which Works application?

The two leaders in this field are **Microsoft Works** and **ClarisWorks**. Of these, once again, Microsoft's offering is the biggest seller by virtue of being bundled with most new PCs as part of the ubiquitous 'free software' package.

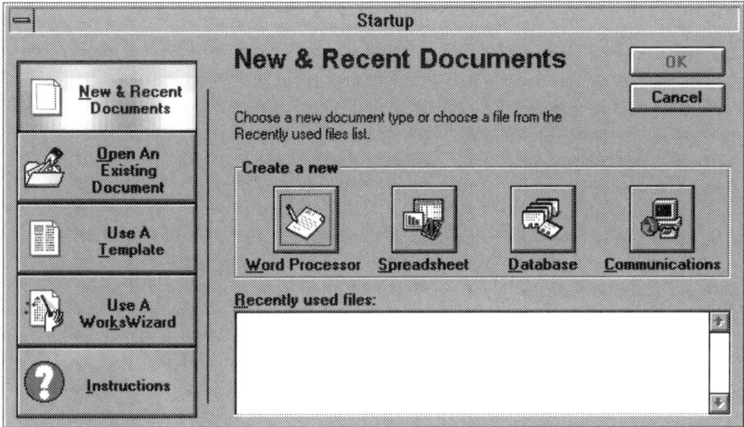

Figure 6.17 The **Microsoft Works Startup** dialog.

Microsoft Works

When you first start Works, you're presented with the dialog shown in Figure 6.17, from which you can choose what to do. Works includes a word processor, spreadsheet and flat-file database, each of which is easy to use and gives good results. The fourth possibility is Communications which allows you to connect to a remote computer or BBS (bulletin board service) using your modem. Like all Office suites and integrated applications, Works offers a huge collection of templates that you can use to get started on particular types of document, or you can use a **WorksWizard** which asks you simple questions about the design, layout and content of the document you want to create and puts it together for you. Each element supports OLE and DDE to let you create impressive-looking compound documents easily. You also get several extra applets including **WordArt** and **Draw** to add graphics to your documents. Works will take roughly 5 Mb disk space and run quite happily with 8 Mb RAM under Windows 95.

▶ *Turn to p. 190 for more details on Microsoft's **WordArt** applet.*

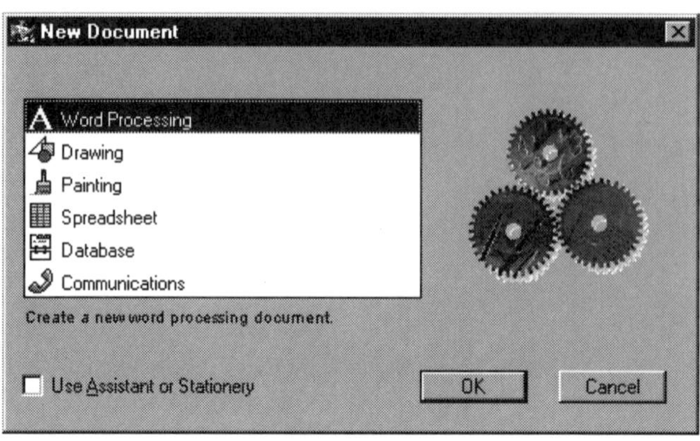

Figure 6.18 Starting work in ClarisWorks.

ClarisWorks

As with Microsoft Works, running the application will present you with a dialog to choose what type of file you want to create, but the choices here are wider: **ClarisWorks** includes both Paint and Draw programs. Either double-click a document type or check the 'Use Assistant' box to work from one of a range of templates. The usual four components are included – word processor, spreadsheet, flat-file database and communications terminal – but the inclusion of the two graphics elements makes for great flexibility. In general terms, the features included are superior to those found in Microsoft Works, and the Paint component could give a few lessons to Windows' **Paint**. ClarisWorks also supports simple slide-show presentations which can use any type of information the package can handle. One drawback, for mouse fans, is that toolbars are 'floating' blocks of buttons termed **Shortcuts** that can't be docked at the top of the screen out of the way. Despite its increased capabilities, ClarisWorks will grab even less hard-disk space than Microsoft Works.

Buyers' guide: Office suites and Works software

- If you need two or more powerful, full-featured applications, an Office suite is a sensible and cost-effective choice. It'll take a large chunk of disk space, but if these are the applications you'll spend most of your time using, this shouldn't matter too much. Make sure you've got at least 16 Mb RAM (more for **Lotus SmartSuite**) to keep things moving at a reasonable speed.
- **Microsoft Office** is the clear winner in terms of popularity and sales, and it's neat, fast and easy to use. However, if you need a database manager you'll need to pay extra for the *Professional* edition (or buy one separately). **Lotus SmartSuite** grabs extra points for including a high-quality

database manager, but promptly loses them again for being extremely slow in operation. **Corel Office Professional** rivals SmartSuite in price and features and is worth a look if you need the inclusion of database facilities at a more reasonable price than Microsoft can manage.

- Integrated applications are far more streamlined in terms of disk space and RAM requirements and are ideal for anyone needing to produce quality output quickly and simply. **ClarisWorks** is a great, flexible package as long as you don't mind those floating toolbars; **Microsoft Works** adds its graphics capabilities in external applets that you can use from any OLE-compliant application and has the benefit of getting you onto the upgrade path for **Microsoft Office** if you have a sneaky feeling that that's what you might need at some future date.

Quickfire software

Over the last few sections we've looked at some of the most common types of software found on the average computer. But in the PC world, as elsewhere, if there's a market for it, there's a product to meet that market – the list of software categories is almost endless. So, moving into quickfire mode, here's a brief rundown of some of the other tricks your PC can do if you feed it the right software!

Personal organizers

The software personal organizer is the computerized version of those little leather binders you can carry around that contain diaries, addresses, notes and so on. The big differences are that the software version is usually cheaper (no leather involved!) and isn't as easy to lose. In geek-speak, the software organizer is known as a **PIM**, short for Personal Information Manager. One of the best (and coincidentally the cheapest) is Starfish Software's **Sidekick**, closely followed by **Lotus Organizer** (included in the SmartSuite Office package) which follows the FiloFax metaphor right down to animated page turning (Figure 6.19).

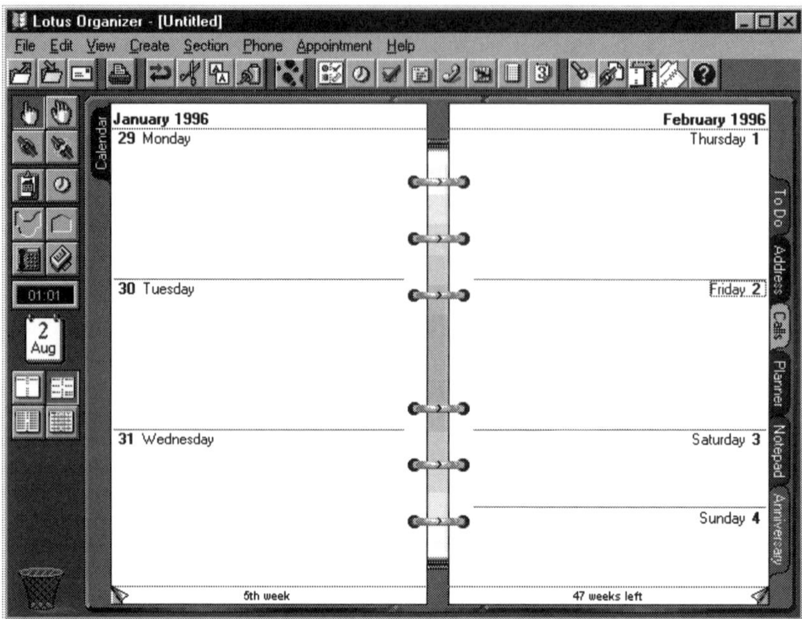

Figure 6.19 Separate tabbed book sections in **Lotus Organizer**.

The features you'll find in these programs include an appointments diary, address and phone book, To Do lists with priority planning, year-planners, and automatic phone-dialling. You can also set an alarm to sound at a preset interval before appointments to remind you, and print out your appointments in organizer-sized pages to carry around in your leather-bound version.

Accounts software

For simple accounting, just adding up lists of income and expenditure, a spreadsheet program can do just fine. But if you have monthly and quarterly standing orders, income paid directly into your bank account, loans and other complications it's easy to lose track of your finances between one statement and the next. Accounts packages allow you to enter all these details once and will then keep the totals balanced for you automatically – you're only job is to remember to enter everything necessary at the start.

The two biggest players in accounts software are Intuit's **Quicken** and **Microsoft Money**. Both are cheap, and can track a variety of bank, building society and credit card accounts, as well as loans and investments. Of the two, **Quicken** is the winner for its ability to handle VAT, but if you don't need to bother about VAT you'll find **Microsoft Money** easier to set up and use. For professional accounting, one of the most popular programs is **Sage Instant Accounting**.

File compression utilities

Once in a while, especially if you download files from the Internet or BBSs (bulletin board services), you'll come across files with the extension **.zip**. These are known as **archives**, and they contain one or more files compressed to take up less space (and thus download faster). There are actually several other types of archive, less frequently encountered, with the extensions **.lzh**, **.arj**, **.tar** and **.arc** but each works in a similar way.

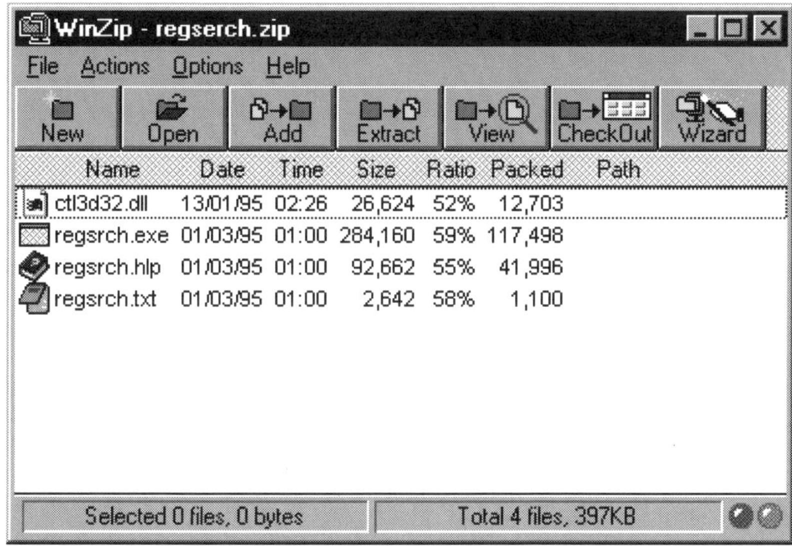

Figure 6.20 **WinZip** displaying the contents of an archive.

In order to decompress (**extract**) the files from an archive, or create new archives, you need a program capable of working with these files, and the undoubted leader in this field is the shareware utility **WinZip** from Nico Mak Computing (shown in Figure 6.20). This can create and open many different types of archive and integrates itself neatly with Windows 95, although a Windows 3.1 version is also available.

Anti-virus software

Viruses are small programs created by people with warped minds. In the worst cases, if a virus finds its way onto your disk it can turn all your files into meaningless gobbledegook in next to no time. Less harmful viruses might just play annoying pranks such as making your PC go 'beep' once a month.

The term 'virus' comes from the way these programs work: they can clone themselves automatically and spread themselves around to infect any disk they come into contact with, often by inserting themselves into an executable file. If you never connect to a network, download files from the Internet or elsewhere, or use files given to you on floppy disk, you're probably quite safe. The odds are that you do at least one of these things once in a while, so you're at risk.

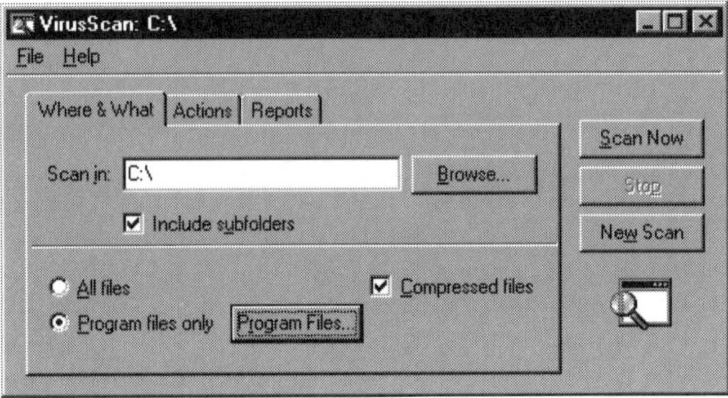

Figure 6.21 The simple but effective **McAfee VirusScan**.

To avert disaster you need an anti-virus utility such as **Dr Solomon's Anti-Virus Toolkit** or **McAfee VirusScan** pictured in Figure 6.21. This will check the boot area of your hard disk every time you switch on your PC to make sure no viruses have wormed their way into your system files. You can also run regular checks of your entire hard disk, check floppy disks before reading any files from them, check any application before running it and (very importantly) any zipped-archive downloaded from a remote computer. Apart from merely discovering viruses, the software should be able to stamp them out before they do any damage, provided you don't skimp on its use.

TIP

In order to work effectively, anti-virus programs need to know what to look for, and new viruses are being discovered all the time. For maximum safety, make sure you update your software regularly according to the details in the manuals.

Replacement shells

Elsewhere in this book we've mentioned that it's possible to edit the **SHELL=** line in your **System.ini** file and change your shell to **Winfile.exe**, **Taskman.exe** or something else if you really can't live with the Program Manager or Explorer interfaces. But a whole industry has grown up to provide replacement shell applications, especially for Windows 3.1 whose Program Manager is almost universally disliked.

Although there are a great many offerings in this arena, together with a vast number of small, simple toolbars that sit on the desktop and offer basic program-launching facilities, there are three clear leaders in this field: **PC Tools** and **Norton Desktop** (both from Symantec) and Starfish Software's **Dashboard**. Another popular shell is **Microsoft BOB**, a family-oriented pictorial desktop consisting of separate 'rooms' full of intuitive clickable objects

▶ *For more details about changing the Windows shell application, turn to p. 279.*

Shareware

Rather than being a type of program, the shareware concept is a way of selling software. Because the cost of packaging, advertising and distributing programs is sky-high, many software programmers and companies allow their creations to be distributed on magazine cover-disks, bulletin board services or the Internet.

The benefit for the consumer is that you get the opportunity to try out the software before you pay for it. A secondary benefit is that the software is usually a lot cheaper than a similar commercial product would be, but the understanding is that you *should* pay for it if you choose to continue using it beyond the specified trial period – this is known as **registering** the software. In return for registering you'll normally receive the latest version plus a manual, and be entitled to free upgrades as they become available. Here are a few variations on the shareware theme:

- *Postcard ware.* Instead of actually paying for the software you send the author a picture-postcard of your town. The author still retains full copyright.
- *Freeware.* Once again the author retains copyright, but this time it doesn't even cost you a postcard to continue use!
- *Nag-ware.* Every time you use the software, a dialog will appear that has to be clicked to make it vanish. This may appear every few minutes, forcing you to either give up or register.

- *Time-limited.* This is a common method employed by larger companies eager to generate sales of more expensive applications. You have full use of the program for a period of around 30 days, after which time it will cease to run.
- *Save-disabled.* The software has no nag-screens or time-limitations, but you won't be able to save or print any of the documents you create.
- *Beta versions.* As new software is developed it goes through various phases. Beta versions are early but working versions of products given away free for anyone to use at their own risk. The benefit for the user is that of having the very latest software; in return, you're expected to report any bugs or problems you experience with the software in some detail to help the company identify and eradicate them. This is known as **beta testing**.

Working with multimedia

What is multimedia?

Multimedia is a rather loosely defined term (and is becoming more so all the time), but it basically refers to the combining of text, graphics, animation, sound and video. A 'Multimedia PC' should, by definition, be able to cope with all of these, but multimedia is an all-encompassing term – recent advances mean that a PC can now act as a TV or radio with the right expansion cards, and that's just more multimedia, so should you feel that your expensive machine is now *not* a multimedia PC because you can't watch *Neighbours* on it?

The most important thing, as always, is what you really want to use the PC for. The main use of multimedia is in software titles such as CD-ROM-based encyclopaedias and references, presentations (as covered on p. 197) and games. Using OLE and DDE you can create 'multimedia documents' – compound documents using embedded or linked graphics, movies and sounds. But the PC is more than just a 'playback' machine. With the right software (and, in some cases, hardware) you can get your hands dirty with multimedia at a more fundamental level. Here's a brief introduction to working with some of these multimedia elements.

Digital audio

Digital audio involves recording sound in much the same way that you would with an ordinary tape-recorder. This is known as **analog** recording. The big difference is that tape is an unreliable medium – the tape heads are in contact during playback and recording and gradually wear away at the tape (or chew it up completely!). The PC's method involves listening to the incoming sound thousands of times every second and converting what it hears into a sequence of numbers (hence *digital* audio). And numbers are reliable: you can keep them for years, edit them, cut and paste them, and they don't suffer any ill-effects.

As long as you have a soundcard (and speakers to play back the result), simple digital recording can be done with Windows' own **Sound Recorder**, either direct from an audio CD, or from a microphone or some other input device plugged into the appropriate input on your soundcard. However, as you already have the soundcard, you'll almost certainly have a more sophisticated application bundled with it with better editing facilities.

When recording digital sound in Sound Recorder, double-click the Tray's Volume Control and make sure the correct input-line channel is high enough. Mute any inputs you're not using to prevent unwanted noise creeping in.

On a professional level, **hard-disk recording** (HDR) is beginning to replace the multitrack analog recording-studio due to its editing flexibility and superior sound quality. This needs a powerful PC with as much RAM as you can shovel into it and, vitally, a large and permanent swapfile. Dedicated HDR software is expensive, and requires a fast disk drive and extra hardware. A cheaper route to take is the **MIDI sequencer**: professional-level sequencers are affordable, easy to use, and can handle multiple tracks of digital sound in combination with MIDI data.

▶ *Turn to p. 368 for more on Windows' Sound Recorder accessory. Skip back to p. 67 to read up on soundcards.*

MIDI

Rather than recording *sound* in the literal sense, MIDI records a collection of instructions. These instructions are then sent to the hardware that contains the sounds to tell it what to do. In a PC this hardware is usually a soundcard, but you can buy a cheap MIDI interface card to connect other devices, such as synthesizers, and use their sounds instead (or as well).

Windows doesn't provide any method of recording MIDI data; Media Player can only play back finished files. For this you need a piece of software called a

sequencer. You'll also need a MIDI-equipped keyboard, guitar, drum kit or similar to play the music into the PC. (You can enter all this data 'by hand', as in a word processor, but it's not a fun experience!)

Two of the top MIDI sequencers, both of which can handle digital audio as well as MIDI data, are Twelve Tone Systems' **Cakewalk Pro Audio** (Figure 6.22) and Steinberg's **Cubase**. Steinberg also offer a sequencer with more advanced digital audio features called **Cubase Audio**.

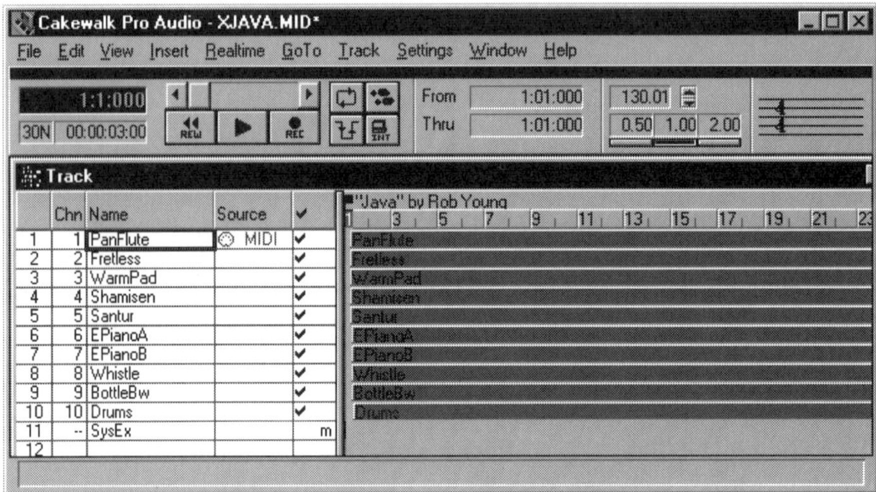

Figure 6.22 The popular **Cakewalk Pro Audio** MIDI sequencer.

Animation

Animation is a more advanced branch of straightforward art and graphics. Instead of creating one picture you create a whole bunch of them and display them quickly one after another. There are many ways to create these pictures: one is to use a simple paint or draw package to create lots of bitmap or vector graphics; another is to take photographs of your subject (perhaps using clay models) with a digital camera such as the **Kodak DC20** or **Canon PowerShot** and sharpen them up with photo-editing software like **Adobe PhotoDeluxe** or **Serif PhotoPlus**.

The trick then, of course, is to string each picture (or *frame*) together to produce an image that appears to be moving, and create a suitable soundtrack. A good suite of programs for this final process (which also includes tools to help in the creation of the soundtrack and images) is **Autodesk Animator Studio**. Common animation formats are **.flc** and **.fli**, but you can also save your creation in Video For Windows (**.avi**) format. As in all graphical fields, 16 Mb RAM should be regarded as a minimum.

Digital video

To record and edit digital video you'll need a video camera, a simple 16-bit soundcard if you want to capture the live soundtrack, and a fair-sized chunk of free hard-disk space. To playback video on your PC smoothly at full screen you need an MPEG card, and there are plenty of these around at reasonable prices. However, to *record* video you'll need the more expensive and less common variety that has recording capability. Compatibility between PC, soundcard, video camera and the video-capture (MPEG) card is imperative – make sure you do your homework before buying anything at all!

JARGONBUSTER

Full-motion video

A term used to describe 'live-action' video shot in real-time, as distinct from *stop-motion video*, in which you'd shoot a single frame at a time and later join them together (or *animate* them) to create a full-motion effect.

To edit and construct a video from the footage you've shot, you'll need a package such as **Asymetrix Digital Video Producer** or **Adobe Premiere**. For a much-increased price there are a few applications in the professional sphere that can add fades and other video effects, titling and graphical overlays, working in tandem with another expansion card.

▶ *For more on sound, MIDI and video file-formats, skip back to pp. 141–142.*

Educational and reference software

The PC's recently acquired multimedia capabilities have certainly added to the enjoyment and friendliness of computing. For example, Windows 95 itself makes full use of multimedia elements by showing small animations while something dull is happening like file copying, and playing wave sounds to coincide with so-called 'system events', as well as having an intuitive clickable interface. But multimedia, in combination with the CD-ROM, has more than just aesthetic value.

There are many educational and reference CD-ROM titles available, and the thing many of them have in common is that they're derived from books. But the CD-ROM has huge advantages over a book: you can quickly search for particular text or topics, and click on words and phrases to follow cross-references. There will also be sound, video and animation clips to illustrate a topic more clearly. Many children's educational titles take an innovative approach to teaching, often using interactive games and puzzles to disguise the 'learning' aspect.

Encyclopaedias

The most popular of the CD-ROM encyclopaedias is **Microsoft Encarta**, shown in Figure 6.23, which is now produced in a 'World English' edition. Encarta has almost 30 000 articles that you can browse alphabetically or by subject; sound, video and MIDI clips; and easy searching and cross-referencing. There's also a Timeline that places world events into historical context, a World Atlas that lets you zoom in on an area through several levels, and many more handy features and locator-tools. A major benefit for Internet users is that monthly updates can be downloaded from the Microsoft Network or Microsoft's Web site.

Figure 6.23 Microsoft's Encarta multimedia encyclopaedia.

The two other main contenders in the encyclopaedia field are **Grolier's Multimedia Encyclopaedia** and the British-designed **Hutchison's Multimedia Encyclopaedia**, both of which are priced similarly to Encarta. Both offer similar search, atlas and timeline tools, but are slower in use and offer shorter articles and fewer multimedia clips. Grolier's has the benefit of offering updates via CompuServe and the Internet. It also contains American spelling, contents and narration.

General reference

There is a huge number of reference CD-ROMs available relating to various subjects, so here's a pick of some of the best.

- *Bookshelf.* A Microsoft product that contains electronic versions of six reference books including thesaurus, dictionary, almanac and dictionary of quotations.
- *William Shakespeare: The Complete Works.* Just about every word ever written by the bard, from shopping lists to historical plays, is in this CD-ROM by Andromeda Interactive, but the real value is its line-notes, background, search facilities, and just about every tool you could ever need for reference or study.
- *Cinemania.* Microsoft's multimedia guide to the movies with reviews, clips, cast-lists and recommendations based upon your tastes.
- *Music Central.* A rock and pop music multimedia reference from Microsoft. Comprehensive in its choice of performers and typically attractive and easy to use, but with comparatively fewer multimedia clips than other Microsoft titles.
- *Dr Schueler's Medical Advisor.* An excellent information and diagnosis provider for all things medical from Health Perfect.
- *3D Atlas.* A multimedia world atlas from Electronic Arts featuring videos, virtual reality tours, quizzes and statistics.

Educational titles

The best educational titles are the ones that children will enjoy using and won't actually *know* they're educational unless you tell them! Above all this means that the software must be interactive and absorbing, offering more than a book or video. Since CD-ROMs are rarely cheap it's worth reading reviews and asking teachers and other parents before buying, but here's a brief selection of popular titles.

- Look out for Dorling Kindersley titles such as *My First Amazing World Explorer* and *My First Incredible Amazing Dictionary.* There's always plenty going on to keep young children interested and almost everything reacts to a mouse-click.

- Broderbund specialize in children's education titles, and have an excellent range of titles in their 'Living Books' series including *Maths Workshop* and *Where In The World Is Carmen Sandiego?*
- Microsoft's *Magic School Bus* series of titles covers a range of subjects such as the Solar System and the Human Body.
- Electronic Arts produce a series of funny, but fascinating, titles such as *The Farm* and *The Airport.*

CHAPTER 7

The Internet

Getting on line

What is the Internet?

The Internet is an *inter*national *net*work of thousands of computers around the world, connected by telephone lines and modems. Although 'internet' has become a major buzzword of the 1990s (along with associated terms like 'cyberspace' and 'web-surfing') the 'Net itself has been around since the 1960s, dreamt up by the US government as a way to allow military and academic establishments to exchange information and files.

In recent years, software companies have designed friendly graphic programs to make all these facilities easy to use once you're connected, and companies have appeared providing easy access to the Internet and its facilities. By dialling in to one of these companies' computers you're connected to the network and can exchange data with computers on the other side of the world for the price of a local phone-call.

What can I use it for?

You've almost certainly come across the phrase 'information superhighway' and it highlights the main value of the Internet. Vast numbers of companies, organizations, research establishments and libraries are connected, offering information on every subject under the sun.

Apart from information gathering, you can exchange e-mail messages with any Internet user in the world, download (copy) files and programs from a remote computer to your own, chat in real time to other users by typing and receiving messages on your screen, buy products from online shopping malls, join e-mail-style discussion groups on topics that interest you, and too much more to list.

What do I need?

First, of course, you need a computer. To take full advantage of the 'Net's increasingly graphical nature, as well as the easy-to-use software available, you'll need to be running Windows 3.1 or 95. You won't need an unusually fast processor or enormous quantities of RAM, so you can regard a 486DX100 with 8 Mb as a safe minimum. To make the most of recent features of the World Wide Web it's worth having a soundcard and speakers along with a display adapter that has at least 1 Mb VRAM, but you can add these anytime you want to.

Second, you need a modem (see p. 72) and a telephone line to plug it into. Bear in mind that no one will be able to call you while you're using the modem so you might choose to install a second line to use for Internet access if you find yourself becoming addicted.

Finally you need to gain access to the Internet itself. Companies specialize in providing links to the Internet via their own computers and there are two ways to do this:

- Connect through an online service such as **CompuServe**, **America Online** (AOL) or the **Microsoft Network** (MSN). This is simple, immediate and requires almost no setting up, but it's a more expensive option.
- Connect through a local **Internet Access Provider** (IAP). There could be a certain amount of initial setting-up needed and you might not be able to connect immediately if the ISP has to process your subscription or send you software on disk, but your online time will be cheaper.

Figure 7.1 Getting on line with CompuServe's WinCIM software.

Using an online service

If you have Windows 95 you can just double-click the **Microsoft Network** icon on the desktop, follow the instructions to subscribe and get on line straight away. Other services give away their software free and the routine is just as simple. You can telephone the service to ask for the software or, in the case of **CompuServe** (Figure 7.1) and **America Online**, you'll find it regularly appearing on PC-magazine cover disks.

TIP

Most online services give you a free trial membership period and make it very easy to sign up. It isn't always obvious how you can *cancel* the subscription if you don't like it enough to start paying for it when your time's up. Make hunting down these details one of your first jobs when you're connected, just in case!

Online services give full access to the Internet, bundling all the software you need together in one automatically installed package. You'll also be assigned (or be able to choose) an e-mail address. In addition to standard Internet access, the software gives access to a range of extra services: you'll usually be able to join discussion groups; get support from software and hardware companies; check news, TV, weather and share-price listings; and browse for particular files or information.

All the details above, taken on their own, make online services the outright winners in the Internet-connectivity race. The downside is the price. As well as the cost of your phone calls (added to your telephone bill like any other phone call), you'll have to pay a monthly subscription charge plus an hourly rate. As most services allow a few hours' free connection per month, online services can be very cheap if you limit your connection time, but once you exceed the free period (and it's easily done when exploring the World Wide Web or downloading files) the cost can rocket.

Whether you choose an online service or an IAP, make sure you can connect by dialling a *local* number. The proliferation of these services means that it should never be necessary to dial outside your local area.

Using an Internet Access Provider

There are countless IAPs to choose from and most charge a single monthly subscription rate (plus a one-off setting-up charge) and allow unlimited access with no extra fees. The monthly charge will be higher than that for one of the online services, but this is a far cheaper option to take if you expect to be connected for more than a few hours per month.

You can usually set up an account with an IAP by telephone with a credit-card number. In some cases you might have to wait for software to be sent to you; in others you may be able to connect to their computer using Windows' **Terminal** or **HyperTerminal** to download the software. If the software is to be sent to you, it should be pre-configured (although it's always worth checking!). This means the company should ask you questions about your computer and the type of connection you'd like and make all the right settings in the software; when it arrives you just need to install it like any other program. If you're asked to choose between a **SLIP** (Serial Line Internet Protocol) or a **PPP** (Point-to-Point Protocol) connection, *always* choose the PPP connection – it's better, and much easier to configure (especially in Windows 95).

If the software isn't pre-configured you'll need to set it up yourself, but most IAPs will be happy to help if you get stuck (since the alternative is that you might just give up and cancel!). There are two aspects to getting connected. First you have to set up a TCP/IP (Transmission Control Protocol/Internet Protocol) stack for your computer to enable it to handle the transmission and reception of data over the Internet. Second, you have to set up the connection itself so that your software knows which number to dial.

Setting up an Internet connection

Let us now have a quick look at the routines for Windows 95 and Windows 3.1.

Windows 95

1. Go to Control Panel/Network. Click **Add**, then click **Protocol** and click **Add**.
2. Choose **Microsoft** in the left pane and **TCP/IP** in the right and click **OK**.
3. Click **Add**, choose **Adapter** and, in the same way, click **Microsoft** and **Dial-Up Adapter** and click **OK**.
4. Click **Dial-Up Adapter/Properties/Bindings**, make sure the **TCP/IP** box is checked. Click **OK** twice and restart the computer when prompted.
5. Go back to the Network applet, click **TCP/IP** and **Properties**. If your provider gave you an IP Address go to the **IP Address** tab, check **Specify an IP Address** enter your IP Address and Subnet Mask. Enter the DNS details you were given on the **DNS** tab.
6. Finally you need to create the connection itself from the **Dial-Up Networking** folder in My Computer. (If you don't have this folder you need to install Dial-Up Networking using Control Panel's Add/Remove Programs applet, and clicking **Windows Setup/Communications/Details**, checking the box and clicking **OK**.) Double-click the **Make New Connection** icon and fill in the connection details provided by your IAP.
7. For ease of use, drag the new icon you've just created onto the desktop to create a shortcut to it (or place one on the **Start** menu). When you double-click the icon a dialog will appear like the one shown in Figure 7.2 to let you know when the connection has been made and keep you posted on your total connection time.

Figure 7.2 A successful connection with Dial-Up Networking.

Windows 3.1

Windows 3.1 doesn't come with its own TCP/IP software so you'll need to install Winsock software (such as **Trumpet Winsock**) that handles the task. This should be provided by your IAP. Follow the installation instructions included with Winsock and then follow these steps:

1. Use **System Editor** to open Autoexec.bat and add the path of your Winsock directory (usually **C:\Winsock**) to the SET PATH= line, remembering to add a semi-colon after the preceding path-entry. Click **File/Save** and close System Editor.
2. Double-click the Winsock icon in Program Manager. A dialog will open displaying text boxes and check boxes. Enter the details you were given by your IAP into the appropriate boxes and ignore the rest. Make sure you check the correct box for SLIP or PPP connection, along with the COM port to which your modem is connected.
3. Click **OK** and you'll see Winsock's terminal window. For the setup to take effect you'll have to go to **File/Exit** and then restart Winsock.
4. Click the **Dialler** menu and click **Login**. In the three dialogs that appear one at a time, enter the phone number of your IAP's computer, your user name and your password.
5. If all goes according to plan, Winsock will connect to your IAP and you'll see a message like Connect 38400 appear. Press *Esc* and you're connected.
6. If instead you see a message like **Script Aborted** you have two options. One is to choose **Dialler/Manual Login** and type **ATD** followed by the phone number to dial and then try to enter the details required by the IAP's computer as the prompts appear. The second is to ask your IAP for a **login script** to automate the process.

TIP

A useful thing to do early on is to send an e-mail message to yourself as a tryout (partly to check you've got your e-mail address right before you start handing it out to friends and colleagues!). It won't necessarily arrive immediately though, so check back after an hour or two.

What next?

Once you've connected to the IAP's computer you're connected to the Internet, but you won't feel the earth move when it happens! To achieve anything at all useful you'll need to run particular programs that will let you send and receive e-mail, download files, or browse the World Wide Web, so let's take a look at some of the Internet's offerings and the software you can use to access them.

The World Wide Web

The World Wide Web (also known as the *Web* or *WWW*) is big news, to the point that you could easily believe it *is* the Internet. In fact the Web is the Internet's new baby and it's a far cry from the unfriendly text-based Internet that had to be navigated prior to the 1990s. The Web provides an intuitive and highly graphical means of finding your way through millions of pages of information on thousands of computers known as **web-servers**.

A 'page' is a single document that can be any length, like a document in a word processor. Pages can contain text, graphics, sound and video clips, and, more recently, advanced effects and controls made possible by new programming languages such as **Java** and **ActiveX**. The most important aspect of the Web is the ability to move around it easily, and this is done by clicking on **hypertext links**. These links are usually words or phrases underlined and highlighted in a different colour from the text around them which, when clicked, will open a different page or lead you to a page on a different web site, possibly on a different continent.

The web browser

To surf the World Wide Web you'll need a piece of software called a **web browser**. The choice in this department really comes down to just two: **Netscape Navigator** (Figure 7.3) or **Microsoft Internet Explorer**. Both are roughly equal in terms of speed, usability and features and both can be downloaded free of charge from their respective web sites (see pp. 244 and 246), so you could even try both to see which you prefer!

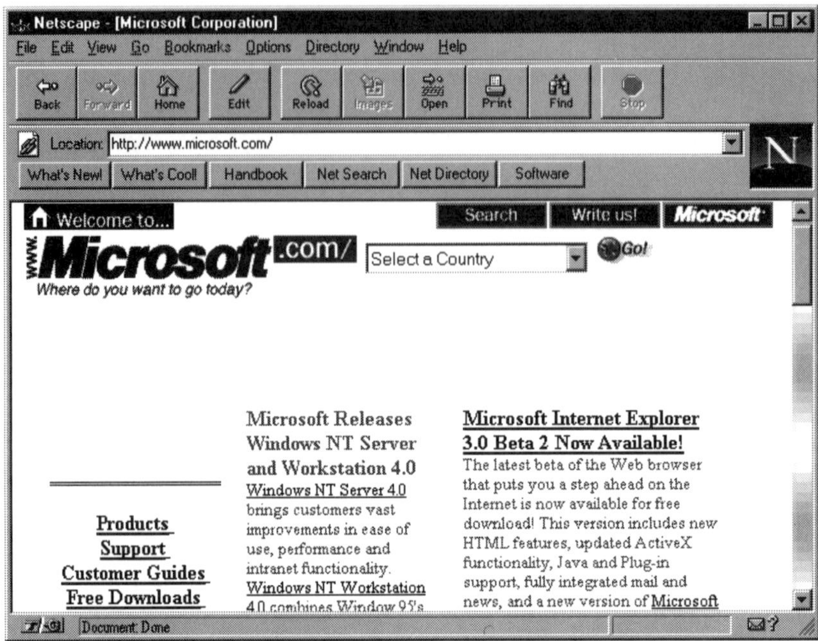

Figure 7.3 Cruising the World Wide Web with Netscape Navigator.

If you want to move to a specific page you can type its **address** into the box on the browser's toolbar and press *Enter*. Web addresses always begin **http://** (short for HyperText Transfer Protocol) as an indication to the browser that it will be receiving a web page. What comes after that can vary, but many UK companies' addresses are in the form **http://www.company-name.co.uk** and US company addresses in the form **http://www.company-name.com**. Other elements that crop up in web addresses are **gov** for government, **ac** or **edu** for colleges and universities, **org** for organisations, and easily recognizable country abbreviations. These addresses work in the same way as paths to folders and files on your own computer, so the full address of a page might be **http://www.company.com/index/products/gadget.htm**. (Note that web addresses use *forward-slashes* in their paths.) Web addresses are also known as **URLs**, short for Uniform Resource Locators.

Here are a few things worth knowing about the Web and browsers:

- Use the **Forward** and **Back** buttons to skip back and forth between pages you've already visited this session.
- Hypertext links referring to pages you've already visited will be a different colour from other links to save you clicking them again in the expectation of finding something new.

- You can stop a page loading at any time by clicking the **Stop** button or pressing *Esc*. Pages load more quickly if you go to the **Options** menu and turn off the display of graphics.
- Browsers use **Cache** folders on your hard disk to store pages you view so that if you return to them some time later they can be loaded from your own disk rather being downloaded again. Use the **Reload** or **Refresh** button to force the page to be downloaded again if you believe it's been changed since your last viewing.
- Beginners often overlook the menu-bar in browsers, but you have many options hidden away here including standard Cut/Copy/Paste facilities, and the ability to save a page as plain text or in its original HTML format (see below).
- If you visit a page you think might be useful in future, you can add its URL to your **Favorites** or **Bookmarks** menu and return to it any time with a single click.
- There are **search-engines** on the Web that help you find information quickly (see p. 245 for their URLs). Just type in one or more words and press *Return* to see a hypertext list of pages that match. Clicking the **Search** button on your browser's toolbar will take you to one of these pages; you can reconfigure it yourself if you'd prefer this button to lead you to a *different* search-engine, or indeed any page at all.
- From the **File** menu you can open a second (or third, or fourth . . .) browser window to let you read a page in one window as other pages are downloading.

Other browser tricks

Your browser will usually turn out to be your most important piece of Internet software. Not just because you'll spend so much time on the World Wide Web either – you can use this program for your other 'Net-related needs. To connect to an FTP (File Transfer Protocol) site you can simply type **ftp://** followed by the site address; to connect to a Gopher site type **gopher://** followed by the site address.

▶ *For more on FTP and Gopher (among others) turn to pp. 236 and 238.*

Publish your own pages

Making pages available on the World Wide Web is known as **publishing** them, and there are several things you'll need to do this. Chiefly you'll need space on a web-server to hold the files you want to publish. Most online services and IAPs provide some free space to their subscribers. If yours doesn't, shop around carefully – there are some good deals to be had in this increasingly competitive area.

Next you'll need either a good knowledge of **HTML** (Hypertext Markup Language) or an authoring application that does a lot of the hard work for you. HTML is a text-based language that uses **tags**, short codes that indicate the size, style and position of text, formulate links and much more. You can create these files in any word processor or text editor, but dedicated software for the job has recently become more plentiful and much easier to use, with friendly graphical interfaces and WYSIWYG displays (although you might still have to play around with a few tags here and there to get things exactly as you want them). Two popular authoring packages are Microsoft's **FrontPage** and **HTML Assistant Pro 2** from Brooklyn North Software Works. If you use Microsoft Word you can download a free copy of **Internet Assistant** from Microsoft's Web site that lets you create HTML documents in Word.

Both Netscape and Internet Explorer have options on their menus that let you see the HTML source code for a page you're looking at. Comparing the code with the finished page can be an excellent way to learn a bit about HTML construction.

E-mail

E-mail is an abbreviation of 'electronic mail', a way of sending messages to other Internet users anywhere in the world in (sometimes) a matter of seconds. In fact it may take longer and your recipient may not receive the message for minutes or even hours, but it's still a lot quicker than using a land-based postal service and may be cheaper too. More usefully still, it's also possible to bundle up other files (such as documents, pictures, zip-files or applications) and send those together with your message.

How does it work?

Sending and receiving e-mail is one of the simplest areas of Internet life. To send an e-mail, run your e-mail software and click a button or menu option often marked **Compose New Mail**. Enter the e-mail address of the recipient and then begin typing your message as you would in a word processor. The only constraint is that e-mail messages are in plain text (ASCII) format, so you can't use any fancy formatting such as bold or italic type, fonts, and so on. You can then usually choose to send the finished mail immediately, or **queue** it to be sent later (you might want to write several messages and send them all in a single phone call).

JARGONBUSTER

Address book

Most e-mail software includes a built-in address book in which you can store all your most-used e-mail addresses. To send e-mail to someone you can just click the required name in the list instead of risking errors (and non-arrival of e-mail) by typing it yourself.

To send the mail, connect to your service or IAP and click the button marked something like **Send All Mail**. The mail will be sent to the service's **mail-server** and then routed to the mail-server belonging to your recipient's IAP. If your recipient is currently online with e-mail software running, the mail might zip straight down the line to his or her computer. Alternatively your recipient might have to click a button marked **Get Mail**. His or her software will then connect to the mail-server, check for e-mail and download any it finds waiting. Most IAPs will leave e-mail messages on their mail-server for several weeks, giving you plenty of time to retrieve it. Once a message has been retrieved it's usually deleted from the mail-server automatically so that its hard disk doesn't get full of messages you've already read.

Most users connect and check for mail every day or two, although some businesses (and users in countries lucky enough to have free local phone calls) remain connected all day and use e-mail software that automatically downloads new e-mail as soon as it arrives at the mail-server, often giving a beep or playing a wave sound to indicate that new mail has arrived. If you subscribe to an online service the e-mail software will be built into the main program, with similar buttons for creating, sending and receiving mail.

▶ *Acronyms and emoticons are commonly used devices in e-mail messages. Take a look at pp. 242–243 for a few samples.*

E-mail software

There are two different protocols in use by mail-servers: **SMTP** (Simple Mail Transfer Protocol), which is an old protocol, and **POP3** (Post Office Protocol 3). Most recent e-mail software uses SMTP to *send* e-mail and POP3 to *receive* it. However, some IAPs include a SMTP account and charge extra for a POP3 account. In most cases the SMTP account is quite good enough, but you'll need to make sure your e-mail software uses this protocol to both send and receive.

Like most of the Internet software you'll come across, the most popular e-mail programs are shareware. A good SMTP program is **Tetrix Reader Plug**, available from many Internet-related FTP sites (look for a file called TRP110.ZIP). This program also doubles as an offline newsreader (see p. 234). Two very popular e-mail programs that use POP3 are **Eudora** and **Pegasus Mail**.

Addressing e-mail

An e-mail address is a mixture of several ingredients, and these vary a little according to the service or IAP you and your recipient subscribe to. If you subscribe to an IAP your e-mail address will be something like **joe@jbloggs.dodgy.co.uk**, where **joe** is the name of your postbox, **jbloggs** is the user name you chose for your subscription (and also the name you login with), **dodgy.co.uk** is your IAP. All the text after the @ is your computer's **domain name**. Alternatively your e-mail address might be **jbloggs@dodgy.co.uk** if your IAP doesn't provide you with your own domain.

Online services assign you a unique subscription name or number (or allow you to choose one) which becomes your e-mail address. For example, CompuServe members are given a number similar to **101355,1436**. To send e-mail from an IAP account to a CompuServe member you have to replace the comma with a dot, so the full address in this example will be **101355.1436@compuserve.com**. To send e-mail from CompuServe to someone on the Internet you have to preface the address with **INTERNET:**, so the full address will be similar to **INTERNET:jbloggs@dodgy.co.uk**.

A lot of the time you won't have to worry too much about this. When e-mail arrives that you want to reply to you can simply click a **Reply** button and the software will insert the correct address in the message for you.

Postboxes

Most e-mail software lets you create 'folders' with particular names into which you can sort your incoming and outgoing mail to make individual messages easier to find later. Some take this a step further by allowing you to create multiple **postboxes**. When new mail arrives at your computer, the software will look at the postbox name in each address (the characters before the @ sign) and sort the messages into the corresponding postboxes. This can be handy if several people use your computer to send and receive e-mail, or you might like to use it to keep your personal and business mail separate.

Sending binary attachments

As well as sending plain text messages by e-mail, you can include other files with your message – anything from a formatted word-processor document to an application. These attached files use a different data format to ASCII text and are known as **binary** files. Many e-mail programs (including the three mentioned above) can handle binary files automatically: click a button marked something like **Attach File** and choose the file(s) you want to send with your mail. The software will convert them to the correct format to be sent, and will automatically decode any binary attachments you receive.

There are two methods of encoding binary files: the most recent is **MIME** (Multipurpose Internet Mail Extensions) which hasn't quite caught on. The older and more popular method is **uuencoding**. This converts 8-bit binary files into 7-bit ASCII format ready for transmission, and is the system built into many e-mail programs.

Netiquette

There are certain rules about behaviour on the Internet, especially in e-mail and newsgroups, known as 'netiquette' (Internet etiquette). In simple terms they boil down to 'Don't waste Internet resources' and 'Don't be rude', but here are a few specific pointers to keep in mind:

- Don't type in capitals. This is termed 'shouting'; it's difficult to read and regarded as rudeness.
- Consider what you say and how you say it very carefully: typing an e-mail doesn't have the formality of a printed business letter but it needs the same care to make sure that your comments will be interpreted as you mean them.
- Don't forward other people's private e-mail without their permission.
- Remember that e-mail is viewed in the same way as land-based mail in the eyes of the law – be careful what you promise and who you libel!

Newsgroups

Newsgroups form a branch of the Internet known as **Usenet**, and these are often called Usenet groups. There are over 17 000 groups (and counting) covering every topic you can think of, many more that you can't, and a few that you probably wouldn't want to. Newsgroups are discussions that take place by e-mail-type messages, but these messages are available for all to see;

you can read the messages posted to a group and reply to any of them you want to.

Newsgroup names

The problem with having over 17 000 groups to choose from isn't *Does a group exist for this subject?* but *What's it called?* Most newsreader programs have a *Search* facility to help you track down a group on a particular topic, but it helps to know how the group names work. True Usenet groups are organized in a carefully structured way, so you can narrow down your search by looking at the first word in the name. Here are just a few to give you the idea:

- **comp** Computer-related newsgroups such as **comp.windows.news**
- **rec** Recreational/sports groups such as **rec.arts.books.tolkien**
- **sci** Scientific groups like **sci.bio.paleontology**
- **misc** All kinds of stuff including items for sale, education, health, investments
- **soc** Social issues groups such as **soc.genealogy.nordic**

The largest collection of groups comes under the **alt** heading. These are 'anything goes' groups that aren't an official part of Usenet. Groups exist here about any and every subject including those mentioned above. As a taste:

alt.culture.kuwait
alt.fan.david-bowie
alt.ketchup
alt.binaries.erotica.fetish
alt.education.disabled
alt.games.dominoes
alt.paranormal.crop-circles
alt.support.spina-bifida

Newsreader software

To access newsgroups you need a newsreader program and these come in two flavours:

- *Online readers.* You read and reply to messages while on line and running up phone (and possibly connection) charges. Not a popular way to do it!
- *Offline readers.* Obviously the opposite of online readers, but these could work in one of two ways. Some programs download every message from your subscribed groups and you can read all, some or none of them. Others download the **headers** (subject-lines of the messages) only, and you can check a box beside the messages you want to read, then reconnect to have these downloaded.

When you come to a message to which you want to respond you can click a **Reply** button as you do when replying to e-mail. This ensures that the message you send has the same header as the message you replied to. Strings of messages with the same header are called **threads** and most programs automatically sort messages into their related threads to help you easily follow particular discussions within a group.

Two of the most popular offline newsreaders are **Free Agent** and **WinVN**, which can be found at many Internet-related FTP sites. Look out for files called **FAGENT***.ZIP** and **WNVN****.ZIP**, where the asterisks will be replaced by numbers corresponding to the latest version-number of the software. Another popular newsreader/e-mail program is **Tetrix Reader Plug**, mentioned in the previous section.

Many newsreaders offer the facility to send e-mail messages too, but some can't *receive* them. Make sure you know what yours can do before you rely on it!

▶ *You should be able to find these newsreaders and many more on the Internet-software FTP sites given on p. 246.*

Subscribing to newsgroups

Before you can start reading and posting messages you need to **subscribe** to the groups that interest you, and before you can do *that* you have to download a list of groups from your IAP's news-server. This could take a few minutes but it's something you'll have to do only once; the list is saved onto your hard disk and most programs will let you know when new groups appear on the server in future and let you add them to the list.

Once the list has been downloaded, disconnect then click a button or menu-option marked **Subscribe**. You can then look through the list and select the groups to which you want to subscribe. 'Subscribing' is the term for letting your software know which groups to download messages or headers from – there are no 'subscription fees'!

Start by subscribing to one group. A common beginners' mistake is to subscribe to about 20 and then spend two hours on line waiting for thousands of dull messages to be downloaded! It's always best to test the water before diving in.

When you first connect and download messages or headers the process might be slow: many servers will keep messages for a long time before deleting older ones and you'll be seeing all of these. In future your newsreader will keep track of what you've seen and what you haven't to prevent you from downloading the same messages over and over again.

▶ *Emoticons and acronyms are used frequently in both e-mail and newsgroup messages. Check out pp. 242–243 for a few examples.*

Newsgroup tips

- Lurk for a while before posting. *Lurking* is the act of reading messages without posting any yourself. A common misdemeanour is to jump straight in and ask a question that isn't relevant to the group, and some groups concentrate on a very narrow field.
- Read the FAQ. Most groups regularly publish a Frequently-Asked-Questions list with answers to save them having to repeatedly use valuable Internet resources answering the same basic questions.
- Don't be afraid to ask for help or advice. Most groups are sympathetic and encouraging to newcomers in their field, and many are frequented by people who simply enjoy helping out and answering questions.
- Don't post the same message indiscriminately to lots of different newsgroups.
- When replying to messages, don't quote more of the original than is necessary to remind readers what the original posting was about.
- Don't post binary files to newsgroups that don't have 'binaries' in their names. Some users with offline readers have no way to avoid downloading them.

Check out the tips given for e-mail messages in the previous section – these apply equally to newsgroup postings.

FTP

FTP (File Transfer Protocol) is a system used for copying a particular file from a remote computer to your own. If you really want to, you can browse the public-access folders on the remote computer looking for interesting files and download an Index of files (which may include descriptions of the files and their sizes) but this isn't like browsing the World Wide Web. Instead you'll be looking through files and folders that use non-intuitive MS-DOS 8.3 names. The main use of FTP is for retrieving a file whose name and location you know.

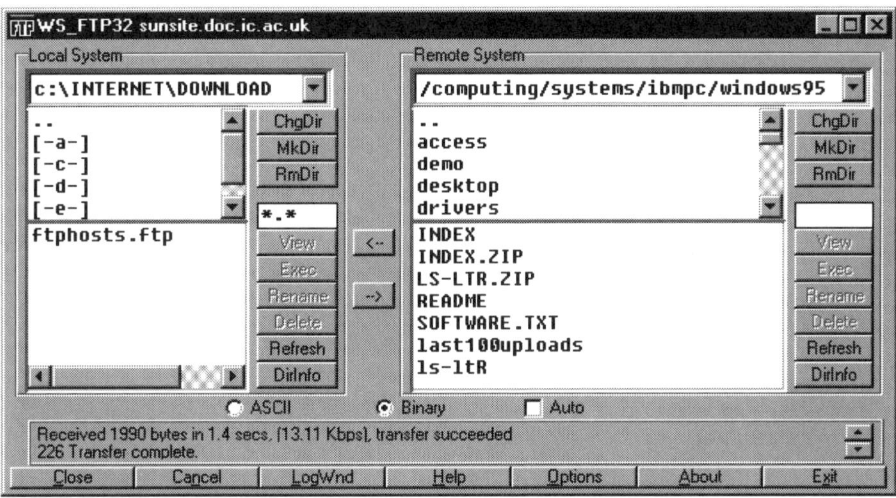

Figure 7.4 The popular WS_FTP.

Making the connection

There are many FTP clients around, but the two most popular are **WS_FTP** and **CuteFTP** (see p. 246 for sites from which these can be downloaded). Most FTP clients use the same layout as WS_FTP, but before you actually see the window shown in Figure 7.4, you have to actually *connect* to the remote computer. To do this you type its domain name (such as ftp.cyberspace.com) or its IP Address (such as 158.152.1.222) into a dialog box. You can also add a path to a particular folder on the remote computer if you know the whereabouts of the file you want, and save these details to make future connections easier, adding your own choice of name for this computer for quick recognition.

If you have a web browser you can connect to FTP sites by typing **ftp://** followed by the remote computer's address rather than using separate software. Note that some addresses actually *start* with the letters 'ftp' so the full line might look something like

ftp://ftp.cyberspace.com/pub/ppp/windows.

Copying files

Once the connection is made to the remote computer, you'll see its folder-listing in the right pane of the window shown in Figure 7.4. In the left pane you can see the folder-structure of your own computer and select a folder to download files into. In both panes, the upper section shows folder names and the lower displays the files in the selected folder. To download files, just click one or more files in the right pane (holding *Ctrl* to select multiple files) and then click the left-facing arrow in the centre of the application. A dialog box will appear to keep you informed of the progress of the download with information about the file size, time taken, expected total download time, and percentage of data copied so far.

Anonymous FTP

You'll often see FTP described as 'anonymous'. Anonymous FTP means that the files stored on the computer are available to anyone who wants to use them (rather than just employees of that company or students at that university). When you log in, enter the user name **anonymous**. When prompted for a password, enter your e-mail address – it isn't strictly necessary, but it's regarded as good netiquette. It's also good netiquette to connect to a remote computer outside its local business hours (as well as being quicker!).

Other Internet services

In addition to the Internet facilities covered in the preceding sections of this chapter, there are many more methods of locating and retrieving information and files or just generally having a good time on the 'Net. Here, briefly, are a few of them.

Gopher

Gopher is a textual menu-based system for locating information. You navigate a series of menus which lead you from computer to computer, but, because the menus remain standard, you won't actually be aware you're zipping around the world like this. It's a bit of a haphazard system: you may find the information you're looking for, or you may just reach a dead-end.

Archie

A method of searching the world (or a large part of it) for a particular file. The program to use is called **WSArchie**. Enter the name of the file you're looking for, using the wildcards * and ? if you're not sure of the exact file name, choose an archie-server from one of many different countries and press *Return* to start the search. Archie will display a list of all the files found that match the name you entered; double-click on one of these and Archie will run your FTP client to download it.

Telnet

Using a Telnet program you can take control of (almost) any remote computer as if you were sitting at its keyboard controlling it directly. What you'll see when you connect will depend on the remote computer – it could be anything from a user-unfriendly Gopher-like menu system to a snazzy graphical interface – you take pot-luck. Windows 95 includes a Telnet program hidden away in the Windows folder.

Internet Relay Chat

Usually abbreviated to IRC, these are real-time discussions held by typing messages into your IRC program's window. In a separate window you can see what everyone else is saying. Because of the delays in transmission, pauses for thought, and two-finger typists, there can be times when no one seems to be saying anything and times when everyone is talking at once, so large gatherings can get a bit confused, but it can also be very addictive once you're used to it. There are many IRC programs around, but a good one to look for is **WS_Chat**.

Finger

This is a small program used to find information about someone on the Internet. Click the **Finger** button and type user name@host (e.g. **jbloggs@dodgy.co.uk**). One of the best Finger clients is **WSFinger**.

Ping

This is another small program used for troubleshooting. You can 'ping' a remote computer by entering its address to see if it responds. This can also be handy for checking your connection: ping a computer you know exists (such as your IAP's own computer). The program to look for is **WSPing**.

Whois

This is one of the few available methods of finding someone's e-mail address by entering their name. It can take some time and effort since there are many whois-servers around the world, and you'll often get no result. The only reliable way of finding someone's e-mail address is to ask them! A whois client is included with **WSFinger**.

Internet software suites

So far in this chapter we've concentrated on the separate pieces of software you can use to take advantage of the Internet, but there's another option you may want to consider – the **Internet Suite**. This is a single integrated application that brings Web browser, e-mail, newsgroup-access and FTP together in one package. Practical as it initially sounds, it isn't the best choice for everyone, so let's take a look at the pros and cons.

Pros

- *Easy to install.* Instead of setting up several different programs, you can simply enter all the necessary information once and start surfing.
- *Complete package.* In most suites, everything you need is included, and some even give you a modem and connection to an IAP.
- *Familiar interface.* Since all the different elements are designed in parallel, it should be easy to learn how to use each one.
- *Ideal for beginners.* If you're new to computers as well as to the Internet, you may be less than excited at the prospect of setting up half-a-dozen different programs and trying to understand them all.

Cons

- *You gotta pay!* Some Internet software is free to home-users, most is cheap shareware. Internet suites cost real money.
- If you don't like one piece of Internet software you can download another and give that a try. With a suite you have to accept the package as it is, good and bad.
- The World Wide Web is growing new features all the time with the popular browsers constantly updating to support them. With an integrated browser you won't be able to use these features.

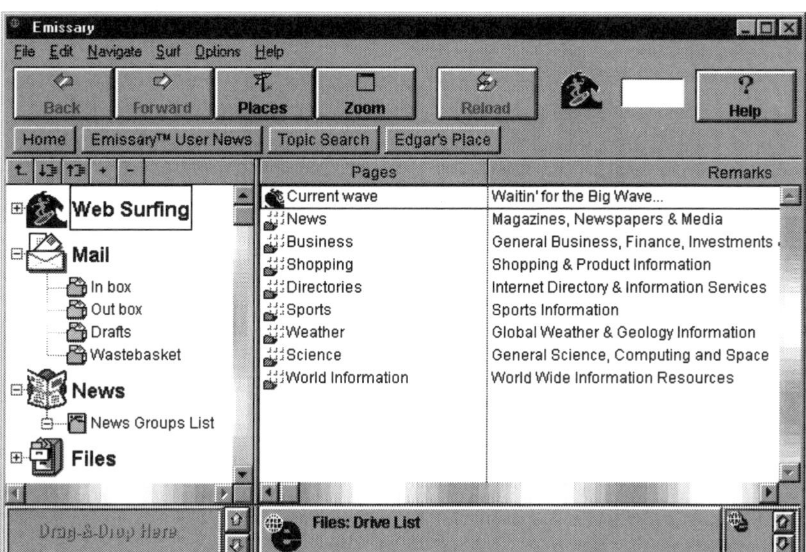

Figure 7.5 Complete Internet access in a single window with Emissary.

Which suite?

There are many suites already available and more arriving, but here are three of the best.

- **Emissary** (shown in Figure 7.5). This includes Web browser, e-mail, newsgroup-access, FTP and Telnet. It offers only the basic software elements, but all are hugely powerful, well-integrated and easy to use, with many clever features not (yet) found in any other Internet software.
- **Internet Chameleon**. This includes the same elements as Emissary plus Archie, Gopher, Ping, Whois, IRC and Winsock for Windows 3.1 users. Chameleon includes easy connection to any US-based IAP, but this is no help to UK users, so setting up is no easier than for any other software. Most of the software elements are neat and easy to use.
- **InterAp**. This includes the same elements as Emissary, plus Ping client. InterAp has an easy-to-use, customizable button-bar for launching Internet and other programs. Excellent e-mail and FTP clients.

If you like the idea of using integrated Internet software, you might want to consider subscribing to an online service such as **AOL**, **CompuServe**, **MSN** or **UK Online** (see p. 223). Although the software provided can sometimes be a bit clunky, it's free and fully integrated, and usually provides the simplest possible way of getting on line.

Emoticon dictionary

Emoticons (otherwise known as 'smilies') are little expressive faces made from standard keyboard characters used to convey feelings or to prevent a phrase or expression being interpreted the wrong way in e-mail or newsgroup messages. Here's a little bundle of the more useful, ubiquitous or amusing emoticons. (If you haven't come across emoticons before, look at them sideways!)

<table>
<tr><td>:-)</td><td>Happy</td></tr>
<tr><td>:-(</td><td>Sad</td></tr>
<tr><td>:-))</td><td>Very happy</td></tr>
<tr><td>:-((</td><td>Very sad</td></tr>
<tr><td>;-)</td><td>Wink</td></tr>
<tr><td>>:-)</td><td>Evil grin</td></tr>
<tr><td>:-D</td><td>Laughing</td></tr>
<tr><td>:'-)</td><td>Crying</td></tr>
<tr><td>:-O</td><td>Surprised</td></tr>
<tr><td>:-&</td><td>Tongue-tied</td></tr>
<tr><td>:-|</td><td>Unamused</td></tr>
<tr><td>:-||</td><td>Angry</td></tr>
<tr><td>X-)</td><td>Cross-eyed</td></tr>
<tr><td>:-#)</td><td>Has a moustache</td></tr>
<tr><td>:-)></td><td>Has a beard</td></tr>
<tr><td>(-)</td><td>Needs a haircut</td></tr>
<tr><td>(:-)</td><td>Bald</td></tr>
<tr><td>:-)X</td><td>Wears a bow-tie</td></tr>
<tr><td>8-)</td><td>Wears glasses</td></tr>
<tr><td>:^)</td><td>Has a broken nose</td></tr>
<tr><td>:-w</td><td>Speaks with forked tongue</td></tr>
<tr><td>:-?</td><td>Smokes a pipe</td></tr>
<tr><td>:-Q</td><td>Smokes cigarettes</td></tr>
<tr><td>*-)</td><td>Drunk or stoned</td></tr>
<tr><td><:-)</td><td>Idiot</td></tr>
<tr><td>=:-)</td><td>Punk rocker</td></tr>
</table>

Acronym dictionary

Acronyms came about as a result of Internet users having to compose their messages while on line and clocking up charges. Speed and conciseness have always been more important in e-mail than grammar, spelling and punctuation, but even though most messages are now composed *off line*, these acronyms have become an accepted part of e-mail style.

In fact most of these aren't acronyms at all, but they fall under the banner of TLAs (Three Letter Acronyms). Er, no, they don't all consist of three letters either.

AFAIK	As far as I know
BCNU	Be seeing you
BST	But seriously though
BTW	By the way
FAQ	Frequently asked question(s)
FWIW	For what it's worth
FYI	For your information
<G>	Grin
GAL	Get a life
IMO	In my opinion
IMHO	In my humble opinion
IMNSHO	In my not-so-humble opinion
IOW	In other words
KISS	Keep it simple, stupid
L8R	Later
LOL	Laughs out loud
NRN	No reply necessary
OAO	Over and out

OIC	Oh I see	ROFL	Rolls on the floor laughing
OTOH	On the other hand	RTFM	Read the f*%£?!# manual
OTT	Over the top	TIA	Thanks in advance
PITA	Pain in the a#%$	TNX	Thanks

Another common need in e-mail and newsgroup messages is to emphasize particular words or phrases, since the usual methods (bold or italic text, or underlining) aren't available. This is done by surrounding the text with underscores (_never_) or asterisks (*never*).

Internet jargon dictionary

Client An application that handles a specific task such as sending and receiving e-mail (an 'e-mail client').

DNS Domain Name Server. The service your access provider has to translate computers' 'Internet names' into dotted decimal names.

Domain The part of your e-mail address that follows the @ sign and specifies your computer's name and location.

Ego-surfing Using search engines or looking through newsgroups to find mentions of your own name.

FAQ Frequently asked questions. Many newsgroups publish a FAQ file that you should read before posting questions that regular posters may be tired of answering. If you don't see it, post a brief message asking for it.

Flame A personal attack on the poster of a message.

Flame bait A message expressly designed to provoke an argument.

Flame war A situation in which there's so much flaming going on that the newsgroup consists of little else.

Gateway A system that translates data between two incompatible networks.

Home Page Originally the first of a group of pages belonging to one individual or company. Now often used generically to refer to the entire group of pages.

Host A computer that lets you connect to other computers on the Internet.

IP Address An individual name that every computer on the Internet has. Noted as an 'Internet name' (bill@dodgy.co.uk) or dotted decimal name (158.152.120.12).

Login The act of identifying yourself when connecting to a service or IAP by entering your user name and password.

Lurking Reading newsgroup messages without posting any yourself.

Newbie Someone new to the Internet or a newsgroup (not necessarily a derogatory term; you can describe yourself this way in appeals for help!).

POP Point of Presence. One of many phone numbers (perhaps in many towns and cities) you can dial to connect to your IAP.

POP3 One of two e-mail transfer protocols in wide use, often for receiving mail.

Server A computer which provides particular data or services such as sending your e-mail (a 'mail-server') or newsgroup messages (a 'news-server').

SMTP Simple Mail Transfer Protocol. The second common e-mail transfer protocol, often used to send mail or to both send *and* receive it.

Snail mail Land-based postal service, whose speed is closer to that of said mollusc than e-mail.

Spamming Sending mail (usually advertising mailshots) to vast numbers of newsgroups and mailboxes regardless of relevance or recipients' interest.

User name The name you selected for your IAP subscription which usually precedes or immediately follows the @ sign in your e-mail address.

Useful Internet sites

The following is an alphabetical list of computer- and Internet-related companies with a presence on the World Wide Web, together with a few additional sites to help you track down the information or software you need.

Software companies

Adobe Systems Inc.	http://www.adobe.com
Asymetrix	http://munin.asymetrix.com
Berkeley Systems	http://www.berksys.com
Borland International Inc.	http://www.borland.com
Brooklyn North Software Works	http://www.brooknorth.com
Claris Corporation	http://www.claris.com
Corel Corporation	http://www.corel.com
Gold Disk Inc.	http://www.golddisk.com
JASC Inc.	http://www.jasc.com
Lotus Development	http://www.lotus.com
Macromedia	http://www.macromedia.com
McAfee	http://www.mcafee.com
Micrografx	http://www.micrografx.com
Microsoft	http://www.microsoft.com
Nico Mak Computing Inc.	http://www.winzip.com
Plasmon Data	http://www.plasmon.com
Quark Inc.	http://www.quark.com
Quarterdeck	http://www.qdeck.com
SoftQuad	http://www.sq.com

Steinberg	http://www.steinberg-us.com
Symantec	http://www.symantec.com

Hardware companies

AMD	http://www.amd.com
Award	http://www.award.com
Aztech	http://www.aztech.com.sg
Canon	http://www.canon.com
Cirrus Logic	http://cirrus.com
Compaq	http://www.compaq.com
Creative Labs	http://www.creaf.com
Diamond Multimedia Systems	http://www.diamondmm.com
Gateway 2000	http://gw2k.com
Gravis	http://www.gravis.com
Hayes	http://www.hayes.com
Hewlett-Packard	http://www.hp.com
IBM	http://www.ibm.com
Intel	http://www.intel.com
Iomega	http://www.careermosaic.com/cm/iomega
Logitech	http://www.logitech.com
Mitsumi	http://www.mitsumi.com
NEC	http://www.nec.com
Olivetti	http://www.olivetti.com
Panasonic	http://www.panasonic.com
Primax	http://www.primax.net
Seagate Technology	http://www.seagate.com
Sony Corporation	http://www.sony.com
Toshiba	http://www.toshiba.com
US Robotics	http://www.usr.com
VideoLogic	http://www.videologic.com

Search pages

Infoseek Search	http://www.infoseek.com
iWorld	http://www.mecklerweb.com/netday
Lycos Search Page	http://www.lycos.com
Savvy Search	http://www.cs.colostate.edu/~dreiling/smartform.html
Starting Point	http://www.stpt.com
The HUGE List	http://thehugelist.com/links.html
WebCrawler	http://www.webcrawler.com
Yahoo Search	http://www.yahoo.com/search.html

Internet software and general sites

Internet shareware	ftp://ftp.cyberspace.com/pub/ppp/windows
More Internet shareware	http://server.net4you.co.at/tucows/t95.html
CuteFTP	http://papa.indstate.edu:8888/CuteFTP
Eudora	ftp://ftp.qualcomm.com
Netscape	http://www.netscape.com
Trumpet Winsock	ftp://ftp.trumpet.com.au
WS_FTP	http://www.csra.net/junodj
General shareware	http://www.islandnet.com/~sword/sharewar.html
Shareware and information	ftp://sunsite.doc.ic.ac.uk
Windows 95 shareware	http://www.windows95.com
More Windows 95 shareware	http://pcwin.com

CHAPTER 8

Using MS-DOS

Introducing MS-DOS

The acronym DOS (pronounced 'doss') simply stands for **Disk Operating System**, so as a general term it could be applied to any operating system and we'd talk about *buying a DOS*. In fact, the term is used almost exclusively to refer to Microsoft's MS-DOS (and, to a lesser extent, IBM's PC-DOS).

Since its inception in the early 1980s, MS-DOS has been through a number of versions and enhancements, arriving at the current version, 6.22, in 1994 (although an updated, compact 'DOS-on-a-diet' is built into Windows 95 as version 7.0, which we'll look at in Chapter 10). Before Windows became popular, DOS was *the* PC operating system and established a huge user-base around the world with no shortage of available software for a multitude of uses. Since the arrival of Windows 3.0, the first popular graphical interface for the PC, DOS has come to be regarded as a difficult, complicated system that has to be grappled with when Windows isn't working properly, and should otherwise be ignored.

DOS alone

In fact, DOS isn't particularly difficult to use, just different. DOS uses a command-line interface in which commands have to be typed from the keyboard. Once you're used to the way these commands are structured, and you start to get a 'feel' for DOS, using it successfully is a simple matter of learning the commands you need to use. More than any other operating system, DOS is just a platform from which to launch the applications you want to use – the only productivity accessory included with DOS being a text editor called **Edit** – and the applications you run under DOS often include support for the mouse, with intuitive menus and toolbars. As a result, you might easily run MS-DOS on your PC and not have to work from the command line at all, other than to run an application or format a disk.

One of the main drawbacks to using MS-DOS as your operating system lies in hardware compatibility – few manufacturers still create DOS drivers for their products now that Windows (and especially Windows 95) has such a firm foothold. A second consideration is that DOS is a **single-tasking** system – only one program at a time can be run. If you need a PC to run one particular program, perhaps an accounts package for a large office, this won't bother you too much. Similarly, most games are still created to run under DOS, and you'd usually only play one game at a time! But if you expect to be using a variety of DOS programs, and would prefer to be able to switch between them rather than having to close one whenever you need to use another, the DOS capabilities built into Windows 95 provide the answer.

DOS and Windows

The relationship between MS-DOS and Windows is an important one to understand. Windows versions from the original 1.0 to 3.11 required a version of DOS to be installed on the PC, which could be run as a stand-alone operating system, allowing the use of DOS-based programs. Windows was then run *from* DOS, in the same way that you'd run any application – when you were working in Windows, DOS was still lurking underneath and keeping the system working. When you'd finished working with Windows you shut it down and were returned to DOS, either to switch off the PC or to continue working with DOS programs.

Windows 95 doesn't need a *separate* version of DOS; it includes its own. Although this new MS-DOS is still there, and still running underneath, Windows 95 hides it behind friendly, colourful pictures as you start and shutdown your PC.

Both Windows versions allow you to run MS-DOS in a window as if it were just another Windows application. In this way, not only can you switch between the DOS window and other windows, you can have several DOS windows open to run multiple DOS programs and switch between them, bringing true multitasking to MS-DOS.

The command prompt

Like any operating system, MS-DOS has a shell program – the program that starts automatically when the operating system loads and gives you a method of communicating with the computer (called an *interface*). The DOS shell is called **Command.com** and its interface consists of just a few characters called the **prompt** on an otherwise blank screen, followed by a cursor that flashes to indicate that it's ready for input (Figure 8.1).

Figure 8.1 The usual MS-DOS prompt and cursor.

By default the prompt displays just the letter name of the currently selected drive and a greater-than symbol (usually **C**>), but it can be set to display different or additional information such as the date and time. Most usefully, it can display the currently selected drive and path (as shown in Figure 8.1) which is the most popular setting.

JARGONBUSTER

Command line

The prompt in MS-DOS is also often referred to as the command line, but this is a term that's encountered more often in Windows. Both 3.1 and 95 have a menu-option in their shell programs called **Run** which provides a dialog box with a blank space into which can be typed a DOS command. The prompt itself isn't shown in this space, but the syntax used is the same.

Everything you want to do in DOS starts from the command prompt, whether it's running an application, looking at the contents of drives and folders or formatting a disk. The command you type on the keyboard appears on the screen beside the prompt, and is carried out when you press the *Enter* key. If you make a mistake in typing you can use the *Backspace* key to delete the command and retype it, but if you press the *Enter* key after entering a wrongly typed command, or one that DOS doesn't understand, an error message will appear on screen followed by another prompt ready for you to type it again (Figure 8.2).

```
C:\REPORTS>dir /i
Invalid switch - /I

C:\REPORTS>_
```

Figure 8.2 MS-DOS shows its dislike of a particular command.

When an application is run it replaces the prompt with its own interface which, as mentioned above, may be a lot friendlier. Nevertheless, the command prompt is still waiting for you: as soon as you exit the application, you're returned to the prompt ready to do something else.

Command structure

A DOS command may consist of up to three distinct elements: a **keyword**, one or more **parameters**, and one or more **switches**, each separated by a space. For a command to be carried out properly, the elements must be in the correct order and, of course, spelt correctly – if a single character in the command is wrong, all you'll get is an error message and an opportunity to try typing it again. On the positive side, this might mean that your typing becomes more accurate after a little time spent working with DOS; on the negative side, it might just mean that your typing slows down to a crawl!

Keywords

The keyword is the part of the command that tells the operating system what to do – you could think of it as actually being the command itself. Indeed, some commands require only a keyword: **cls**, for example, clears all text from the screen apart from the prompt, and needs no parameters or switches to do it. In many cases, the keyword is an abbreviation of the command name (**del** being the keyword for the Delete command); in others it may be an alternative (either **ren** or **rename** may be used as the keyword for the Rename command).

Parameters

The parameter is the element that indicates what the command should be applied to. For example, **del** or **ren** can do nothing by themselves: **del** needs a parameter identifying the file to be deleted; **ren** needs two parameters, the first indicating the file to be renamed, the second indicating the name it's to be given. In the same way, the Format command needs to be told which drive to format.

Switches

This third element of a command is used to adjust the way in which the command is carried out. Think of these as ways of *switching on* the options you want to use with a certain command. Most commands will work without switches but may not produce the result you want. The Format command, used with a parameter specifying your floppy drive, will automatically try to format the disk as a high-density (1.44 Mb) disk. If it's a 720 K disk, you'll need to add the switch **/f:720** after the parameter. The **dir** command will display the entire contents of the specified folder (directory) in a list of file and folder names, one per line. Switches can be added to the command to show only files with particular attributes, or to group files in a particular order, or to present the list in different ways.

Running DOS programs

Running a program in MS-DOS follows exactly the same rules as any other command. The **keyword** is the path and name of the program to be launched; the optional **parameter** is the file you want to open in that program; **switches** may be added to alter how the program is run, which will be listed in the program's manuals. Thus

c:\programs\grafik.exe c:\files\mydog.jpg

would run a program called **Grafik.exe** and open a file called **Mydog.jpg** in it.

There are also a few labour-saving options available that can reduce the amount of typing you have to do:

- To run any program, there's no need to include its **.exe**, **.com**, **.bat** or **.pif** extension in the command – DOS will look for a program with that name. In the example above, typing just **c:\programs\grafik** would start the program. However, if your Programs folder contained a Grafik.exe and a Grafik.bat, DOS would run the **.exe** file; if you wanted to run Grafik.bat you'd have to include the **.bat** extension.
- If the path to the program you want to run is specified in the SET PATH= line in your Autoexec.bat (see p. 262), you need only type the program's name. So if the path **C:\Programs** were specified, you could start this program by typing **grafik** whatever the current folder.
- If the path to the program is specified in the SET PATH = line, *and* you're in the folder containing the document file you want to open, you can avoid typing either path. The full command can be shortened to **grafik mydog.jpg**.

Types of command

MS-DOS comprises two types of command: internal and external. An **internal** command is one built into the operating system itself for fast access. These are the commands most needed in day-to-day use. **External** commands are supplied by the other program files in the DOS folder (**C:\DOS**). Over the next few pages, we'll take a look at some of the commands used in MS-DOS versions 6.2/6.22, describe what they do and give a few examples of use. In all cases, the use of keyword, parameters and switches must always be separated by one space, and the *Enter* key must be pressed to run the command you've typed.

TIP

None of these commands is case-sensitive, so there's usually no need to use the *Shift* key other than for inputting the colon (:) in the drive name. Because you'll usually choose to enter commands in lower-case, that's the way they're noted here.

Internal commands

Prompt

When used by itself, the keyword **prompt** returns the command prompt to its default setting, displaying the current drive and greater-than sign (**C**>). To change the prompt involves adding to the keyword a parameter made up of the following settings in any combination:

$d today's date

$t current time

$p current drive and path

$l less-than sign (<)

$g greater-than sign (>)

**$$** dollar sign ($)

$q equals sign

The usual prompt setting is current drive and path followed by greater-than sign, which is set by entering

prompt pg

This enables you to tell which folder you are currently in just by looking at the prompt.

Change directory

The keyword for this command is **cd**, used to change the folder you're currently working in (usually shown by the prompt, as above). The command always requires a parameter to specify which folder to change to.

cd c:\letters\business

would switch to the folder called Business, which is a subfolder of Letters on your C drive. If Business contained a subfolder called Recent, you can simply type

cd recent

and the system will automatically look for this folder in the current folder. If you arrive in C:\Letters\Business\Recent and you want to return to the Business folder again, there's another shortcut – just add two dots to the keyword

cd..

which will automatically move you up to the parent folder. If you want to switch to a folder on a different drive, you first have to change drive. This is done simply by typing in the drive's name (including the colon). To switch to your floppy-disk drive, for example, type

a:

You can then use the **cd** command to switch between folders on this drive.

If you prefer not to use the **pg** prompt to show the folder you're working in, you can display its name and path by typing **cd** by itself.

Copy

The **copy** command makes a copy of a file somewhere else, and therefore needs two parameters: the first is the path and name of the file to be copied, the second is the path to which the copy should be made. To copy a file called Whatsup.doc from the Business folder mentioned above to the root folder of a floppy disk, type

copy c:\letters\business\whatsup.doc a:

To copy the same file to a folder called Temp on your C drive, type

copy c:\letters\business\whatsup.doc c:\temp

The copy command has another trick up its sleeve – you can give the copy a different name from the original! For example:

copy c:\letters\business\whatsup.doc c:\temp\dry.doc

would once again copy the file to your Temp folder, but would give it the name Dry.doc. And, of course, you can create a copy with a different name in the *same* folder if you want to:

copy c:\letters\business\whatsup.doc c:\letters\business\dry.doc

TIP

To avoid the vast amount of typing needed at times like this, and preclude the possibility of mistakes, it's quicker to use the **cd** command to change to the folder containing the file. You can then leave out the path, and simply type

copy whatsup.doc dry.doc

Delete

Not unexpectedly, this command deletes (erases) a file, using the keyword **del**. The parameter required, of course, is the name (and path if necessary) of the file to be deleted:

del c:\letters\business\whatsup.doc *or* **del whatsup.doc**

Rename

The Rename (**ren**) command needs a file to rename (including path if necessary) and a new name for the file. Because it isn't possible to move a file elsewhere while renaming it, there's no need to re-enter the path in the second parameter:

ren c:\letters\business\whatsup.doc dry.doc *or*
ren whatsup.doc dry.doc

Make directory

You can choose between two keywords for this one, **mkdir** or **md**. This command creates a new folder at the specified location. If no location is specified, the result will be a subfolder of your current folder. To create a folder called Personal inside our Letters folder, type

md c:\letters\personal *or* **md personal**

Remove directory

Decision time again – for extra typing exercise, use **rmdir**; otherwise go for **rd**. Either way, this command deletes an empty folder. If the folder isn't empty, or if you're trying to delete the folder you're currently in, you'll receive an error message. To delete the empty Personal folder we just created, enter

rd c:\letters\personal *or* **rd personal**

Directory contents

The **dir** command lists the contents of the folder you specify (or the current folder if no parameter is entered). To view the contents of the Letters folder, type

dir c:\letters

Of all the commands given in this section, **dir** is the one for which it's handy to know a few switches: one of the problems with this command is that if your parameter is a folder containing lots of files they can't all fit on one screen, so you'll see them whizzing by, leaving you with just the last few on the screen.

- **/w** This switch presents the folder contents in *wide* view, with up to five files or folders per line.
- **/p** This one *pauses* the list on each screen-full and prompts you to press any key when you're ready to view the next bunch.
- **/s** Also shows the contents of each *subfolder* of the folder you specified, which will almost certainly require the use of the **/p** switch as well. This can be useful when you're trying to locate a file and you only know its approximate location.

These switches can be used in combination with a space between each, such as:

dir c:\letters /w /s /p

Quickies

Here are a few other internal commands that can be useful at odd times:

- **time** Displays the current time and prompts you to change it and press *Enter*. If you don't want to change it, just press *Enter*.

- **date** Displays the current date in exactly the same way.
- **type** Followed by the path (if necessary) and name of a file, this displays the contents of the file on the screen.
- **ver** Displays the current MS-DOS version.
- **path** Displays the path setting specified in your Autoexec.bat.
- **set** By itself, displays variable settings such as Temp folder, Path line and prompt setting. These can be changed by typing, for example, **set temp=c:\temp**. These settings are retained until either you reset them again in the same way, or you restart your computer and the settings in Autoexec.bat are reloaded.
- **Ctrl + Break** This is not a DOS command, but a key combination used to stop a lengthy ongoing process. If, for example, you typed **dir/s/p** in a folder containing hundreds of files and subfolders and then saw the file you were looking for in the very first screen, you could press *Ctrl + Break* to cancel the process and return you to the prompt.

► *For details of Autoexec.bat and variable settings, turn to p. 262.*

External commands

External commands in MS-DOS each have a **.com** or **.exe** file in the DOS folder whose name matches the keyword. These are all fairly small files – most are well under 100 K which is tiny by today's standards – but if you like to keep all your folders clutter-free you can delete any of these you don't want (or, for preference, move them to floppy disk).

Move

The move command is actually an amalgamation of Copy and Delete, giving the impression of moving a file from one place to another. The first parameter is the path (if needed) and name of the file to be moved, the second is a path to its desired location:

move whatsup.doc c:\temp

By adding a new name to the desired location you can also use **move** to *rename* a file:

move whatsup.doc c:\temp\dry.doc

Xcopy

A command for copying multiple files, including those in subfolders and the subfolders themselves (although **Xcopy** doesn't copy files with the System or

Hidden attribute). Adding the switch **/e** specifies that *empty* subfolders should also be copied. For example, the command

xcopy c:\letters c:\temp /e

will copy all the files in C:\Letters, together with its subfolders and their contents if they have any, to C:\Temp.

▶ *See below for use of the **attrib** command, or p. 145 for more on file attributes.*

Deltree

This is a command that deletes a folder *and* its contents. Remember that its contents includes any subfolders and *their* contents as well! To remove our entire Letters folder, losing all our letters in the process, together with our Business subfolder and its contents, type

deltree c:\letters

Because this is quite a radical action to take, you'll always receive a prompt asking if you really want to do it. You'll have to type **y** and *Enter* for 'Yes' or **n** and *Enter* if you've changed your mind.

Format

This is used chiefly to format floppy disks. In addition to the keyword, a parameter is needed to specify the drive containing the disk to be formatted, followed by a switch to indicate the disk's capacity. To format a double-density disk in Drive A, type:

format a: /f:720

To this you can add the switch **/q** to specify a *quick* format for previously formatted disks.

Sys

This creates a boot disk (also known as a system or startup disk) by copying the vital operating system files to a floppy disk. You can use this disk to start your PC if you develop a problem with your hard disk or accidentally delete one of these files (see p. 34). Assuming your floppy drive is Drive A, type

sys a:

Diskcopy

This command copies the contents of one floppy disk to another, and requires two parameters: the *source* drive (containing the disk to be copied) and the *destination* drive. In most cases these will both be Drive A, and you'll be prompted to remove the first disk after its data has been read, and insert the second so that it can be written. To copy a disk in this way, you'd enter

diskcopy a: a:

A useful switch to add on the end is **/v**. This *verifies* that the data is copied correctly, but the whole operation will take longer to complete.

Attrib

This is used to view or change the attributes of a file. To view the attributes of Whatsup.doc in your Letters folder, type

attrib c:\letters\whatsup.doc *or* **attrib whatsup.doc**

The result will show the initial letter of any of that file's attributes: **A** for Archive, **R** for Read-only, **H** for Hidden, **S** for System.

To change the attributes for a file, these initials are used again, together with a + or – sign to add or remove the attribute respectively. For example, to add the Archive and Read-only attributes to this file, and remove the Hidden attribute, you'd type

attrib +a +r –h c:\letters\whatsup.doc

▶ *File attributes are explained on p. 145.*

Subst

This command substitutes a path with a drive letter. The main use of this command is if you find yourself working in several folders that each have very long paths, such as C:\Letters\Business\Memos\1995\July. If you get into a situation in which you have to keep retyping these paths at the prompt, turn each into a 'virtual drive' for a while. For example, to assign the path above the name Drive W, type

subst w: c:\letters\business\memos\1995\july

Now if you want to work with a file in this July folder called **Sales.txt**, instead of typing that tedious path every time you can simply refer to it as **W:\Sales.txt**.

You must, of course, pick a drive letter that isn't currently in use, either for one of your *physical* drives or for another virtual drive. To find out which letters you've already assigned to virtual drives, just type **subst** with no parameters at the prompt.

Edit

This is the one program included with MS-DOS that lets you create something. It's a simple text editor, very similar to Windows' **Notepad**, that supports the mouse and has Windows-like menus sporting Open, Save, Save As, Print, and Cut/Copy/Paste options.

To run the editor from the command prompt, just type

edit

You can also follow the keyword with a path (if needed) and file name to be opened in the editor. To open your Autoexec.bat file, for example, you'd type

edit c:\autoexec.bat

TIP

If you specify a file name that doesn't exist, the editor will create a file with that name at that location as it opens, meaning that you can just *save* your file when you've finished typing it, rather than having to navigate the **Save As** dialog and pick a location and name.

Help

This is sure to be one of the commands you'll use most, especially in your early dealings with DOS. To get a little assistance, just type

help

at the prompt and you'll see a screen similar to the one pictured in Figure 8.3, listing all the DOS programs and keywords in alphabetical order. You can navigate through the list using the arrows keys (or press the initial letter of the command you want to reach first in the list with that initial). When the entry you're interested in is highlighted, press Enter to open its page. These entries, surrounded by green brackets, are called **jumps**, and each leads to a different page.

TIP

Although the **Syntax** page carries all the main information about each command's options and construction, it isn't put together in a way that makes it easy for beginners. Make full use of the **Examples** page to get a clearer idea of how the command works.

If you know which command you'd like help with, you can bypass the contents page altogether. To open the help page for **attrib** straight from the command prompt, type

help attrib

```
File  Search          MS-DOS Help: Command Reference                     Help
Use the scroll bars to see more commands. Or, press the PAGE DOWN key. For
more information about using MS-DOS Help, choose How to Use MS-DOS Help
from the Help menu, or press F1. To exit MS-DOS Help, press ALT, F, X.

<What's New in MS-DOS 6.22?>

<ANSI.SYS>                 <EMM386.EXE>               <Multi-config>
<Append>                   <Erase>                    <Nlsfunc>
<Attrib>                   <Exit>                     <Numlock>
<Batch commands>           <Expand>                   <Path>
<Break>                    <Fasthelp>                 <Pause>
<Buffers>                  <Fastopen>                 <Power>
<Call>                     <Fc>                       <POWER.EXE>
<Cd>                       <Fcbs>                     <Print>
<Chcp>                     <Fdisk>                    <Prompt>
<Chdir>                    <Files>                    <Qbasic>
<Chkdsk>                   <Find>                     <RAMDRIVE.SYS>
<CHKSTATE.SYS>             <For>                      <Rd>
<Choice>                   <Format>                   <Rem>
<Cls>                      <Goto>                     <Ren>
<Command>                  <Graphics>                 <Rename>
<CONFIG.SYS commands>      <Help>                     <Replace>
<Copy>                     <HIMEM.SYS>                <Restore>
<Country>                  <If>                       <Rmdir>
<Ctty>                     <Include>                  <ScanDisk>
<Date>                     <Install>                  <Set>
<Dblspace>                 <Interlnk>                 <Setver>
<Debug>                    <INTERLNK.EXE>             <SETVER.EXE>
<Defrag>                   <International commands>   <Share>
<Del>                      <Intersvr>                 <Shell>
<Deltree>                  <Keyb>                     <Shift>
<Device>                   <Label>                    <SIZER.EXE>
<Device drivers>           <Lastdrive>                <Smartdrv>
<Devicehigh>               <Lh>                       <SMARTDRV.EXE>
<Dir>                      <Loadfix>                  <Sort>
<Diskcomp>                 <Loadhigh>                 <Stacks>
<Diskcopy>                 <Md>                       <Submenu>
<DISPLAY.SYS>              <Mem>                      <Subst>
<Dos>                      <Memmaker>                 <Switches>
<Alt+C=Contents> <Alt+N=Next> <Alt+B=Back>                      N 00034:047
```

Figure 8.3 Online Help from MS-DOS.

Quickies

Another little collection of useful commands:

- **label** Displays the label and serial number of the specified (or current) drive and allows you to assign a new label with a maximum of 11 characters. To assign a label (name) to a disk in your floppy drive, type **label a:** (not forgetting the colon).
- **keyb** Sets your keyboard to send out the correct language characters for your country. For UK English enter **keyb uk**. Without the **keyb** command, the keyboard will default to the US English layout.
- |**more** This is a switch that works just like the **/p** switch in the **dir** command. For any command that delivers a long stream of output, use this switch to force it to display one screen at a time. You move to the next screen by pressing any key.

Using wildcards

Wildcards are a common labour-saving device in MS-DOS (also useful in Windows and certain Windows applications). They are used to select multiple files or to locate files whose full name you can't remember, by allowing you to substitute characters in the file name with the wildcard characters * and **?**. The asterisk (*) represents multiple letters and the question-mark (**?**) represents a single letter. These are best demonstrated by example.

To delete all files with the extension **.txt** in a folder called C:\Letters, type
del c:\letters*.txt

- To add the Read-only attribute to all files in the current folder, type
  attrib +r *.*
- To see a list of all **.doc** files in C:\Reports whose names end with the characters 'net' (such as Internet.doc), type:
  dir c:\reports*net.doc
- To locate any file with 1995 in its name, type
  dir *1995*.*
- To locate any **.txt** file whose third and fourth letters are *sp* (such as Suspect.txt) type
  dir ??sp*.txt
- To show all files with a four-letter name beginning with J (such as July.doc and Jack.txt), type
  dir j???.*
- To change the extension of all **.txt** files to **.doc** in the current folder, type
  ren *.txt *.doc

Autoexec.bat and Config.sys

There are two files whose names are often spoken in the same breath: Autoexec.bat and Config.sys. These two files are processed as you boot your computer, containing commands to load drivers for your hardware, configure memory and set up user-preferences. These files can be edited to tailor the system to your own taste, or to add extra device drivers (if the hardware setup program doesn't do that for you), or to tweak the memory settings.

In this section we'll take a look at some of the entries you'll find in these files and what they're all about, but to do more than skim the surface would be beyond the scope of this book – the exact entries in *your* system files depend upon your installed software and hardware, whether or not you use Windows 3.1 or Windows 95, and what types of program (if any) you run under DOS.

TIP

Whether you use MS-DOS or Windows 3.1 you'll have both of these files in your root folder. In Windows 95 neither are required, but both have their uses so you might still have them. Make sure you have backups of these files on a floppy disk before editing them. In Windows, try to use **System Editor** (Sysedit.exe) to edit them, since this utility creates an automatic backup of an edited system file, giving it the extension **.syd**. (For more on System Editor, see p. 309.)

Autoexec.bat

The **.bat** extension indicates that this is a **batch file**, which is a type of program that runs under DOS. The difference between batch programs and the more usual **.exe** and **.com** programs is that batch programs are text based – you can create them yourself in a text-editor such as Windows' **Notepad** or DOS's **Edit**. This particular batch file is executed automatically when DOS starts – hence its name!

An example of a typical MS-DOS Autoexec.bat is shown in Table 8.1.

Table 8.1 A typical MS-DOS Autoexec.bat

Autoexec.bat
@ECHO OFF SET PATH = C:\;C:\DOS;C:\WINDOWS;C:\WINDOWS\SYSTEM; SET TEMP = C:\TEMP SET DIRCMD = /W rem sets dir command to wide mode. PROMPT PG rem sets prompt to display current drive and path. KEYB UK,,C:\DOS\KEYBOARD.SYS C:\DOS\MSCDEX /D:NEC_CD /M:20 /E L:F LOADHIGH C:\DOS\SMARTDRV.EXE 1024 128

The Autoexec.bat file contains many of the settings needed to prepare the operating system for use, together with commands to load particular programs into memory. These programs are known as **memory-resident** programs, since they remain in memory while you work rather than shutting down when the operating system has finished booting. These are often referred to as **TSRs**, an abbreviation of 'Terminate and Stay Resident'.

To open your Autoexec.bat in MS-DOS's text editor, type

edit c:\autoexec.bat

Here are a few of the entries you might find in your Autoexec.bat, together with a few you might want to add. These entries are not case-sensitive: any entries added by DOS itself are always upper-case, but there's no requirement to follow DOS's lead. You might prefer to add your own entries in lower-case to help distinguish them from the others.

set path=

This specifies a list of paths that DOS will search for executable files (**.exe**, **.com**, **.bat** and **.pif** files). Ordinarily to run a file called Vampire.bat in your C:\Games\Vampires folder, you'd either have to use **cd** to switch to that folder and type **vampire**, or you'd have to enter the full path: **c:\games\vampires\vampire**. But if this path is already specified in your **Path**= line, you can just type **vampire** whatever your current folder, and DOS will be able to find and run the program. A common path statement will look something like:

set path=c:\;c:\dos;c:\programs;c:\games;c:\games\vampires;

The paths follow on one after another, with no spaces, each path separated by a semi-colon (;). You can include paths to compressed drives, but don't use paths to floppy disk or CD-ROM drives. The path statement can be a maximum of 128 characters in length – any characters after the 128th will be ignored.

set temp=

Many Windows programs create temporary files while they're running, often in order to keep track of edits you make to a file. When the file or program is closed, these files are automatically deleted. To do this they need a folder to use, which is specified by entering a path in the **set temp**= line. When Windows is installed, it creates a folder called C:\Windows\Temp and adds this path to Autoexec.bat, but many users prefer to have their Temp folder in C:\ where they can get at it more easily to check that their programs really have deleted their **.tmp** files, so you might like to change this entry to

set temp=c:\temp

set dircmd=

This is a useful one for DOS users. Because the **dir** command by itself displays the contents of folders in a long list, you might often find yourself typing **dir/w** or **dir/w/p** on the command line. If so, you can use the **set dircmd**= line to add these switches automatically every time you type **dir**. For example, if you always want the **dir** command to display a folder's contents in wide mode, one screen at a time, enter the line

set dircmd=/w/p

Anytime you want to use the **dir** command in normal (list) mode, you can override this Autoexec.bat setting by using the switch **/-w**.

prompt

This sets the command prompt the way you want it without having to do it from the command line every time you start DOS. To make the usual setting (drive, path and greater-than sign), enter

prompt pg

keyb uk,,c:\dos\keyboard.sys

By default, the computer keyboard is configured for United States English. UK users will find the results of their key-presses don't match the labels on the keys themselves. This command reconfigures the keyboard for UK English. (Note the double-comma in the command!)

win

This should be the last command in the Autoexec.bat file. It runs a file called **Win.com** which loads Windows. Obviously if you don't have Windows you won't use this command. If you have Windows 95, the **win** command is built into the operating system and shouldn't be included in Autoexec.bat – if it is included, every time you try to boot to DOS, this command will be processed and you'll shoot straight past DOS and into Windows 95!

rem

This is a useful item to remember when working with both Autoexec.bat and Config.sys. **Rem** is short for remark, and allows you to add comments to either file for your own reference that won't be processed along with the commands. On a new line in the file, type **rem** followed by a space and your comment. If you want to type a paragraph, make sure you type **rem** and a space at the start of each new line. You can also use this for troubleshooting: if you think a particular command in one of these files is causing problems, insert **rem** and a space at the beginning of the line to turn it into a remark, re-save the file, and then reboot the computer to see if the problem goes away.

Config.sys

The primary role of Config.sys (see Table 8.2) is in loading device-drivers and configuring memory, which is traditionally a knotty problem in MS-DOS. The memory-setting options you might use in Config.sys are covered in the next section, but here are a few other entries worthy of a mention.

Table 8.2 A typical MS-DOS Config.sys

Config.sys
DEVICE=C:\DOS\HIMEM.SYS DEVICE=C:\DOS\EMM386.EXE RAM AUTO DOS=HIGH,UMB BUFFERS=15,0 FILES=40 STACKS=9,256 COUNTRY=44,,C:\DOS\COUNTRY.SYS DEVICEHIGH=C:\CDROM\CD12J27.SYS /D:NEC_CD rem loads the dos cd-rom driver into upper memory rem to free up conventional memory. DEVICEHIGH=C:\DOS\DRVSPACE.SYS /MOVE

country=44,,c:\dos\country.sys

Along similar lines to the **keyb** entry in Autoexec.bat, this line sets UK conventions for displaying date, time and currency.

numlock=

This specifies whether you want the *Num Lock* key on your keyboard's numeric keypad switched on (activating its numeric keys) or off (activating the keys' secondary uses). Follow the equals sign with **on** or **off**.

device=drvspace.sys/move

If you have one or more compressed drives, this driver must be loaded into memory to let you access the files they contain. The **/move** switch moves the driver from its original position in memory (as MS-DOS started) to a different position that keeps it out of the way of other drivers that need to use this area of memory. The **device=** section of the line can be replaced with **devicehigh=** to load the driver into upper memory (see p. 266).

files=

This specifies how many files can be open in MS-DOS at any one time, by simply typing the required number after the equals sign. The range can be anywhere between 8 and 255, but a typical value here would be 30 to 40.

▶ *Windows 3.1 and 95 have their own system files in addition to Autoexec.bat and Config.sys.* *Turn to pp. 272 and 306 for Windows 3.1 details, and to p. 379 for Windows 95.*

MS-DOS memory

The PC's memory is a rather complicated affair. Quite simply, there sometimes isn't enough of it, and juggling things around to try to free more takes knowledge, or patience, or both. At this you're probably thinking, *But I've got 8 Mb RAM – how much more do I need?* The problem is that although Windows can make good use of your 8 Mb, DOS mostly has to work with just the first 1 Mb of that. And when you try to load more data into RAM under Windows, it can use its virtual memory capabilities to send some currently unused data off to disk temporarily; DOS doesn't have that luxury. In addition, of this 1 Mb memory available to DOS, a certain amount must be used to hold DOS itself, device drivers, TSR programs and so on.

Nevertheless, most of the programs you use under DOS will run quite happily. DOS programs are considerably smaller than Windows programs, and many are tiny. The problems of configuring memory arise mostly when trying to run arcade-style games which, even in these days of Windows, often run under MS-DOS and tend to stretch its capabilities to the maximum.

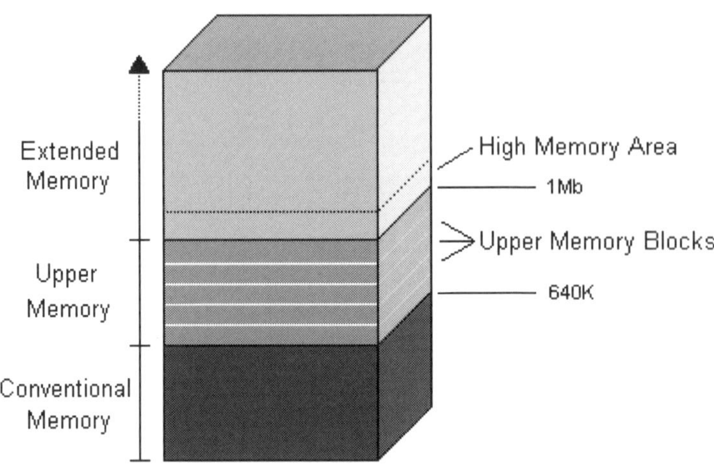

Figure 8.4 The assignment of memory in the PC.

Memory types

To picture what and where the different types of memory are, picture your PC's memory as a tall rack of shelves into which chunks of data can be slotted. As shown in Figure 8.4, the shelves nearest the ground can hold 640 K of data; the few shelves above them can hold 384 K of data (a total of 1 Mb so far); and the remaining shelves will be able to hold 7 Mb of data (if your PC has 8 Mb installed).

Conventional memory

This is the name given to the first 640 K of memory in your PC. By default, DOS itself loads into this area of memory, together with all the programs you run, and any installed device drivers. This might leave you with too little conventional memory for the program you want to use.

Upper memory

This is the next 384 K of memory, and is divided into blocks known as **UMBs** (Upper Memory Blocks). The UMBs contain a certain amount of system data, but empty blocks can be used to hold device drivers and TSR programs that would normally reside in conventional memory, thus freeing more conventional memory for running your program. Device drivers are loaded into upper memory from Config.sys by replacing the word **DEVICE**= with **DEVICEHIGH**= in the appropriate lines. Programs are loaded into upper memory from Autoexec.bat by inserting **LH** or **LOADHIGH** and a space at the beginning of the appropriate line. To load programs and drivers into UMBs requires the use of a program called **Emm386.exe** which comes with MS-DOS. You'll also need the line **DOS**=**UMB** in your Config.sys file.

Extended memory

After the first 1 Mb used for conventional memory and UMBs, the remaining RAM in your computer is known as Extended memory (abbreviated to **XMS**). For example, if your PC has 16 Mb RAM installed, you have 15 Mb of XMS. For DOS to be able to use XMS, you must use a memory-manager program such as **Himem.sys** which is included with MS-DOS. This is installed by adding the line: **device = c:\dos\himem.sys** to your Config.sys file.

High memory area

This is almost always abbreviated to **HMA**. The High Memory Area is the first 64 K of your Extended memory. If **Himem.sys** is installed as above, DOS can use this first little chunk of XMS to load a program into. Since only one program can be loaded here, it's usual to make that DOS itself by adding the line **DOS = HIGH** to Config.sys. If you load DOS into HMA in this way, you'll regain about 46 K of conventional memory.

Expanded memory

Expanded memory (abbreviated to **EMS**) also needs **Emm386.exe** to be loaded, and uses an area of the UMBs to give access to more of your huge reserves of Extended memory. It does this by squirrelling away chunks of data in Extended memory, and logging the locations of these chunks in the area of the UMBS it uses. These 'chunks' of data are called **pages**, and the 64 K area of the UMBs used to track their whereabouts is called the **page frame**. This means that to get access to Expanded memory you have to sacrifice 64 K of UMBs to create an EMS page frame.

TIP

To maximize the memory you have, don't load unnecessary drivers or programs in your system files. For example, if you need more memory to run a program that doesn't use your soundcard or CD-ROM drive, unload their drivers and the Mscdex.exe file: edit Autoexec.bat and Config.sys to place a **rem** before the appropriate lines and then reboot the computer. As an example, rem-ing out the **keyb** line in Autoexec.bat will regain 7 K of conventional memory (if you don't mind learning a slightly different keyboard layout!).

Dos and don'ts

Understanding how all this works isn't easy; piecing it together so that it really *does* work can be a bit of a pain, often involving making a few changes to your system files, rebooting the PC and trying to run the program again. The process can be helped along by ensuring that you follow a few rules.

To gain the maximum conventional memory you'll want to enable all types of memory, give DOS access to them, and (usually) load DOS into HMA. You'll also want to use **devicehigh=** and **loadhigh/lh** commands to move drivers and programs out of conventional memory. This entails the use of **Emm386.exe**, **Himem.sys**, and the **DOS=** commands. These should always be placed in your Config.sys file, and in the following order:

```
device=c:\dos\himem.sys
device=c:\dos\emm386.exe ram auto
dos=high,umb
```

These three lines must come before any line beginning with **devicehigh=**, but for simplicity, it's easiest to make these the *first* three lines of your Config.sys. It's important to remember that commands in the system files are processed in the order they appear, so nothing can be placed in upper memory until **Emm386.exe** has been loaded. The **dos=high** and **dos=umb** lines can be merged, as shown in the third line above.

The inclusion of the **ram** switch in the **Emm386.exe** line ensures that the maximum available space will be used for UMBs and EMS when needed; the **auto** switch specifies that this space should only be used when it really *is* needed. If the program you want to run doesn't need EMS, remove both switches and use the switch **noems** instead. This will prevent Emm386.exe using its chunk of upper memory to supply expanded memory, meaning that you'll get your missing 64 K of UMBs back.

Programs are loaded from Autoexec.bat. To load a program into upper memory (UMBs), you preface the command line with **LOADHIGH** (or just **LH**) followed by a space, such as:

```
lh c:\dos\smartdrv.exe
```

Driver files are loaded from Config.sys, and can be loaded into UMBs using **DEVICEHIGH=**, such as:

```
devicehigh=c:\dos\drvspace.sys /move
```

One last point to consider: only *whole* files can be loaded into upper memory. You can place **LH** or **DEVICEHIGH=** in front of all the appropriate lines in your system files, but they won't necessarily all be able to fit into the available UMBs, so some might still remain in conventional memory. However, because the system files are processed line by line, you might be able to fit the most important files into the UMBs by rearranging the order they occur in your system files so that the largest files appear first.

CHAPTER 9

Using Windows 3.1

Introducing Windows 3.1

Windows, from 1 to 95

The history of Windows has been a slightly curious one: to look at the early success of MS-DOS you'd think it hardly surprising that Microsoft is still at the top of the operating systems tree with Windows. In fact Microsoft was slow to pick up the idea of a graphical user interface and start running with it, even when Apple produced a WIMP machine called **Lisa** that proved popular. Only after a company called Digital Research had released a graphical interface for the PC called **GEM** (Graphical Environment Manager) did Microsoft sit up and take notice, and Windows version 1.0 appeared in 1985.

Although PC users were waiting for a friendly graphical interface, this, apparently, wasn't the one they were waiting for and they carried on using GEM. Windows 2 arrived to a similarly unspectacular reception, and Microsoft joined forces with IBM and released OS/2 in 1988. Although OS/2 received the same level of undisguised apathy as Windows, this partnership proved useful to IBM: the shared technology agreement between the two companies enabled IBM to keep its PC-DOS development running in parallel with MS-DOS, and ensured that later versions of OS/2 (which IBM has continued to develop alone) were largely compatible with Windows, even to the point of containing Windows code.

It was in 1989 that Microsoft released Windows 3.0, and this time they struck gold: *this* was the friendly graphical interface everyone was waiting for, and they bought it. The release of version 3.1 consolidated its position to make Windows *the* operating system for the PC. Finally, in 1993, a few enhancements brought version 3.11, together with a sister version called Windows for Workgroups 3.11 (see Figure 9.1) which added networking, mail and fax facilities. Although the various Windows 3s have been superseded by Windows 95 (a departure in version numbering for what would have been Windows 4.0), they're still widely used and widely available with a vast amount of software to be found.

Windows 3.x has the additional advantage that it will run reasonably happily on a 386SX25 computer with as little as 4 Mb, whereas Windows 95 really needs a minimum of a fast 486 with 8 Mb. Bear in mind, however, that use of graphics-intensive applications, large files, and multitasking all put extra strain on system memory – every 4 Mb RAM you add, up to about 16 Mb, makes a huge difference to performance.

JARGONBUSTER

Windows 3.x

Much of the detail that applies to Windows 3.1 applies equally to Windows 3.0, 3.11 and Windows for Workgroups. As a form of shorthand, the collective term Windows 3.x is often used to refer to the entire version 3 series.

Bits and modes

Like previous versions, Windows 3.1 is a **16-bit operating system**. This means that it can access memory in 16-bit (2 byte) chunks at a time, as can programs designed to run under it (you'll often see these referred to as '16-bit applications'). In comparison, Windows 95 is largely 32-bit, accessing chunks of memory 4 bytes at a time for increased speed and giving rise to the term '32-bit applications'. Among the enhancements built into Windows 3.11 was a small amount of early Windows 95 code for 32-bit disk access, making disk operations faster under 3.11 than they were under 3.1.

Another term frequently encountered when discussing Windows 3.1 is **real mode**. This is one of the two modes in which memory can be addressed, and is the operating mode used by Intel processors. The result of real mode is that one program can access the memory being used by another which might cause one of the programs to crash, or (more frequently) cause Windows itself to crash. This might be indicated by a dialog telling you that a **General Protection Fault** (GPF) has occurred, or the entire system might just 'hang' and refuse to accept any input. The GPF dialog will give you the option to ignore the error and continue, but the program is rarely able to recover. If it *does* recover, immediately save any unsaved files, shut down Windows, and restart the computer.

If a program hangs it may be possible to close it by pressing *Ctrl+Esc*, selecting the offending program and choosing **End Task**. More often Windows itself will hang and you'll have to restart the computer.

▶ *In contrast with Windows 3.1, Windows 95 is principally a 32-bit operating system and runs in protected mode – p. 317.*

Figure 9.1 The Windows on-screen startup logo.

Starting Windows

As we've already mentioned briefly, Windows requires a version of MS-DOS to be installed. Windows is started from DOS in the same way you'd start any DOS program – by typing the program's name and pressing *Enter*. The program that starts Windows is called **Win.com**, so simply typing **win** at the command prompt will do the trick.

Both Autoexec.bat and Config.sys still exist in your root folder, usually C:\, as covered on p. 261, and do exactly the same job. However, when Windows is installed, the **win** command is added as the last entry in Autoexec.bat so that Windows is loaded automatically without pausing in DOS; all you have to do is switch on your PC and wait.

TIP

In Windows 3.11 you can bypass the startup logo (shown in Figure 9.1) and thus load Windows a little faster by typing **win/n** at the command prompt or adding the **/n** switch to the **win** command in your Autoexec.bat. (In Windows 3.1, use **win:** instead.)

If you prefer, you can delete the **win** command (or type **rem** and a space before it) to boot to DOS instead, and decide whether or not to load Windows. An alternative method is to insert an extra line before the **win** command containing the single word **pause**. When the boot-process has loaded MS-DOS, the screen will display

Press any key to continue

Pressing any key will load Windows; if you want to work in DOS for a while, hit *Ctrl+Break* instead and the **win** command will be ignored.

Shutting down Windows

When you've finished working in DOS, you can just save the file you were working on and turn off your PC – no complications. Windows is a slightly different story – it isn't complicated, but it *is* important: because Windows and its applications keep a certain amount of data on disk in the form of virtual memory and temporary (**.tmp**) files, just switching off when you've finished can result in loss of data and a build-up of temporary files that should have been deleted.

TIP

Although shutting-down properly should cause **.tmp** files to be deleted, it's worth checking your Temp folder once in a while and deleting any you find. A system-crash or a badly behaved application might leave files there hogging disk space.

To shut down in an organized way, first close any running applications (saving any open files if you need to) and return to Program Manager. Either choose **File/Exit** or press *Alt+F4* and you'll see the **Exit Windows** dialog, shown in Figure 9.2. Click on **OK** and you'll be returned to the DOS prompt, where you can either continue working in DOS, type **win** to reload Windows, or switch off the PC.

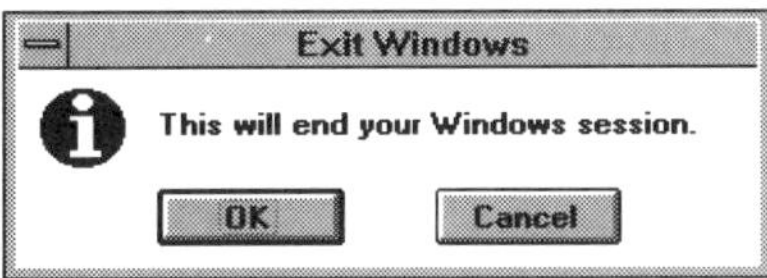

Figure 9.2 If you don't see this dialog when you stop working in Windows, you're doing it wrong!

Program Manager

Program Manager (**Progman.exe**) is the shell program of Windows 3.1, and is what you'll see on the screen when Windows has finished loading. The Program Manager window contains several smaller windows known as **group windows** displaying icons for the accessories installed with Windows itself together with any other software you have installed. Windows creates groups called **Main**, **Accessories**, **Games**, **StartUp** and (in Windows for Workgroups) **Network**. Other installed applications will usually create their own groups named after the software.

Open group windows can be resized by moving the mouse pointer onto a corner or edge of the window (so that it turns into an arrow) and dragging. A group can also be minimized to an icon (like those at the bottom of the window in Figure 9.3) or maximized to fill the entire Program Manager window. Groups and icons can be renamed or deleted, new groups and icons can be created, and you can save the layout of the Program Manager window when you've arranged it the way you like it.

When you minimize a group, it doesn't necessarily end up at the bottom of the screen – the icon might hide behind one of your open group windows! If an icon goes missing, minimize the other windows until you find it, and drag it to somewhere it'll be visible.

The icons in Program Manager groups are **shortcuts** – each icon acts as a pointer to a file on your hard disk to save you trawling through your folders and files to locate the program you want to run. So deleting an icon (or an entire group) doesn't delete the file itself, it just removes your quick method of getting at it.

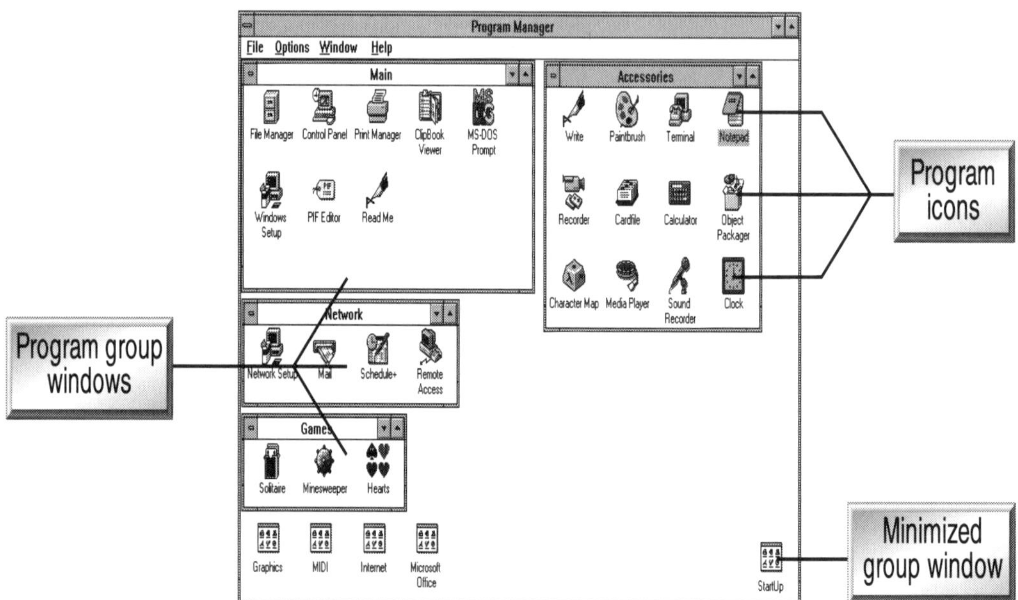

Figure 9.3 Program Manager.

Working with groups and icons

To run a program that has an icon in Program Manager, just double-click the icon with the mouse. If the group window containing the icon is minimized, double-click the group icon first to open its window. To run a program using the keyboard, hold *Ctrl* and press *Tab* repeatedly until the required group's title-bar is highlighted, then either use the arrow keys to navigate to the icon you want or press its initial letter on the keyboard; press *Enter* to run the highlighted item.

An icon can be deleted from any group by clicking once on it to select it, pressing *Delete*, and clicking *Yes* (or pressing *Enter*) in the inevitable confirmation prompt. To delete an entire group the group window must be minimized – you can then select its icon and delete it in the same way.

You can move an icon from one group to another by dragging it with the pointer; if you want to *copy* an icon to another group, hold *Ctrl* and drag. The target group doesn't have to be open – you can drop an icon onto a minimized group to move or copy it there. To move or copy using the keyboard, highlight an icon, press *F7* or *F8* respectively, and choose the target group from the dialog.

Creating a new program group

To create a new Program Manager group, choose **New...** from the **File** menu, choose Program Group, and click **OK**. Another dialog will appear with two boxes for **Description** and **Group File**. Type any name for the group you like in the **Description** box, which will be displayed in its title-bar. You can ignore the **Group File** box and click **OK** – Windows will create a group file automatically in C:\Windows using the first eight letters of your chosen name and the extension **.grp**. Your new group window will appear and you can start creating icons in it.

TIP

If you end up with so many program groups that it gets hard to find what you want, create a new group and move all your most-used icons into it. Minimize all the other groups and arrange the window of this new one so that you can still see the other minimized groups for when you need to open one of them, then save the settings.

Creating a new program item

The quickest way to create a new item in a group is to hold *Alt* and double-click any white space in the group window – the **Properties** dialog will appear (see Figure 9.4), saving you the trouble of going to **File/New/Program Item**.

Program Item Properties

Description: CardFile

Command Line: CARDFILE.EXE

Working Directory: c:\winprogs\cards

Shortcut Key: Ctrl + Alt + C

Run Minimized

OK

Cancel

Browse...

Change Icon...

Help

Figure 9.4 The **Properties** dialog.

1. In the **Description** box, type your own choice of name for the item.
2. In the **Command Line** box, type the path and name of the file for which you want a shortcut. Alternatively, click on **Browse** and use the standard file dialog to find and double-click the file.
3. Enter a **Working Directory** if you want one (see below). If you don't, Windows will automatically assign the directory (folder) containing the target program.
4. Enter a **Shortcut Key** in the next box if you want one (see below).
5. Click **OK**, and you've got a new icon in your group!

You can also create a new item by finding the file in File Manager and dragging it into a Program Manager group. This is most easily done by arranging the File Manager and Program Manager windows side by side.

Working Directory

Let's say you've got a shortcut to a word processor called Myword.exe, and its path is C:\Programs\Myword.exe. When you're using this program and you want to open or save a file, the **Open** and **Save As** dialogs will offer you C:\Programs as the default folder. If all your word-processing documents are in a folder called C:\Docs, enter this path in the **Working Directory** box and this folder will be presented as the default Open/Save folder, saving you a lot of clicking around in the dialogs.

Shortcut Key

You can assign a hotkey combination to a shortcut that will let you run it by pressing three keys on the keyboard instead of finding and double-clicking the icon. Click once in the **Shortcut Key** box to select it (or use *Tab* to move the cursor to it) and enter your choice of hotkey. If you press a single key, such as 'D', your hotkey combination will automatically be *Ctrl+Alt+D*. If you'd prefer to use *Ctrl+Shift+D* or *Alt+Shift+D* you must press these keys too. The advantage of hotkeys is you don't have to have a group window open to run an item inside it – very handy for non-mouse-lovers!

To help you remember the hotkeys you've assigned, rename the icons adding the hotkey combination in the **Description** box.

Shortcuts to files

Shortcuts aren't limited to programs – you can add a shortcut icon to any file at all! For example, if you've got a file called **Business.crd** that you use regularly, enter its path in the **Command Line** box; **.crd** files are associated with **Cardfile.exe**, so double-clicking this icon will run Cardfile with this file loaded. It's a lot quicker than clicking your Cardfile shortcut, then using Cardfile's **File/Open** dialog to search for **Business.crd**.

Renaming groups and icons

A common problem with the groups and icons created by software installations is that they often use ridiculously long names which overlap one another. To rename an icon, hold *Alt* and double-click the icon, then type a different name in the **Description** box. To rename a group, first minimize it, then click it once to highlight it. (If a control menu appears, click the icon a second time to get rid of it, or press *Esc*.) With the group icon highlighted, press *Alt+Enter* and type a new name in the **Description** box.

Run Minimized

If you check the **Run Minimized** box on an item's Properties dialog, the program will open as an icon on the desktop instead of a window – you'll see it appear at the bottom of the screen unless Program Manager is covering that portion of the screen. When you want to use that program, either double-click the icon (if you can see it) or use *Alt+Tab* to switch to it.

Usually, of course, when you start a program you want to use it immediately. This checkbox really comes into its own when used with the **StartUp** group.

Even if you haven't checked this box, you can force a program to start minimized by holding *Shift* while you double-click it.

The StartUp group

Windows creates an empty group called **StartUp** when it's installed. Any shortcuts placed in this group (whether files or programs) will be started automatically when Windows finishes loading. This is particularly useful if there are programs you find yourself using in every Windows session (such as File Manager or a word processor), or you like to have certain accessories running, such as the Clock. You can move or copy existing shortcuts into the StartUp group, or create new ones here in the usual way.

TIP

If you want Windows to ignore the **StartUp** group and not load any of these items, press *Shift* when Windows starts to load (i.e. the logo appears) and hold it until the 'Busy' pointer turns to its usual arrow shape.

The Run line

Windows offers a DOS-type command line for running programs: select **Run...** from the **File** menu, and type in the path (if necessary) and name of the program to be run. Some programs have switches to alter how they're run, so even if you already have a Program Manager icon for the program, the Run line can be useful if you ever need to run it with different options selected.

The Options menu

Program Manager's **Options** menu has three entries, each of which will display a tick when switched on.

- *Auto Arrange.* When selected, the icons in each group window will be neatly arranged in straight rows and columns. If you prefer your groups to have a random look, turn off this option.
- *Minimize on Use.* If you select this option, as soon as you double-click an icon in a group, Program Manager will minimize to an icon at the bottom of the desktop (unless the program you're starting is set to run minimized).
- *Save Settings on Exit.* This specifies that the layout of Program Manager should be saved every time you quit Windows. You'll usually want to leave this unchecked so that you can arrange everything the way you want it, save it, and keep it that way.

After you've set all your group window sizes and positions (and the positions of any iconized groups) you could save the settings by checking the **Save Settings on Exit** option, quitting and restarting Windows, and then unchecking the option. A far niftier way to do it, however, is to hold *Shift* and select **File/Exit** (or press *Shift+Alt+F4*). This will save your settings immediately without shutting down Windows.

Changing the Windows shell

Although Program Manager is Windows 3.1's shell program by default, you can change this easily to another program. For example, a popular option is to use File Manager (**Winfile.exe**) as the shell.

1. Open **System Editor** (C:\Windows\System\Sysedit.exe) and click on the title-bar of **System.ini** to bring it to the top of the stack.
2. In the [**boot**] section, near the top of the file, you'll see a line that reads **SHELL=PROGMAN.EXE**. Change this to **SHELL=WINFILE.EXE**.
3. Select **File/Save** in System Editor, then exit and restart Windows. Instead of Program Manager appearing, you'll see File Manager.

Another popular shell program to use is **Taskman** (C:\Windows\Taskman.exe). Whatever program you choose as the shell, whenever you try to exit that program you'll be presented with the **Exit Windows** dialog (see Figure 9.2) – in other words, closing the shell program will close Windows.

The **SHELL=** line can also be useful if you have limited memory and you just use your computer for one particular task such as word processing: change the line to load your word processor as the shell (including the program's path if it's not specified in your Autoexec.bat). If you need to run other programs, you can call up Taskman by pressing *Ctrl+Esc*, or by minimizing your word processor and double-clicking on the desktop.

File Manager

File Manager (Winfile.exe) is Windows 3.1's program for viewing the files and folders on your disks. When you first open it (by double-clicking its icon in Program Manager's **Main** group) you'll see something similar to Figure 9.5 – a two-pane view of your 'C' drive, with the folder tree in the left pane and the contents of the selected folder in the right.

Clicking any folder in the left pane will 'open' it, and its contents will be displayed in the right pane, including any subfolders. If you were to double-click the folder in the left pane, the result in the right-pane would be the same, but the tree would expand to show that folder's subfolders if it had any. You can also open a folder shown in the right pane by double-clicking it, which will also expand the tree view.

ee at a glance which folders in the left pane contain subfolders, select **Indicate Expandable Branches** from the **Tree** menu: those that are expandable will have a small cross added to their icons.

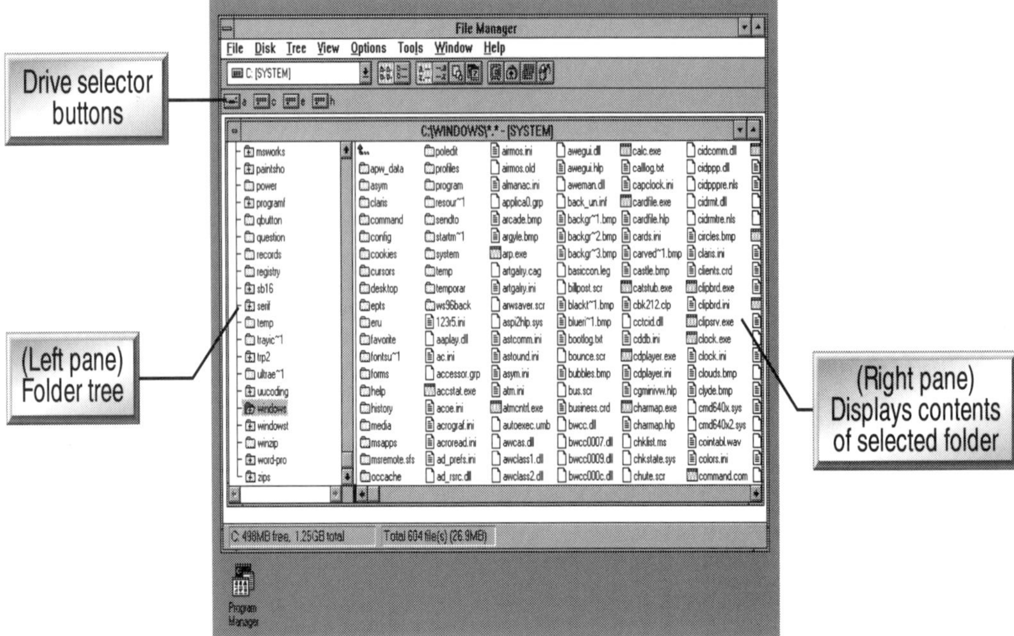

Figure 9.5 File Manager displaying a single window.

If you want to view the contents of a different drive, click one of the drive-selector buttons or press *Ctrl+drive letter* (for example, to view the contents of Drive A, press *Ctrl+A*). If you have several windows open (see below), the drive's contents will be displayed in the currently selected window. To open a drive *and* have the tree fully expanded automatically, hold *Shift* while you click a drive-selector button, or press *Ctrl+Shift+drive letter.*

If you use the MS-DOS's **Subst** command to substitute a path with a drive letter (see section **8.4**), the drive letter will appear as an icon on the drive-bar for extra-quick access.

▶ *The Properties pages of files and folders in File Manager were explained on p. 143. For more on File Manager's icons and file-associations, return to p. 120.*

Opening multiple windows

One extremely useful feature of File Manager is its multiple document interface (MDI), which lets you open multiple drives and folders in different windows. This makes it easy to move or copy files and folders from one drive to another.

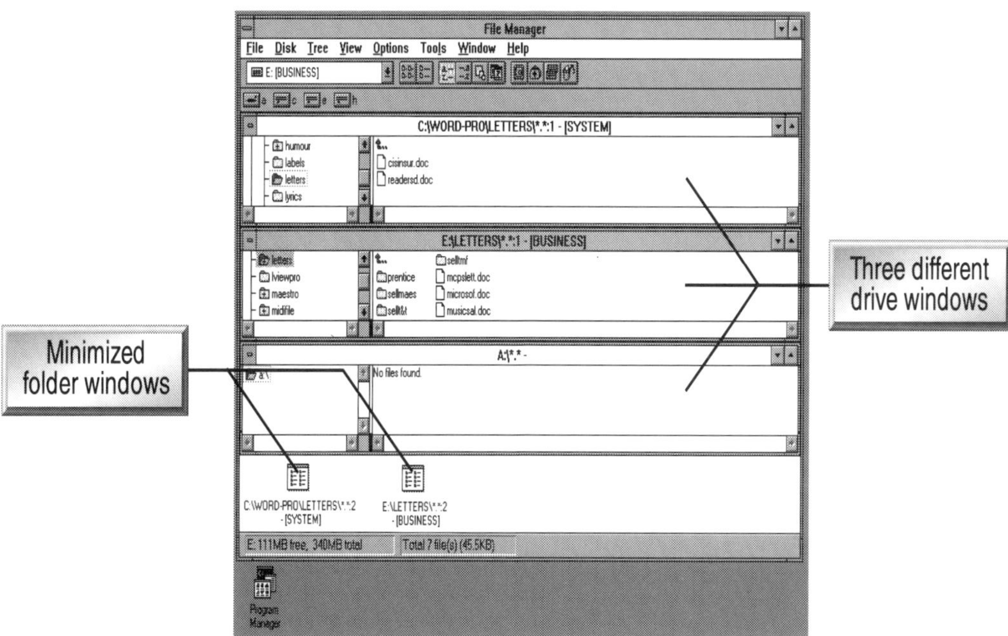

Figure 9.6 File Manager's multiple document interface.

For example, if you're looking at Drive C in a window and you want to view Drive D as well, just *double-click* the drive-selector button for D and it'll open in a new window. You can also open *folders* in a new window: to open a folder from the left pane in a new window, hold *Shift* as you double-click it; to open a folder from the right pane, click it once to highlight it, then *Shift+double-click*. You can maximize any of these 'child windows' to fill File Manager's main window, or minimize them so they become icons at the bottom of the window, as in Figure 9.6.

TIP

To move up from the current folder to its parent, double-click the little green arrow in the upper left corner of the right pane. If you want to view the parent folder in a *new* window, click once on the arrow to highlight it, then hold *Shift* while you double-click it.

Moving and copying

You can move or copy files and folders from one place to another using Drag & Drop. For this to work, of course, you've got to be able to see the item you want to drag as well as the place you want to drop it. If you want to drag an item to somewhere on the same drive, this is quite simple: after making sure the item is visible in the right pane, use the scroll-bar to bring the target folder into view in the left pane. You can just drag the item from the right pane and drop it on the folder icon in the left pane. If you drag it to a drive-selector button it will automatically be placed in that drive's root folder, which can be useful for copying files to floppy disk for example.

There is just one complicating factor: when using Drag & Drop, if you drag a file or folder to somewhere on the *same* drive it will automatically be *moved*; drag to somewhere on a *different* drive and it'll be *copied*. To get around this, here's a good habit to get into: if you want to move an item somewhere, hold *Shift* while you drag; if you want to copy it somewhere, hold *Ctrl*.

TIP

When you drag and drop an item, keep an eye on the mouse pointer. As you move the pointer, a little page icon moves with it. If the page icon is blank, the item will be moved; if it has a small cross in the middle, the item will be copied. If you start dragging and realize you're not going to get the result you wanted, press *Esc* and the whole action will be cancelled.

For keyboard fans, highlight an item and press *F7* if you want to move it, and *F8* to copy it. A dialog will appear prompting you to enter a path to the target drive and folder.

Selecting multiple items

Sometimes, of course, you want to move, copy or delete several items in one go, so how do you select them all?

- To select every item in an open window, press *Ctrl+/*. If you want to deselect them all again, press *Ctrl+*.
- To select several items that occur one after the other, click on the first one, then press and hold *Shift* and click on the last – all those in between will also be selected.
- To select several items that don't form a continuous list, press *Ctrl* each time you click on one. The items you've already selected will *stay* selected, and you can use the scroll-bars to move around in a window to find other items to add to the collection.

Using any of these methods, if you select a file you didn't mean to, there's no need to start all over again: just press *Ctrl* and click it a second time – this will *deselect* it. Keep this in mind if you want to select all but a few items in a window: use the first method above to select every item, then use *Ctrl+click* to deselect the ones you don't want.

To find a file quickly in a folder, click somewhere in the right pane, then type the initial letter of the file you're looking for repeatedly until it's selected.

▶ *Skip back to p. 116 for details on creating new folders in File Manager, and p. 124 for information on deleting files and folders.*

Finding files

File Manager has two built-in methods to help you find the files you're looking for. The first is **Search...** on the **File** menu, which allows you to search for files by name. In the **Search For** box, either type the name of a file to be found or use wildcards (see p. 260) to locate a group of files. In the **Start From** box, enter a path to be searched. If you know exactly which folder the files are in, type this path and remove the check-mark from **Search All Subdirectories** to speed up the search.

The resulting list of files can be used in the same way as files in a normal File Manager window – you can double-click a file to open it, select one or more files to move or copy somewhere, delete files, and so on.

The second method is to use File Manager's *masking* facility by selecting the **View/By File Type...** option, shown in Figure 9.7. By checking or unchecking boxes, you can remove different types of item from view:

- *Directories.* Uncheck this box and your directories (folders) will be displayed in the left pane only.
- *Programs.* Choose whether you want to see **.exe**, **.com**, **.bat** and **.pif** files displayed.
- *Documents.* Refers to any file with an association (i.e. those with 'written-page' type icons).
- *Other Files.* Refers to files with no association (those with 'blank page' icons).
- *Show Hidden/System Files.* You can choose to hide any file with the System or Hidden attributes to prevent it being accidentally deleted or to keep it private.

In the box at the top of the dialog, you can type in a particular extension (such as ***.txt**) to see only files with that extension displayed. When you've finished working with files masked in this way, don't forget to go back to this dialog and enter *.*, or you'll be wondering where all your files have gone!

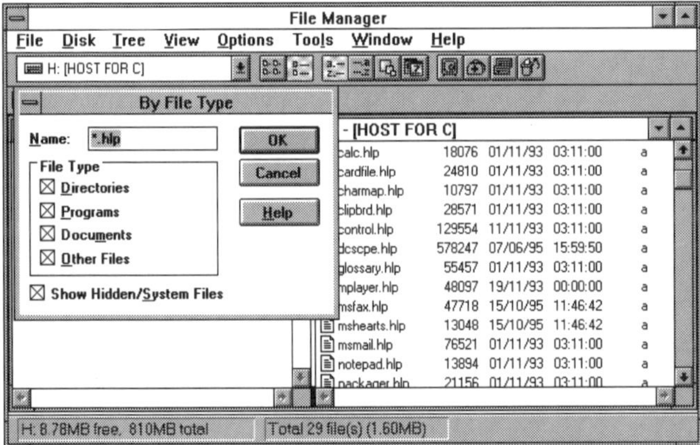

Figure 9.7 Choose which files you want displayed in File Manager windows.

TIP

If you forget what a particular button on File Manager's toolbar does, click it with the mouse but *don't release it*, then look at the status-bar for an explanation. If it doesn't do what you want, move the pointer away from the button before releasing it. (These buttons don't appear in version 3.1.)

Useful File Manager features

- To rename a file or folder, highlight it, go to **File/Rename...** and type a new name. Folders can have up to 11 characters in their names, but you'll have to type a dot after the eighth.
- If you get tired of being asked 'Are you sure...?' every time you try to do something in File Manager, go to **Options/Confirmation...** and remove the check-mark from the appropriate boxes.
- To print a file, highlight it and go to **File/Print**. (This will work only if the file extension has been associated with a program, and that program has a **Print** option on its own **File** menu.)
- To change the font used in File Manager, go to **Options/Font...** and choose a new font and point size. You can also choose whether to display titles in all upper-case or all lower-case characters.

Formatting a floppy disk

After putting the disk in your floppy drive, go to **Disk/Format**. Choose the correct drive from the drop-down list, usually **Drive A**. In the **Capacity** box, choose **1.44 Mb** for a high-density disk or **720 K** for a double-density disk. If you've previously used the disk and want to re-format it, check the box marked **Quick Format** to speed up the process. Click **OK**.

Saving your settings

File Manager has the same **Save Settings on Exit** option as Program Manager and it works in exactly the same way. If you've spent ages setting up the layout so that all the drives and folders you want to see are open and tiled or minimized, uncheck this entry on the **Options** menu, then press *Shift+Alt+F4* to save the settings and prevent them being accidentally changed.

TIP

Don't save your settings with a window open on your floppy-disk drive: next time you start File Manager, if there's no disk in the drive, you'll hear a lot of grinding and churning as Windows searches for one!

Control Panel

The **Control Panel** is a single program containing a collection of **applets**, small programs that have to be run from the main Control Panel program Control.exe. Each applet enables you to carry out a single task, such as configuring your mouse or keyboard, customizing the way Windows looks or sounds, tweaking system settings, and so on (see Figure 9.8).

The Control Panel lives in Program Manager's **Main** group. Double-clicking its icon will open its window, which will be followed by a pause of a few seconds while its constituent applets are loaded, each represented by its own icon. You can get a rough description of what each applet does by clicking once on its icon and looking at the status-bar, but here's a slightly more detailed overview coupled with a few tips for use. (Depending upon which version of Windows you have, and what software you have installed, your Control Panel may contain more or less applets than detailed here. Any applets added by an application's installation routine should be explained in its manuals.)

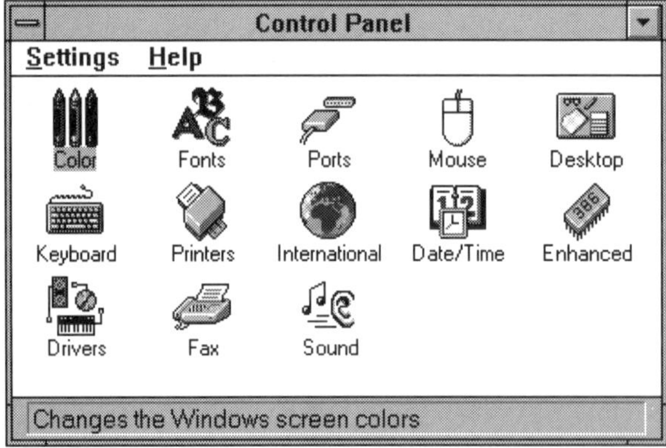

Figure 9.8 Windows 3.1's standard Control Panel.

International

The International applet is where you specify which country you're in, which language you use, which time/date/currency format you want, and the keyboard layout that matches your country and language. These settings are usually entered during Windows' installation process, but you can change them any time you want to.

If you never (or rarely) use MS-DOS, remove the **keyb** line from your Autoexec.bat file to save a little memory. Windows has its own setting for keyboard layout in International. If you ever need to work in DOS, just type **keyb uk** at the command prompt. (The keyboard has a US layout by default, so American users can ignore the **keyb** command altogether.)

Keyboard

Only two settings to play with here: the **Delay Before First Repeat** slider lets you choose how long you should hold a key before the character starts repeating; **Repeat Rate** specifies how fast the character should repeat. You can test your settings by clicking once in the **Test** box then holding down a key.

Mouse

The Mouse applet is where you fine-tune the behaviour of your mouse. The **Mouse Tracking Speed** is the rate the pointer moves across the screen in relation to the movement of your hand. **Double-Click Speed** lets you choose how far apart two clicks of the mouse can be before they cease to be recognized as a double-click – go for a slow speed to begin with if you're a mouse beginner, and give your finger a chance to limber up! Double-click in the TEST box to practise – if you're successful, the box will change colour.

On a high-resolution screen you'll probably need to move the **Tracking Speed** slider further to the right to help the rodent crawl around. A fast speed on a low-res screen can make it difficult to position the pointer precisely over small objects.

The **Swap Left/Right Button** checkbox allows left-handed users to make the right button their primary button. Click a button in the box above and you'll see the 'L' or 'R' flash to match the button you clicked. **Mouse Trails** (also known as 'mouse droppings') makes the pointer leave little trails of 'ghost pointers' everywhere it goes. This can give the irritating impression that the pointer is moving slowly, but it can be useful on a Notebook screen or any mono screen to prevent your rodent getting lost.

TIP

You can change the number of 'droppings' your mouse leaves behind it. Use System Editor to open **Win.ini** and add a new line to its [**windows**] section that reads **MouseTrails=7**. (The number can be anything from 1 to 7 inclusive.)

Date/Time

This allows you to change the system date and time of your PC. Either use the spin buttons or double-click on a number and type in a different one. The date/time setting is used by the **Clock** accessory, and used by Windows itself to mark the creation date of files and folders on their Properties sheet.

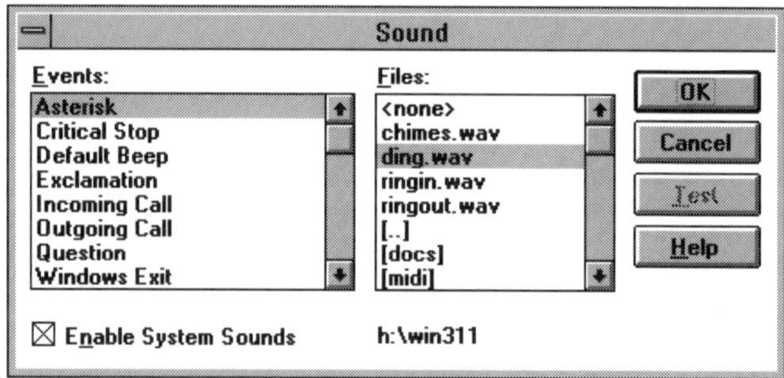

Figure 9.9 Let Windows serenade you as you try to get some work done.

Sound

This is a neat little customization applet that lets you assign sounds (in the form of **.wav** files) to Windows events such as different types of dialog, or starting and exiting Windows (Figure 9.9). Choose the **Event** in the left pane and the sound file you want to play in the right. By default, Windows' own small collection of sounds is displayed, but you can switch to the folder containing any others you have on your system by double-clicking [**..**] to move up to the parent folder, or double-clicking folder names in square brackets. Uncheck the **Enable System Sounds** box if you want to override this memory-hungry luxury. (If you want to hear sounds, you'll need a soundcard and speakers!)

Drivers

This displays the list of sound, video and multimedia drivers installed on your PC. Some of these may be device drivers for hardware on your system, others will be software *codecs* (short for compression/decompression) that enable Windows to work with some of the compressed video and graphics file formats.

To install a new driver, click on the **Add** button. If the driver you want to install is listed, click it and click **OK**. If it isn't, select **Unlisted or Updated Driver**, click **OK**, and type in the path to the new driver file in the **Install Driver** dialog (or use the **Browse** button to locate it).

To change the settings of a driver (such as IRQ or base-address of a soundcard), click the **Setup** button with the correct driver selected. Windows 3.1 isn't very helpful in this department, but it will often tell you if you've selected an incompatible setting.

▶ *For more on installing device drivers and making resource settings for hardware, see p. 39.*

Printers

The Printers applet shows the printers connected to your system. In most cases this will be just one hardware printer, but you might have additional 'software printers', such as Microsoft Fax, that grab the output from an application and fax it to someone by sending it to the modem instead of the printer. You can change the settings for a printer by highlighting it in the **Installed** list and clicking the **Setup...** button.

The **Default Printer** will usually be your hardware printer, so that whenever you select the **Print** option in an application, the data will be printed on paper (set this by highlighting the required printer in the **Installed** list and clicking **Set As Default Printer**). To send the data to a different printer, click your application's **Print Setup** option (usually on the **File** menu) and select the printer you want from the drop-down list box.

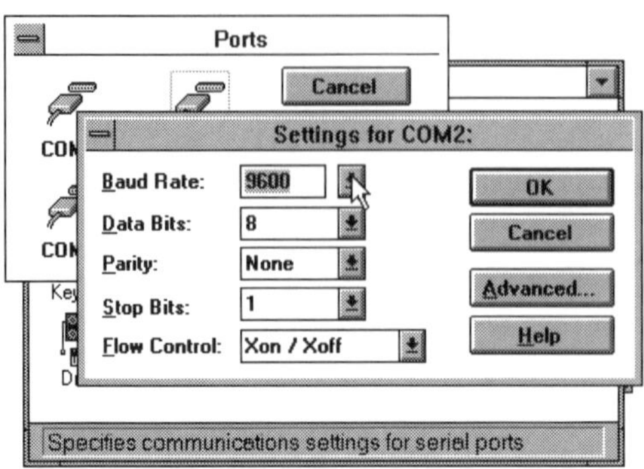

Figure 9.10 Making the most of port-speeds.

Ports

The Ports applet, shown in Figure 9.10, is where you make the settings for your COM (serial) ports, of which you'll usually have two, named COM1 and COM2. If you have a serial mouse, it should ideally be connected to COM1 and you shouldn't need to alter the settings. Your modem, if you have one, will often be connected to COM2, and these settings might need a bit of tweaking. The details of **Baud Rate**, **Data Bits**, **Parity** and **Stop Bits** are given on pp. 74–75. Leave the **Flow Control** setting at **Xon/Xoff** unless you experience problems in data transmission or reception, or you need to connect to a computer that specifies a different type of flow control.

Desktop

This is a fun applet packed with interesting buttons and checkboxes that let you change the look of your desktop.

- *Pattern.* Select a pattern from the drop-down list to cover your desktop (though you'll only see it in its full glory when Program Manager and all your other windows are minimized).
- *Wallpaper.* This places a picture, pattern or logo from the list in the middle of your desktop (if the 'Center' option is selected), or 'Tiles' it to cover the whole desktop. You can use any **.bmp** or **.rle** file as your wallpaper by copying or moving it to your Windows folder. Wallpaper can be used together with *Pattern*, but a tiled wallpaper will cover the whole desktop, pattern and all.

TIP

If your PC is short on memory, avoid using a **Wallpaper**. By the same token, if you run Program Manager maximized, and don't use the **Minimize on Use** option, your Wallpaper and/or Pattern will be hidden almost as soon as Windows loads!

- *Screen Saver.* To prevent burn-in on your monitor when you don't use it for a while (see p. 47), select a screensaver from the list and set a **Delay** time to specify when it should kick in. Click **Test** to preview a saver; move the mouse or press the spacebar to stop it.
- *Icons.* **Icon Spacing** determines how far apart icons will be placed in Program Manager (if you have **Auto Arrange** selected on Progman's **Options** menu). **Wrap Title** ensures that a long icon caption automatically wraps to a new line rather than overlapping the caption of the icon beside it.

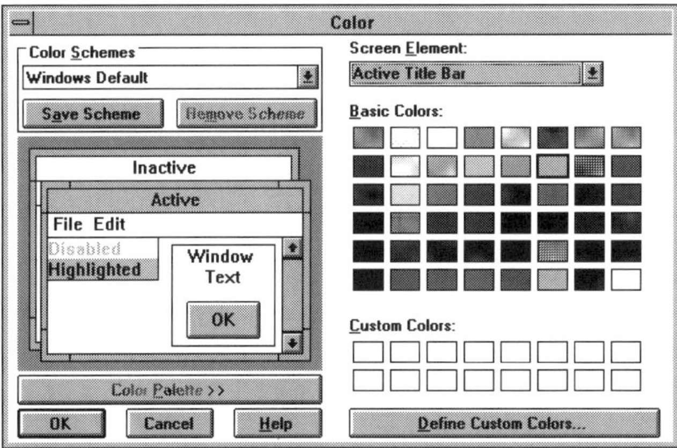

Figure 9.11 Customize your entire Windows colour-scheme.

Color

This allows you to select a new preset colour scheme. Select a scheme from the **Schemes** box and you'll see it previewed in the window below. When you find the one you want, click **OK** to apply it. If you want to create your own, click the **Color Palette** button and the window will expand, as shown in Figure 9.11. When creating a new scheme (or editing an existing one) you can select screen elements from the drop-down list, but there's a far better way: the preview window is interactive – just click on the various elements and text in the preview to select them, then pick a colour from the palette and the preview will update to show the result. Click on anything you can see – almost everything in the preview can have its own colour! (In particular, the large button marked **OK** has *four* different colours assigned to it – keep clicking it to change the colour of each element.) If you like your result and want to save it, click the **Save Scheme** button and type a unique name in the dialog that appears.

TIP

When you want to preview the preset schemes, click once on the list-box's arrow, then use your keyboard's arrow buttons to move through the schemes one by one – it saves a lot of fiddly clicking in the drop-down list!

▶ *Control Panel's **Fonts** applet was covered on pp. 151–154. To change your virtual memory settings using the **Enhanced** applet, turn to p. 308.*

Help

One of the first things you're going to need when you start working with any operating system is help. Whether you read the manuals carefully before starting, or just pile in and experiment, there are sure to be things you can't remember or answers you can't find. And on top of that, there are all your other software to get to grips with too! Fortunately, you're not just left to get on with it alone, Windows gives you help. If fact, Windows gives you **Help!**

Help comes in the form of a program called **Winhelp.exe** and a bunch of files with the extension **.hlp**. Windows itself provides an array of help files for Program Manager, File Manager, and its various accessories and utilities, which you'll find in your Windows folder – you can open any one of these by double-clicking it. If there's a particular help file you find yourself referring to a lot, you could even create an icon for it in one of your Program Manager groups.

But the main asset of the Help system is that you *don't* have to ferret around in File Manager to locate the files when you need them: wherever you are, and whatever you're doing, Help is close at hand!

Help on the menu

Almost any program you're working with will have a **Help** entry on its menu-bar. This is true of all the accessories and utilities installed with Windows *and* any other software you have that runs under Windows, and the **Help** menus contain at least four entries:

- *Contents.* This is the first page of the help file, which works just like the Contents page in a book.
- *Search for Help on . . .* This helps to find a particular help topic quickly.
- *How to Use Help.* This opens Help's own help file to tell you how it works.
- *About. . .* (usually followed by the name of the program you're using). This option usually presents a dialog box displaying the program's copyright and version details.

TIP

Remember that the Help window is a completely separate program from the one whose Help menu you clicked – there's no need to shut the Help window when you want to return to your program. You might find it useful to keep it open while you work and use *Alt+Tab* to switch to it when you next need it.

Windows Tutorial

Program Manager's Help menu has one extra little trick up its sleeve – the Windows Tutorial. If you're a newcomer to Windows this should definitely be one of your first ports of call. Not only does it explain how to carry out the basic tasks (running programs, opening and closing windows, using menus, and so on), it prompts you to do these things yourself, and offers clues and demonstrations when you're doing it wrong. This is an especially handy training-ground for anyone needing a bit of mouse practice.

Links and pop-ups

If you've used MS-DOS's Help program, you'll know how to use the Windows version as soon as you see it. Windows Help uses **hypertext links** – green underlined words and phrases – which you can click on to see related information. Anything with a solid underline takes you to a whole new topic;

anything with a dotted underline calls up a small box called a **pop-up** that usually contains a brief explanation or definition of the phrase you clicked on. (You can make these pop-up boxes vanish by clicking again.)

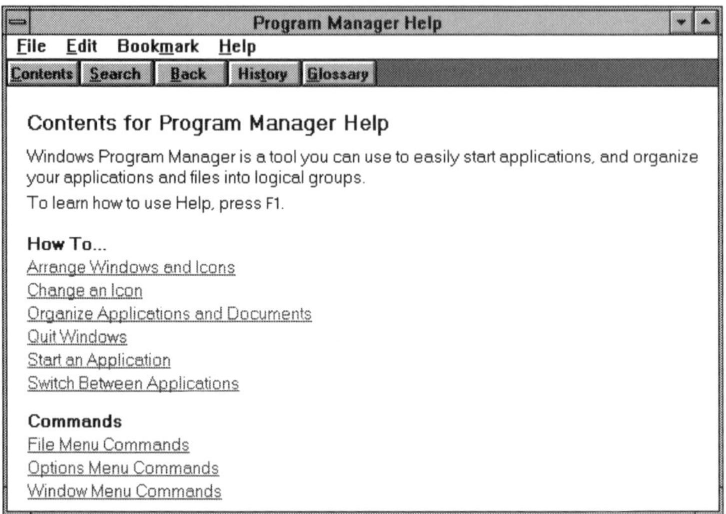

Figure 9.12 The Contents page of a typical Help file.

Working with the Contents page

Selecting **Help/Contents** from any program's menu-bar will present a window like the one shown in Figure 9.12. Just click on any green text to skip to the corresponding topic. Since most topics contain hypertext links of their own, this can start you on a major exploration, but you can return to the Contents page by clicking the **Contents** button any time. If you want to return to the topic you were just reading, click the **Back** button. (Some help files also have buttons marked « and » which you can use to step through topics in the order the file's author meant you to read them.)

Keyboard fans, keep an eye out for those underlined letters: holding *Alt* while you type the letter will take you to the corresponding option.

History

Clicking the **History** button opens another tiny window containing a list of the topics you've visited on your travels. If you want to *revisit* one, just double-click it. When you do this the History window vanishes behind the main Help window, but it isn't closed: you can bring it back to the surface by clicking the button again or using *Alt+Tab*.

Glossary

The **Glossary** button opens another small window with a long alphabetical list of Windows terms. These are all pop-ups – click one to see its definition, then click again to close it. Just like the **History** window, you can keep the Glossary window open as you read through the help file. The Glossary is actually a completely separate file, so if you find it useful, you can add a shortcut to it in one of your Program Manager groups: use the command line **glossary.hlp**.

Bookmark

Another useful feature of the Help system is its **Bookmark** menu. Any time you come across a topic you know you'll want to refer to again, you can add a bookmark to this menu that will take you back to it with a single click. Click on **Bookmark/Define** and a dialog box will appear with a suggested name for the bookmark – click **OK** to accept this name, or type in any name that will help you remember what the topic was about, then click **OK**. Next time you need the topic in a hurry, just click its name on the **Bookmark** menu.

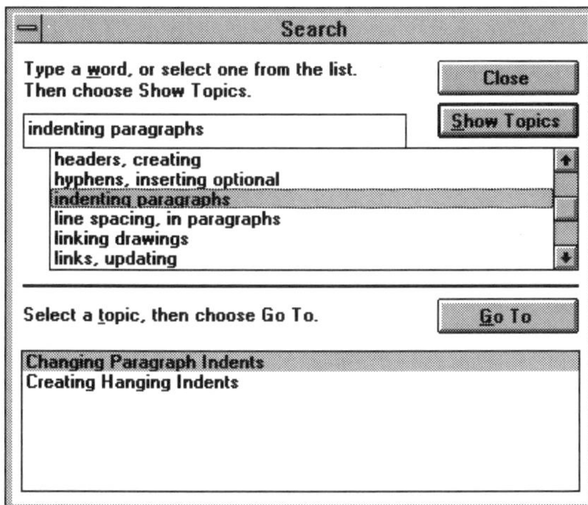

Figure 9.13 The Search page.

Using Search

A quick way to find help on a specific subject is to click **Search for Help on...** from the **Help** menu, or click the **Search** button in Help itself. This brings up a new window like the one shown in Figure 9.13 which you can use in two ways. One way is to type a word or a few letters into the topmost box. The contents of the middle box will scroll downward to find an entry that begins with the same letters. This is rather a hit-and-miss approach – the topic may exist, but the Help file's author may not refer to it the same way you do. The other method is to scroll through the middle box until you find an entry that looks promising. Whichever method you decide to use, when you've selected an entry in the middle box click **Show Topics**. One or more topics will appear in the box at the bottom of the page – choose the one you want and click **Go To**.

Context-sensitive help

Apart from the **Help** menus in programs, many applications (including Windows itself) offer *context-sensitive* help – that is, help related to what you're trying to do, or what you're currently looking at. For instance, many dialog boxes have a button marked **Help** – if you're not sure what to do when a dialog pops up, click the **Help** button and a window will open to reveal all.

TIP

Remember the magic key: *F1*. Wherever you are, whatever you're doing, and whether or not you can see a button or menu marked 'Help', press the *F1* key. If Help is available, this key will call it up!

Accessories

Add and remove components

If your PC arrived with Windows 3.1 already installed, or if you installed Windows yourself but didn't select the 'Custom' option, you may be missing a few of the juicy extras that came with the software. To find out what you've got and what you've not, double-click the Windows Setup icon in Program Manager's **Main** group and choose **Options** and **Add/Remove Windows Components**.

Before you do this, make sure you've got your Windows installation disks handy – Setup will need these to copy any files you want to install.

The next window you'll see contains five categories each with its own check-box. If a check-box is empty (which is unlikely) you don't have any of the files from that category installed. To see which files are in each category, click the button to its right marked **Select Files** – any uninstalled components are shown in the left-hand box. To install one, click it and then click the **Add** button. If you want to *uninstall* a component, select it from the right-hand box and click the **Remove** button (you might want to consider junking some of those Readme files, or any unneeded Help files from the Accessories category to grab back some disk space!).

When you've selected the additions and removals from one category, click **OK** to return to the original Add/Remove window and, if you want to, click the **Select Files** button for a different category. When you've worked your way through all the categories you want to, click the **OK** button in the main window. All the changes you made will be carried out, whether they were additions, removals, or a mixture of the two.

Cardfile

Cardfile is an apparently simple little accessory for storing addresses, phone numbers and other details. When you first start it you're presented with a single blank card to type text into. You can index the card by pressing *F6*, and add another card by pressing *F7*. On the surface it seems like that's all there is to it, but Cardfile knows a few other tricks too.

- If you have a modem, you can make Cardfile dial your phone for you. Select a card containing a phone number (with no spaces or symbols) and press *F5* – the first number found on the card will be dialled.
- If you have several **.crd** files, you can merge their contents together to create one larger file by selecting **File/Merge** and choosing a file to merge with the one currently open.
- Cardfile's powerful search facilities make it a handy place to catalogue just about anything: records and videos; books; floppy disks and CD-ROMs; recipes. Just press *F4* and type the index (or part of the index) of the card you want to find, or select **Search/Find** and type a few characters that you know are on the card itself. If Cardfile doesn't find the right card first time, press *F3* to find the next occurrence.

TIP

To find a card fast, hold *Ctrl+Shift* and type the first letter of the card's index-label repeatedly until it reaches the front of the pack.

Calculator

A totally ordinary basic calculator accessory with one little twist: go to the **View** menu and choose **Scientific** and Calculator switches to 'complicated mode'! You can use the mouse to click the buttons if you're that fond of your rodent, but the easiest way is to use your keyboard's numeric keypad (with the *Num Lock* button switched on).

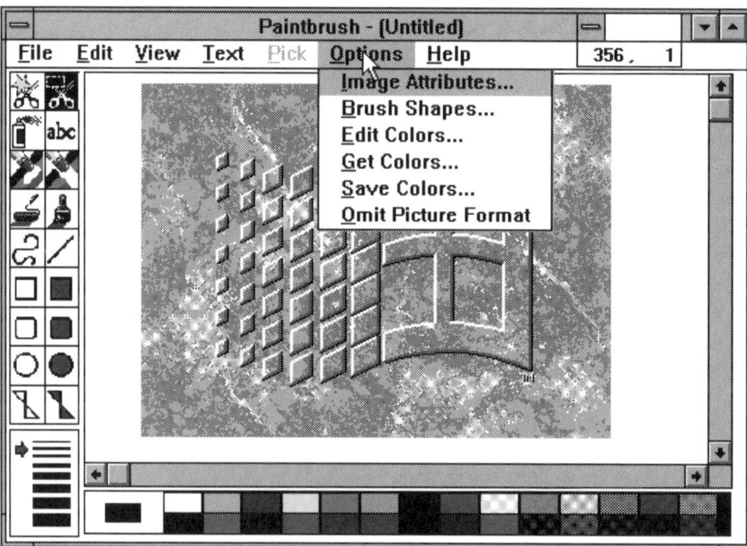

Figure 9.14 Paintbrush.

Paintbrush

Paintbrush is Windows' own paint-and-draw program for opening, editing, and creating **.bmp** and **.pcx** files. Choose a Tool or Shape from the toolbar on the left, click on a colour from the palette at the bottom, and start drawing. The Linesize chart at the bottom-left is used to choose the width of line when using the brush, line or shape tools. The Eraser will erase anything you swipe it over; the Colour-Eraser removes any instance or the foreground colour (selected by left-clicking a colour from the palette) and replaces it with the background colour (selected by *right-clicking* a colour). The Scissor and Pick tools at the top of the toolbar are used to select an area of the drawing for cutting, copying, moving, or saving as a file in its own right.

You can use **Paintbrush** to create your own windows wallpapers by saving your creations into your Windows folder with the **.bmp** extension and using Control Panel's Desktop applet to select them.

Here are a few hints for productive painting:

- For detailed work, turn on **Cursor Position** from the **View** menu – a little box will appear in the top right corner of the window to show your position (see Figure 9.14).
- To save a section of your picture as a file, select it with Scissors or Pick, go to **Edit/Copy To**, and choose a name and location for the file.
- To paste a file you've already created into the current picture, go to **Edit/Paste From**, find and double-click the file, then position it where you want it.
- To view an image full-screen, either double-click the Pick tool or press *Ctrl+P*. To return to normal viewing, click once or press *Ctrl*.
- To make sure you get a perfectly straight line, circular circle, or square square, hold *Shift* as you draw.
- To move an area of your picture selected using the Pick or Scissors tools, move the pointer inside the box and drag it. To make a copy, hold *Ctrl* as you start to drag.
- When you've selected part of an image using Pick or Scissors, the **Pick** menu comes alive: you can flip, tilt and resize the selection by clicking and dragging (which can create some weird and wonderful effects if you selected text!).
- To zoom in on an area of the image, press *Ctrl+N* and click on the area of the image you want to view. To zoom out again, press *Ctrl+O*.

To conserve disk space, avoid saving an image as a 256-colour bitmap file: a 16-colour **.bmp** file will be less than half the size. If you need better quality than 16 colours allows, saving the file as a **.pcx** gives good quality at a smaller file size than a 256-colour bitmap.

Clock

Clock is pretty much what you'd expect it to be – it's a clock! By clicking its control menu (in the top left-hand corner) you can set it to be **Always on Top** of any open windows. In its **Settings** menu you can choose between the Analog and Digital varieties, decide whether you want seconds and date displayed, and choose a font for the Digital clock. When you've set it how you want it, click **No Title** from the **Settings** menu, then resize its window and move it to where you want it. To make sure this setting is saved, press *Alt+F4* to close it, find **Clock.ini** in your Windows folder and check the **Read Only** box on its properties sheet before running Clock again.

The Clock is a good candidate for the Program Manager's **StartUp** group – just drag its icon from the **Accessories** group to **StartUp** (holding *Ctrl* if you want to *copy* it).

Write

Write is Windows 3.1's surprisingly capable word processor. Apart from standard options like font-selection, bold and italic text, and paragraph alignment, Write supports running indents, headers and footers, page numbering, find and replace, OLE, and lots more, with the result that you produce a sophisticated-looking document without paying a sophisticated price for a word processor. By default, Write opens and saves files with the **.wri** extension, but you can also work with plain text (**.txt**) files.

Here's a quick way to move a block of text in **Write** which bypasses the clipboard leaving its contents intact: highlight the text you want, scroll to the part of the document in which you want it to be placed, hold *Alt* and click once. (If you want the text to be copied instead, hold *Shift+Alt* as you click.)

▶ *OLE (Object Linking and Embedding) is explained on pp. 256–260.*

Notepad

Notepad is a simple text editor, opening and saving files with the **.txt** extension. These are ASCII files and have no character or paragraph formatting, but Notepad provides a quick'n'dirty method of typing short messages and notes. These files have the advantage that they can be loaded into any word processor on any computer (including MS-DOS's **Edit**).

One drawback to Notepad is that it works with a limited file size: if a file is over 50 K you'll just get a message telling you to use another editor to open the file. This leads many Windows 3.1 users to associate the **.txt** extension with **Write** instead of Notepad – Write takes a little longer to open, but it least it *can* open the file! If you choose to do this, click on the **No Conversion** button when prompted. (In Windows 95 this problem has been sorted – if a file is too large for Notepad to cope with, a dialog offers to open it in Wordpad instead.)

TIP

When you use Notepad's **Word Wrap** menu-option to keep all the text within the window and then try to close the file after reading it, a dialog tells you the file has changed and prompts you to save it. And, of course, it *has* changed, but the **Word Wrap** setting isn't saved even if you do follow Windows' advice, so you might as well just click *No* to this kind offer!

Being a plain-text editor, Notepad can be used to edit system files such as Autoexec.bat and your **.ini** files. Find a file with one of these extensions in File Manager and select it, then go to **File/Associate . . .** and choose Notepad from the list. (Make sure you always make a backup of a system file before editing it in Notepad. For **Autoexec.bat**, **Config.sys**, **Win.ini** and **System.ini** it's preferable to use System Editor – covered on p. 309 – which creates backups automatically.)

▶ *For information on setting and changing file associations, go back to p. 120.*

ClipBook Viewer

Depending whether you use Windows 3.1 or 3.11, you'll have either Clipboard Viewer or ClipBook Viewer. Clipboard Viewer is the simpler of the two: whenever you use the **Cut** or **Copy** options on an application's **Edit** menu, the information is placed on the clipboard – if you start Clipboard Viewer, you'll see it sitting there. You can even save the clipboard's contents as a **.clp** file, and reopen it any time you need to **Paste** it into another document.

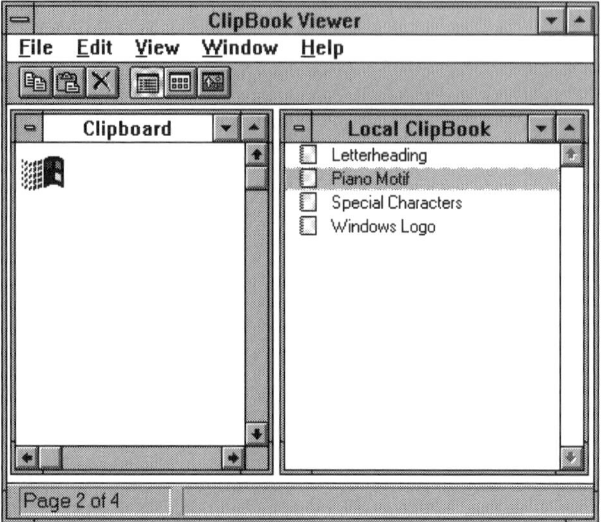

Figure 9.15 ClipBook Viewer's two windows, displaying the current Clipboard contents and a little bunch of saved clips.

ClipBook Viewer is a more advanced program with two windows (Figure 9.15). The Clipboard window works the same way as Clipboard Viewer, displaying the current clipboard contents. With the Clipboard window selected you can save the contents as a **.clp** file in the same way, or open other **.clp** files.

The ClipBook window is the clever one: click inside this window and press *Ctrl+V* (**Paste**), choose a descriptive name for the clip, and the current clipboard contents will be added to the clipbook. Every time you start the ClipBook Viewer program, any clips added in this way will be displayed. If you want to Paste one of these into a document, just click it and press *Ctrl+C* (**Copy**) and its contents will be placed on the clipboard. To view the contents of one of your clips, double-click it; to return to the list of clips, double-click again.

► ***Character Map, Media Player, Sound Recorder****, and a few other Windows 3.1 accessories, found their way into Windows 95 virtually unchanged – find out about them on p. 362.*

Windows 3.1 and DOS

Although thousands upon thousands of Windows programs are available, you may have a few MS-DOS programs that you can't bear to part with, or you may be a fan of computer games (these continue to be created for DOS rather than for Windows). The trouble is, you don't want to have to exit Windows and return to DOS just to run one program. Fortunately, Windows has taken care of this: you can run DOS programs from Windows itself, and easily switch back and forth between the DOS program and any other programs you have running.

If your MS-DOS programs were already on your computer when you installed Windows, the installation procedure would have found these and set them up for you automatically, placing icons for them in Program Manager. If you want to install a new one, however, you have to create your own icon. This involves much the same process as creating a Program Manager icon for a Windows program, but has one small complication – some DOS programs will work only if they have a **PIF** (see Figure 9.16).

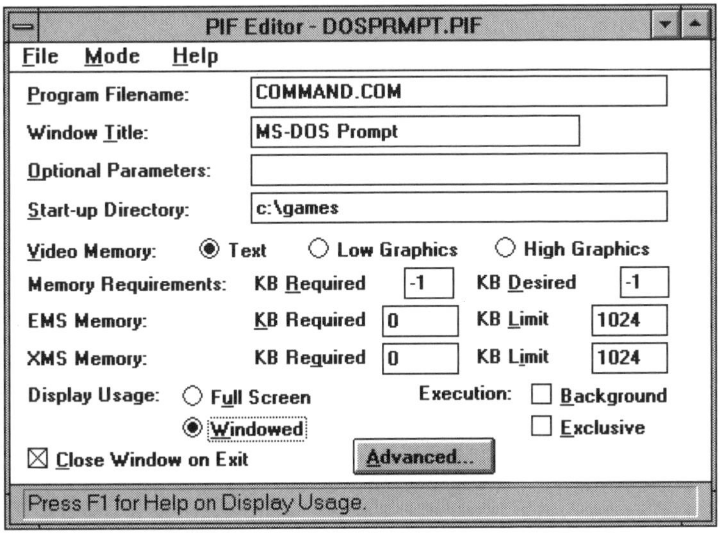

Figure 9.16 The Windows 3.1 PIF Editor.

What is a PIF?

PIF is an acronym for **Program Information File**, a file with a **.pif** extension containing information about a DOS-based program that helps Windows to run it properly. A lot of DOS software has its own ready-made PIF when installed – it's well worth looking in the folder containing the program's files to see if one exists. If it does, create a shortcut to it in one of your Program Manager groups and double-click it to run the program. If there's no PIF in the folder, double-click the **.exe** or **.bat** file named after the software – if the program runs successfully, you could create a shortcut to this instead and escape the whole PIF business!

Creating a PIF

Most DOS-based productivity software will run quite happily without its own PIF; Windows uses a PIF by the name of **_default.pif** as a substitute which should work adequately. Most *game* software, however, does need a PIF to run because games are very fussy about their memory requirements, the size of their window, and whether they have to share resources with any other programs.

Windows 3.1 provides a **PIF Editor** for the purpose (shown in Figure 9.16), so let's run through the PIF-creation process. (If you need extra help, click on the box or button you're not sure about, and press *F1* for context-sensitive Help.)

1. Start PIF Editor by double-clicking its icon in Program Manager's **Main** group.
2. In the **Program Filename** box, type the path and name of the **.exe**, **.com** or **.bat** file that starts the program (for example, if you bought a game called 'Vampires', the file would probably be called **Vampire.exe** or **Vampire.bat**.
3. In the **Window Title** box, type a name you'd like displayed in the window's title-bar as it runs, such as Vampires. (You won't see this name if you choose **Full Screen** in step 5). If you leave this box blank, Windows will insert the same name as the program file you entered in step 1.
4. In the **Optional Parameters** box you can add any additional DOS parameters or switches you want added to the program's command line when you run it. You can leave the **Start-up Directory** box blank, or enter the name of a folder that DOS should work from if you use files from a particular folder with this program.
5. Choose whether you want the program to run in a window (that looks like any other window but has DOS's usual black background), or full-screen so that Windows vanishes behind it. Most games will only run in **Full Screen** mode, but you could try the **Windowed** setting first and change it if it doesn't work. Choose **Close Window on Exit** if you want to return to Windows when you've finished using the program.
6. You can use the three **KB Required** memory boxes to enter the amount of each type of memory your program needs if necessary, but try running

the program first – if it works, you might be able to avoid dealing with these! If the program reports that it doesn't have enough memory to run, check the manuals for its memory requirements and type them in these boxes. **Memory Requirements** refers to Conventional memory – this and the other two types are explained on p. 266 in section **8.6**. Entering **0** in one of these boxes specifies that *no* memory should be reserved for the program; entering **-1** means 'as much as possible'.

7. You could also check the **Exclusive** option to give the program the maximum amount of processor-time available, but you'll need to run the program **Full Screen** for this to have the full effect – in a DOS box Windows must hold onto some resources to run itself and any other applications. Many games will have an intense dislike for sharing resources with Windows, so **Exclusive** and **Full Screen** modes will probably be inevitable.
8. Choose the **Video Memory** mode required: a word processor, for example, would usually run fine in **Text** mode, whereas an arcade shoot-em-up game will probably need the **High Graphics** setting.
9. Go to **File/Save As . . .** and choose a location and name for this file which will have the extension **.pif**.
10. Create a shortcut to this PIF in one of your Program Manager groups so that you can start the program by double-clicking it instead of searching through File Manager for it.

You can edit this PIF (or any other) by starting PIF Editor and using **File/Open . . .** to find and open the file.

TIP

If you have a DOS program for which you like to use different options at different times, you can create more than one PIF for it, as long as each PIF has a different name. For example, you could create another PIF that has different switches set in the **Optional Parameters** box, or perhaps one PIF set for **Full Screen** and the other **Windowed**.

The MS-DOS Prompt icon

Windows also gives you a quick way to get at the command prompt by including a shortcut in Program Manager's **Main** group labelled **MS-DOS Prompt**. Double-clicking this will open a DOS window that works exactly as if you were in 'real' DOS (often referred to as a 'DOS box'). This icon is actually a shortcut to a PIF called **Dosprmpt.pif** in your Windows folder.

With the DOS prompt running in Windows, you can toggle backwards and forwards between a window and full screen by pressing *Alt+Enter* or *Alt+Return*.

If you use the MS-DOS Prompt icon regularly, there are a couple of changes you might like to make to Dosprmpt.pif which you can carry out using PIF Editor once again.

- Choose whether you want your prompt to start **Windowed** or **Full Screen**.
- Choose which folder (directory) you want to be in when the Prompt appears by typing its path into PIF Editor's **Start-up Directory** box.

Managing the system

Adding Windows 3.1 to your system is rather like adding another floor to your house – it should improve your life, but it's going to give you a bit more cleaning up to do! In this section we'll take a look at some of the things you should do to avoid locking yourself out and to keep your system running smoothly.

Backup system files

Because MS-DOS is still running and Windows is running *on top*, you still have Autoexec.bat and Config.sys in your root folder (usually C:\) and they're just as vital as they were under a DOS-only system. Windows has its own pair of important files, called **System.ini** and **Win.ini**, both of which live in your Windows folder.

The **.ini** extension is an abbreviation of *initialization*, and most of the Windows-based software you install will create an **.ini** file the first time you run the program (usually placing it in your Windows folder, though some programs place them in their own folders). These files contain details of all the options, settings and preferences you've selected for the program so that they can be set up each time the program starts. Any changes you make while you use the program will be saved to its **.ini** file when you close it again.

With some programs (such as Windows' **Clock.exe**) the file is quite small and doesn't contain much that's important – if you accidentally deleted it, you'd have to set up your Clock preferences again, but that's about as serious as it gets. In others, such as a suite of Internet software, the **.ini** file may contain a lot of settings and preferences that took time to set up and were tweaked and perfected over several months' use. To lose this would be very irritating indeed.

Follow this procedure to make backups of all these important files.

1. Put a floppy disk in your floppy drive (usually **A**:) and open **File Manager**.
2. Hold *Ctrl* and click on Autoexec.bat and Config.sys in your root folder.
3. With these two files selected, press *F8* and type **a:** in the **To:** box and press *Enter*.
4. Now select **File/Search . . .** In the **Search For** box type ***.ini**. Make sure the **Start From** box shows **C:** and that **Search All Subdirectories** is checked, and press *Enter*.
5. A new window will appear when the search is finished listing all the **.ini** files on your C drive. Press *Shift+End* and the whole list will be highlighted.
6. Once again, press *F8* and type **a:** in the **To:** box and press *Enter* to copy all these files to your floppy disk.

Carry out this operation every few weeks to ensure that you've got up-to-date copies of these files (and copies of the **.ini** files for any new software you've added since), but make sure you do this only if your system is running properly!

Create a system disk

A system disk (often called a startup disk or boot disk) is a vital thing to have if something goes wrong with your system; if you put this disk in your floppy drive when you start or reboot your PC, the startup files will be read from here instead of your hard disk (see p. 34). Just pop a disk in the drive, open File Manager, choose **Disk/Make System Disk . . .** and leave File Manager to get on with it.

If your hard disk is compressed using **DoubleSpace**, however, File Manager won't copy the all-important DoubleSpace driver to the floppy, so the system won't be able to see your compressed files. In this case, open a DOS-window and type

format a: /s /f:720

Before storing the disk away somewhere, make sure it really works by restarting your PC with this disk in the drive. Having a system disk that doesn't work is just a slightly more expensive way of having *no* system disk!

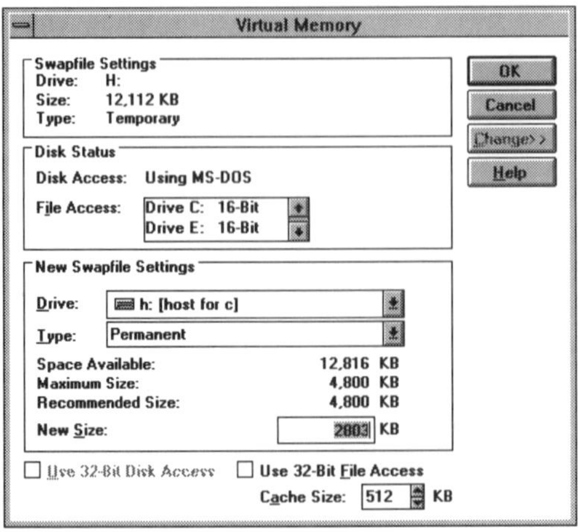

Figure 9.17 Creating a permanent swapfile.

Change Virtual Memory settings

Virtual Memory is a system that Windows uses to supplement RAM by using an area of your hard disk to store data temporarily. It's this system that allows you to have several applications running at the same time. Without Virtual Memory, a PC with 4 Mb RAM would be unable to run more than about two programs. Virtual Memory allows data occupying RAM to be sent off to hard disk when it's not being used, making room for another file or application to be opened; next time you need that data, it swaps places with some of the data in RAM.

Windows handles all this by creating a hidden file named **win386.swp** (known as a **swapfile)** whenever it needs to use Virtual Memory, and moves the data in and out of this file. However, this *temporary* swapfile isn't the most productive way to run things. Follow the steps below to create a faster, more effective, *permanent* swapfile.

Before making your swapfile permanent, exit Windows and type **defrag** at the DOS prompt to defragment your hard disk. This ensures that Windows will be able to find a long enough chain of empty clusters to create a sufficiently large swapfile.

1. Open **Control Panel** and double-click the **Enhanced** icon. Click the **Virtual Memory** button, then the **Change** button to see the dialog shown in Figure 9.17.
2. In the **New Swapfile Settings** part of the dialog, open the drop-down box labelled **Type** and click on **Permanent**.
3. If you want to increase or decrease the size of the swapfile, type a new figure into the box marked **New Size**. (The current size is shown near the top of the dialog.) If you're not sure what size your swapfile should be, cancel the whole operation, and run the programs you'd be using in a normal day's work. Use *Alt+Tab* to return to **Control Panel** and rerun the **Enhanced** applet to check what size of swapfile Windows has had to create to run these programs. Add a megabyte or two to the figure for headroom, and type it in the **New Size** box.
4. Click **OK** to confirm the change.

TIP

This dialog shows a 'Recommended Size' for your swapfile. If you type a larger figure into the **New Size** box, a dialog will appear telling you that Windows won't use more virtual memory than the recommended size, and asking you if you're sure. In fact, this is quite untrue – if you *do* want a swapfile of this size, ignore the warning and click **OK**.

Use System Editor

Although it's perfectly permissible to use **Notepad** (or MS-DOS **Edit**) to view and edit your system files (and with some of these files you have no choice), **System Editor** is a good choice whenever you want to edit Autoexec.bat, Config.sys, System.ini or Win.ini. When the program starts, it automatically loads each of these files into a separate window – you can choose which one you want to edit by clicking its title-bar or choosing it from the **Window** menu.

The other nifty feature of **System Editor** is that it creates automatic backups of any of these files you edit and save. For example, if you make a change to **System.ini**, you'll find a file called **System.syd** in your Windows folder which is a copy of your **System.ini** file before being changed. In the event of trouble, you can delete **System.ini** and replace this **.syd** extension with **.ini**.

To start **System Editor**, choose the **File/Run** from File Manager or Program Manager, type **sysedit** and press *Enter*. If you find yourself using this a lot, create an icon in Program Manager with **sysedit** as the command line.

Quick tips

Here's a little collection of hints and tips for Windows 3.1 users to make your computing life more productive, or more enjoyable, or to ease some of those 'Windows pains'. A few of the following tips require you to edit your system files, so if you choose to follow them, make sure you copy the necessary file(s) to a floppy disk or different folder first, in case it all goes wrong!

Performance tips

- If you don't have any DOS programs (or you never use more than one DOS program at a time), run Windows in Standard mode rather than the default Enhanced mode to get a little extra speed: either type **win /s** when you start Windows or add the **/s** switch to the **win** line in your Autoexec.bat.
- If you've recently used the **Edit/Copy** or **Edit/Cut** command in a program to place a large amount of data on the clipboard, empty the clipboard again as soon as you've pasted it – it's hogging valuable memory while it's there! The easiest way to 'empty' the clipboard is to **Copy** something very small, such as a single character in a word processor.
- The **Win.ini** file is loaded into memory when Windows starts, and remains there until you quit, so the smaller this file is, the better. If you've installed and removed a variety of software you've probably got a variety of bracketed sections referring to software no longer installed – these can be deleted. Check the [**Extensions**] section for file extensions belonging to programs you've no longer got as well.
- Here are a few ways to maximize your available Windows memory: have fewer icons in Program Manager; don't use wallpaper; have fewer fonts installed; user fewer screen colours and a lower screen resolution; don't use system sounds; don't run any background accessories (TSRs) that you don't really need.
- And here are a few ways to maximize your available disk space: use **View/By File Type** to isolate and delete **.tmp** files; get rid of any Help files and Readme files you never use; move unused **.bmp** files to floppy disk; uninstall any programs you never use; remove any screen savers (**.scr** files) you don't use.
- If you have a serial mouse, make sure it's connected to COM1. If it's connected to COM2, Windows will spend a long time searching for it as it starts up.

MS-DOS Prompt tips

- If you're tired of seeing the boxed-text telling you how to exit the DOS prompt every time you start it, use **System Editor** to open **System.ini** and add the line **DOSPromptExitInstruc=Off** to the [**386Enh**] section.
- If you're thwarted by the size of the DOS box but you don't like Full Screen mode, add **ScreenLines=50** to the [**NonWindowsApps**] section of **System.ini**.
- If none of your DOS programs needs expanded memory (EMS), add the **NOEMS** switch to the **Emm386.exe** line in Config.sys (see section **8.6**), and add the line **NoEMMDriver=True** to the [**386Enh**] section of **System.ini**.
- If there are any programs in your DOS folder that you like to use regularly, create PIFs for them and add shortcuts to the PIFs in a Program Manager group. For example, to format a disk with a double-click, create a PIF with **format** in the **Filename** box, **a: /f:720** in the **Optional Parameters** box, and select **Windowed** and **Close Window on Exit**. Save this as **Format.pif** and create a Program Manager icon for Format.pif.

General tips

- When you make changes to a system file you have to restart the system for the files to be re-read and the changes to take effect. But that doesn't necessarily mean rebooting the computer from scratch: if the file you edited belonged to Windows rather than DOS (i.e. it's in the Windows folder), you can just exit to DOS, and type **win** again immediately.
- In any program that has buttons on its toolbar, you can find out what they do by *holding* them down and reading the entry in the status-bar. If you're happy to continue, release the button; if you're not, move the pointer away from the button first.
- When you press *Ctrl+Esc*, or you double-click on the desktop, up pops Taskman. Bearing in mind you can use *Alt+Tab* and *Alt+Esc* to switch between programs, Taskman isn't that useful. If you'd prefer to have a different accessory or application start when you press *Ctrl+Esc*, add the line **TASKMAN.EXE=** (followed by the path, if necessary, and program you want to run) to the [**Boot**] section of **System.ini**.
- You can add sound-effects to **Minesweeper** by opening **Winmine.ini** in **Notepad** and adding the line **Sound=3**.
- If you're having a clear-out of unused fonts, don't get rid of **WingDings** – the Windows-logo symbol is used to make the Flying Windows screensaver!

- You can use **Write** to find the minimum margin-size your printer can use: go to **Document/Page Layout...** and set all four margin boxes to **0** and click **OK**. A box will pop up immediately telling you what the minimum settings are for the current printer.
- Change the size of text used for your Program Manager icons by adding the line **IconTitleSize = 10** (or whatever size you like) to the [**Windows**] section of **Win.ini**.
- Change the font used for Program Manager icons by adding the line **IconTitleFaceName =** (followed by the name of the font) to the [**Windows**] section of **Win.ini**.
- Maximize or Restore a window quickly by double-clicking on its title-bar.
- If **Print Manager** is running (either in a window or minimized on the desktop) you can drag and drop files from **File Manager** onto it to print them.
- Use the *PrintScreen* (or *PrtSc*) key on your keyboard to copy the entire screen to the clipboard. Holding *Alt* at the same time will copy just the *active* window to the clipboard. In a DOS window, you can send the screen-contents straight to the printer by pressing *Shift+PrintScreen*.
- To move or resize a window using the keyboard, press *Alt+Spacebar* followed by *M* for move or *S* for size, then use the arrow keys to make the changes you want. (For finer movements, hold *Ctrl* while using the arrow keys.) When you've positioned the window the way you want it, press *Enter*.
- If you want **Program Manager** to be the active window after Windows has finished loading, select **Run Minimized** on the properties sheets for all the items in your **StartUp** group.
- In a similar way to adding **rem** and a space before entries in Autoexec.bat and Config.sys, you can force entries in your **.ini** files to be ignored by placing a semi-colon (;) at the beginning of each line.
- You can troubleshoot startup problems by pressing *F8* as soon as you see the **Starting MS-DOS...** message appear on your screen. The entries in your Autoexec.bat and Config.sys files will be shown one at a time and you'll be asked whether to execute each line. This gives you the chance to leave out any commands you think may be causing a problem (or to leave out the final **win** command and remain in DOS).

Clicks and keystrokes

General keystrokes

Get Help anywhere	*F1*
Copy selection to the clipboard	*Ctrl+C*

Cut selection	*Ctrl+X*
Paste selection	*Ctrl+V*
Open properties sheet for selected item	*Alt+Enter* (or *Alt+double-click*)
Open the Control Menu	*Alt+Spacebar*
Switch focus to menu-bar	*F10 (and move using arrow keys)*
Open a drop-down menu, button or command	*Alt+underlined-letter*
Select a menu option	*Underlined letter*
Maximize a window	*Alt+Spacebar, X*
Minimize a window	*Alt+Spacebar, N*
Restore a window	*Alt+Spacebar, R*
Close a window	*Alt+F4*
Switch to a different MDI 'child window'	*Ctrl+F6*
Close a MDI 'child window'	*Ctrl+F4*
Switch between running programs	*Alt+Tab*
Switch between open windows	*Alt+Esc*
Call up Taskman	*Ctrl+Esc* (or *double-click desktop*)
Run a program or open a file	*Enter*
Print from an application	*Ctrl+P*
Open a file from an application	*Ctrl+O*
Save a file in an application	*Ctrl+S*
Undo last action	*Ctrl+Z*

Program Manager keystrokes

Switch between program groups	*Ctrl+Tab*
Switch between program items in a group	*Arrow keys* or *press initial letter*
Save Program Manager settings	*Shift+Alt+F4*
Tile open group windows	*Shift+F4*
Cascade open group windows	*Shift+F5*
Move a program item	*F7*
Copy a program item	*F8*
Open the Run command	*Alt+F, R*

File Manager keystrokes

Switch to a different drive	*Ctrl+drive letter*
Open an expanded view of a drive	*Ctrl+Shift+drive letter*
Open a folder	*Enter*
Open a folder in a new window	*Shift+Enter*
Toggle between left pane, right pane, and drive-bar	*F6*
Expand one level of the current folder	+
Expand all levels of the current folder	*
Collapse the current folder	–

Expand the entire tree	*Ctrl+ **
Move to start/end of tree or folder contents	*Home/End*
Select folder contents from current position to end (*or* beginning) of list	*Shift+End* (or *Shift+Home*)
Select contiguous files	*Shift+arrow keys*
Select individual files	*Ctrl+click each required file*
Deselect a single file	*Ctrl+click the file not required*
Move one or more files/folders	*F7* (or *Shift+Drag*)
Copy one or more files/folders	*F8* (or *Ctrl+Drag*)
Update (refresh) the window contents	*F5*
Save File Manager settings	*Shift+Alt+F4*

Write keystrokes

Move forward or back one word	*Ctrl+arrow keys*
Jump to end of current line	*End*
Jump to beginning of current line	*Home*
Scroll up *or* down through the document	*Page Up* or *Page Down*
Jump to a different page	*F4*
Select text by character or line	*Shift+arrow keys*
Select text by word or line	*Ctrl+Shift+arrow keys*
Select to end (*or* beginning) of current line	*Shift+End* (or *Shift+Home*)
Select to end (*or* beginning) of document	*Ctrl+Shift+End* (or *Ctrl+Shift+Home*)
Select multiple lines	*Ctrl+Shift+Up/Down arrow keys*
Insert page break	*Ctrl+Enter*
Toggle bold type on/off	*Ctrl+B*
Toggle italic type on/off	*Ctrl+I*
Toggle underlining on/off	*Ctrl+U*
Return to regular type	*F5*

Paintbrush keystrokes

Move between colour-bar, toolbar, line sizes and drawing area	*Tab*
Select a tool or line size	*Arrow keys, Insert*
Select a foreground colour	*Arrow keys, Insert* (or *click colour*)
Select a background colour	*Arrow keys, Delete* (or *right-click colour*)
Draw	*Insert+arrow keys*
Zoom in	*Ctrl+N*
Zoom out	*Ctrl+O*
View picture full screen	*Ctrl+P*
Switch from full screen to normal	*Ctrl*

Cardfile keystrokes

Add a new card	*F7*
Edit index of current card	*F6*
Autodial first number on current card	*F5*
Jump to a different card	*F4*
Scroll through cards with same initial letter	*Ctrl+Shift+initial letter*

Calculator keystrokes

Enter numbers and calculations	*Numeric keypad (Num Lock on)*
Delete last digit entered	*Backspace*
Clear current entry [CE]	*Delete*
Clear calculation [C]	*Esc*
Square root	*@ [Shift+']*
Percent	*% [Shift+5]*
+/− [change sign]	*F9*
1/x [reciprocal]	*r*
MR [recall memory contents]	*Ctrl+R*
M+ [add to memory contents]	*Ctrl+P*
MS [store current value in memory]	*Ctrl+M*
MC [clear contents of memory]	*Ctrl+L*

CHAPTER 10

Using Windows 95

Introducing Windows 95

What's new in 95?

Windows 95 is the latest version to hit the streets, arriving in August 1995. Although its appearance is different it follows many of the traditions of Windows 3.1, albeit with a greater emphasis on speed and ease of use. One of the main watchwords in Windows 95 is *choice*. For almost anything you want to do, there will be several methods of achieving it. In some cases you might find just one you like and stick with it; in others, you'll want to use one method in one situation, and a different method in another.

In the coming sections we'll be taking a look at the new or updated features of Windows 95, together with a few tips to help you get the most out of the operating system, but here's a brief résumé of the major changes:

- *Right-click*. The right mouse button suddenly becomes useful for accessing options, using Drag & Drop, and working in Windows 95-compatible applications.
- *Long Filenames*. Gone are the days of **Jlyslrpt.doc**, and it's hello to **July Sales Report.doc**.

- *Taskbar.* All your open windows and applications are represented by a button on the Taskbar at the bottom of the screen – click a button to bring the window to the foreground.
- *Start Menu.* Instead of your program groups vanishing behind the first window you open (as in Windows 3.1), they're gathered together on the permanently accessible Start Menu, opened by clicking the Start button on the left of the Taskbar.
- *Shortcuts.* Shortcuts are no longer the sole domain of Program Manager, nor are they limited to files. You can create shortcuts to a particular folder or drive whose contents you use regularly, and place the shortcut almost anywhere you want it.
- *Context menus.* Almost any icon or object in Windows 95 has a context menu – a list of options that appears when you click it with the right mouse button (known as *right-clicking*). This is so named because the options that appear on the menu will depend on what object you click and what else is happening at the time.
- *Recycle Bin.* All your 'deleted' files are placed in the Recycle Bin in case you delete something you didn't mean to. You can search the Bin and retrieve a file with just a couple of clicks.
- *Properties sheets.* Almost all icons you come across in Windows 95 have properties sheets that let you see more details about the item or customize it in various ways.
- *Tooltips.* Tooltips are tiny pop-up messages that appear over a button on a menu-bar when you hold your mouse pointer over it for a moment to tell you what that button is for.
- *Support for Windows 3.1 users.* If you've upgraded from Windows 3.1 and feel a bit daunted by it all, Program Manager (Progman.exe) and File Manager (Winfile.exe) are still in your Windows folder if you need to see a familiar face, albeit one that's had a bit of surgery.

The technical stuff

Windows 95 is a (mostly) **32-bit** operating system, meaning that it can access memory in 32-bit (4-byte) chunks instead of Windows 3.1's 16-bit chunks. The result is that Windows 95 is faster and more efficient when working with applications built for it (referred to as '32-bit applications'). However, Windows 95 has had to compromise slightly in this area to ensure that ex-Windows 3.1 users can still run their old 16-bit applications after upgrading.

The other phrase that pops up frequently alongside '32-bit' is **protected mode**. Windows 95 supports this mode of memory addressing which, for the user, is important in one particular respect: an area of memory being used by one particular application is *protected* from other rogue applications trying to access the same area. The result is that programs are less likely to crash, and if they do they're unlikely to take down the whole operating system with them.

Starting Windows 95

Despite promises to the contrary, Windows 95 hasn't managed to free itself completely from the shackles of MS-DOS, but it *has* taken a few steps in the right direction. Instead of requiring a version of DOS to be installed, Windows 95 comes with its own cut-down version (MS-DOS 7.0, which we'll look at more closely on p. 388). And in order not to worry the beginner, it hides all this unfriendly looking DOS stuff behind several different logo screens as the computer boots or shuts down. So when you switch on your PC you'll see the BIOS do its thing for a few seconds, followed by a message that reads **Starting Windows 95...** . The screen will then by filled by the Windows logo on a background of clouds until Windows 95 has finished loading and the Desktop appears.

Figure 10.1 The logo screen to wait for before you switch off.

Shutting down Windows 95

When you've finished work for the day and it's time to switch off, it's important to shut down Windows 95 correctly – just turning off the PC could result in loss of data or mucked up system files.

1. First close all running applications, saving any open files if necessary.
2. Click the **Start** button, click on **Shutdown** and click **OK** (or press *Enter*).
3. Another of those logo screens will appear asking you to **Please wait while your computer shuts down**. After a few seconds, the rather dull-looking screen shown in Figure 10.1 will tell you **It's now safe to turn off your computer** – always wait to see this screen before hitting that power switch!

The **Shutdown** dialog that appears in step 2 will contain at least two other options: you can choose to *restart the computer* or *restart the computer in MS-DOS mode.*

Start Menu and Taskbar

When you start Windows 95, the first thing you'll see is a plain green expanse called the **Desktop** with a few icons on it, and a grey strip across the bottom of the screen. This grey strip is called the **Taskbar**, and it's one of the central features of Windows 95. On the surface it doesn't look very exciting, but it doesn't look too complicated either. If you've just upgraded from Windows 3.1, however, it probably looks worrying: *If there's no Program Manager, where did all my program groups go?*

The Programs Menu

The rather clumsy Program Manager has been scaled down to a single button marked **Start** which sits at the left-hand end of the Taskbar. If you click the Start button the **Start Menu** will open. Move the pointer up to Programs and another menu will pop out called the **Programs Menu**, shown in Figure 10.2. (Menus that 'pop out' from another menu like this are called **submenus**.) On this submenu you'll find several more entries called Accessories, Games and StartUp containing icons for the programs installed with Windows 95. If you upgraded from Windows 3.1, you'll see a separate entry here for each of your old program groups too. Moving the pointer onto one of these entries will open its submenu to display icons for your programs.

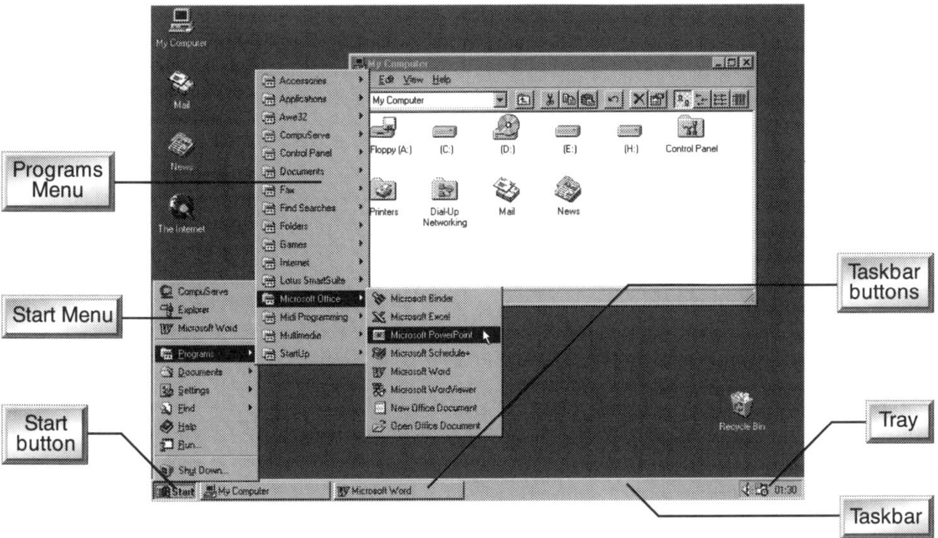

Figure 10.2 The components of Windows 95's Taskbar.

TIP

You can easily tell which items on a menu will open a submenu when you move the pointer onto them – they have a right-facing arrowhead beside them. Any entry *without* an arrowhead will immediately run a program, open a window or carry out a particular command when clicked.

The Documents Menu

The **Documents Menu** keeps track of the last 15 documents you opened, working on the assumption that you might like to use some of them again soon. Just click on the document you want, and the application it's associated with will open and load that document for you automatically.

TIP

If you're using 16-bit applications with Windows 95, any files you open or create from *within* one of these applications won't be listed on the **Documents Menu**. Only files that you open by double-clicking their icons in **Explorer** or **My Computer** will appear here.

The Settings Menu

The Settings Menu contains three entries: **Control Panel**, **Printers** and **Taskbar**. The Control Panel entry opens a window containing icons for the various applets you can use to configure and customize Windows – we'll take a closer look at these on p. 349. Clicking on Printers opens a window to display icons for your printer(s), plus an extra icon that helps you through the process of adding a new printer to the system if you need to. The Taskbar option opens a dialog that lets you change the appearance of the Taskbar (see '*Customizing the Taskbar*' below).

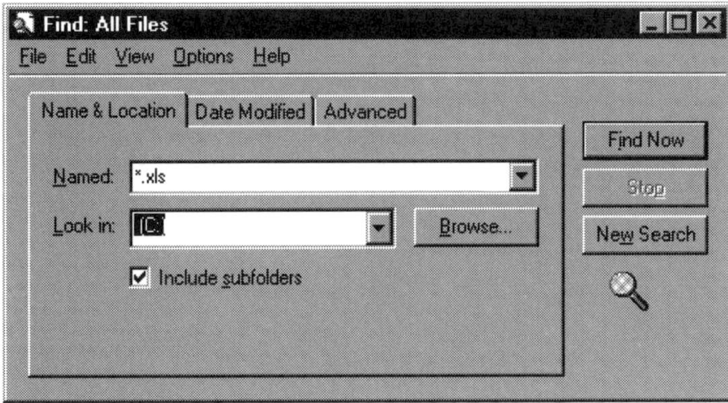

Figure 10.3 Searching for files using the **Find** dialog.

The Find dialog

Choosing **Start/Find/Files or Folders...** will open the dialog shown in Figure 10.3. The first tabbed page, marked **Name & Location,** allows you to find files or folders with a particular name anywhere on your system: just type the name into the **Named** box and a folder from which to start the search in the **Look In** box (or click **Browse** and double-click the folder you want to start from). Click on **Find Now** and the window will expand downwards to display the list of items found with that name.

Find is quite a powerful piece of work, so here are a few tips to help you make the most of it:

- You can use the wildcards * and ? in the **Named** box (see section **8.4** for more on wildcards), and you can search for several different files at once: for example, entering ***.txt;*.doc** would find all the files in the selected folder with the **.txt** or **.doc** extension (note the semi-colon separating the two entries).
- You can search several folders or drives at once: to search Drive C and Drive E, for example, type **c:;e:** in the **Look In** box.
- When the search has finished, click **File/Save Search**. A file named after your search will be placed on the Desktop. You can look at the list of files that were found any time you want to by double-clicking this file.
- After choosing where to search in the **Look In** box, click the **Advanced** tab. In the **Containing text** box you can type a word or phrase and **Find** will list all the files it locates that contain that text. (Make sure you type in the correct case if **Options/Case Sensitive** is switched on!)

- You can choose how you want the results sorted in the lower window: click one of the bars labelled **Name**, **In Folder**, **Size**, **Type** or **Modified**. Clicking **Name**, for example, will sort the results alphabetically. Clicking the same bar again will sort them counter-alphabetically.
- You can open the **Find** dialog more quickly by clicking once on the Taskbar and pressing *F3*.

The Run command

Clicking **Start/Run** will open a small box in which you can type a command, rather like the MS-DOS command prompt. You can type the name of a program here such as **taskman** or "**c:\program files\accessories\wordpad.exe**", the name of a document such as **internet.txt**, or the name of a folder such as **windows**.

Whenever you type a command on the **Run** line that uses a long filename (anything longer than eight characters) you must enclose the whole command in quotes ("). The term *long filename* also applies to folders, as in "**c:\ program files**".

Help

The Help entry starts Windows 95's own Help files which we'll look at in more detail on p. 358. You can also start **Help** by clicking once on the Desktop and pressing *F1*.

The Taskbar

The Taskbar is the device that makes multitasking easy (not to mention irresistible!) in Windows 95. Every time you open a program or a folder, a corresponding button appears here displaying the name of that folder or program. Because the entire Taskbar will usually be visible whatever you're doing, you can always see at a glance which windows are open behind the one you're working in. If you want to switch to one of these windows or applications, just click its Taskbar button.

TIP

When switching between open windows and programs, you can still use the *Alt + Tab* and *Alt + Esc* key combinations covered in section **5.11**. *Alt + Esc* is especially useful if you have any dialog windows or Control Panel applets open which don't appear on the Taskbar.

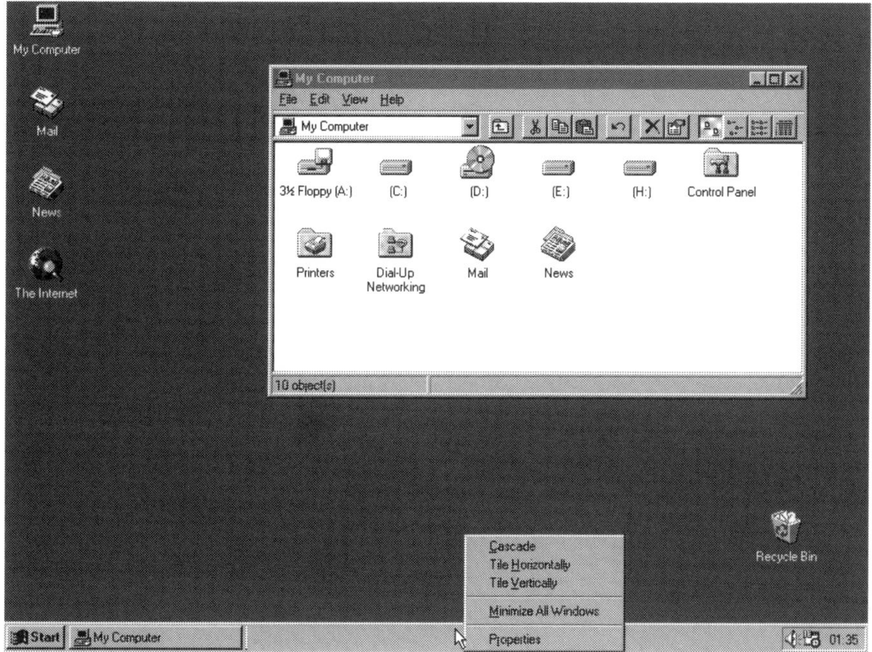

Figure 10.4 A single open window with its corresponding Taskbar button, and the Taskbar's own context menu.

Like almost every item in Windows 95, the Taskbar has a **context menu**, a menu of options that relate to the Taskbar and its contents. The context menu is opened by right-clicking on any *empty* area of the Taskbar. To select an option, just click it in the normal way; to make it go away again without selecting an option, either click somewhere outside the menu or press *Esc*. Here's what those context options do:

- *Cascade*. This moves and resizes all your open windows so they're stacked in a pile, with each window's title-bar visible and clickable. The *Cascade* and *Tile* options apply only to non-minimized windows – if you've minimized a window but you want it to be tiled or cascaded with the rest, click its Taskbar button first to *restore* it.

- *Tile Horizontally*. This moves and resizes open windows to place them side by side across the screen. Both *Tile* options are useful for comparing information in two windows or dragging items from one window to another.
- *Tile Vertically*. This is similar to *Tile Horizontally*, but places windows one above the other.

If you've tiled or cascaded your windows, and you then open another or run an extra program, right-click the Taskbar and select the option again. Windows will take another look at these windows and rearrange things to slot this new one in.

- *Minimize All Windows*. This is a super-quick method of minimizing every open window with one click instead of clicking each window's Minimize button individually. If you right-click the Taskbar again after selecting this option, you'll see an extra entry, *Undo Minimize All*, which will restore all the windows to their previous size and position.
- *Properties*. Almost every object you see in Windows 95 has its own Properties sheet. This option opens the sheet for the Taskbar. (Selecting **Start/Settings/Taskbar** is another way to do the same thing.)

Customizing the Taskbar

You can customize the way your Taskbar behaves by opening its Properties sheet using either of the two methods described above. Decide which options you want by checking or clearing each of the four check-boxes:

- *Always on top*. If this box is checked, the Taskbar will always be visible while you work. Maximized windows will sit above it instead of covering it up. If you want windows to be able to cover the Taskbar, click the box to clear it. If the Taskbar is covered you don't have to minimize your window to see it again – just press *Ctrl* + *Esc* followed by *Esc* again.
- *Auto hide*. Checking this box will make the Taskbar slide downwards and vanish when you're working on the Desktop or in a window and, once again, allows a maximized window to have the whole screen to itself. Any time you want to see your Taskbar, just move your pointer to the bottom of the screen and it will reappear.
- *Show small icons on Start Menu*. This determines whether the icons next to the entries on the Start Menu should be large or small, including those you add yourself (see 'Customizing the Start Menu' below). If you opt for

small icons by checking this box, you'll be able to fit more entries on the menu.

- *Show Clock*. Clear this box if you don't want the clock shown in the Tray.

Customizing the Start Menu

To customize the Start Menu and Programs Menu, it helps to understand how they work. The Start Menu is actually a folder called **C:\Windows\Start Menu**, which contains the **Programs** folder. All the menus contained in the Programs Menu are separate subfolders of **C:\Windows\Start Menu\Programs** and they each contain shortcuts to files on your system and, perhaps, even more subfolders.

You can open the Start Menu folder by right-clicking on the Start button and choosing either **Open** or **Explore** from the context menu.

By default the Start Menu folder doesn't contain any shortcuts, but you can place shortcuts here if you want to for extra-quick access. (If you skip back to Figure 10.2 you'll see that three shortcuts have been added to the menu above **Programs**.) The easy way to add more shortcuts here is to drag them from a folder and drop them onto the Start button – Windows will take care of the rest.

You can add new folders and shortcuts to the Start Menu or Programs Menu by opening the Taskbar Properties sheet, clicking the **Start Menu Programs** tab, and following these steps:

1. Click the **Add...** button.
2. Type the path to the file or program you want a shortcut for, or click the **Browse** button to track it down and double-click it. Click **Next**.
3. Click on the folder you want to place the new shortcut in. If you want to create a new folder, click the folder in which you want to create it and click the **New Folder** button. A folder will appear with its name highlighted – type in any name for this new folder. Click **Next**.
4. Type in any name for the shortcut and click **Finish**.

Just as you can add *shortcuts* to the Start Menu itself, you can add folders to it as well by clicking on the Start Menu folder before clicking the **New Folder** button when you get to step 3.

The **StartUp** folder on the Programs Menu functions in just the same way as Windows 3.1's StartUp group – any shortcuts placed in here will be run automatically when Windows finishes loading.

The **Start Menu Programs** page also has a **Remove** button which is worth keeping in mind: most of the software you install will add a folder to your Programs Menu, and its own little bunch of icons, many of which will be unnecessary shortcuts to help files and manuals that you don't really need shortcuts for. The **Remove** button is a handy tool to stop your menus getting so full that they become almost impossible to navigate quickly.

You can remove icons and folders from the Start Menu or Programs Menu by right-clicking the Start button, choosing **Open**, and deleting the offending icons just like any other file. Remember that deleting shortcuts doesn't affect the file they point to at all – you can recognize shortcuts by the little black-and-white arrow attached to their icons.

The Tray

The Tray (also rather pretentiously known as the *notification area*) is the indented area on the right of the Taskbar containing the Clock, a little speaker icon, and perhaps one or two other icons. When you use your printer or modem, icons for each of these will appear here, and some applications add a Tray icon when installed. Here are a few Tray tips:

- Hold your mouse pointer over an icon to find out what it is, or what it's doing, displayed in a little message called a **tooltip**. Hovering over the clock will present a tooltip showing the date. Double-click the clock to run the **Date/Time** applet from Control Panel.
- Click once on the speaker icon and a slider will appear to let you adjust the volume of your soundcard. Double-click it to open a full mixing desk.
- When your printer is busy, a printer icon will appear. Hovering over it will tell you how many documents are waiting to be printed. Double-click it to open the printer window, from which you can pause or cancel printing.
- When you're using your modem, hold the pointer over the icon that appears in the Tray for information about the total data received and transmitted. Double-click the icon to see a more graphic depiction with constant updates on data flow.
- Right-click on any Tray icon to open its context menu. Selecting the entry n **bold** type will give the same result as double-clicking the icon, but many

icons have other options here too. For example, if you right-click the speaker and choose **Adjust Audio Properties**, this opens the Audio page from Control Panel's **Multimedia** applet (see p. 351).

Explorer and My Computer

Explorer (Explorer.exe) is Windows 95's replacement for File Manager, the program that lets you see the files, folders and drives on your system. To open Explorer, click the **Start** button, go to the **Programs Menu** and click on **Windows Explorer**.

Ex-users of Windows 3.1 will notice little difference in the appearance of Explorer after File Manager: the folder tree is still displayed in the left pane with the contents of the selected folder in the right, although the left pane now displays all the drives on your system together with several other icons such as Control Panel and Recycle Bin. Folders in the tree that contain subfolders have a small cross beside them to indicate that they're *expandable* – either click the cross to expand the folder, or double-click the folder icon itself to expand the folder *and* view its contents in the right pane. When a folder is expanded, the plus sign becomes a minus sign: either click the minus sign or double-click the folder icon to collapse the folder again.

To find out what all those buttons on Explorer's toolbar are for, hold your pointer over each one for a moment – a little tooltip explanation will appear. This tip works for almost *any* button you come across in Windows 95.

Opening new windows

Like most of Windows 95, Explorer sports many shiny new features, but there's one thing missing – no MDI! In the old File Manager you could open new drive and folder windows, tile them side by side, or minimize them at the bottom of the File Manager window; in Explorer, quite simply, you can't. What you can do, however, is right-click on any drive or folder icon (in either pane) and choose **Open**. The contents of that folder will be displayed in a new *single-pane* window, with no folder tree. You can skip back to your Explorer window and open as many of these new windows as you want to in the same way. These windows are entirely independent of each other – you can close the Explorer window or any of the others and the rest will stay open.

Choose your views

Almost everything in Windows 95 is hugely customizable – you can tailor the way things look or work to suit your own taste, or your level of experience. Here's a quickfire list of a few options you might want to play with:

- The four buttons on the right-hand end of the toolbar are the **View** buttons which alter how icons are displayed in the right pane: you can choose between **Large Icons** or **Small Icons** (in rows across the Window), **List** (in columns) or **Details** (in columns with information about each item's Size, Type and Modification date).

Using Explorer in **Details** view, you can click one of the bars at the head of each column to sort the folders' contents alphabetically by Name or Type, by Size from smallest to largest, or by Modification date from latest to earliest. Clicking the same bar a second time will reverse the order.

- Open the **View** menu and click on **Options**. The **View** tab contains two option buttons from which you can choose to **Show all files** or to **Hide files of these types**. If you select the second option, all your system files will be hidden from view to prevent accidental deletion, together with any file or folder you've marked as **Hidden** on its properties sheet (see p. 145 for more on the 'Hidden' attribute).
- Once you're comfortable with Windows 95's use of icons and can distinguish between one type of file and another, you can return to **View/Options/View** and check the box marked **Hide MS-DOS extension for file-types that are registered**. This means that a file called **Letter To Bob.txt** will appear as just **Letter To Bob**. You'll be able to tell that this is a text file because it will have the same icon as **Notepad**, with which text files are associated (or *registered* in Windows 95 parlance).

If you choose to hide extensions to try to look cool and capable, and find yourself floundering sometimes, use **Details** view – the **Type** column will give you a few clues as to what types of file you're looking at.

- Choose whether you want to see Explorer's toolbar and status-bar by opening the **View** menu and selecting the option you want.

Copying or moving files and folders

In keeping with the whole Windows 95 philosophy of *choice*, there are several ways to move and copy files and folders – using the keyboard, clicking toolbar buttons, or employing our two buddies, Drag & Drop. If you opt for the Drag & Drop method, make sure you can see whatever you want to drop the item on before you start dragging – whether it's a folder or drive in the left pane or another window or application.

Drag & Drop

Click on a file or folder with the left mouse button and drag it to where you want it, then release the mouse button. If you drop a file onto an application's title-bar it will be opened in that application; if you drop a file or folder onto a folder *on the same drive* it will be moved to that folder; if you drop a file or folder onto a folder *on a different* drive it will be copied. To complicate matters still further, if you Drag & Drop a program file this way, a **shortcut** will be created rather than the file being copied or moved!

Drag & Drop using the right mouse button

This is a far more user-friendly method that lets you choose whether you want to copy or move the item. Click it with the right mouse button and start dragging; when you release it, a context menu will appear to let you choose what you want to do (shown in Figure 10.5) – just click on the option you want.

Figure 10.5 The context menu that appears when you Drag & Drop using the right mouse button.

Using the toolbar buttons

Explorer's toolbar contains three buttons commonly found on applications' **Edit** menus: **Cut**, **Copy** and **Paste**. You can now use these with files and folders in just the same way as you can with information in a document: select the items you want, then click the **Cut** button if you want to move them somewhere else, or **Copy** if you just want to copy them, then open the folder you want to place these items in and click the **Paste** button.

If you've selected multiple files and/or folders, Cut, Copy and Paste will apply to all of them – there's no need to copy items one at a time. If you're using the context-menu method, right-click on *any* of the highlighted items and choose **Cut** or **Copy**.

Using the context menu

The **Cut**, **Copy** and **Paste** options also feature on the context menu for files and folders. After selecting the file you want to copy or move, right-click it and choose **Cut** or **Copy**. You now have two options: if you can see the icon for the folder you want to place the file in, click it with the right mouse button and click **Paste** on the context menu. If the folder's window is open already, right-click on any white space in the window and click **Paste**.

Using the keyboard

Just as in applications, you can select the **Cut**, **Copy** and **Paste** options by pressing *Ctrl + X*, *Ctrl + C* or *Ctrl + V* respectively. Follow exactly the same procedures mentioned above, but use these keystrokes to replace the clicks.

If the window you want to drop an item into is hiding behind your other windows, or it's minimized, you can use its Taskbar button instead, but don't drop the icon onto it – that just gets Windows annoyed! Instead, drag the item onto the Taskbar button and hold it there for a moment. The corresponding window will magically appear so that you can drop the item into it.

▶ *Another way to copy and move items is to use the Send To option – see p. 342.*

Renaming files and folders

As usual there are several methods you can use to rename files and folders. Whenever you choose to rename an item, an outline appears around its name, and the name is highlighted with a flashing cursor after the last character. There's no need to delete the current name, just type in the new one to replace it.

- Right-click on the icon and click **Rename** on the context menu.
- Highlight the item, and go to **File/Rename**.
- Highlight the item and press *F2*.
- Click once on the item, then click its label. (These two clicks can be reasonably close together, but don't *double-click* or you'll just open the file or folder!)

Deleting files and folders

Once a folder is deleted it's gone to folder-heaven for ever. This is no big deal – you can create a new one with the same name in the same location easily (see p. 116). Any files you delete are sent to the **Recycle Bin**, covered in the next section, and you can retrieve them again if you need to. Here are the deletion methods available to you once you've selected the item or items you want to be rid of:

- Right-click on the item (or one of the selected items) and click *Delete* on the context menu.
- Press the *Delete* key on the keyboard.
- Select **Delete** from the **File** menu.
- If you can see the **Recycle Bin** on your Desktop, click on the item (or one of the selected items), drag it to the Bin and let go.
- If you can't see the **Recycle Bin**, use one of the **Cut** methods listed above, then find your way back to the Desktop, right-click the Bin's icon and click **Paste** on the context menu.

TIP

Explorer's toolbar has an **Undo** button that can reverse the last action. Holding your pointer over the button will show a tooltip with a brief description of what you're about to undo, such as **Undo Rename**. However, for a more detailed description, right-click on any blank area in the window and move the pointer down to the **Undo** entry on the context menu. If you look at Explorer's status-bar, you'll see a full description of the action that can be undone, including the name of the file or folder in question.

Selecting multiple files and folders

Explorer offers two handy ways of selecting multiple items from a window. The first is to press *Ctrl + A* which selects every item in the current window. (If you want to *deselect* one or two of these afterwards, click the ones you don't need while holding *Ctrl*.) The second method is useful if you want to select *almost* every item in the window – select the items you don't want instead, then click on **Edit/Invert Selection** and Explorer will deselect the items you clicked and select all the others.

▶ *You can also select multiple files and folders in Explorer just the same way as in File Manager, explained on* *pp. 282–283*.

Find in Explorer

The **Find** command found on the **Start Menu** can also be reached from Explorer by pressing *F3*, but with a slightly new twist. Whatever folder you're currently viewing in Explorer will be automatically entered in the dialog's **Look In** box to help you find a file in the current folder or one of its subfolders.

TIP

If you want to search for a file in a particular folder or drive, but you don't want to waste time opening it first, just right-click it – you'll see a **Find...** entry on the context menu which will open the **Find** dialog with that folder entered as the starting point for the search.

Go To

Want to look at the contents of a folder but don't fancy the exertion of all that clicking? Press *Ctrl + G* (or click **Tools/Go To...**) and the **Go To** dialog will appear. Just type in the path (if necessary) and folder name, press *Enter* or *Return*, and Explorer will switch to it for you. Unlike the **Run** command, there's no need to use quotes when typing long folder names in **Go To**.

My Computer

There's a metaphor going on here, and it's got all the subtlety of a sledgehammer – you have a desktop, just like Windows 95, and on your desktop sits *your computer*. Inside *your computer* is a bunch of files, folders and other stuff. This is why, on Windows 95's Desktop, you have an icon with the rather banal name **My Computer**.

In fact, My Computer is just like **Explorer**, with the exception that the window that opens doesn't contain the tree-view of your drives and folders. Instead you have a single-pane view that shows icons for your drives, a pair of folder-like icons for the **Control Panel** and the **Printers** folder, possibly a **Dial-Up Networking** folder and a few other icons, depending on which options you selected when you installed Windows 95.

If you've had enough of being faced with an icon labelled **My Computer** every time you start work, right-click it, click **Rename**, and type in something better!

Double-clicking any of these icons will open another single-pane window to show the contents of the selected drive or folder. Since My Computer is showing you exactly the same things as Explorer, most of its options and customizations work in the same way too. Nevertheless, there are a few extra points of interest:

- Every time you double-click a folder in My Computer, a new window opens to show its contents. You'll soon have a huge stack of open windows (Figure 10.6). To close *all* these windows with one simple action, hold *Shift* while you click the close button on the uppermost window (or press *Shift* + *Alt* + *F4*).

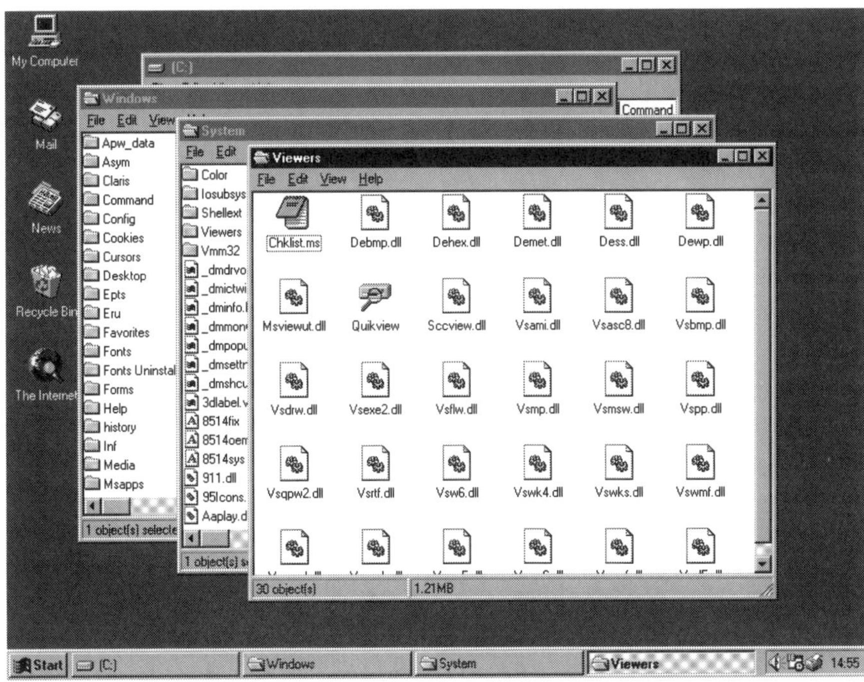

Figure 10.6 The stack of windows that appears in My Computer's default view.

- If you don't like having all these separate windows opening, go to **View/Options**. In My Computer, the **Options** menu has gained a new first page called **Folder**. Just click the lower of the two option buttons. From now on, every time you double-click a drive or folder icon, its contents will be presented in the same window. If you want to go back and view the contents of the parent folder, click the arrow button on the toolbar or press *Backspace*. (You can use the *Backspace* key in Explorer too.)
- If you've followed the previous tip to reuse the same window, you can still open a drive or folder in a *new* window by holding *Ctrl* while you double-click it.
- Although there's no **Tools** menu in My Computer, and the **Go To** command has vanished along with its *Ctrl + G* hotkey, you can still open the **Find** dialog routed to a particular folder by pressing *F3* or right-clicking the folder you want to search.
- If you want to open a drive or folder in an **Explorer-window** (with the tree-view in the left pane), just right-click on the icon and choose **Explore** from the context menu.

Format a floppy disk

You can reach the **Format** command by right-clicking your floppy disk icon whenever you see it – in My Computer's window, in either pane of an Explorer window, or a shortcut you might have put on the Desktop. Choose the correct capacity for the disk in the drive (**1.44 Mb** for a high-density disk or **720 K** for a double-density). Choose whether you want a Quick or a Full format by checking the appropriate option – a new disk will need a full format, a previously used disk can be quick-formatted to save time. If you want to give the disk a label (name), type up to 11 characters in the **Label** box. Click on **Start**. If you've got a bunch of disks to format, you can save some time by removing the check-mark from **Display summary when finished**.

▶ *Details of opening the Properties pages of files and folders, and changing their attributes, are covered on pp. 143 and 145.*

The Desktop and shortcuts

As we've already seen, the Windows 95 **Desktop** is a metaphor for your own desk upon which sits *your computer*. Although technically *under* your desk, there's a bin for all your trash called the **Recycle Bin**, and the **Taskbar** corresponds to the jumble of papers on your desk that you pick up and work with for a while before filing them away (closing a window or application) or putting a document down and picking up a different one (clicking a button to switch tasks).

The Desktop folder

The concept that seems a little weird when you're starting out with Windows 95 is that the Desktop is actually a folder, **C:\Windows\Desktop**. And just as you can put files or folders into any other folder on your system, you can put them in this Desktop folder. The difference is that any file or folder in C:\Windows\Desktop will have its icon displayed *on* the Desktop. Likewise, you can create new files and folders on the Desktop and, although you don't realize you're doing it, you're actually creating them in this folder.

Recycle Bin

The Recycle Bin is a storage place for files deleted using any of the methods listed in the previous section. Although the keyboard key and the menu options all say **Delete**, what you're actually doing is moving these files to a folder called **Recycled**. This folder can have a potential capacity of 10 per cent of your hard disk, so if you have a 500 Mb hard disk, this folder can hold 50 Mb of deleted files. This, of course, is bad news for your disk space, but like any bin you'll want to empty it before you're knee-deep in trash!

To empty the Bin (thus deleting its contents permanently), right-click it and click **Empty Recycle Bin** on the context menu. If you want to sift through its contents first, double-click the icon or right-click and choose **Open**. If you choose to you can permanently delete just a few items – select them in the usual way, press *Delete* then *Enter* when the inescapable confirmation dialog appears.

You can also retrieve files from the Bin that you deleted by accident. Select the file or files you want to retrieve and either choose **File/Restore** or right-click one of the selected files and click **Restore** on the context menu. The restored file will be moved back to the folder from which it was deleted. If that folder no longer exists (perhaps you deleted the folder along with its contents), Windows will recreate it.

TIP

You can find out which folder a file will be restored to by double-clicking it, or highlighting it and pressing *Enter*. Its properties sheet will open and the folder name is shown beside the **Origin** entry. You can also see its size, and the date of its creation and 'deletion'.

If you'd prefer the file to be restored to somewhere different than its original location, you can move it by choosing **Cut** from the **File** menu or context menu, then **Paste** in the desired folder, or by dragging it to the desired folder or the Desktop using the left mouse button.

Be careful not to take the Bin for granted: files deleted from a floppy disk won't be placed here, and the same goes for files deleted at the MS-DOS prompt.

Customizing the Bin

You can change how your Bin does its job by making changes to its properties sheet. This properties sheet, like any other, can be opened in several ways: right-click the Bin and choose **Properties**; hold *Alt* and double-click it; highlight it and press *Alt + Enter*.

The properties sheet has at least two tabs: the first is called **Global**, the second will be named after your 'C' drive. Any others will be named after any other hard disks or compressed drives you have on your system. Here's a summary of the Recycle Bin's properties:

- You can change how much of your hard disk the Recycle Bin can use to hold 'deleted' files by dragging the slider left or right and watching the percentage noted underneath. (This should usually be unnecessary – you'll probably empty your Bin long before it gets full!)
- You can bypass the Bin entirely if you want to and force all files to be deleted immediately and permanently – check the box labelled **Do not move files to the Recycle Bin**. In this case, you'll always get a confirmation dialog when deleting.

If you opt to store your 'deleted' files in the **Recycle Bin**, you can still permanently delete a file any time you want to. Just hold *Shift* while you drag the file to the Bin, click **Delete** on one of the menus, or press the *Delete* key on your keyboard.

- Every time you delete a file, a confirmation dialog appears to ask if you really want to send the file to the Recycle Bin. To stop these prompts appearing, clear the check box marked **Display delete confirmation dialog**.

It's easy to delete files with the **Read Only** or **System** attribute set on their properties sheets in Windows 95, especially if you turn off Delete Confirmation. Be very wary of deleting anything from C:\ , C:\ Windows, or any subfolders of C:\ Windows.

Shortcuts

As we've seen from looking at the **Start Menu** on p. 325, shortcuts are just little 'pointer' files that tell Windows where to find the item you want. In effect, having shortcuts to a file is like having lots of copies of the file in different places, but while the file itself might be several megabytes in size (and you wouldn't want unnecessary copies of a file that size hanging around your hard disk!) a shortcut is roughly 360 bytes.

Here are a few useful things to remember about shortcuts:

- You can create shortcuts to almost anything on your system: a drive, a folder, a program, a document, an applet from Control Panel, a printer, whatever!
- You can create as many shortcuts to the same drive/file/folder as you want to, so it's accessible from wherever you are, whatever you happen to be doing.
- Just as in Program Manager, you can add hotkeys to shortcuts that you've placed on the **Desktop**, **Start Menu** or **Programs Menu**. The difference is that these hotkeys are *always* available, even when you're working in an application.
- Shortcuts always have a small black-and-white arrow attached to their icons to distinguish them from a 'real' file or folder (shown in Figure 10.7). Deleting a shortcut has no effect on the item it points to.

Figure 10.7 Shortcuts on the Desktop, indicated by their icons' arrow-attachment.

Creating shortcuts

For mouse users, one of the easiest ways to create a shortcut is by Drag & Drop. Click the item with the right mouse button, drag it where you want it and click on **Create Shortcut(s) Here** from the context menu (shown in Figure 10.5). As the inclusion of **(s)** in **Shortcut(s)** suggests, you can drag multiple items if you want shortcuts to each of them in the same place.

Another method is to select the item and *copy* it to the clipboard by pressing *Ctrl + C*, or right-clicking and choosing **Copy**. You can then find the folder you want to put the shortcut into, right-click on its icon (or on a blank space inside it), and choose **Paste Shortcut**. If you're not a big fan of right-clicking, you'll also find this option on the folder's **File** menu.

Last, but not least, there's the Shortcut Wizard. Right-click on the Desktop, inside a folder window, or on the icon of the folder in which you want to create a shortcut, and choose **New/Shortcut**. The Wizard will open and help you do it in two easy steps. First, type in the path (if necessary) and file name of the file for which you want a shortcut or click the **Browse** button to search for and double-click it. Click **Next**, and the Wizard will suggest a name for

GETTING STARTED page 13
Major group tests
PCs for the home office
Fax/printer/copiers
Personal organisers
Budget accounts software
Computer class
Working from home
Double CD pack
Get on the Internet for FREE
office
AUGUST 1996 £2.95

GETTING STARTED page 13
WHAT PC?
AND SOFTWARE
Major group tests
Luxury notebooks
Presentation packages
Image editing software
Computer class
Working from home
Special report
Dangers on the Internet
Get On line
We test twelve super-fast fax/modems
Win
The UK's biggest and best buyer's tables
SEPTEMBER 1996 £2.95

GETTING STARTED
WHAT PC?
AND SOFTWARE
major group tests
Reference software
Mid-range colour notebooks
Personal laser printers
CD-ROM drives
EXCLUSIVE
Psion's new Series 3c and Siena palmtops
PCs
Win
Two Canon Multipass 10 printer-fax-scanners,
plus 15 copies of Print Shop Deluxe
The UK's biggest and best buyer's tables
OCTOBER 1996 £2.95

MICROSOFT OFFICE 97
All-new versions of Word and Excel
PLUS
Lifestyle/leisure software
Upgrade your hard disk: a step-by-step guide
best-selling PCs, software & peripherals
getting started
Two Visioneer PaperPort document
NOVEMBER 1996

THE ESSENTIAL BUYER'S GUIDE
WHAT PC?
AND SOFTWARE
Group tests
17in monitors
Drawing software
Document scanners
Computer classes
Upgrading: processors and memory
Making music part one
Budget PCs
Complete Pentium systems for under £1,200
and 10 copies of the Collins Electronic Dictionary

THE ESSENTIAL BUYER'S GUIDE
WHAT PC?
AND SOFTWARE
Group tests
Christmas goodies
DTP software
Keyboards
200MHz Pentiums
Top of the line systems compared
Computer Class
Making music part 2
Get Personal
Pocket computers with the power to organise your life

your shortcut. Type in a different one if you don't approve of the suggestion, and click **Finish**. (Remember that any paths involving long file names must be enclosed in quotes if you type them yourself. If you use the **Browse** button to locate the file, Windows will put in the quotes itself if they're needed.)

You can create a shortcut to a folder using the Wizard just as you would a file: just type the path (if it's not included in the SET PATH = line of Autoexec.bat) and name of the folder.

Customizing shortcuts

More than any other type of file on your system, the shortcut can be customized by changing its properties sheet. A shortcut's properties sheet consists of two tabbed pages headed **General** and **Shortcut** (Figure 10.8). Most of the excitement happens on the second of these: the first applies to the shortcut (**.lnk**) file itself, showing its size, location and other information. Move to the second tab and it's a whole new ball-game:

- Hold your pointer over the entry for **Location**, and a tooltip will appear to show the full path of the file or folder.
- The **Target** box shows the full command line for the shortcut – if you want to make the shortcut point to a different file or folder, you can change it here instead of deleting it and creating a new one.
- Click the **Find Target...** button to open the folder that contains the item.
- Enter a hotkey in the **Shortcut Key** box following the procedure given under the 'Shortcut key' heading on p. 276. If the shortcut is on your Desktop or Start Menu, or in one of your Programs Menu folders, you can use this key combination to access it any time you need it.
- The **Run** drop-down list gives you the choice of **Normal Window**, **Maximized** or **Minimized**. Most of the time you'll want a normal window. **Maximized** can be useful if an application opens with a particularly small window and you can't find any other way to make it start larger. Select **Minimized** if you want the program to start as a button on the Taskbar rather than in a window.
- The **Start In** button is useful in shortcuts to applications. As an example, if you keep all your word-processor documents in a folder called **C:\Word-Pro**, create a shortcut to your word processor and type **C:\Word-Pro** in this box. Whenever you want to open a file or save a newly created one, the word processor will offer you this folder in its **Open** and **Save As...** dialogs, saving you a lot of clicking or key pressing!

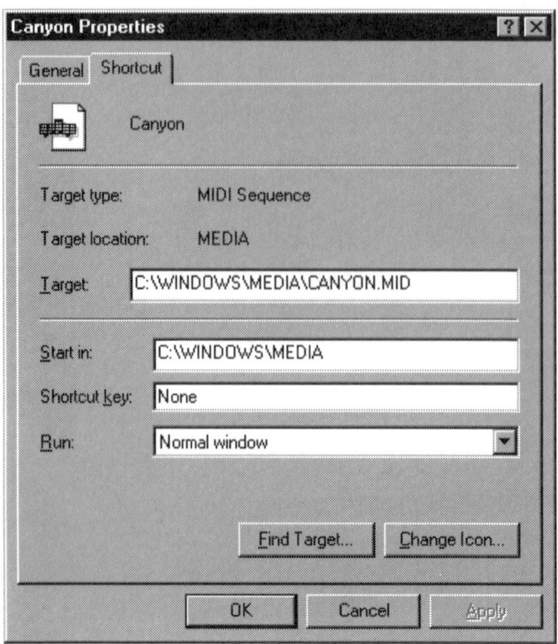

Figure 10.8 The feature-packed second tab on a shortcut's properties sheet.

- You can use a different icon for any shortcut, including shortcuts to folders and drives. Click the **Change Icon** button, and either double-click an icon from the list or click on **Browse** and go looking for a different icon file. Use the **Files of type** box to choose which type of file you want to see: **Icon Files** (the default) shows programs and libraries; **Program Files** often contain one or more icons; **Libraries** are **.dll** files that sometimes contain icons but, more often, don't; **Icons** are single-icon files with the extension **.ico.** Double-click a likely looking file and you'll see its icons displayed, if it contains any. If the file you chose contains no icons, a dialog will tell you so, and you can click **Browse** again and try a different one.

To reduce the hit-and-miss aspect of finding icon files, try these first: **Shell32.dll** and **Cool.dll** in your Windows\ System folder; **Progman.exe** and **Moricons.dll** in your Windows folder.

Shortcut suggestions

So what are shortcuts good for? Here's a few ideas for shortcuts you might find useful:

- Open **My Computer** and drag each of your drive icons out to the Desktop. A dialog will tell you can't move or copy them here and offer to create a shortcut – click **Yes**. You can now open your drives quickly without first opening **My Computer**.
- Open **My Computer** and your **Printers** folder, and drag your printer-icon to the Desktop in the same way. To print a file fast, just drag it onto this icon.
- If you have files that you use regularly, such as an appointments file or a list of regular contacts, create a shortcut to the file on the Desktop or somewhere on the Start Menu.
- Create shortcuts to the folders you use most often to save yourself piling through Explorer or My Computer to find them. Just drag them to the Desktop from one of these windows using the right mouse button, and choose **Create Shortcut(s) Here**.
- If you find yourself using **Control Panel** a lot, drag its folder out of My Computer in the same way as the drive icons. Or, if you use just a couple of Control Panel applets regularly, drag out the icons you want.

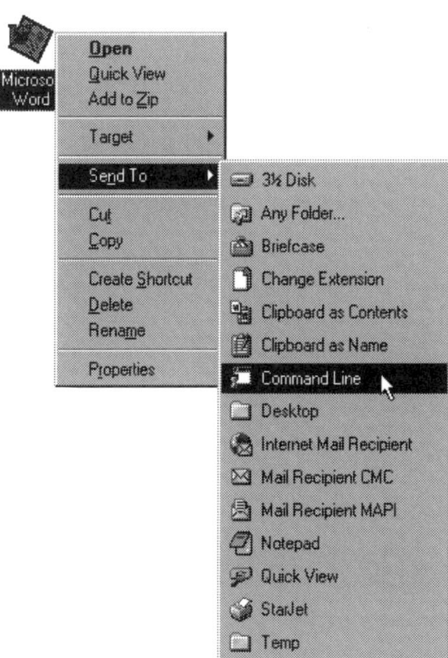

Figure 10.9 The Send To option and its submenu.

The Send To folder

Windows 95 has one more powerful feature that makes use of shortcuts, and its full potential is often overlooked by beginners. If you right-click on any file or folder you'll see a **Send To** entry (Figure 10.9) on the context menu whose submenu contains an icon for your floppy-disk drive and perhaps two or three more entries (depending on the accessories you chose when installing Windows 95).

The **Send To** option works like an automated Drag & Drop, sending the item you clicked to the drive, folder or program you chose from the submenu. For example, if you click on **3½ Floppy (A:)** the file or folder you selected will be copied to the disk in your floppy drive. The aspect that gets overlooked is that you can customize the options that appear on **Send To**'s submenu by adding shortcuts to the folder **C:\Windows\SendTo**. To outline the uses of the Send To option, here are a few suggestions for shortcuts you might want to add to this folder:

- Add a shortcut to **Notepad** (C:\Windows\Notepad.exe). Any time you come across a text-based file with an unusual extension you can open it in Notepad by right-clicking it and choosing **Send To/Notepad**. This is also handy if you *don't know* whether it's a text-based file or not – you'll soon find out!
- Add a shortcut to your printer by dragging it from **My Computer/ Printers**. You can print a file by 'sending' it. This is useful if you have more than one printer and need to choose which one to use for a particular file.
- If you have certain folders that you seem to keep moving things into, put shortcuts to these folders in Send To. If the folder is on the same drive as the item you 'send', the item will be moved; if the folder is on a different drive it will be copied.
- Add a shortcut to your Desktop (C:\Windows\Desktop). You can then move all the files you want to work with at the beginning of a Windows session so that they're sitting right in front of you.

Files and file types

Most of the information you need to work with files and folders in Windows 95 has been covered in Chapter 5 – creating, opening, saving and printing files, associating filename extensions with programs, and so on. But, as usual, Windows 95 has a few tricks of its own to make some of the basic tasks a little easier than they were under Windows 3.1, and these are the main focus of this section.

Open and Save As

These two options are still found on applications' **File** menus, and still lead to dialogs that let you choose a file to open, or select a location and name for the file you want to save (as explained on pp. 124–130). But the dialogs themselves have a few enhancements to make navigation easier and more intuitive, following a similar layout to a **My Computer** window.

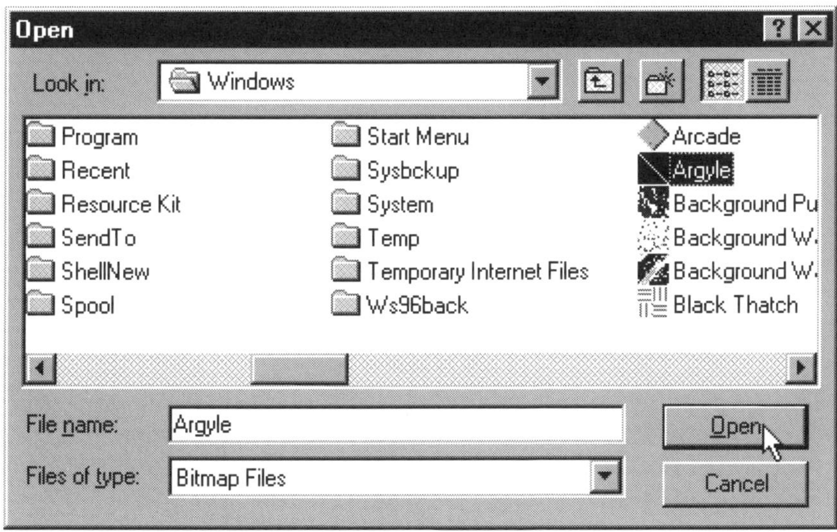

Figure 10.10 A standard Windows 95 Open dialog.

The **Open** and **Save As** dialogs are both laid out in the same way, as shown in Figure 10.10, with the exception that the **Open** button becomes a **Save** button in **Save As** dialogs. Choose a drive from the **Look In** drop-down box and its folders will be displayed in the window below. Double-click a folder to see its contents and the name of the folder will be displayed in the **Look In** box to help you track where you are. If you want to move up to the parent folder, click the arrow button beside the **Look In** box. To open a file, double-click its icon, or select it and click **Open**.

If you know the precise path and name of the file you want to open, or the location and name you want to save to, you can type it into the **File name** box irrespective of which folder is currently displayed.

To save a file in the current folder, type a name in the **File name** box and click **Save**. Windows will add the file extension itself according to the file type shown in the box labelled **Files of type**. If you want to save with a different extension, type the dot and extension after the file name.

Here's a quickfire list of some of the other features found in these dialogs:

- The two buttons on the right of the toolbar let you swap between **List** and **Details** views as in **Explorer** (see p. 328).
- You can create a new folder in the current folder (shown in the **Look In** box) by clicking the shiny-folder button rather than dashing off to Explorer to do it.
- Right-clicking on any file or folder will show the same context menu you'd find in Explorer, with options such as **Cut**, **Copy**, **Rename**, **Delete** and **Properties**.
- You can right-click on any white space in the window to bring up the context menu for the current folder. The entries here include the two remaining **View** options (large or small icons), **Paste**, **Properties** and **New** (see below).

The inclusion of the context menus in these dialogs means that you can carry out complete file-management tasks without leaving your application. For example, if you select **My Computer** in the **Look In** box, you can right-click on your floppy-disk drive and format or copy a disk!

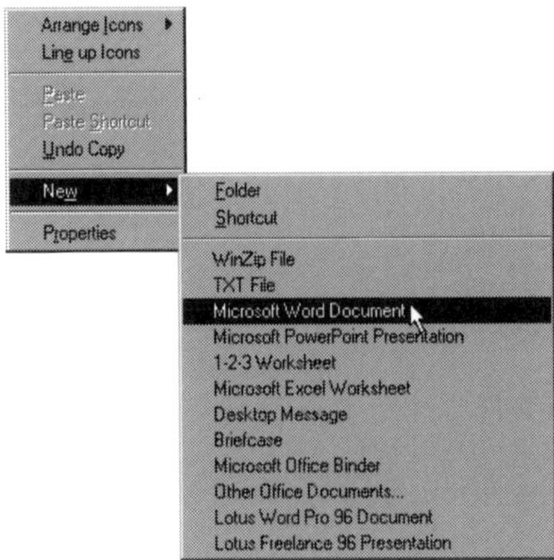

Figure 10.11 Create a new blank file wherever you want it.

Creating new files and folders

The context menu that appears when you right-click on the Desktop or a blank space in a folder window includes the entry **New** (Figure 10.11). One of the items you can create from here is a shortcut, and the Shortcut Wizard himself will appear to guide you through the process (see section **10.4**). The other option you'll have is to create a new folder in the current location – just click **New/Folder**, type a name for the folder in the box below its icon and press *Enter* (or click somewhere outside the box).

You'll have several other entries on this menu which create new blank files – many applications designed for Windows 95 add their own file types to this menu when they're installed, so you might have quite a few. You can create a new file wherever you want it in the same way as a new folder, give it a name, and double-click it to open the associated application.

File Types

Windows 95's use of File Types and matching icons has been introduced in section **5.3**, but it can be helpful to know how to create a new type or edit an existing one. As part of their drive to make Windows 95 easier to use, Microsoft have removed references to file extensions wherever possible and replaced them with more friendly sounding *types*, such as **Bitmap Files** as shown in Figure 10.10. The different types of file that can be opened or saved by a particular program can be viewed and selected from the **Files of type** drop-down list on **Open** and **Save As** dialogs. You can find out which *type* a file belongs to by choosing **Details** view in My Computer or Explorer, or by looking at the file's properties sheet, and you can tell which application that type of file is associated with by its icon.

▶ *The basic details relating to files, file names and extensions were explained on p. 116. Turn to p. 119 for more on file associations, file types and icons.*

Viewing File Types

You can find the details of all the File Types on your system by selecting **View/Options** in any Explorer or My Computer window and clicking the **File Types** tab. To see which extensions belong to a particular file type, click the appropriate entry in the window and you'll see the information displayed below, together with the name of the program with which this type of file is associated. Three buttons beside the window let you edit or remove a file type, or create a new one.

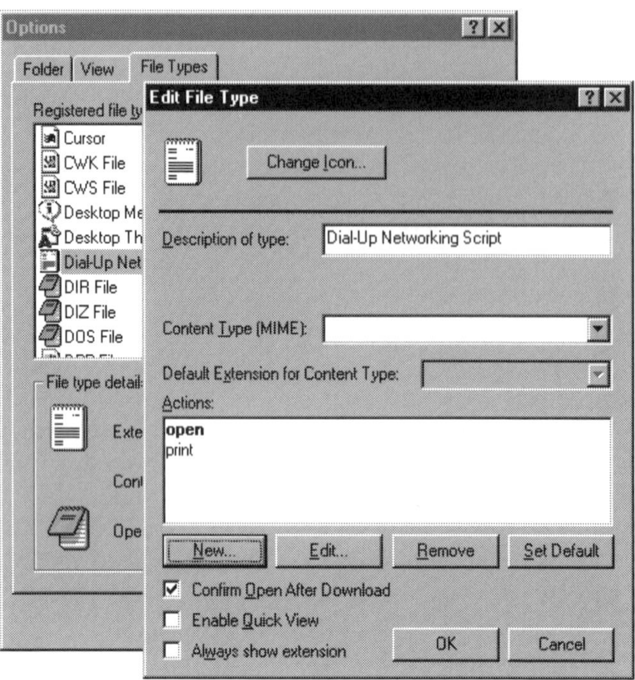

Figure 10.12 The File Types tab, and the dialog that appears when you choose the Edit or New Type button

Create a new type

Clicking the **Edit** or **New Type** buttons on the **File Types** tab will open a dialog similar to the one in Figure 10.12. The following steps describe how to create a *new* type, but you can easily use this information to modify an existing one if you want to. Let's assume you want to create a new type for files with the extension **.zzz** that will open in **Notepad**.

1. In the box marked **Description of type**, enter anything you like, such as **ZZZ Files**. This is the description that will appear in the main File Types list and on properties sheets.
2. In the **Associated extension** box, type **.zzz**. If you want to include several extensions in this type, enter each in this box, separated by a comma and a space, such as **.zzz**, **.yyy**, **.xxx**. A major oversight is that the **Edit** dialog doesn't have this box – you can't just add an extra extension to an existing type, or delete one that you want to associate with a different program; instead you have to remove the whole type and create a new one. Rather than making this easy for beginners, Microsoft have chosen to make it so complicated that beginners won't try. If you *do* try and it all goes wrong, click **Cancel** in every dialog until you're returned to your folder window.

3. Click the **Change Icon** button to select an icon for the type (or to change an existing icon). If you don't do this, Windows will automatically assign this type of file the same icon as the application that it opens with.

Bear in mind that if you enter multiple extensions in step 2, all the files with these extensions will have the icon you choose in step 3. This is a good argument for creating a new file type for each extension separately.

4. The next task is to create **Actions** for the new file type. Actions are shown in the large window at the bottom of the dialog, and the two usual actions are **Open** and **Print**. These actions will appear on the context menu for files of this type. Click on the **New** button, and you'll see the dialog shown in Figure 10.13. Type a name for the action in the upper box such as **Open**. In the lower box, enter the path and name of the application that this type of file should open in; in the case of our **.zzz** files, you'd enter **c:\windows\notepad.exe**. Click **OK**.

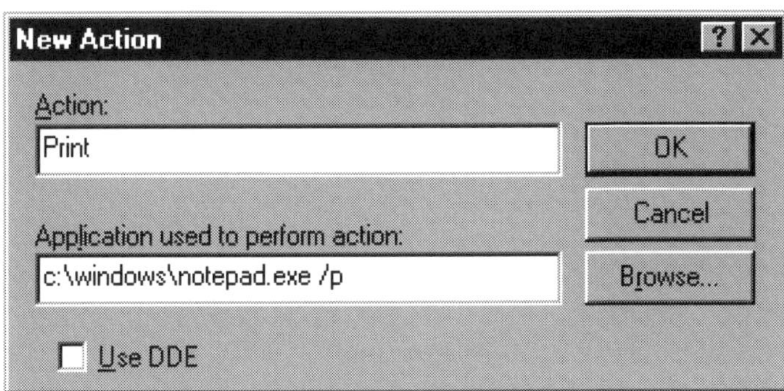

Figure 10.13 Adding an action to a file type.

5. Now add a **Print** action by clicking **New** again, typing **Print** in the upper box and **c:\windows\notepad.exe/p** in the lower. The **/p** switch is used by most applications to denote the 'print' command. (Adding this as an action lets you print a file by right-clicking it and choosing the option from the context menu instead of having to run the application and choose it from the **File** menu.) Click **OK**.
6. You'll see your two actions listed in the **Actions** window. Click once on **Open** and click the button marked **Set Default** – the **Open** action will change to bold type. This indicates that this is the action that will be taken when you double-click one of these files in a folder window (and

the action will also appear in bold type at the top of the files' context menus). Finally, click **OK** to exit the **File Types** tab.

Open With...

The **Open With...** dialog has two uses. Its first use is for opening a file in an application other than the one it's associated with. To do this, click once on the file to highlight it, then hold *Shift* and right-click it and you'll see the **Open With...** option on the context menu. Select this option, choose the application you want to use from the list that appears and it will open and load the file. If you don't see the application you want in this list, click the **Other...** button to locate and double-click it in a standard file dialog.

The second use of **Open With...** is to change the application associated with a particular file type. If you wanted the **ZZZ Files** type to automatically open in **WordPad** instead of **Notepad**, select one of these files and choose the **Open With...** option as above, click on **WordPad** in the list of applications, check the box marked **Always use this program to open this type of file** and click **OK**. From now on, any time you double-click a **ZZZ File**, it will open in **WordPad**.

Bear in mind, however, that some file types contain several extensions relating to several file formats. If you change the association for a file type, the application you choose may not be able to work with all these formats. If you're unsure, take a look at the extensions listed for this type on the **File Types** tab, then check the application's Help files and manuals to make sure they're compatible.

Naming files and folders

One of the most popular additions to Windows 95 is the ability to handle long file and folder names. A long name can be up to 255 characters, and can use any letter, number or symbol except:

\ / : * ? " < > |

In addition, you can now use mixed upper- and lower-case letters and spaces, so a name can be as descriptive as you want it to be. All this is good news, but, like any silver lining, it has a cloud. Only yourself and other Windows 95 users will be able to see these long names, so Windows also assigns items one of the old-style MS-DOS names consisting of eight characters, a dot, and a three-character extension (known as an *8-dot-three* or MS-DOS name). To do this, it takes your long file name, strips out any spaces and characters that can't be used in 8.3 names, then uses the first six characters followed by a tilde and a numeral (such as **~1**). If any other files in the same folder have the same six initial characters, Windows will use a different numeral for each.

This means that if you give a file called **Latest Sales Report.doc** to someone using Windows 3.1, what that person will see is a file called **LATEST~1.DOC**. Worse still, if you gave him or her another two files called **Latest Share Prices.doc** and **Late Start Due To Bad Light.doc**, they'd appear on the same disk as **LATEST~2.DOC** and **LATEST~3.DOC**. The information they contain would be unchanged, but how would your colleague know which one was which? If you plan to share files in this way, consider the first six characters of your long names carefully.

TIP

If you're not sure what the 8.3 name of a file or folder would be, right-click it, choose **Properties**, and look at the entry beside **MS-DOS Name**.

You'll find the same thing happening if you use 16-bit applications created for use with Windows 3.1. Any files you save with these applications will have to be given 8.3 names. You could, for example, save a file as **SALESRPT.DOC** in one of these applications. If you then renamed it in Explorer to **Sales Report.doc** it would look more understandable, but when you needed to reopen it in your application, the name would be shortened to **SALESR~1.DOC** which is a lot less easy to work out than the original 8.3 name!

TIP

When you save a new file in a 16-bit application, decide first what you want its *long* name to be, then use the first eight characters of that (excluding spaces). For example, if you want the long name to be **Sales Report.doc**, save the file as **SALESREP.DOC** then go and rename it in Explorer. If you then look at the file's properties sheet, you'll see that these eight characters have been retained as the MS-DOS name.

Control Panel

Just like its counterpart in Windows 3.1, the **Control Panel** consists of a collection of separate applets that are loaded into one window by a program called **Control.exe**. To open the Control Panel, click on **Start/Settings/Control Panel**, or click its icon near the bottom of the tree-view in Explorer, or double-click it in My Computer. Run an applet by double-clicking its icon.

In Windows 95, each Control Panel applet functions as a separate entity, so you can have as many of these open at once as you want to.

Because Windows 95 gives you so much more scope to customize than earlier versions did, tabbed pages are much in evidence in Control Panel and most applets have a daunting array of windows, check boxes and buttons. You can find out what each applet does by clicking it once and looking at Control Panel's status-bar, but when you come to navigating these pages and changing settings, use the context-sensitive Help to find out what each element on a page is for (see p. 361).

Date/Time

The Date/Time applet is where you set or alter your computer's system date and time. One of the few differences between this and the Windows 3.1 version is the addition of a **Time Zones** tab showing a graphical map of the world – this should have been set up correctly when Windows 95 was installed, but you can have some fun clicking it and watching it scroll, and it makes a useful reference if you're planning an international phone-call!

If you need to change your time zone, make sure you click the **Apply** button before clicking **OK**. If you don't, Windows won't actually update your system time and date to reflect the change!

Mouse

A multi-paged epic with plenty of options to give your rodent a makeover. The first tab, labelled **Buttons** is the practical one: from here you can switch mouse buttons for left-handed use and set the double-click speed. The **Motion** tab lets you adjust the speed your mouse moves across the screen, and gives you the option to show pointer trails (ghost pointers that follow your mouse around to help you see where you are) and to adjust their length.

The **Pointers** tab is one of Windows 95's many 'scheme' pages: from this tab you can choose which types of pointer (or *cursor*) you want to assign for different actions, and save this as a scheme that can be recalled anytime. You can choose which scheme to use from the drop-down list at the top of the page, or create your own by clicking one of the pointer types in the window and using the **Browse** button to find and select one of the pointer or animated-cursor files on your hard disk. When you've chosen all the pointers you want, click **Save As...** and type your own choice of name for the scheme, which will be added to the list in the **Schemes** box, and click **OK**.

For maximum choice, make sure you've got Windows 95's cursor-collection installed. Run Control Panel's **Add/Remove Programs** applet, go to **Windows Setup/Accessories**, click the **Details** button and check the box beside **Mouse Pointers**. Click **OK** to install them. (You'll need your Windows 95 installation disks for this.)

To use animated cursors you must have at least a 256-colour, 800 × 600 display. You can make these settings on the **Settings** tab of Control Panel's **Display** applet, but make sure your monitor and display adapter support them first.

Joystick

A simple applet from which you can select the joystick you want to use for a particular game. You can choose settings for up to 16 different joysticks here and switch from one to another with two clicks. If a particular joystick configuration isn't listed, you can click **Custom** and create your own by checking the appropriate boxes.

Multimedia

Another applet with multiple tabbed pages from which you can set up and tweak the multimedia settings of your PC.

- *Audio.* Choose the overall volume levels to use for playback and recording of digital audio (such as audio CDs and **.wav** files). You can also create your own formats for recording digital sound and save them for future use.

If you prefer to use the volume control on your speakers or an external amplifier, you can get rid of the speaker icon in the Tray – just clear the check box beside **Show volume control on the taskbar** on the **Audio** page.

- *Video.* Choose the screen size for playback of **.avi** video files. For best results choose **Original Size**. Avoid choosing fractions of screen-size from the drop-down list, and go for either **Double original size** or click the **Full screen** option button if you want a larger video-window.
- *MIDI.* Lists the MIDI-compatible devices attached to your PC. On a standard multimedia computer the upper box will relate to your soundcard. If you have more than one sound device (such as a MIDI interface card), these will be shown in the upper box and you can choose which one should be used by selecting it and clicking **OK**. If you want to use two or more sound devices at once, click the **Custom Configuration** button, click **Configure**, and assign different MIDI channels to different devices by highlighting the channel, clicking **Change...** and choosing a device. You can create multiple configurations and save each one as a 'scheme'.

TIP

If you only have a soundcard it's still worth looking at the MIDI tab. Most soundcards offer several different types of sound synthesis, and some will be better than others. These will all be listed in the upper box – try selecting a different one, clicking **OK**, and using **Media Player** to play one of the MIDI (**.mid**) files from C:\ Windows\ Media.

- *CD Music.* This tab contains two simple controls. One is a master-volume setting for the headphones socket on your CD-ROM drive; the second shows the drive-letter assigned to this drive. If you have *two* CD-ROM drives, this second setting can be useful, allowing you to specify which should be used for audio CDs.

Printers

The Printers folder contains an icon for each printer on your system, including 'software' printers such as Microsoft Fax. Double-click the printer icon to open its window and view details about which documents are queued. Right-clicking a document in the window allows you to pause, resume or cancel printing.

To change the settings for your printer, right click it and choose **Properties** (or highlight it and press *Alt* + *Enter*) then go to the **Details** tab. This page shows the port to which your printer is connected, and the device driver it uses. Clicking the **Settings** button for a hardware printer will lead you to another tabbed page from which you can alter the default paper size and orientation, colour intensity and resolution for graphics, and print quality.

The Printers folder also contains an icon labelled **Add Printer**. Double-clicking this icon starts the **Add Printer Wizard** which helps you through the process of installing a new printer. After pausing for a few seconds to build a database of printer drivers included with Windows 95, the Wizard presents you with a two-pane dialog. Choose the manufacturer of your printer from the left window and the model from the right and the Wizard will set it up for you. If your printer isn't listed, click on **Have Disk...** and direct the Wizard to the floppy disk containing the drivers that came with your printer.

TIP

If the precise model of your printer isn't listed and you don't have a disk, don't worry! Choose a model that seems to be a close match judging by its name and any other information given and try it. If the results aren't good, you can delete the printer from your Printers folder and try another one.

Keyboard

The primary settings for your keyboard haven't changed since Windows 3.1 (see p. 287), probably because the keyboard itself hasn't changed either – the same sliders for **Repeat Rate** and **Repeat Delay** are here, with a text box you can use to test the settings before quitting the applet. There's also a slider for **Cursor Blink Rate** which determines how fast the insertion-point cursor should flash in text-based applications.

A second tab, labelled **Language**, adds the ability to switch languages and keyboard-layouts quickly. Click the **Add...** button and add the languages you want to use, then highlight them one at a time and click **Properties** to change the keyboard layout for each. You can specify a hotkey to switch between languages, or check the box marked **Enable indicator on taskbar**. The indicator is a two-letter abbreviation of the currently selected language – click once to display a menu of your chosen languages and select one to switch to, or right-click the icon and choose **Properties** to get back to this **Language** tab quickly.

Figure 10.14 Adding sound effects to system events.

Sounds

Sounds is another single-page applet that works in a similar way to the **Pointers** tab in the **Mouse** applet, allowing you to assign sound effects to system events and dialogs (see Figure 10.14), such as Maximizing or Minimizing a window, starting or quitting Windows, or the ever-amusing program crash (listed as 'Critical Stop'). This is another 'scheme' applet – choose the collection of sounds you want to assign, and save the result to build up a list of your own sound schemes. To use one of Windows' own schemes (or one you made earlier) choose it from the **Schemes** box at the bottom of the page and click **OK**. Or follow these steps to create your own scheme:

TIP

System sound effects are something of a luxury item – apart from needing a soundcard and speakers to hear them, they use valuable resources that you might want to use for more practical purposes!

1. In the **Events** window, click an event for which you want to assign a sound (you don't have to assign a sound for all of them unless you want to).
2. Click the arrow beside the drop-down list box labelled **Name** to display the **.wav** files in C:\Windows\Media. Click on one of these entries and click

the 'Play' button (with the arrow icon) beside the **Preview** window to hear it.

3. If none of the sounds from the Media folder is suitable, click **Browse** and search your hard disk for other **.wav** files – you can preview these in the same way using the same button at the bottom of the **Browse** dialog. Click **OK** when you find the one you want to use.
4. Repeat steps 1 to 3 to assign sounds to other events. If you choose a sound from a different folder, the contents of this folder will be listed in the **Name** box for you to choose the next from.

If you don't have any **.wav** files, open Control Panel's **Add/Remove Programs** applet, and click your way to **Windows Setup/Multimedia/Details**. The **Sample Sounds** entry adds a small collection of sounds to your Media folder. There are also several preset sound schemes you can install, but keep an eye on the sizes of these schemes – they range from 0.7 Mb to over 3 Mb! Check the items you want to install and click **OK**.

5. When you've selected sounds for all the actions you want, click **Save As...**, type a name for the scheme and click **OK**.
6. Click **Apply** and/or **OK** to put the new scheme into effect.

Regional settings

This applet has five tabs from which you can choose the appropriate country and language, and a range of settings for the way you like numbers, currency, time and date to be presented in applications that use these settings. In most cases the choice you make on the first page will set up the remaining options the way you'd want to see them anyway, but if you have particular preferences you can choose them from simple drop-down list boxes on the remaining pages.

Display

This is a four-tab applet that customizes the look of Windows 95 (Figure 10.15). The basics are little changed since Windows 3.1, but the methods have altered a little and more options have been added. The **Background** tab lets you choose a **Pattern** for your Desktop to spice-up its otherwise plain colour. (The colour is selected by choosing 'Desktop' on the **Appearance** tab.) You can also choose a **Wallpaper** which will appear over your pattern if you selected one, or on your Desktop if you didn't. If you choose a pictorial wallpaper, choose the **Centered** option; if the wallpaper is a design of some sort it will look more effective **Tiled** to cover the entire Desktop, but this will of course obliterate your Pattern! Bear in mind that Wallpapers use valuable memory, and your Desktop will probably spend most of its time covered in application windows!

You can use any bitmap (**.bmp**) file from any folder as wallpaper – just click the **Browse** button to locate the file you want to use and double-click it.

The second tab is where you choose and set up your **Screensaver**. Select a screensaver from the drop-down list, and click the **Settings** button to see any customization options included by its creator. To check out the result, click the **Preview** button; move the mouse or press a keyboard key to stop the preview. The screensaver will kick in automatically if you don't touch the keyboard or mouse for a preset period of time; you can adjust the time in minutes by entering a new figure in the **Wait** box. Alternatively, you can activate energy-saving options on this page, if your monitor supports them, by checking the appropriate boxes at the bottom of the page and entering delay times. The **Low-power standby** option functions like a screensaver – just

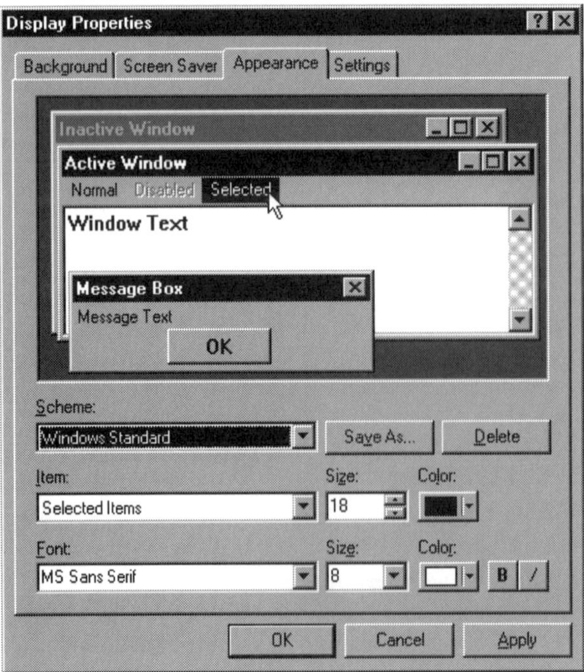

Figure 10.15 All the tools you need to customize the way Windows looks.

move the mouse or press a key to bring your screen back to life. Check your monitor's manuals for details on its implementation of the **Shut off** option. Energy-saving options take precedence over any screensaver you set up.

The **Appearance** tab allows you to define colour schemes that are used throughout Windows, choosing different colours and sizes for screen elements such as active title-bars, menus, buttons, and the Desktop itself. You can also change the font type and size used for menus and title-bars, and a whole host of other things. As in Windows 3.1, the preview window is interactive – you can click on an element and its name will be displayed in the **Item** box ready to be altered – but there are certain elements that don't appear in the preview and have to be selected from the Item box itself such as Tooltips and Icon Spacing.

TIP

You can open the **Display** applet quickly by right-clicking on the Desktop and clicking **Properties**.

There are various attributes that can be changed for various items including colour and size of objects and text, and bold or italic text. When these are unavailable for a certain screen element they'll appear *greyed-out* and you won't be able to click them. As usual, you can save your own creations as schemes by clicking the **Save As...** button and entering a name.

TIP

When you're experimenting with different schemes or altering screen elements, make the most of the **Apply** button: this lets you see what difference the changes make to the whole of Windows as if you'd clicked **OK**, but if you're not happy with the result you still have the page open in front of you to change it.

The **Settings** tab lets you change Windows' display settings. The **Color Palette** drop-down list lets you choose the number of colours used for the display. If you change this setting you'll have to restart your computer before it will take effect. Check your manuals carefully before choosing a higher colour setting – if you choose one that's incompatible you could end up with a blank screen when Windows loads (see 'Booting in Safe Mode' on p. 381).

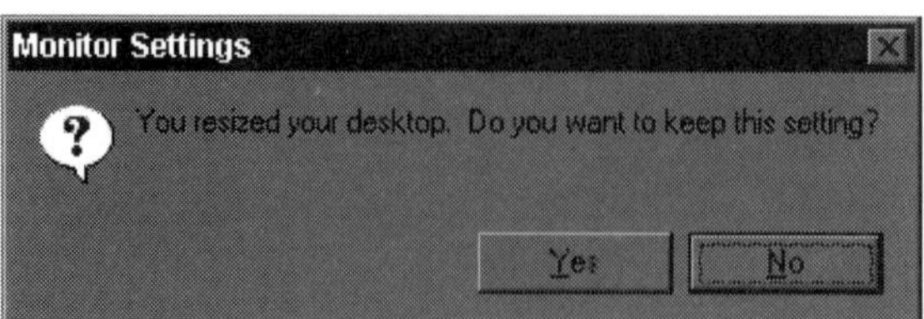

Figure 10.16 A vital dialog. But you can just ignore it.

You can also change the screen resolution, using the slider marked **Desktop Area**. Windows 3.1 users who tried this kind of thing and still bear the scars might have shied away from this one. This time, however, it's painless. When you change the setting and click **OK** the screen will blank. Within a couple of seconds the screen should return at the new resolution and Windows will then bring up a dialog to ask if everything went okay (shown in Figure 10.16). If it did, click the **Yes** button. If it didn't, of course, you won't see the dialog. Provided you don't start blindly clicking mouse buttons at this point, Windows will return you to the original resolution after a few seconds, wiser but unharmed.

► *You can also change your monitor and display adapter from the **Settings** tab. Turn to p. 378 for details.*

► *Several applets escaped coverage in this section: you'll find the **Network** applet on p. 225; the **Fonts** folder on pp. 151–154; the **System** and **Add New Hardware** applets on pp. 373–381; and the **Add/Remove Programs** applet on p. 362.*

Help

The Windows 3.1 **Help** program (Winhelp.exe) is still included with Windows 95 for compatibility with older programs: these Help files function in the same way as described in Chapter **9** although the program itself has a slightly updated appearance. The main enhancement comes in the form of added menu options allowing you to **Keep Help on Top**, or change the size of the font used in the files. You can also now use the right mouse button to click inside a Help window (though not inside a pop-up) and choose options straight from the context menu.

But Windows 95 also has a shiny new Help system which comes in the form of three tabbed pages labelled **Contents**, **Index** and **Find**. Applications built for Windows 95 will use this new Help program, and it continues to be accessed by clicking the **Help** menu on an application's menu-bar or pressing *F1* anywhere in the application.

To open Windows 95's *own* Help file, click **Help** on the **Start Menu**, or click once on the Desktop and press *F1*. The 'Ten Minutes to using Windows' tour is a sensible place to start for new users, taking you step by step through all the basic procedures in an interactive presentation, with a friendly **Show Me** button you can click if something doesn't make sense. The 'If You've Used Windows Before' option is a brief, graphical question-and-answer session for ex-Windows 3.1 users that points out some of the changes to the new operating system.

Contents

The **Contents** page follows the structure of a book's contents page. Topics are represented by 'page' icons, with groups of these icons gathered together in 'books'. Double-click a book to open it and see the topics it contains; double-click it again to close it.

This Help program uses two windows – the topics themselves are displayed in a different window when you double-click them, and the hypertext links are gone. Instead the topics come in the form of step-by-step tips with a clickable button at the bottom of the page marked **Related Tips** which displays titles of more topics that may be of interest. As soon as you double-click a topic on the Contents page and the Topic window appears, the Contents page vanishes – to bring it back, click the **Help Topics** button (see Figure 10.17).

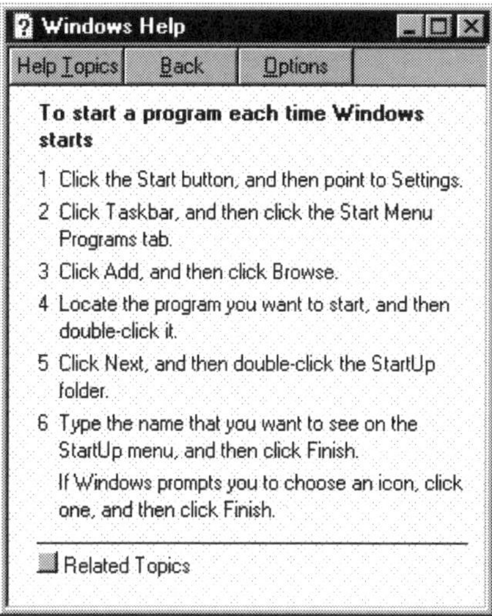

Figure 10.17 The new look of the Help topic.

Index

The **Index** tab is a straight lift from the **Search** option used in the old Help program, but it's become a lot easier to use. Type a word, or the first few letters of a word, into the upper box, and the lower box scrolls to find an alphabetical match. If you type a single letter, for example, the lower box will scroll to the first entry that begins with that letter. To display a topic either double-click it, or highlight it and press *Alt+D*.

Find

Find is a new and powerful addition to the Help program, but it works in a very simple way: the first time you select the **Find** tab for a new Help file, the program builds a database of all the words contained in the file. You're presented with a dialog from which you can choose how thorough the search for words should be, but the **Minimal** option is almost always thorough enough. (If you select one of the others, bear in mind that its database will take longer to create, more space to store, and longer to load every time you click this tab in the future!)

There are three separate elements to locating the topic you want from the **Find** tab, shown in Figure 10.18. First, type one or more words that you'd expect to find in a topic dealing with the subject you're interested in. In the second window, you'll see a list of matching or derived words, and the third window will display all the topic titles that contain these words. To narrow the search, click on any entries in the second window that don't fit the topic you were looking for to remove their highlight. Then choose from the likely looking topics in the third window. If you choose one of these and it doesn't contain the information you were looking for, click the **Help Topics** button and the **Find** tab will reappear with the same results displayed.

Troubleshooters

Another new aspect of this Help system is the addition of **Troubleshooters**. The easiest way to find them (and other troubleshooting help) is to click on the **Index** tab and type **trouble** – you'll see a long list of entries on just about every Windows 95-related issue you could ever get into trouble with! Troubleshooters work by asking you questions about the problem and giving you several possible answers to choose from, each with its own button, that lead either to another question or a suggestion to try something and see if it works. These windows remain on top of any others, so you can nip off and try Windows' suggestion and then come back and click the **No, I am still having trouble** button.

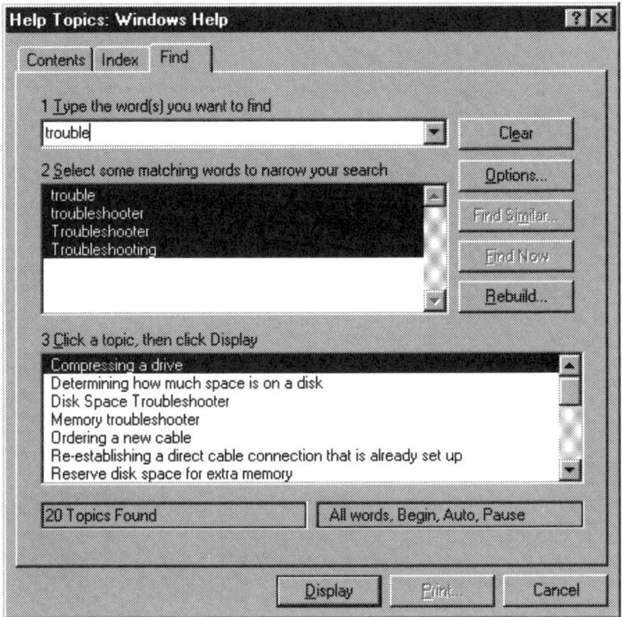

Figure 10.18 Help's new **Find** tab.

What's This?

A final addition to the program is an enhancement of context-sensitive help. In Windows 3.1, many dialogs had a **Help** button you could press for explanations. In Windows 95 these have been replaced by a smaller and neater type of help in Tooltip form, similar to the pop-ups used in old-style Help files.

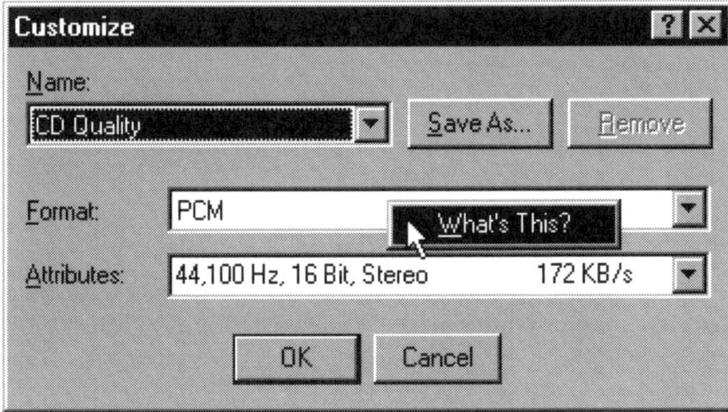

Figure 10.19 The question-mark button and 'What's This?' context menu.

There are three different ways of opening these tooltips. If a window's title-bar contains a button with a question-mark icon, click the button and then click the item you want explained. If there's no button (or if there is, but you prefer this method!), right-click on the item and a tiny context menu will appear with the words **What's This?** on it – just click the context menu. The third option is to click the item once to select it and then press *F1*. There are times when this third method is no use: for example, if the item in question is a button, by the time you've clicked it, it'll be too late to press *F1* – for better or worse, you'll have just found out what the button does!

Accessories

Add and remove Windows 95 components

If your PC came with Windows 95 pre-installed, or you chose the 'Typical' installation option, you may be missing out on a few useful accessories. To see what else is available, add extra components, or remove any you don't need, open Control Panel, double-click **Add/Remove Programs** and click the **Windows Setup** tab.

All the components are collected into groups under headings such as **Accessories**, **Multimedia** and **Communications**. Click one of these group names and click on the **Details** button to see which components the group contains (see Figure 10.20). You can *add* a component from this group by checking the box beside the component's name, or *remove* it from your system by clearing the check box. When you've made all the selections you want from one group, click **OK**, then choose another group from the list to look at.

When you've worked your way through each group in this way, click **OK** on the main **Windows Setup** page and Windows will carry out all the additions and removals you've chosen. Depending what you selected, you may be prompted to restart Windows when all this is finished; if so, click the **OK** button and be patient – it might take a little longer than usual to restart while Windows updates the system.

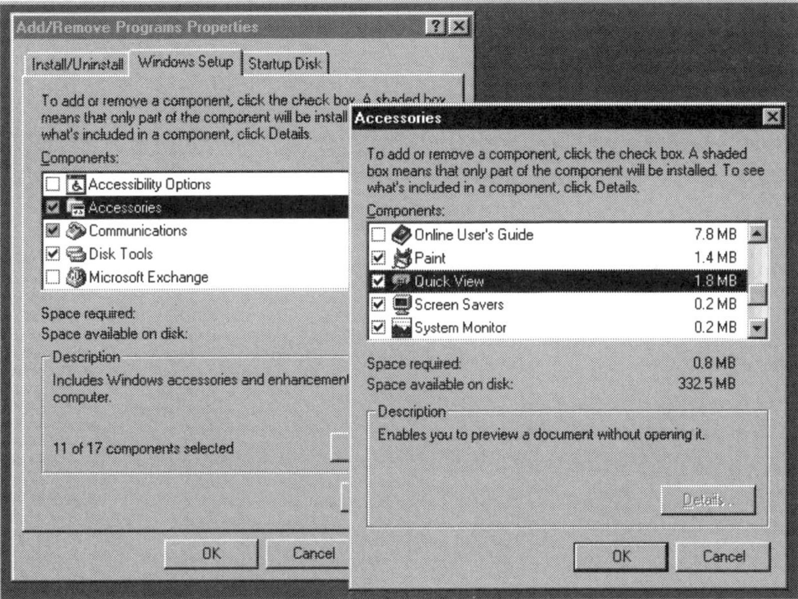

Figure 10.20 Installing **Quick View** from the Accessories group.

TIP

If you bought Windows 95 as a set of floppy disks rather than a CD-ROM, a bunch of items will be missing (including some of those mentioned in this section). Ask any friendly software retailer about the so-called **fulfilment disks** containing these extra components, or download them from Microsoft's Web site using the URL given on p. 244.

Installing and uninstalling software

The **Add/Remove Programs** applet serves a second useful purpose – most of the software you install that was designed for Windows 95 will add itself to the list of programs on the **Install/Uninstall** page. There's no need to use this page to actually *install* the software; just follow the instructions included with the software itself. But if you ever want to *uninstall* it, and it doesn't have an uninstall option of its own, always take a look at the **Install/Uninstall** list to see if the program has logged itself here before you resort to the unsatisfactory solution of deleting its files and folders manually.

If the software *is* listed here, highlight it and click the button marked **Add/Remove**.

▶ *For more details on installing and uninstalling software go back to p. 163.*

WordPad

Windows 3.1's excellent **Write** word processor has been replaced with **WordPad** in Windows 95, a cut-down version of Microsoft's top-of-the-line **Word** application. For compatibility purposes, WordPad can open files created with Write, but it saves files with a **.doc** extension compatible with Word. You can also open and save files in plain text (ASCII) format, or in rich-text format. Rich-text (**.rtf**) files contain all the formatting and layout detail of the original document and can be opened by almost any word processor, but a rich-text file will be larger than the same document saved in Word (**.doc**) format, so it's a format to be avoided if you're saving files for your own use (or for the use of someone who has either WordPad or Word).

Like most of Windows 95's accessories, **WordPad** supports the right mouse button and context menu – right-click inside its window for formatting options, Cut, Copy and Paste, and OLE object editing.

WordPad has the usual text and paragraph formatting options you'd expect to find in any word processor such as bold, italic and underline; left-aligned, right-aligned and centred text. It also has a few neat additions such as coloured and bulleted text and can handle documents many megabytes in size. Its one failing is its lack of support for page breaks and numbering, which relegates it from the ranks of 'word processor' to 'jotter'.

On the positive side, WordPad supports OLE (see p. 156), allowing you to include logos and drawings in your documents, or add DDE links to other files. This OLE compatibility means that you can open a file by dragging it from a folder and dropping it in WordPad's window, and it offers another neat little feature too – scraps! Highlight a section of text, then use the left mouse button to drag it to the Desktop, and an icon will appear with the name **Document Scrap (???)** where the question marks will be replaced with the first 16 characters of text to help you remember what each scrap contained. You can drag these scraps back into this or any other WordPad document and drop them wherever you want them.

Instead of using Cut, Copy and Paste in a **WordPad** document, just highlight a section of text and drag it to a different position in the document to move it, or hold *Ctrl* and drag to copy it.

▶ *For more on Text (ASCII) and Rich-text formats, go back to p. 140.*

Character Map

Character Map is an accessory from Windows 3.1 that's found its way into Windows 95 completely unchanged. The whole reason for its existence is to give you access to special characters and symbols such as ©, $\frac{1}{2}$ and ± that you can't type into a document in the normal way. You start by choosing a font from the drop-down list box and hunting through the characters in the window below to find the one you want. (If you can't find anything suitable, try a different font – the type and quantity of characters vary from one font to another.) There are two methods of importing these characters into your documents:

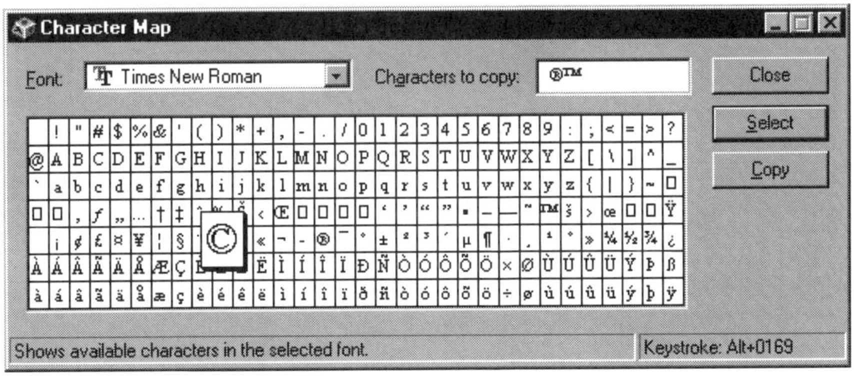

Figure 10.21 Character Map with two symbols already selected, and another highlighted.

Insert by pasting

After clicking the character you need, click on **Select**. If you need other characters, do the same for each – they will all be added to the **Characters to copy** box. When you've selected all you want, click **Copy**. Return to your document and select **Paste** from the **Edit** menu, or press *Ctrl* + *V*. The characters will be pasted at the insertion point. You can then delete the characters you don't want at that particular position. (Provided you don't subsequently Cut or Copy anything else, these characters will remain on the clipboard to be pasted again.)

Insert by typing

After clicking the required character, note the **Keystroke** in the lower right corner of the window (e.g. the copyright symbol is *Alt + 0169*). Return to your document and position the cursor where you want to insert the symbol. Making sure *Num Lock* is on, hold *Alt* and type *0169* on the numeric keypad. (For some symbols, you'll have to select the same font in your document as you had in **Character Map**.)

The symbols in **Character Map** are quite small, and it can be difficult to see what they look like. To get around this, click on any symbol and then use the arrow keys to move around – the symbols will be shown double-size.

Paint

Paint is Windows 95's updated and enhanced version of Windows 3.1's **Paintbrush** program. All the features of Paintbrush still apply to Paint (with the exception of the *Ctrl + P* hotkey, which is now used for **Print**), so return to p. 298 for more information. Here are a few points that relate just to **Paint**:

- If you draw with the right-mouse button the background colour will be used, which means that you can swap between two colours easily by switching from one button to the other.
- Paint can still open **.pcx** files for compatibility with Paintbrush, but can no longer save in that format.
- After saving a file, go to the **File** menu and choose one of the two **Set As Wallpaper** options to use your creation as Desktop wallpaper.
- Create your own icons for use with your shortcuts: start Paint, press *Ctrl + E*, set units to **pels** and enter **32** into the **Width** and **Height** boxes. Press *Ctrl + PageDown* to zoom in, *Ctrl + G* to turn on the gridlines, and start creating. When you've finished, save the file as a 16-colour bitmap and give it any name you like, plus the extension **.ico**.
- With the Pick, Scissors or Text tool selected, you can right-click on the canvas to open the context menu.

- The toolbar and colour-bar are both detachable: click to the extreme left of the toolbar or the top of the colour-bar and drag them to where you want them. To 'dock' them again, drag them back to either side, top or bottom of the window.
- When you're working on a large or detailed drawing in zoom mode, go to **View/Zoom/Show Thumbnail** to open a small window that gives you an overview of what the whole drawing looks like as you work on it.

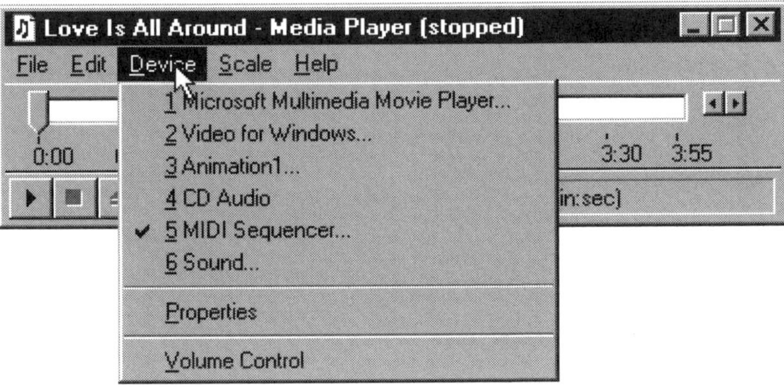

Figure 10.22 Media Player and its list of compatible devices.

Media Player

Media Player is a Windows 3.1 utility that's arrived in Windows 95 largely unaltered. Its precise capabilities will depend upon what multimedia hardware and software you have installed, but it can potentially handle **.mmm** movie files, **.avi** video, **.flc** and **.ani** animations, **.mid** and **.rmi** MIDI files, **.wav** digital audio files, and audio CDs. To play CD and wave sound you'll need a soundcard installed; MIDI files need either a soundcard or a MIDI interface card and an external MIDI device. (And to play an audio CD, of course, you won't get far without a CD-ROM drive!)

The remaining types will depend upon software: to play **.avi** videos in Windows 3.1 you'll need to install Microsoft's free Video For Windows software. In Windows 95 you'll have to install **Video Compression** from the **Multimedia** group in **Windows Setup** (see 'Add and remove Windows 95 components' earlier in this section). Here are a few tips on **Media Player** use:

- Although you can use **File/Open** to open a file, it's easier to use the **Device** menu to choose the type of file you want to open – an **Open** dialog will appear displaying the last folder you looked in when using that particular device.
- **Media Player** is an OLE server – you can embed media clips or whole files in documents and Media Player will replay them when they're clicked. You can use **Edit/Options** to change the way an embedded clip should look and behave in a document, and use the **Start Selection** and **End Selection** buttons to mark and copy a section of a file to link or embed. (If you do this with an audio CD track, you'll need to have the same CD in the drive when you want to replay the clip!)
- When a particular device is selected (checked) on the **Device** menu, clicking **Properties** on the same menu will open the corresponding page of Control Panel's **Multimedia** applet.
- Using the **Scale** menu, you can choose to view the progress of a video or animation in **Frames** rather than seconds and minutes, and an audio CD by track.

Sound Recorder

Sound Recorder is a simple program for playing, recording and editing wave sound (**.wav**) files. To play a file, double-click the file's icon or use the **File/Open...** dialog to locate it. When it comes to saving a file, the standard **Save As...** dialog has an extra line of information at the bottom displaying the file format – clicking the **Change** button allows you to choose a different format and set attributes from the dialog shown in Figure 10.23.

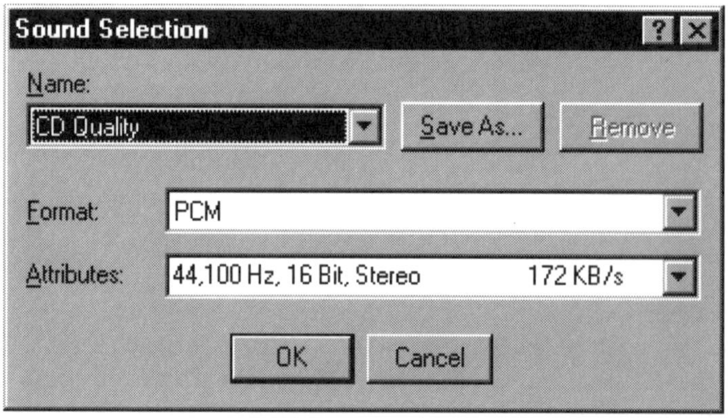

Figure 10.23 Choosing a new data format and attributes for a wave sound file.

Sound Recorder records all sound in PCM format which is fully editable and provides a clear output. For a smaller file you can convert to a different format by choosing it from the **Format** box, but the quality will suffer. You can also choose a set of attributes from the lower list box. These are arranged from lowest to highest quality, with **44,100 Hz**, **16 Bit**, **Stereo** being a crystal-clear CD-quality sound. Keep an eye on the entry to the right of this list which indicates the disk space needed per second of sound – CD quality sound uses 172 K per second, which equates to roughly 10 Mb per minute. If there's a particular combination of attributes and format that you expect to use again, click the **Save As...** button on the **Sound Selection** dialog and type a name for this combination.

TIP

If you can spare the disk space temporarily, save the file several times using different attributes, under different names. (Save in highest quality first and work your way down.) You can then play them back one at a time and stick with the smallest file whose quality is good enough for your purposes.

Here are a few creating and editing ideas for sound recording:

- If some of the sounds you've assigned to system events using Control Panel's **Sound** applet seem much louder than others, load them into Sound Recorder and use **Effects/Decrease Volume** to quieten them down, then re-save them. (You may have to select the **Decrease Volume** option several times before you reach the volume you want.)
- If recordings seem distorted, click **Edit/Audio Properties** and move the slider in the **Recording** section slightly to the left.
- You can use the **Insert File...** and **Mix With File...** options on the **Edit** menu to create quite complex wave files. Move the slider to the desired position, then choose either option and select a **.wav** file from the dialog. **Insert** will replace the current file with the inserted one for its duration; **Mix** will layer the two files.

CD Player

As long as you have a CD-ROM drive and soundcard, CD Player does just what you'd expect it to do – it plays your audio CDs. Its controls and features are similar to those found on hardware CD players, offering continuous play (endlessly cycling through the disk), random play (randomizing the order of tracks), and intro play (playing the first few seconds of each track).

TIP

A new feature in Windows 95 is **Autoplay**: as soon as you insert an audio CD, **CD Player** loads and starts to play it. If you load a CD-ROM, Windows searches it for a file named **Autorun.inf.** If it finds one, the CD's GUI program will run automatically (as the Windows 95 installation CD does). To override both Autoplay and Autorun, hold the *Shift* key as the drive tray closes and keep it depressed for about five seconds while Windows reads the disk information.

One of the great features of CD Player is the ability to set up playlists for your CDs. Place an audio CD in the drive and wait for CD Player to start, then follow these steps:

1. Click on **Disc/Edit Play List**.
2. Type the artist's name and CD title in the boxes at the top of the dialog.
3. Click in the box at the bottom, marked **Track 01**, type the title of the first track on the CD; press *Return* and type the title of track two, and so on.
4. Finally, hold *Ctrl* and click on all the tracks you don't like in the **Playlist** window, and click **Remove**. Alternatively, click **Clear All** to clear the **Playlist** window, then create your own playlist by selecting tracks one at a time from the **Available Tracks** window and clicking **Add**. (You can even add the same track over and over again if you want to!)

All the titles you entered are stored in CD Player's initialization file (**Cdplayer.ini**), so you'll see them displayed automatically every time you insert this disk into the drive. Any time you want to you can re-edit the playlist to replace titles you removed or to remove others.

HyperTerminal

HyperTerminal is a communications accessory that allows you to connect to another computer via your modem to send and receive (*upload and download*) files and view textual information. This might be a bulletin board service (BBS), an online service that supports one of HyperTerminal's terminal emulations, or a friend's computer if he or she has a modem.

By default, when HyperTerminal is installed, a shortcut to its folder is placed in **Start/Programs/Accessories**. Click this shortcut to open the folder and double-click the icon labelled **Hypertrm** to start HyperTerminal. Follow these steps to connect to a remote computer:

1. When HyperTerminal starts you'll see a dialog labelled **Connection Description**. Type any descriptive name for the connection you're going to make (such as the name of the BBS or service) and choose an icon from the window. Click **OK**.

2. In the next dialog, enter the area code and phone number you want to dial to, and make sure the correct modem is selected if you have more than one.
3. In the third dialog, click the **Dial** button to make the connection.
4. The connection you've just created is like any file you'd create in an application: you can save it from the **File** menu, and you'll be prompted to save it when you shut HyperTerminal. If you do save it, you can reconnect to the same computer by simply double-clicking the icon for the connection (or choosing the connection from **File/Open** if HyperTerminal is already running).

TIP

If you have an external modem and one set of lights is enough for you, you can get rid of the little modem icon that appears in the Tray when you make a connection. With the connection file open, go to **File/Properties/Configure/Options** and clear the check box beside **Display modem status**.

Quick View

One of the main problems with Windows 95 applications is their size – even **WordPad** is a slow loader – and this can be frustrating when all you want to do is glance quickly at a file to see what it contains. **Quick View** is a little utility that makes this possible by using conversion files to 'translate' data from a range of different files types and let you see the files in a fast-loading window.

If you don't have Quick View on your system, you can install it from the **Accessories** group in **Windows Setup** (see 'Add and remove Windows 95 components' earlier in this section). To 'quick view' a file, right-click it and select **Quick View** from the context menu. If you want to edit the file, or view it in its original application, click the button on the left of the Quick View toolbar.

Quickies

- **Resource Meter** (Rsrcmtr.exe) is a tiny optional accessory that installs as an icon in the Tray and keeps you informed about available system resources – if the meter goes into the red you're overdoing it! Double-click the meter for a slightly more detailed view.

- **Phone Dialer** (Dialer.exe) is just what it says: provided you have a modem, you can use this little accessory to dial a number using the keyboard's numeric keypad. Like any decent phone, you can also assign regularly used numbers to 10 speed-dial buttons.
- **Calculator** (Calc.exe) is largely unchanged since its Windows 3.1 days (see p. 298), still sporting both standard and scientific versions. The big improvement is the addition of tooltip help – right-click on any button and click the **What's This?** context menu and the tooltip will explain what the button does and tell you the keyboard shortcut for it.
- A handy new applet is included with Windows 95 called **Fontview**. Double-click on any font file, whether in your **Fonts** folder or elsewhere, and Fontview will display examples of the font in a variety of point sizes. Click **Done** to close the window, or **Print** to print out a copy of the page (useful for building up a catalogue of the fonts on your system).
- **System Editor** is included with Windows 95 and lives in C:\Windows\System as Sysedit.exe. It functions exactly as it did in its Windows 3.1 incarnation (see p. 309), but now opens two extra files, **Msmail.ini** and **Protocol.ini**. If you find yourself working with any of these files regularly, it's worth creating a shortcut to Sysedit.exe somewhere accessible.

▶ *Two of Windows 95's accessories, **Notepad** and **Clipboard Viewer**, started life in Windows 3.1. To recap on them, go back to section **9.6. Clipbook Viewer**, also covered in this section, can be found hiding on the Windows 95 CD-ROM. You can install it using the **Add/Remove Programs** applet, clicking **Have Disk** and navigating to D:\Other\Clipbook. The file name to look for is **Clipbook.inf**.*

Adding and configuring hardware

Adding new hardware to your computer has traditionally been viewed as something you shouldn't do on a full stomach. It's not the physical installation of the device that causes the problems – it usually just slips into an expansion slot, or plugs into a port – it's the configuration of the thing once it's there. Windows 95's support for Plug & Play has made the configuration of new devices much easier than it was in most cases, but with so many manufacturers selling so many products, instant success isn't guaranteed.

In this section we'll begin by looking at the automated methods of installing and configuring hardware and lead on to some of the manual changes you might have to make in order to get everything working as it should.

Installing with Plug & Play

The idea of Plug & Play is that the first time you start your computer after installing new hardware, Windows 95 will notice this new device, decide what it is, and add the necessary drivers for it automatically. If all goes smoothly, you should see just a brief on-screen message as your Desktop appears announcing that a new device has been detected and is being configured. As well as installing driver files, the Plug & Play system covers the allocation of resources for the device, such as assigning correct and non-conflicting DMA channels and IRQs if necessary (see pp. 39–40).

Microsoft supplies its own drivers for a huge range of hardware: you might be prompted to insert your Windows 95 installation disks or CD so that the required files can be copied to your hard disk. If Windows detects a Plug & Play device but can't provide a driver for it, you'll be prompted to insert the disk containing the driver files that you received with the hardware.

Windows 95's drivers are usually at least as good as those created by the manufacturer, so if Windows installs its own driver automatically and everything seems to function correctly, you might as well stick with it unless you have a more recent driver from the manufacturer. If you want to swap drivers, you can use the **Add New Hardware Wizard** from Control Panel to do it (see 'Changing hardware drivers' below).

Full Plug & Play support relies on having a Plug & Play BIOS as well as Plug & Play hardware. Nevertheless, if one or both of these items are non-Plug & Play compatible, Windows 95 will still have a brave try at identifying the new device. If neither is Plug & Play compatible, however, you'll probably find you need to get your hands dirty in **Device Manager** to assign non-conflicting resources. This will always depend upon the type of hardware you're installing, and what's installed already (see 'Resource settings' below).

Changing hardware drivers

Despite its name, the **Add New Hardware Wizard** in Control Panel lets you *change* hardware drivers as well as install new hardware (Figure 10.24). If Windows didn't manage to detect your device, or you want to install an updated driver, go to Control Panel and run the wizard, then follow these steps:

Figure 10.24 Choose the type of device you want to install and configure.

1. Click **Next** in the first dialog to begin the process. In the second dialog click the **No** button to prevent Windows searching for the device.
2. On the next page, double-click the type of hardware for which you want to change or install drivers.
3. If Windows failed to detect your hardware, look at the **Manufacturers** and **Models** lists to see if the device is listed. If it is, select it and click **Next** to install it. If you want to install an updated driver, or the driver that came with the software, click **Have Disk...** and direct Windows to the location of the files.
4. Installing new drivers will always require that you restart the computer for the change to take effect.

▶ *Although you can add a new printer from the **Add New Hardware Wizard,** the more compact **Add Printer** wizard in Control Panel's Printers folder is a neater option to take. See 'Printers' on p. 352.*

Installing an unrecognized device

Sometimes Windows just hasn't got a clue what your device is: it can't detect it, and doesn't list a driver for it. If the manufacturer didn't package a driver with the hardware, all is not lost! Many drivers will work with different devices, so use the **Add New Hardware Wizard** to try a few. It's a trial-and-error process, so it could involve a lot of booting and rebooting, but you'll usually get there in the end.

If there are devices of the same type as yours listed by the same manufacturer, start by trying those, following steps 3 and 4 above. If none of those works (or your manufacturer isn't listed at all), try the range of generic drivers supplied for most device types: after clicking the **No** radio button as in step 1 above, double-click **Other devices** in the **Hardware types** list.

You'll see a list of bracketed entries in the left pane such as (**Standard display types**) and (**Standard mouse types**). Click the correct type and choose what you think is the closest match in the right pane, then click **Next** to continue the installation.

Device Manager

Almost all the nitty-gritty of your system that affects (or is controlled by) Windows 95 can be found in Control Panel's **System** applet. You can either double-click this icon or, for quicker access, right-click on **My Computer**, and choose **Properties**.

Following the basic information on the **General** page, the first tab you come to is **Device Manager**. This follows the familiar 'tree-structure' used in Explorer's left pane. From this page you can:

- view all the devices connected to your computer
- add/remove or disable/enable devices
- see which drivers are used for particular devices and change them
- check and change settings, addresses and IRQs
- check and alter port settings (mouse, modem, printer, etc.)
- make sure that each device is working properly.

It's well worth taking a browse through **Device Manager** even as an inexperienced user: expand trees, select devices and choose the **Properties** button for each. Provided you don't actually change anything, this is risk-free. For the nervous, the simple way to change nothing is: never click **OK** – always use **Cancel** to close a dialog.

By selecting the **Computer** entry at the top of the **Device Manager** list and clicking **Properties**, you can view devices by resource: for example, click the **Interrupt Request** radio button to see which IRQs are in use, and by which devices – useful information to have if you need to find a free IRQ to allocate to a newly installed device.

Windows 95 provides a friendly Help-based Hardware Conflict Troubleshooter which aims to solve conflicts in question-and-answer style. Run **Help** from the Start Menu, click the **Contents** tab, then double-click **Troubleshooting** and **If you have a hardware conflict**.

Resource settings

Assuming your computer has a Plug & Play BIOS, when you install a Plug & Play device, Windows 95 allocates the resources for it automatically. On the **Resources** tab of a device's **Properties** page in **Device Manager** you should see that the **Use automatic settings** box is checked. This lets Windows juggle resources around between different devices if you install more Plug & Play hardware, so this box is always best left checked.

With a Plug & Play BIOS, Windows will still try to allocate correct resources for a *non*-Plug & Play device, but these may not always suit the hardware itself. If they don't, you'll need to clear the **Use automatic settings** check box and specify your own settings instead.

If neither hardware nor BIOS is Plug & Play compatible, the **Use automatic settings** box will be greyed out and you'll have to identify and set the resources yourself.

Setting Resources manually

Different hardware will require different resources, such as **IRQ** (Interrupt Request), **DMA** (Direct Memory Access) channel, **I/O** (Input/Output) range and **Memory address**. The following steps explain how to carry out the common operation of changing the IRQ setting. The procedure is the same to change the setting for one of the other resources – just select the resource you want to change in the **Resource Settings** window.

1. Highlight the offending device in **Device Manager** and click **Properties**.
2. Click the **Resources** tab, and highlight the **Interrupt Request** entry in the **Resource Settings** window.
3. Make sure the **Use automatic settings** box isn't checked; if it is, clear the check box.
4. Click the **Change Setting...** button.
5. Change the interrupt setting in the **Value** box, keeping an eye on the lower box for an indication that you've picked a non-conflicting setting (see Figure 10.25).

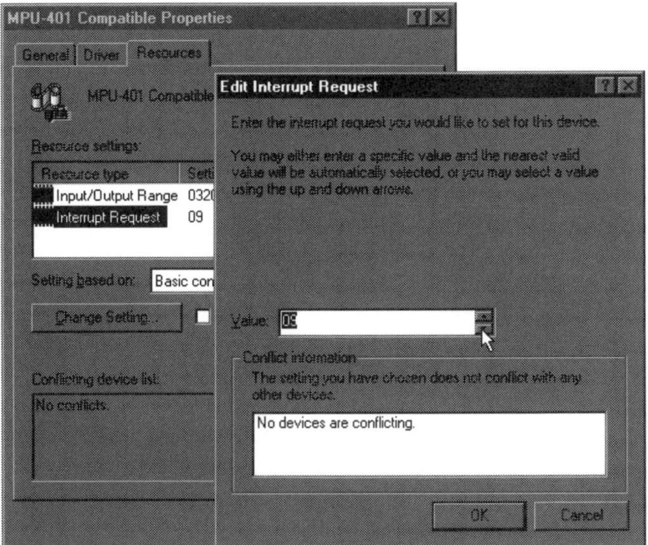

Figure 10.25 Assigning a different Interrupt Request to a device.

Of course, not only do you have to choose an IRQ that doesn't conflict with other installed devices, it must be one that your device can respond to, and some devices respond to a very limited number. You might be able to juggle IRQs for other devices to free-up a compatible one, but it's possible you'll have to replace the device itself with one with greater IRQ support.

If you can find an available IRQ that *is* compatible with your device, you may have to alter jumper or DIP switch settings on the hardware accordingly – check the device's manuals for details.

Some devices offer different preset configurations: before modifying any resource settings, take a look in the drop-down list titled **Setting based on**. A different configuration may give you the settings you need, or may let you change settings that were fixed in a different configuration.

▶ *For more details on resource types and settings, take another look at pp. 39–40.*

Adding a new monitor

The monitor is one of the only pieces of hardware that can't be added from either **Device Manager** or the **Add New Hardware Wizard**. Instead this has to be done from the **Settings** tab of Control Panel's **Display** applet. You can also change your display adapter from the same tab. Click the **Change Display Type...** button, and a new dialog will appear to show the current adapter and monitor, with a **Change...** button for each.

To install a new adapter or monitor, click the appropriate **Change...** button. Devices regarded by Windows 95 as compatible are displayed. To use an unlisted device, either click **Show all devices** and choose one from the full list, or select **Have Disk...** and direct Windows to the installation files that came with the device. In troubleshooting or desperation, try the Standard VGA or Super VGA types shown at the top of the **Show all devices** lists.

Bear in mind that Windows doesn't necessarily know which devices are compatible: if you've been assured by a manufacturer or retailer that a particular device will work properly, don't be deterred if this device isn't included in the main **Models** box.

Managing the system

In this section we'll take a look at the system utilities bundled with Windows 95 and how and when to use them, together with some of the other methods of optimizing your PC's performance. But let's start with the absolute essentials – which files you need to make backup copies of, and how to get the system working again in times of crisis!

Create a startup disk

When you installed Windows 95 you were given the option of creating a startup floppy disk to boot the system in the event of a serious crash. If you didn't (or if your computer arrived with Windows 95 pre-installed thus denying you the prompt), grab a couple of high-density disks and your Windows 95 installation disk(s) and do it now:

1. Start the **Add/Remove Programs** applet in Control Panel.
2. Click the **Startup Disk** tab and then click on **Create Disk**.
3. Once the disk has been created, shutdown and restart the computer (not Windows) with this emergency disk in the drive to make sure it works. You should arrive at the DOS command prompt (**A:\>**). If you do, it works.

Remove the disk from the drive and restart the computer normally. Write-protect the emergency floppy, label it **DOS Boot Disk** and keep it somewhere safe.

▶ *For more on boot disks, return to p. 34.*

Backup the .ini files

Windows 95 has largely replaced the old Windows 3.1 initialization (**.ini**) files with the **Registry**, but they still can't be phased out entirely and those that remain are just as important as ever. Grab a floppy disk and follow these quick steps to back them up:

1. Click the Taskbar and press *F3* to start **Find**.
2. Type ***.ini** in the **Named box** and click **Find Now** to start the search.
3. When the search has finished, every **.ini** file on your system should be listed in the window below. Press *Ctrl* + *A* to select all files, then right click on any of them and choose **Send To/Floppy Disk** from the context menu.

Backup the Registry files

The Windows Registry consists of two files: **System.dat**, which contains all the settings and configurations for your PC itself, added hardware, applications and file types; and **User.dat**, which contains your own personal preference settings such as colour and sound schemes, Start Menu layout and so on. Both files are important (**System.dat** is vital) so it's important to have up-to-date backups of both. The two files should fit on a high-density (1.44 Mb) disk.

1. If you choose to keep your system files *hidden*, go to Explorer/View/Options/View and check the **Show all files** option.
2. Open your Windows folder and copy **System.dat** and **User.dat** to your floppy drive.
3. Return to the **View** page and check **Hide files of these types** to hide your system files again if you choose to.

After installing new hardware or software, wait a day or two until you're sure everything is working properly and then replace these backups with new ones.

Virtual Memory settings

Virtual Memory is a special type of memory used by Windows 95 to supplement the physical memory (RAM) installed on your PC by moving pages of data from RAM to a file on your hard disk called the **swapfile**. It chooses which data to move out of RAM on a 'recently used' basis, first paging out the data that hasn't been accessed recently.

Windows 95 handles Virtual Memory slightly differently from its predecessors. In Windows 3.1 it was usual to create a permanent swapfile to ensure maximum efficiency. In Windows 95 the swapfile is permanent, but *dynamic* – it grows and shrinks according to the demands made upon it. Often, as you're sitting in front of your PC pondering on the meaning of life, or the whereabouts of a particular file, your hard disk will suddenly start to whirl as Windows takes the opportunity to resize the swapfile.

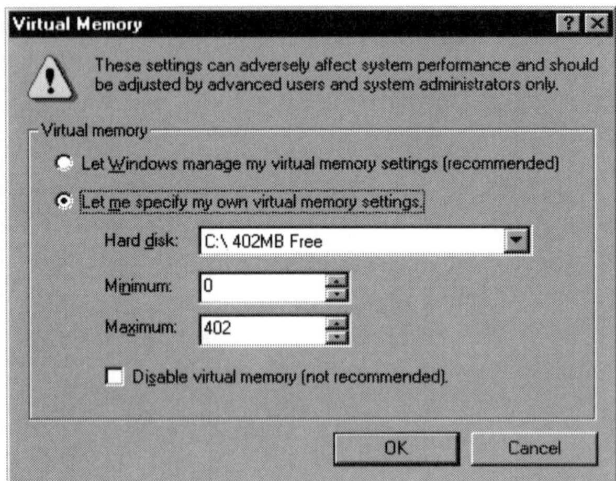

Figure 10.26 The Virtual Memory settings dialog.

Because Windows is now able to determine virtual memory requirements more skilfully, it's recommended that you leave it alone to do so (see Figure 10.26). If you start Control Panel's **System** applet and click your way to **Performance/Virtual Memory** you can check that the upper of the two option buttons is selected in the **Virtual Memory** dialog.

However, some uses of the PC need large amounts of virtual memory, and a few applications actually require a *fixed-sized* swapfile rather than the dynamically sized one. If you record audio or video in real-time to hard disk, for instance, Windows can't resize its dynamic swapfile fast enough to cope with the huge quantities of incoming data. In situations like this the application may fail or the system may crash, making a fixed swapfile imperative.

If you create a fixed-size swapfile, it's important to get the size right. A good way to pick a size is to run **System Monitor** (C:\Windows\Sysmon.exe) for a few hours during normal-to-heavy computer workloads, and look at its **Swapfile Size** and **Swapfile In Use** measurements regularly. Choose the maximum size reached during this period and add several megabytes for a little extra leeway. Bear in mind you can come back and resize it again anytime you need to.

To create a fixed swapfile, check the button marked **Let me specify my own virtual memory settings**. To fix the size, enter the same figure in both the **Minimum** and **Maximum** boxes. Click **OK** to restart the PC when prompted.

Before creating a fixed swapfile, or moving your swapfile to a different drive, run the Disk Defragmenter (Defrag.exe) to make sure the file is fully optimized.

Another change you might want to make, particularly if you stick with the dynamic swapfile, is to use a different drive for the swapfile. If the drive that contains your dynamic swapfile is badly fragmented or almost full, Windows will find it hard to locate space to expand into, which will affect system performance noticeably. If you have a drive with more free space, select this from the drop-down list marked **Hard disk** but don't change the settings in the **Minimum** or **Maximum** boxes. After making this change you'll have to restart Windows.

You can move your swapfile to a DriveSpace-compressed drive without reducing its performance in any way.

Booting in Safe Mode

With a normal 'doing it by the book' installation of Windows 95, you simply switch on your computer, wait 30 seconds or so, and the Windows 95 Desktop appears. Most of the time this is exactly what you want, but there are times when it's the *last* thing you want! A common example is finding you've installed an incompatible display driver and the screen blanks instead of displaying the Desktop.

At times like this you can boot in a special mode called **Safe Mode**, in which Windows loads generic drivers for display and mouse and disables any non-essential drivers to display a low-resolution 16-colour screen, giving you the chance to put the problem right and reboot normally.

To boot to Windows in Safe Mode, follow the steps below. We'll do it the hard way, assuming you've arrived in Windows with a completely blank screen; if you've got a different problem and you can still see the Desktop the routine will be even easier.

1. Wait until the hard disk stops working and you know Windows 95 has finished loading. Press *Ctrl + Esc* to (invisibly) open the Start Menu, press the up arrow key once to select the shutdown option, and then press *Return* twice to shutdown.
2. When Windows has been through its shutdown procedure (still invisibly of course!), press your PC's reset button.
3. Watch the screen carefully with your finger poised. As soon as you see the message **Starting Windows 95...** press the *F5* key. Windows will load in **Safe Mode** which will take at least twice as long as usual.
4. Once you've put the problem right you can choose the shutdown option again, click on **Restart The Computer**, and Windows will restart normally.

Other boot options

The other thing you might need to do in times of trouble is to boot to MS-DOS. You do this in a similar way to starting Safe Mode Windows. Wait for the **Starting Windows 95...** message to appear and then press *F8*. A menu will appear labelled the **Windows 95 Startup Menu**, listing a variety of boot options. Each of these has a number beside it – type the number corresponding with the option you want to select and press *Enter*. Here's what each of these options does:

- *Command prompt only.* Boots in the normal way but stops at the MS-DOS prompt instead of loading Windows 95.
- *Safe Mode command prompt only.* As above, but doesn't process Autoexec.bat or Config.sys.
- *Step-by-step confirmation.* Asks you for confirmation before each command in Autoexec.bat, Config.sys and Io.sys to let you bypass any commands you think may be causing problems.
- *Logged.* Boots to Windows 95 in the normal way, and creates a file called **Bootlog.txt** in your root folder listing the startup sequence.
- *Normal.* Boots to Windows 95 in the usual way.

- *Safe Mode.* As described in 'Booting in Safe Mode' above.
- *Safe Mode with network support.* Boots in Safe Mode but loads network drivers. You may want this option if you need to use files from the network to correct a configuration problem.

ScanDisk

This is a new Windows 95 version of a program that had to be run under MS-DOS by Windows 3.1 users. **ScanDisk** checks your files and folders for lost clusters, or clusters somehow orphaned from the file, and either reports back to you when it finds an error or fixes it automatically. It can also check the disk surface itself for damaged sectors.

To run ScanDisk, use the Run command and type the command line **scandskw** or create a shortcut to C:\Windows\Scandskw.exe somewhere accessible. Choose the drive you want to check from the upper window, or hold *Ctrl* and click multiple drives. Choose whether to perform a Standard or a Thorough test, and check the box labelled **Automatically fix errors** if you want ScanDisk to get on with it and not prompt you if it finds an error. You should run a Standard test weekly, and substitute it with a Thorough test once every 4–6 weeks.

You can also run **ScanDisk** and **Defrag** by right-clicking a drive's icon in Explorer or My Computer, choosing **Properties/Tools** and clicking the appropriate button. This page also tells you how long it's been since you last ran these utilities.

Disk defragmenter

When a disk is formatted, the formatting process divides it into *tracks*, and divides each track into smaller compartments called *sectors*. Whenever you create a new file and save it to disk, the data in the file is split into small, identically sized chunks called *clusters* to be placed onto the disk. The size of these clusters will depend upon the total capacity of your hard disk, the operating system being used, and whether you used a disk-compression utility or not – cluster size can range between a tiny 512 bytes and a hefty 32 K. When the file is saved, each cluster is placed in the first available space on the disk which should, in a perfect world, mean that all your files' clusters form a continuous chain, one file after another.

In fact, that doesn't happen. Sooner or later, you'll delete a file and the space in the chain that its clusters filled will be used by the next file you save. And if this new file is larger than the one you deleted, some of its clusters will fill up this space, and the rest will be placed at the end of the chain. Similarly, you might open an existing file, add a few paragraphs to it and save it again: this file can no longer fit in the space it occupied before, so some of it will be placed elsewhere.

Soon you'll have little pieces of file scattered far and wide on your hard disk – in techno-speak, the disk is *fragmented* – which means that the disk's read/write head has to chase around to find all the pieces when you need to open a file, or to locate free clusters when you need to save one, effectively slowing down your system. The defragmentation program sorts out this mess by rebuilding the chain and grouping each file's clusters together. To run the defragmenter, type **defrag** on the Run line, or create a shortcut to C:\Windows\Defrag.exe.

To get a clearer idea about clusters and fragmentation you can watch the utility moving the clusters around by clicking its **Show Details** button. To find out what the differently coloured clusters represent, click the **Legend** button.

Defrag should be run weekly, but in its default setup it won't bother to tidy a disk that's less than 5 per cent fragmented and will instead display a dialog asking if you really want to bother.

Backup

Backup.exe is an optional accessory installed from the **Disk Tools** group of **Windows Setup** (see 'Add and remove Windows 95 components' ion p. 362) and lives in C:\Program Files\Accessories. You can use Backup to select all the files and folders on your system that you want to keep backup copies of, and save this list as a **.set** file that you can run anytime you want to update your backups (see Figure 10.27). Backup comes with a default file called **Full System Backup.set** which you can use if you have a high-capacity drive such as a tape drive or optical disk, but if you create your backups on floppies this isn't a sensible option. Follow these steps to create a backup set containing all the important files on your system:

1. Using the Explorer-type tree structure, check the boxes beside single files or entire folders to be added to the list. Checking the box for a folder automatically checks the boxes for all the files it contains. If you change your mind, uncheck the box again.

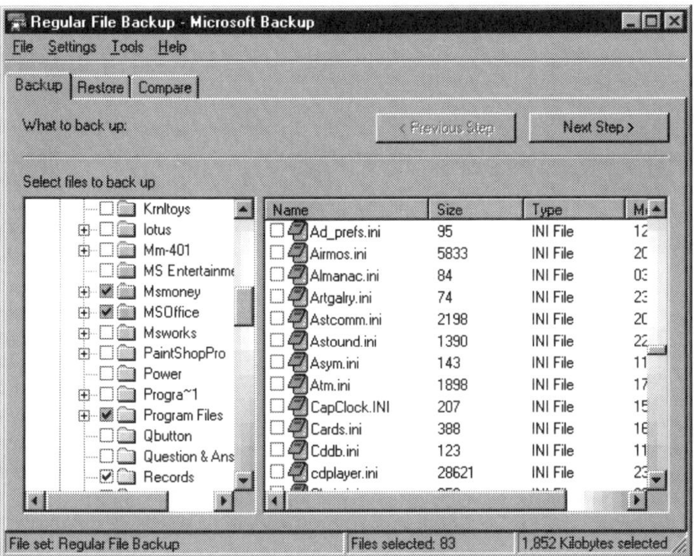

Figure 10.27 Selecting files and folders in Backup.

2. Click the button marked **Next Step** and select the drive (such as **A:**) or the folder to which these files should be backed-up by clicking on it.
3. Click your way to **Settings/Options/Backup** and choose the settings you want to use. The **Quit Backup after operation is finished** option is worth taking as an aid to automating the process; choosing the appropriate **Always erase...** option ensures that your drive doesn't become full of out-of-date backups.
4. Now choose **File/Save As...** and type a name for the selection file (the **.set** extension will be added automatically).
5. Click on **Start Backup** and you'll be prompted to enter a name for the backup file. For convenience, give this exactly the same name you gave to the selection file.

You can back-up the same files anytime you want to by double-clicking the selection (**.set**) file, or you could create a shortcut to it somewhere handy.

DriveSpace

This is yet another DOS program that's woken up to find itself in Windows. DriveSpace is a disk-compression utility (see Figure 10.28) that can give you at least 50 per cent more disk space by compressing the files on your hard disk. To run DriveSpace, type **drvspace** on the Run command line, or create a shortcut to C:\Windows\Drvspace.exe and double-click it.

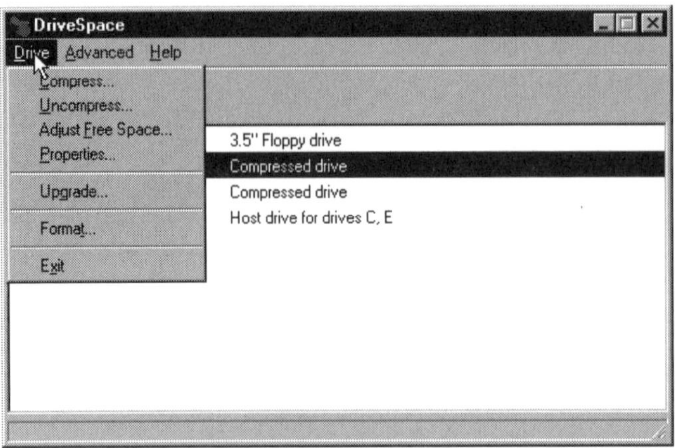

Figure 10.28 The DriveSpace disk-compression utility.

When you compress your hard disk (**C:**), the compression utility creates an extra drive on your disk and asks you to choose a letter name for it. This drive is called the **host drive** and contains certain system files that can't be compressed. Your C drive is still there, and still used in exactly the same way as before, but its contents are all stored in one large file on the host drive called **Drvspace.000**, so whatever you do, *don't delete this file!* This file is referred to by the technical sounding name **Compressed Volume File** (CVF), because it's a *file* containing the *compressed* contents of a *volume* (disk).

To compress your hard disk, highlight it in DriveSpace's window and go to **Drive/Compress...** . The next dialog will tell you what the resulting size of that drive will be, which drive-letter will be assigned to the host drive, and how much free space will be left on the host drive. To change any of these, click the **Options** button at the bottom of the dialog. To begin compression, click on **Start**. The final dialog gives you a button you can click to backup your files, and it's sensible to take this option in case something goes wrong along the way. Finally, click **Compress Now**. Windows will close your running programs and switch into a special mode to carry out the compression, which may take several hours.

JARGONBUSTER

Logical drive

A term used to refer to a drive created by compression software that doesn't actually *exist* as a piece of hardware like a floppy drive; the operating system just treats it as a separate drive.

There are other compression options you may want to use after compressing your hard disk, so here they are in brief:

- The **Adjust Free Space** option on the **Drive** menu lets you move space between a compressed drive and your host drive. You might want to reduce the host drive to just a few megabytes in order to have the maximum available compressed space. Alternatively you might want to move some empty space from the compressed drive back to the host drive and use it create an *empty* compressed drive.
- You can uncompress a drive by selecting it in DriveSpace's window and choosing **Drive/Uncompress**.
- You can change the drive name assigned to a drive by clicking **Advanced/Change Letter**.
- You can create a new compressed drive using free space on the host drive by highlighting your host drive in DriveSpace's window and choosing **Advanced/Create Empty**. (This is a far quicker process than *compressing* a drive since there are no files to compress!)

If you're halfway through a **DriveSpace** operation such as compressing a drive and your computer goes down for some reason, don't panic. Windows can remember what was going on and should resume when you restart the computer. If it doesn't, just run DriveSpace again – it'll remember it had been busy and will give you the opportunity to cancel, defer, or continue the task.

Program crashes

If an application hangs, press *Ctrl + Alt + Del* and you'll see the **Close Program** dialog, containing a list of the currently running applications. Select the offending application from the task list and click the **End Task** button to kill it without having to restart the whole system. (Be patient at this point: Windows sometimes has to grapple with the program for a while before it can show you a confirmation dialog.)

The task list itself can be a useful tool at any time to find out what accessories and utilities are running in the background that don't appear on the Taskbar. If you're only accessing it for information, however, make sure you close the dialog by clicking **Cancel** or pressing *Esc*.

Pressing *Ctrl + Alt + Del* a second time while the **Close Program** dialog is on the screen will restart the computer. This should be regarded as a last resort in the unlikely event that you lose all control over Windows 95 and can't access **Shut Down** on the Start Menu to quit safely.

Windows 95 and DOS

When Windows 95 is installed, its own version of DOS, MS-DOS 7.0, is installed along with it. This version is considerably smaller than earlier versions, simply because it no longer has to be an operating system in its own right – programs previously bundled with DOS such as **Defrag**, **ScanDisk** and **DriveSpace** have all become Windows utilities, and other external DOS commands were regarded as unnecessary and given the push. In fact, they've been given the push to the extent that, if you installed Windows 95 over an existing MS-DOS/Windows 3.1 installation, some of those 'unnecessary' commands were removed from your DOS folder! This leads to another change: MS-DOS 7.0 is installed into a subfolder of your Windows folder called Command, rather than the traditional C:\DOS.

Although the detail has changed, the basic implementation of DOS remains the same as it was with Windows 3.1, in that you can open DOS boxes in Windows, or you can leave Windows and channel all your resources into DOS and the program you're trying to run. Similarly, the DOS commands that remain still function exactly as they did in previous versions of DOS, so skip back to sections pp. 252–260 if you need to use them!

Three types of DOS

The main point to grapple with is that there are actually *three* ways to run DOS on your PC as a Windows 95 user:

- *The MS-DOS Prompt.* Just as in Windows 3.1, you can open a DOS window to run commands and DOS programs and switch back and forth between the window and your other applications whenever you want to. You'll often see this referred to as 'Windows-DOS'.
- *MS-DOS Mode.* A special mode for running DOS programs that don't like to share resources with Windows or any other programs. Essentially, this is Windows 'faking' MS-DOS.
- *MS-DOS itself.* By choosing the appropriate option from the StartUp Menu (see 'Other boot options' on p. 382) you can boot to 'real' MS-DOS 7.0 to run DOS programs without Windows being involved at all.

The MS-DOS Prompt

The DOS window is opened from **Start/Programs** by clicking the entry labelled **MS-DOS Prompt**. This is simply a shortcut to the MS-DOS shell program **Command.com**, and you can create shortcuts to DOS programs just as you do with Windows programs.

Apart from the inevitable white-on-black colouring, the window itself looks similar to any other – the Maximize, Minimize and Close buttons still appear on the title-bar, and the window has its own toolbar (Figure 10.29).

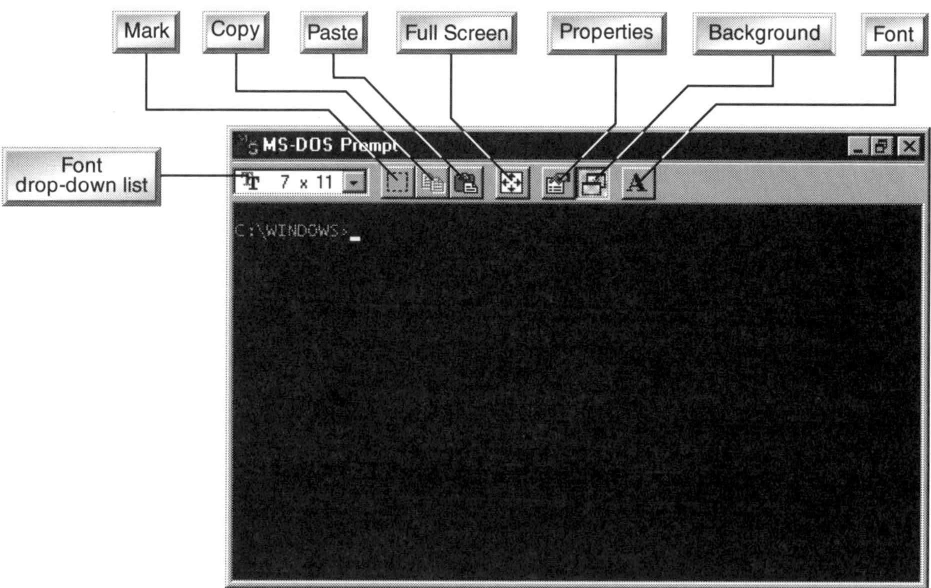

Figure 10.29 The MS-DOS Prompt window and toolbar buttons.

- *Font drop-down list.* Choose the font size you want to use from this box. The window is automatically resized to suit the font size you select.
- *Mark.* Clicking this button enables you to select text from the window to be copied to the clipboard.
- *Copy.* Places the marked text on the clipboard.
- *Paste.* Pastes the text currently on the clipboard at the insertion point. This text may have been copied from a Windows application or the DOS window.
- *Full Screen.* Switches the DOS box to full-screen mode, removing its title-bar and toolbar in the process. You can use either *Alt + Enter* or

Alt + *Return* to do the same job, and that's worth remembering – with no toolbar in full-screen mode, the hotkey is the only way to switch back to a window!

TIP

If you're running DOS in a window but you have no toolbar, right-click on the title-bar and click the **Toolbar** entry to bring it back.

- *Maximize button.* Does the same as the Full Screen button.
- *Minimize button.* Switches the window to a button on the Taskbar as with any Windows 95 window.
- *Close button.* This closes the prompt window. However, if a program other than **Command.com** itself is running (i.e. you can't see the prompt), you'll get a dialog warning that the window can't be closed until you exit the program. In fact, it can, but you should regard this as a last resort for use only if the program has stopped responding. Click **No** in this dialog and exit the program to return to the prompt first.
- *Properties.* This opens the properties sheet for the program running in the window.
- *Background.* With this button depressed, you can open other DOS windows and run different programs in each.
- *Font.* Opens the **Font** page of the current program's properties sheet.

Properties sheets

All MS-DOS programs now have properties sheets, just like any Windows file, which can be opened by right-clicking them and choosing **Properties**, holding *Alt* and double-clicking, or highlighting them and pressing *Alt* + *Enter*. In addition, if the program is already running in a DOS window, you can click the **Properties** button on the toolbar. The properties sheet for a DOS program differs from that of a Windows program by having five tabs containing some useful options for changing the appearance or behaviour of the prompt window:

- Clicking the **Font** tab (or the dedicated Font button on the toolbar) lets you choose whether to use bitmap or TrueType fonts, or both. As you select different font sizes from the list, two preview windows indicate the actual size of the text you'll see and the relative size and position of the window on your screen.
- From the **Screen** tab you can choose whether the program should open in a window or in full-screen mode. (You can also use the **Run** box on the

Program tab to choose between Normal Window, Maximized and Minimized).

- The **Program** tab has a check box marked **Close on exit**. If this is checked, exiting the program you were running will close the window.
- Checking the **QuickEdit** box on the **Misc** tab means that you can mark text to be copied in a DOS box without first clicking the **Mark** button. If you do this, however, you won't be able to use your mouse to *click* items in the window.

Any changes you make to a DOS program's properties sheet are saved into a file with the same name as the program and the extension **.pif**, which is created automatically when you make a change on the sheet and click **OK**. Windows 3.1 users will remember the PIF (Program Information File) and its dedicated PIF Editor with varying degrees of dread, but Windows 95 has managed to take a lot of the pain out of configuring DOS programs by building the PIF into the properties sheet. The tighter integration between the new MS-DOS and Windows means that most DOS programs will run quite cheerfully from the default settings, and you'll rarely need to make new settings for a particular program.

▶ *The exception here is games designed to run in MS-DOS which might still need some tweaking on the properties sheet as a result of their memory requirements or dislike for sharing resources with other programs. Turn to the next section for some hints on running games and other problematic DOS programs.*

MS-DOS Mode

MS-DOS Mode is a special operating mode in which Windows shuts down (except for a small amount of data which remains in memory), together with any other programs you're running, and switches to full-screen, single-mode DOS. In this mode you can run only one DOS program; when you've finished using this program, type **exit** at the command prompt and Windows will automatically restart.

There are two methods of switching to MS-DOS Mode:

- After shutting down all running programs, select **Shutdown** from the Start Menu, click **Restart the computer in MS-DOS mode**, and click **OK**. You can then run any program using the usual DOS commands.
- On the program's properties sheet, go to **Program/Advanced** and check the box marked **MS-DOS Mode**. Whenever you try to run the program, Windows will display a warning that all running programs will be closed (although you should save any work first and close them yourself). Click

OK and Windows will shut down and start the program for you automatically.

Because of Windows 95's improved support for running DOS there should rarely be a need to use MS-DOS Mode. Being rather a long-winded and messy way to run a program, it's preferable to try all the configuration possibilities available for running the program *within* Windows before taking this route.

New DOS commands

To make up for removing some of the old commands from MS-DOS, Windows has added some new ones:

- To replace the now-departed Help program, you can now type a space and **/?** after a command's keyword for an explanation and syntax. For example, if you want help on the **dir** command, type **dir /?** and press *Enter*.
- You can still use the double-dot to move up to the parent directory (**cd..**), but Windows has extended this even further: to move up two levels type **cd...**; to move up three levels type **cd**.... and so on.
- You can use long file names and folder names in a command, provided you enclose the entire path in quotes ("), such as:

cd "c:\program files\accessories"

Having to use quotes around paths using long names can be annoying, particularly since you have to retype the whole command again if you forget them. There's no real escape from the leading quote, but for almost everything you do at the DOS prompt (and on the Run command line) you can leave out the closing quote mark.

- The **dir** command now displays folders' long names at the right of the screen.
- The new **/v** switch has been added to the **dir** command to show additional details about folders including attributes and date of creation. Each entry will take two screen lines, so its best to add the **/p** switch to view one screen at a time (**dir/v/p**).

The Start command

A brand new DOS command, **start**, has been added to give access to Windows programs from the DOS prompt. Here's a few examples of use:

- To open an Explorer window for the current folder, type **start.**
- To open an Explorer window for the parent folder, type **start..**
- To open an Explorer window for another drive (such as your floppy-disk drive), type **start A:**
- To run a Windows program, type its path (if necessary) and name just as if it were a DOS program.
- To run a program maximized, use **start /max** (e.g. **start/max notepad**).
- To run a program minimized, use **start /m** (e.g. **start/m notepad**).
- The **start** command makes use of Windows' file-type associations too: type something like **start tips.txt** to run Notepad with this file opened.
- To run a DOS program, but have it open in a new DOS window, prefix the command with **start**.

TIP

If you've never had a version of DOS on your PC, you can find some of the external commands (plus the MS-DOS 6.22 **Help** program and file) in the **Other\Oldmsdos** folder of the Windows 95 installation CD-ROM. Just copy them into your **Windows\Command** folder to make them available for use.

Running DOS games in Windows 95

GUI-based operating systems are memory-hungry beasts, and Windows 95 has a particularly voracious appetite. For this reason, game producers still create games that run in MS-DOS in order to have maximum resources at their disposal. Of course, there are many non-game DOS programs out there still being used (and the tips in this section apply equally to them) but for the most part these will run in a DOS window with consummate ease. Games, on the other hand, often come with a frightening-looking list of memory demands in their manuals, all couched in acronyms, which often take varying degrees of experimentation, inspiration, and pure luck to set up correctly.

Getting a game to work might, on occasion, be a struggle, but the good news is that once you've managed to fix the settings you need they can be retained for the next time you play, and you shouldn't have the worry of whether your other games will still run after all that tweaking!

Since a collection of variables is involved, there can be no concrete solutions given here: the appropriate settings will depend on the game, your installed hardware and drivers, and your available memory. For this reason, it's best to approach this section with a particular game in mind and a list of its requirements in front of you.

Will it, won't it?

After carrying out any installation of the game software that may be necessary, look in Explorer for the file used to start the game (with an **.exe** or perhaps a **.bat** extension) and create a shortcut to it somewhere accessible. Right-click the shortcut's icon and choose **Properties**. On the **Program** tab check the **Close on exit** box to ensure you'll be returned to Windows when you've finished playing; on the **Screen** tab click the **Full Screen** button (most games won't run in a window). Provided you're not intending to run other applications in the background, clear the check box for **Dynamic Memory Allocation** to help channel available resources to the game.

Now, the moment of truth – double-click the shortcut, and see what happens! If the game runs, you're done (although you may want to consider a few of the tips later in this section to see if you can make any useful modifications).

Hide Windows

The usual reason a game won't run is through lack of memory: if you had any Windows programs running when you tried the game, shut them down and try again – some Windows applications use a small amount of Conventional memory which might make the difference.

Before tweaking memory settings, let's try something else. Since most DOS games expect to have exclusive rights to system resources, just a sniff of Windows 95 can send them into a sulk. Go back to the **Properties/Program** tab and click the **Advanced** button. Check the box marked **Prevent MS-DOS-based programs from detecting Windows**, and make sure **Suggest MS-DOS mode as necessary** is also checked. Click **OK**, and try running the game again.

To make maximum memory available in DOS sessions, start **System Editor** and select **System.ini**. Find the section of the file headed [386Enh] and add **LocalLoadHigh=1** on a new line.

Fixing memory

If the previous tip didn't do the trick, it's time to look at the settings shown in the game's manual. Go back to **Properties** and click the **Memory** tab. There are three types of memory you're concerned with here: Conventional, Expanded (EMS) and Extended (XMS). By default these are all set to **Auto** allowing dynamic allocation of resources (see Figure 10.30), but you can set the amount of each type of memory required for an individual program in these boxes.

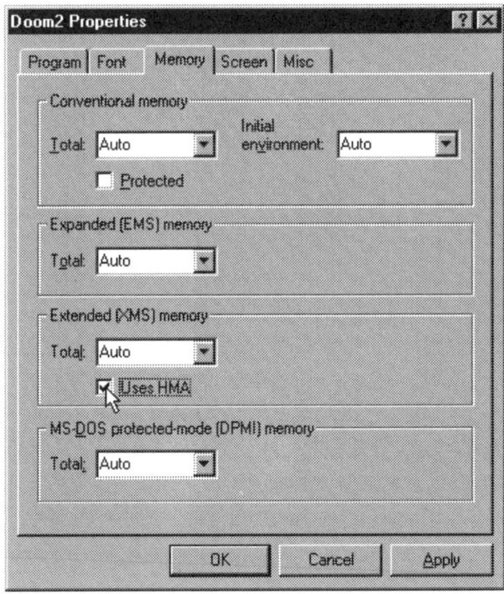

Figure 10.30 The memory settings tab on a DOS program's properties sheet.

Following the memory requirements given in the game's manual, type the figures into the appropriate boxes for Conventional memory, EMS and XMS. Clear the **Protected** check box under Conventional memory to gain a little extra performance from the game. Click **OK** and run the program again.

TIP

To find out how much of the various memory types you have free, open a DOS window and type **mem /c** and press *Enter*. If you manage to find and remove some unnecessary TSRs and drivers from your system files, take a look at these results again after rebooting your computer, paying particular attention to **Largest executable program size** – this is the amount of Conventional memory you have available, and it's probably increased.

▶ *For more details on the PC's memory types, take a further look at p. 266.*

Using MS-DOS mode

If you've run through the previous tips and your game is still resolutely refusing to run, it's time to try MS-DOS mode. Head back to the **Properties/Program** tab and click the **Advanced** button. Check the box marked **MS-DOS mode**, and ensure the **Warn before entering MS-DOS mode** box is checked too: the warning is usually worth having since this is a single-application mode so all currently running applications are shut down when you use it. Now click **OK** and try running the program – you might just avoid some more intimate dealings with memory settings.

If you're still having no luck, Windows 95 has another trick up its sleeve that should do the job. Go back to **Properties/Program/Advanced** and click the radio button marked **Specify a new MS-DOS configuration**. This lets you create custom Autoexec.bat and Config.sys settings for the program by typing them directly into the boxes below. Whenever you run this program, Windows will read these files and use the settings they contain in place of your usual system files.

The following suggestions cover entries you can include to maximize the three types of memory.

▶ *Autoexec.bat and Config.sys are explained on pp. 262–265.*

Gaining Conventional memory

To gain the most free Conventional memory you need to be sure you're not loading unnecessary drivers. For example, if your game doesn't run from CD-ROM, don't bother loading your CD-ROM driver in these 'customized' system files. Similarly, if you can bear to run the game without sound, that's another chunk of memory kept available for the game itself.

Those items you do have to use should be loaded into upper memory (making sure you've included the **EMM386.SYS** statement in your Config.sys file, as covered below).

- Programs should be loaded in Autoexec.bat, using the LOADHIGH (LH) command, e.g. **LH C:\WINDOWS\MSCDEX.EXE /S /D:MSCD001 /M:10**.
- Device drivers should be loaded in Config.sys using DEVICEHIGH= (but make sure they're placed after the **EMM386.SYS** reference), for example **DEVICEHIGH=C:\SB16\DRV\CTMMSYS.SYS**.

Notice that the LOADHIGH (or LH) command is followed by a space rather than the = sign.

If you have a hard disk compressed with DriveSpace, make sure you load the DriveSpace driver into upper memory with the Config.sys line

DEVICEHIGH=C:\WINDOWS\COMMAND\DRVSPACE.SYS /MOVE.

TIP

The DriveSpace driver uses memory wherever you put it, of course. To get around this problem, move your game and all its constituent files to your host drive, and leave out the reference to **Drvspace.sys**. This will free up extra memory, but you won't be able to access your compressed drives while playing.

Using Upper Memory Blocks

The point of this tip is to allow the use of UMBs (Upper Memory Blocks) to load real-mode device drivers and parts of DOS itself. When these are loaded into Upper memory, they're releasing valuable space in Conventional memory.

As long as your program doesn't require Expanded memory (EMS), place the following lines at the top of your custom Config.sys in this order:

DEVICE=C:\WINDOWS\HIMEM.SYS

DEVICE=C:\WINDOWS\EMM386.EXE NOEMS

DOS=HIGH,UMB

The reference to HIGH in the third line specifies that DOS is loaded into high memory (HMA), saving another 40+ kilobytes of Conventional memory.

If this works as it is, fine. If not, replace **NOEMS** with **FRAME=NONE** at the end of the second line to add another 64 K to your available Conventional memory. If you do this, start **System Editor**, find **System.ini** and also add the following line to the [**386Enh**] section:

NoEMMDriver=TRUE

Using Expanded memory

The point of this tip is pretty much the same as the last: to make use of HMA and UMBs to free up as much Conventional memory as possible. The difference is that the entries below sacrifice a little upper memory in order to provide Expanded memory (EMS). If your program needs EMS, place these lines at the beginning of Config.sys in this order:

DEVICE=C:\WINDOWS\HIMEM.SYS

DEVICE=C:\WINDOWS\EMM386.EXE RAM AUTO

DOS=HIGH,UMB

Another option is to specify a minimum setting for EMS by adding a space and **MIN=???**, replacing the question marks with the required figure. The default is 256 (for 256 kilobytes), so only use the **MIN**=addition if you need more. Extra experimentation may still be needed – you might have to raise the figure some way beyond the program's quoted requirements before it works.

Quick tips for DOS programs

- If you're running a joystick-controlled DOS game under Windows 95, make sure you disable your screensaver – most screensavers don't check for activity from the joystick port, and might kick in while you're playing. Go to the **Properties/Misc** tab and clear the check box marked **Allow screen saver**.
- If your DOS program won't run for lack of memory, take a look at the Clipboard by running **Clipboard Viewer**: if the last thing you cut or copied was particularly large (perhaps a bitmap image?) it could be filling enough memory to make the difference. Clear the Clipboard by pressing *Delete* and clicking **Yes**, or by copying something small such as a single character to replace it.
- If your game doesn't seem to be performing as well as you'd hoped, open the **Properties/Misc** page and drag the **Idle sensitivity** slider to the left ('Low'). This ensures that maximum processor-time is allotted to the game rather than any other programs running in the background.

- If you have an SCSI device installed on your system, you might need to enter the line

  DEVICE=SMARTDRV.EXE/DOUBLE_BUFFER

  in your Config.sys file before any **DEVICEHIGH** lines.

- Some games use a variety of keyboard combinations for some of their functions which might conflict with combos used by Windows (such as *Ctrl+Esc*). Go to your game's **Properties** page, click the **Misc** tab, and take a look at the 'Windows shortcut keys' section: remove the check mark from any of these that might be used in the game. If in doubt, remove everything except *Alt+Tab* which can be useful to switch to a Windows program quickly if you need to.

Quick tips

Windows 95 has an almost inexhaustible supply of customization possibilities, options and shortcut methods that can make the operating system and its accessories easier, faster or more enjoyable to use. Here's a few of them.

Desktop tips

- If you don't like the Taskbar at the bottom of the screen, click on a blank space (not a button) and drag it to the top or either side of the screen.
- If your Taskbar is so full of buttons that you can't read the captions on them, hover your mouse over a button briefly to see a descriptive tooltip. And if that's not good enough, move the pointer to the upper edge of the Taskbar until it turns into a double-headed arrow, then click and drag upwards to double (or triple, or quadruple...) its height. You can drag it back down again later if you want to.
- Experiment with your Tray icons – many have different options on their menus depending whether you click with the left or right mouse button. The option shown in bold type is the action that occurs if you just double-click the icon.
- If you want your screensaver to start immediately you leave your desk, create a shortcut on your desktop to one of the **.scr** files found in C:\Windows. You can just double-click it to start it running.
- When you select the **Shutdown** command from the Start Menu, you have the option to **Restart the computer**. If you only want to restart Windows 95 itself (which is much faster), select **Restart the computer**, then hold *Shift* as you click on **OK**.

- The previous tip can also be used if a dialog appears telling you to restart the computer: once again, hold *Shift* as you click on **OK**. Usually this will work, but on occasions Windows needs to reboot completely so your attempt to cheat will be ignored!

Explorer tips

- If you delete, copy, move, or rename something accidentally, press *Ctrl* + *Z* immediately to undo it. (Note: this won't work for a file deleted by using the *Shift* key for permanent deletion!)
- If you don't like using the right mouse button to get some control over your Drag & Drop actions, try using these in conjunction with the *left* button: hold *Ctrl* to force a copy; hold *Shift* to force a move; or hold *Ctrl* + *Shift* to create a shortcut.
- When viewing any list in Windows – whether in Explorer, My Computer, Find, Open With or anywhere else – type the first three letters of the entry you want (in quick succession) to move straight to it.
- When you use **Details** view in Explorer, long file names are often truncated and end with an ellipsis (. . .), with other details vanishing out of the right side of the window. To put this right, move the pointer up to the 'sort' bars and position it between two bars so that the pointer turns into a vertical beam intersected by a horizontal arrow, then double-click. The column to the left will resize itself to the perfect minimum width! (You can use this tip wherever you see these 'sort' bars, including **Find** and **Backup**.)
- If you've opted to hide file extensions by clicking the appropriate option on Explorer's **View/Options/View** page, you can still turn them on just for certain types of file (this can be useful if a particular *file type* encompasses several different file extensions, giving each one the same icon). Go to **View/Options/File Types**, click the type you want to see extensions for and click **Edit**. At the bottom of the dialog, check the box marked **Always show extension**.
- You can hide any file or folder by opening its properties sheet and checking the **Hidden** box, but to make them disappear from view you must check **Hide files of these types** on the **View/Options/View** page. You'll then only be able to open a hidden file (or a file in a hidden folder) by typing its full path in **Open** dialogs, DOS windows or the **Run** command. To save a file to a hidden folder you'll have to type the full path and desired name for the file in **Save As** dialogs. To view hidden items in Explorer once again, return to the **View** tab and check **Show all files**.

Accessories tips

- If you start a video clip (**.avi** file) by double-clicking its icon, you can open **Media Player** by double-clicking the video window's title-bar. To close Media Player again, double-click Media Player's title-bar. More fun than watching the video!
- If you want to re-run a particular Search in **Find** or command in **Run**, click the arrow beside their drop-down list boxes and choose an entry from the list.
- Before running **DriveSpace** to compress a drive, empty your Recycle Bin so that you're not wasting time by compressing files you're about to delete.
- Before running any system utilities (**DriveSpace**, **ScanDisk** or **Defrag**), override your screensaver to prevent the process being botched or restarted.
- If you've got a nice pictorial wallpaper and the icons on your Desktop spoil it, use **Paint** to create 'blank' icons! Start Paint, and immediately go to **File/Save As**, choose a location, and save as **Blank.ico**. You can then assign this icon to all the shortcuts on your Desktop. (The icon is invisible, but still there – you can still click in that space above the icon-label.)
- Select the **Run** command from the Start Menu, type **winver** and click **OK** to see one of Microsoft's less interesting, but entirely bug-free, programs!

General tips

- If your **Send To** menu is getting too full, you can turn it into a mini-Start Menu! Just go to C:\Windows\SendTo and create new folders inside it, then start dragging items into it from the **SendTo** folder to organize them into groups. This is useful if you've created Send To shortcuts to lots of different folders on your system – create a folder called **Folders** and drag all these shortcuts into it to keep them separate from the other items.

- Getting back to your Desktop when you've got a bunch of windows open can be a pain. One way out is to right-click the Taskbar and choose **Minimize All Windows**. A neater way is to create a shortcut to your Desktop (C:\Windows\Desktop) and put it on the Start Menu. You can then open a window containing your Desktop's contents any time you need to.
- If you follow the tip above, the important item missing from this window will be My Computer. Right-click My Computer and choose **Create Shortcut**, then highlight this shortcut and press *Ctrl* + *X*. Go to C:\Windows\Start Menu and press *Ctrl* + *V* to put this shortcut within easy reach.

- It shouldn't happen, but it does (occasionally). If your Taskbar vanishes but the computer doesn't shut down and your wallpaper and Desktop icons are still there, hit *Ctrl + Esc*. This should open the Start Menu allowing you to shut down properly. If that doesn't happen, Taskman will appear which is even better: select **File/Run Application**, type **Explorer** and the Taskbar will reappear, giving you the chance to close applications before shutting down or restarting the computer.
- Another one from the *'It shouldn't happen, but it does'* stable. Sometimes icons in Control Panel or Explorer seem to swap places, or be exchanged for icons you've never used for anything before. This is an unexpected 'feature' of Windows 95 (unexpected to its creators too), and should just be ignored. They'll sort themselves out before long; in the meantime they'll continue to function just as they're supposed to.

Clicks and keystrokes

General keystrokes

'Right-click' on selected item	*Shift+F10*
Context-sensitive Help (in tabbed pages and dialogs)	*F1*
Open the Start Menu	*Ctrl+Esc*
Close the Start Menu	*Esc*
Navigate the Start Menu	*Arrow keys*
Open or run the selected item	*Enter* or *Return*
Move to (next) item beginning with ? [*initial letter/s*]	*?* [initial letter/s]
Run command	*Ctrl+Esc then R*
Find command	*Ctrl+Esc then F*
Iconic list of currently open windows and applications	*Alt+Tab (+Tab to select)*
Cycle through currently open windows, applications and dialogs	*Alt+Esc*
Close a window or quit an application	*Alt+F4*
Open a file	*Ctrl+O*
Save a file	*Ctrl+S*
Print a file	*Ctrl+P*
Cut selected item	*Ctrl+X*
Copy selected item	*Ctrl+C*
Paste selected item	*Ctrl+V*
Open a menu	*Alt+underlined letter*
Select item from menu	*Underlined letter*

Close a menu or dialog without making a selection	*Esc*
Scroll through list of recent commands in **Find** and **Run**	*Up/Down arrow keys*
Drop-down the **Open** box in **Run**	*F4*
Drop-down the **Named** box in **Find**	*F4*
Drop-down the **Drives** box on a window's toolbar	*F4*
Open the **Look in** and **Save in** boxes in **Open/Save As** dialogs	*F4*
Defeat CD Autoplay or Autorun	*Hold Shift+insert CD*
Move between options/buttons in a dialog box	*Tab*
Move backwards between options/buttons in a dialog box	*Shift+Tab*
Move through tabbed pages	*Ctrl+Tab*
Move backwards through tabbed pages	*Ctrl+Shift+Tab*
Toggle DOS prompt between window and full-screen	*Alt+Enter* or *Alt+Return*
Shut down Windows	*Alt+F4, Enter* or *Ctrl+Alt+Del, S*
Restart the computer	*Alt+F4, R, Return*
Restart Windows	*Alt+F4, R, Shift+Return*
Restart in MS-DOS mode	*Alt+F4, M, Return*
Close programs and log on as a different user	*Alt+F4, C, Return*

Boot keystrokes

To prevent display of startup logo	*Esc*
To display Windows 95 Startup Menu on system startup	*F8*
To start Windows 95 in Safe Mode	*F5*
To boot to the command prompt	*Alt+F5*
Boot with step-by-step confirmation of system file entries	*Shift+F5*
To prevent Windows loading StartUp folder items	*Hold Ctrl as Windows starts*

Desktop and Explorer keystrokes

Windows 95 general Help	*F1*
Rename the selected item	*F2*
Send the selected item to Recycle Bin	*Del*
Delete the selected item, bypassing Recycle Bin	*Shift+Del*
Open the **Find** command	*F3*
Show the context menu for the selected item	*Shift+F10*

Show the properties page for the selected item	*Alt+Enter*
Move the selected item	*Ctrl+X then Ctrl+V*
Create a copy of the selected item	*Ctrl+C then Ctrl+V*
Create a shortcut to the selected item	*Shift+F10 then S* or *Ctrl+C then Shift+F10, S*
Refresh (update Desktop or Window contents)	*F5*
Undo last action	*Ctrl+Z*
Select all items	*Ctrl+A*
Open parent folder	*Backspace*
Step from item to item	*Arrow keys*
Open the selected folder in a new window	*Ctrl+Enter*
Access the **Open With** dialog for the selected item	*Ctrl+Shift+F10 then E*
Close current window and all parent windows	*Shift+Alt+F4*
Cancel a 'Drag & Drop' manoeuvre	*Esc*

Dual-pane Window keystrokes

Select and expand the drive list	*F4*
Switch between left and right panes	*F6*
'Go To' a particular folder	*Ctrl+G*
(Left pane) Expand the selected folder (one level)	*+sign (NumLock On)* or *right arrow (NumLock off)*
(Left pane) Expand the selected folder (all levels)	**(NumLock On)*
(Left pane) Collapse the selected folder	*– (NumLock On)* or *left arrow (NumLock off)*

Notepad keystrokes

Find *or* Repeat last search	*F3*
Insert date and time	*F5*

WordPad keystrokes

Centre selected text	*Ctrl+E*
Right-align selected text	*Ctrl+R*
Left-align selected text	*Ctrl+L*
Find	*Ctrl+F*
Find Next	*F3*
Replace	*Ctrl+H*
Select All	*Ctrl+A*
Toggle Overtype mode on and off	*Insert*

Paint keystrokes

Undo	*Ctrl+Z*
Redo	*F4*
New (Clear Canvas)	*Ctrl+Shift+N*
Show Toolbox	*Ctrl+T*
Show Colour Bar	*Ctrl+A*
Zoom In	*Ctrl+PageDown*
Zoom Out	*Ctrl+PageUp*
Show Gridlines	*Ctrl+G*
View Full Screen	*Ctrl+F*
Select All	*Ctrl+L*
Attributes dialog	*Ctrl+E*
Flip/Rotate dialog	*Ctrl+R*
Invert Colours	*Ctrl+I*
Stretch/Skew dialog	*Ctrl+W*

Windows 95 keyboard keystrokes

If you have one of the Windows 95 keyboards with its additional keys, here are a few extra keystrokes you can use to speed up access to frequently needed options:

Open the **Run** command	*Win+R*
Minimize all windows	*Win+M*
Start **Explorer**	*Win+E*
Open the **Find** dialog	*Win+F*
Start the Windows 95 Help file	*Win+F1*
Cycle through Taskbar buttons	*Win+Tab*
Open Control Panel's **System** applet	*Win+Break*

Mouse clicks and combos

Move the selected item	*Shift+Drag*
Copy the selected item	*Ctrl+Drag*
Create shortcut to the selected item	*Ctrl+Shift+Drag*
Choose from Copy, Move or Create shortcut	*Right-click+Drag*
Show the Properties page for the selected item	*Alt+Double-click*
Choose selected items from a window or list	*Ctrl+click each item*
Choose contiguous items from a window or list	*Click first item, hold Shift+click last*
Open a folder in a new window	*Ctrl+double-click*

Close current window and all parent windows	*Shift+click close button*
Open a folder in a dual-pane window	*Highlight, Shift+ double-click*
Add the **Open With** option to the context menu	*Highlight, Shift+right-click*
Toggle a window between maximized/restored	*Double-click on title-bar*
Cancel a Drag & Drop manoeuvre	*Click opposite mouse button*
Open the **Find** command anywhere	*Click the Taskbar, press F3*
Start Windows 95 Help	*Click the Desktop, press F1*
Open Control Panel's **Display** applet	*Right-click Desktop, Properties*
Open Control Panel's **System** applet	*Right-click My Computer, Properties*
Open Control Panel's **Date/Time** applet	*Double-click Clock*

Directory

Choosing an Internet Access Provider

One of the most important aspects of choosing an IAP is to make sure you can connect by dialling a local phone number (known as a **POP** or Point of Presence). Most IAPs allow unlimited connection time in return for their monthly fee, so your *only* ongoing expense is your telephone bill. However, this isn't the only important aspect. Here are a few other points to check:

- *Connection speed.* Many IAPs now support 28.8 Kbps modems on all their POPs and others are already shifting to the latest 33.6 Kbps modems. If you've got a fast modem you don't want to dial in on a slower line.
- *How do you pay?* Most IAPs will need a credit card number to take payment automatically each month.
- *Cancellation details.* What are the terms for cancelling your subscription?
- *Software.* Is software provided? Is it preconfigured or must you set it up yourself? Is it free or will you have to pay extra for it? (Some IAPs provide shareware software that you must register if you choose to use it.) Make sure the software will run on your version of Windows.
- *Which e-mail protocol?* Is a POP3 account included in the price or do you have to pay extra for it? You'll have a much wider range of e-mail software to choose from if you have a POP3 account.
- *Choose a user name.* When you take out a subscription you'll be asked what user name you want to use (often a maximum of eight characters).

Choose two or three in advance so you're not caught on the hop if your first choice is unavailable.

- *SLIP or PPP.* Make sure you're getting a PPP connection rather than a SLIP connection, *especially* if you're using Windows 95.

You might also want to ask whether the monthly rate includes space on the IAP's Web-server for you to publish your own pages, and if so, how many megabytes. (Most IAPs will still charge for the space if you intend to use it for business purposes though.) It's also worth finding out what sort of technical support they offer. It doesn't hurt to ask if you can have a month's free trial too!

UK Internet Access Providers

Use the list below to find an IAP with the services and prices you're looking for and a local POP, then give them a ring and check some of the details mentioned above. All IAPs noted here offer the basic services of e-mail, World Wide Web, FTP, Telnet, Gopher, IRC and newsgroup access. Extra details are included under *Notes*.

Bear in mind that this isn't an exhaustive list, and these details change regularly – for example, more and more IAPs are starting to offer free Web space – so it doesn't hurt to ask if the details don't exactly match what you want. Prices quoted here include VAT and relate to a standard dial-up account, but most IAPs have special packages for business users and other connection options available.

Company	E-mail and WWW site	Setup charge	Account charges	POPs	Notes
ACE Tel: 01670 528204	info@ac.co.uk www.ace.co.uk	£14.10	£11.75/month	Ashington	Free Web space
Aladdin Tel.: 01489 782221	info@aladdin.co.uk www.aladdin.co.uk	£23.50	£11.75/month	Portsmouth, Southampton	Free Web space; POP3 e-mail; FTP archive
Almac Tel.: 01324 666336	info@almac.co.uk www.almac.co.uk	£29.38	£18.79/month	UK coverage	Free Web space
AngliaNet Tel.: 01473 211922	tony@anglianet.co.uk www.anglianet.co.uk	£20.72	£13.81/month	Ipswich	Web space available; POP3 e-mail
Aspen Internet Tel.: 01672 511388	admin@aspen-internet.net www.aspen-internet.net	£17.63	£14.10/month	Blackpool, Swansea, Swindon	Web space from £9.79/month; Site design service; POP3 e-mail; domain registration
Atlas Tel.: 0171 312 0400	mail@atlas.co.uk www.atlas.co.uk	£29.38	£14.10/month	UK coverage	Web space £58.75 setup + £8.23/month
BT Internet (British Telecom) Tel.: 0800 800001	info@bt.net www.btinternet.com	£20	£15/month or £150/year	UK coverage	Free Web space; POP3 e-mail as standard; domain registration
Celtic Internet Services Tel.: 01633 811825	enquiry@celtic.co.uk www.imaginet.co.uk/cnet/index.html	£20	£11.75/month	Swansea	
Cerbernet Tel.: 0171 3608010	sales@styx.cerbernet.co.uk www.cerbernet.co.uk	£29.38	£14.10/month	London	Free Web space; FTP archive; OLR for e-mail only
CityScape Tel.: 01223 566950	sales@cityscape.co.uk www.cityscape.co.uk	£58.75	£17.63/month	UK coverage	Free Web space; POP3 e-mail
Colloquium Tel.: 0141 849 0849	smith_j@cqm.co.uk www.colloquium.co.uk/www	£17.63	£14.10/month	Glasgow	Free Web space
Connect Ireland Tel.: 00353 1 6711687	info@connect.ie www.connect.ie	£29.38	Free	Dublin	Free Web space
Cyber Network Systems Tel.: 01925 494949	sale@cyber.co.uk www.cyber.co.uk	£15	£12/month	Macclesfield, Warrington	Free Web space; POP3 e-mail as standard; FTP space available; FTP archive
Delphi Internet Tel.: 0171 757 7080	ukservice@delphi.com www.delphi.co.uk	Free	£11.75/month	London (UK coverage via GNS Network.)	Wire services; games; conferencing; ASCII text WWW access only
Demon Internet Tel.: 0181 371 1234	sales@demon.net www.demon.co.uk	£14.69	£11.75/month	UK coverage	Web space £58.75 setup + £28.38/£28.38/month; Web site design available; FTP archive
Direct Connection Tel.: 0181 297 2200	sales@dircon.co.uk www.dircon.co.uk	£8.81	from £11.75/month	UK coverage	Web space £58.75 setup + £28.38/month; FTP archive; Conferencing

Company	E-mail and WWW site	Setup charge	Account charges	POPs	Notes
Dungeon Network Systems Tel.: 01638 711550	info@dungeon.com www.dungeon.com	Free	£117.50/year or £11.75/month	Ipswich, Mildenhall	Web space available
Easynet Tel.: 0171 209 0990	admin@easynet.co.uk www.easynet.co.uk	£29.38	£14.99/month	UK coverage	Unlimited free Web space
Eclipse Networking Tel.: 01392 202345	eclipse@eclipse.co.uk www.eclipse.co.uk	£17.63	£9.40/month	Exeter	Web space £3.53/month; POP3 e-mail; FTP archive
Edinburgh Network Tel.: 0131 466 7003	info@ednet.co.uk www.ednet.co.uk	Free	£11.75/month	Edinburgh	Free Web space; FTP space available; FTP archive
FastNet International Tel.: 01273 677633	sales@fastnet.co.uk www.fastnet.co.uk	Free	£12.99/month	Brighton	Web space from £7.05/month; 15-day free trial
Foobar Internet Tel.: 0116 233 0033	sales@foobar.co.uk www.foobar.co.uk	£14.69	£11.75/month	Edinburgh	Free Web space; BBS; OLR for e-mail only
Frontier Internet Services Tel.: 0171 242 3383	info@ftech.net www.ftech.net	£29.38	£11.75/month in London; £15.28/month outside London	UK coverage	Web space from £25 setup + £50/year
Garden CityNet Tel.: 01462 485624	colinb@gardencitynet.co.uk www.gardencitynet.co.uk	£35	£14.99	Hitchin, Letchworth, Luton, Royston, Welwyn Garden City	Web space from £125/year
Gifford Internet Tel.: 0117 939 7722	admin@gifford.co.uk www.gifford.co.uk	n/a	£9.99/month	Bristol	Web space from £4.70/month; FTP space available; POP3 e-mail standard
Global Internet Tel.: 0181 957 1008	info@globalnet.co.uk www.globalnet.co.uk	£11.75	£11.75/month	UK coverage	Web space from £23.40/month
Hiway Tel.: 01635 550660	info@inform.hiway. co.uk www.hiway.co.uk	£17.63	£17.63/month	Edinburgh	Free Web space; FTP archive and space; Web page design
IBM Global Network Tel.: 0800 973000	internet_europe@ vnet.ibm.com regsvr01.fl.us.ibm.net/cgi-bim/ fees?150=gb	Free	£11.75/month for three hours	Bristol, Edinburgh, Glasgow, Leeds, London, Manchester, Nottingham, Portsmouth, Warwick	Other subscription options available
KENTnet Internet Services Tel.: 01580 890089	sales@kentnet.co.uk www.kentnet.co.uk	£19.99	£14.99/month	Ashford, Hastings, Heathfield, Maidstone, Rye, Staplehurst, Tunbridge Wells	Free Web space; FTP archive; domain registration; conferencing
MANNET Tel.: 01624 623841	postmaster@mcb.net www.mcb.net/mannet	£23.49	£9.39/month	Isle Of Man	Web space from £5.88/month

Company	E-mail and WWW site	Setup charge	Account charges	POPs	Notes
Netforce Group Tel.: 01245 257788	sales@netforce.net www.netforce.net	£35.25	£176.25/year	UK coverage	Web and FTP space available; FTP archive
.netKonect Tel.: 01420 542777	info@netkonect.net www.netkonect.net	Free	£11.75/month	UK coverage	Web space from £29.38/month
North West Net Tel.: 0161 950 7777	info@nwnet.co.uk www.nwnet.co.uk	£23.50	£12/month	Liverpool, Manchester	Free Web space
Onyx (Octacon) Tel.: 0345 715715	onyx-support@octacon.co.uk www.onyxnet.co.uk	£29.38	£11.75/month	Belfast, Teeside, Tyneside	Web space from £5.88/month
Paradise Internet Network Services Tel.: 01256 414863	sales@pins.co.uk www.pins.co.uk	£17.63	£9.40/month	Basingstoke	FTP and Web space available; 33.6 Kps lines
Paston Chase Tel.: 01603 502061	mail@paston.co.uk www.paston.co.uk	£17.63	£10.58/month	Norwich	Web space £58.75 setup + £29.38/month
Pavilion Internet Tel.: 01273 607072	info@pavilion.co.uk www.pavilion.co.uk	£17.63	£14.75/month	Brighton	Web space £58.75 setup + £11.75/month
Pipex Dial (Unipalm) Tel.: 0500 474739	sales@pipex.com www.unipalm.pipex.com	£13.51	£194/year	UK coverage	Free Web space; FTP space
Power Internet Tel.: 01908 503126	info@powernet.co.uk www.powernet.co.uk	£17.63	£14.10/month	Birmingham, Milton Keynes	Free trial offers; free Web space
Rednet Tel.: 01494 513333	sales@rednet.co.uk www.rednet.co.uk	£29.38	£17.63/month	UK coverage	Free Web space; POP3 e-mail standard
Technocom Tel.: 01753 673200	sales@technocom.co.uk www.technocom.co.uk	Free	£17.63/month	London, Maidenhead, Slough	Free Web space; free trials available
Total Connectivity Providers Tel.: 01703 366364	sales@tcp.co.uk www.tcp.co.uk	£8.23	£14.10/month	UK coverage	Web space available; FTP archive
Voss Net Tel.: 01753 737800	info@vossnet.co.uk www.vossnet.co.uk	Free	£11.75/month	London, Slough	7-day free trial offer
Wave Rider Internet Tel.: 01564 795888	info@waverider.co.uk www.waverider.co.uk	£18	£12/month	Birmingham	Free Web space; FTP archive
WorldScope Tel.: 01734 521000	info@worldscope.net www.worldscope.net	£14.69	£11.75/month	UK coverage	Web space available
Zetnet Services Tel.: 01595 696667	info@zetnet.co.uk www.zetnet.co.uk	£25	£6/month	UK coverage	Free Web space; 33.6 Kbps access

Choosing an online service

Online services offer full Internet access together with a range of other information sources not available to non-members. The software is free, fully integrated and usually easy to use: just double-click an icon to install it on your hard disk, then double-click another icon to run the sign-up program and enter your details. You'll then be connected to the service automatically so that your subscription can be logged and you'll receive a user name or number (which will form part of your e-mail address) and a private password. Follow the instructions to enter these into the main software program and you're done.

Choosing an online service is easier than choosing an IAP in several respects. First of all, the list is a lot shorter! More importantly, most online services offer a month's free trial membership – if you don't like it, just cancel before you've run up any charges and try a different one. All the same, there are still a few points worth checking:

- Find out *how* you cancel if you don't like it. It's always easy to sign up, but online services don't make much noise about the cancellation routine!
- Make sure your local POP matches or exceeds the speed of your modem.
- Have your credit card handy when you run the software that signs you up to the service. Although you won't pay for the first month, you won't be able to connect without it.
- Don't forget the user name or password you're assigned when you run the connection software – write them clearly on a piece of paper straight away.

The following is a list of the online services available. If you don't have the free software required to subscribe, give them a call and ask for it. Each of these services has other subscription schemes that might suit you better and (with the exception of MSN) offers free Web space to its members.

Company	E-mail and WWW site	Setup charge	Monthly charge	Online charges	POPs
America Online (AOL) Tel.: 0800 279 1234	queryuk@aol.com www.aol.com	Free	£5.95	First 5 hours per month free; £1.85/hour thereafter	UK coverage
CIX Tel.: 0181 2969666	sales@compulink.co.uk www.compulink.co.uk	£11.75	£17.63 (25 hours maximum)		UK coverage
CompuServe Information Service Tel.: 0800 289378	70006.101@compuserve.com www.compuserve.com	Free	$9.95 (roughly £6.50 depending on exchange rate)	First 5 hours per month free; £1.85/hour thereafter	UK coverage
Europe Online Tel.: 0800 106610	www.europeonline.com	Free	£3.95	First 3 hours free; £1.85/hour thereafter	All major UK cities
Microsoft Network (MSN)* Tel.: 0345 002000	www.msn.com	Free	£14.95	None	UK coverage
UK Online Tel.: 01749 333333	sales@ukonline.co.uk www.ukonline.co.uk	Free	£14.99	None	UK coverage

* MSN software is included with Windows 95

UK software companies

Some of the companies in the following list have been singled out earlier in the book as producers of high-quality and/or very popular software titles in particular areas of computing. In these cases, the products named are listed with the company's details for easy reference. This shouldn't be taken as an implication that these are the only products produced by that company, nor that they're the only *good* products produced by that company!

Company	Telephone	Products
Adobe Systems	0181 606 4000	Acrobat, Premiere, PhotoDeluxe
Aldus	0131 451 6888	
Andromeda Interactive	01235 529595	William Shakespeare: The Complete Works
Attica Cybernetics	01865 200892	
Autodesk	01483 303322	Autodesk Animator Studio
Avalon	01624 627227	
Borland	01734 320022	Paradox
Broderbund	01753 620909	Print Shop Deluxe, Living Books series
Brooklyn North Software Works	0500 284177	HTML Assistant Pro 2
Central Point International	01628 788580	
Claris	0181 756 0101	ClarisWorks, FileMaker Pro
Corel	0800 581028	CorelDRAW, Quattro Pro, PerfectWorks

Company	Telephone	Products
Delrina	0181 207 7033	Fax and communications software
Digital Workshop	01295 258335	Illuminatus
Dorling Kindersley	0171 753 3488	Children's CD-ROM titles
Electronic Arts	01753 549442	3D Atlas, The Farm, The Airport
Gold Disk	01753 832383	Astound
Gremlin Games	0114 275 3423	
GSP	01480 496789	DesignWorks, PressWorks, MONEYmatters
Guildsoft	01752 895100	
Health Perfect	0181 200 8897	Dr Schueller's Medical Advisor
IBM Software Enquiries	01329 242728	OS/2
Interplay	01235 821666	
Intuit	0181 990 5500	Quicken Deluxe, QuickBooks
Lotus Development	01784 455455	Lotus SmartSuite, Approach, WordPro, 1-2-3
Macromedia	0181 358 5857	Authorware
Micrografx	0800 626009	
MicroProse	01454 329510	
Microsoft	01734 270001	Windows, Word, Excel, Encarta, Office, Works
Mirage	01260 299909	
MoneyBox Software	01392 429424	
Ocean	0161 839 0999	
Pegasus Software	01536 495000	
Psygnosis	0151 282 3000	
Quark Systems	01483 454397	Quark Xpress
Quarterdeck UK	01245 494940	Cleansweep, QEMM
Sage	0191 255 3000	Instant Accounting
S&S International	01296 318700	Dr Solomon's Anti-Virus Toolkit
Serif	0800 924925	PagePlus, DrawPlus, PhotoPlus, Publishing Suite
Softkey	0181 789 2000	
SoftQuad	0181 236 1001	
Starfish Software	0181 875 4455	Sidekick, Dashboard
Symantec	01628 592222	Norton Tools, PC Desktop
TopLevel Computing	01453 753944	
Wang UK	0181 568 9200	

UK hardware companies

Company	Telephone	Products
AMD	01256 603121	Processors
Apricot Computers	0121 717 7171	PCs
Brother UK	0161 330 6531	Printers
Compaq	0181 332 3888	PCs, Notebook PCs
Conner	01294 315333	Hard drives
Creative Labs	01734 344322	Soundcards, Multimedia peripherals

Cyrix	0800 137305	Processors
Diamond Multimedia	01753 501400	Display adapters, Multimedia peripherals
Epson UK	01442 227478	Printers
Fujitsu	0181 573 4444	Hard drives, Printers, Scanners
Hayes	01252 775533	Modems
Hercules	01635 861122	Display adapters
Hewlett-Packard	01344 369369	Printers
Hitachi	0181 849 2087	CD-ROM drives, Monitors
IBM	0345 500900	PCs, Notebook PCs
Iiyama	01438 745482	Monitors
Intel	01793 431144	Processors
Iomega	0800 898563	Archive and backup drives
IPC Corp UK	01282 618866	PCs, Notebook PCs, Peripherals
JVC	0181 896 6000	CD-ROM drives
Kodak	01442 61122	Scanners, Digital cameras
Kyocera Electronics UK	01734 311500	Printers
Lexmark International	01628 488200	Printers
Logitech	01344 891313	Mice, Trackballs, Scanners
Matrox	01793 614002	Display adapters
Microsoft	01734 271000	Mice, Trackballs, Keyboards
Microvitec	01274 390011	Monitors
Mitsumi	01276 29029	CD-ROM drives
NEC Computer Products	0181 993 8111	PCs, CD-ROM drives
Nikon	0181 541 4440	Scanners
Olivetti	0800 447799	PCs, Notebook PCs, Printers
Orchid Europe	01256 844899	Display adapters
Packard Bell	0800 314314	PCs
Panasonic	01344 853508	Monitors, Printers, CD-ROM drives
Pioneer	01753 789731	CD-ROM drives
Plasmon Data	01763 262963	Recordable CD drives
Primax	01235 536374	Scanners
Psion	0171 258 7376	Palmtop computers
Roland UK	01792 702701	Soundcards, MIDI hardware
Seagate	01628 474532	Hard drives
Sony UK	0181 784 1144	CD-ROM drives, Monitors
Star Micronics	01494 471111	Printers
Toshiba	01932 785666	CD-ROM drives, Printers, Notebook PCs
Trust Peripherals	01376 500770	Scanners, Modems, Multimedia peripherals
US Robotics	01734 228200	Modems
VideoLogic	01923 271300	Display adapters
Visioneer	0181 358 5850	Scanners
Western Digital UK	01372 360055	Hard drives

UK retailers

Company	Telephone	Products
Byte Direct	0121 766 2565	PCs/Peripherals
Choice Peripherals	01909 530 242	Peripherals/Components/Software
Dabs Direct	0800 558866	PCs/Peripherals/Software/Components/Consumables
Dan Technology	0181 830 1100	PCs
Dart Computers	01794 511505	PCs
Dell	0500 500111	PCs
Elonex	0181 452 6666	PCs, Notebook PCs
Fox Computers	01621 744500	PCs/Peripherals/Components
Gateway 2000	0800 342000	PCs, Notebook PCs
Memory Bank	0181 956 7000	Memory/Peripherals/Software/Components
Mesh Computers	0181 452 1111	PCs
MrPC	01282 777888	PCs/Peripherals/Software
Multimedia Direct	01635 873000	Multimedia hardware
Novatech	0800 777500	PCs/Peripherals/Software/Consumables
PC World	0990 464464	PCs/Peripherals/Software/Consumables
Pico Direct	01483 202022	Notebook PCs/Notebook peripherals
Plug & Play Technology	0181 341 3336	PC Cards/Notebook peripherals
Roldec	01902 456464	Peripherals/Components
Silica Systems	0181 309 1111	PCs/Peripherals/Software
Simply Computers	0181 498 2130	PCs/Peripherals/Components
SMC Computers	01753 550333	PCs/Peripherals/Components
Software Warehouse	01675 466467	Software/Peripherals/Components/Consumables
Stak Trading	01788 577497	PCs/Peripherals/Components
Taurus Component Shop	01978 312372	Components/Peripherals
Tech Direct	0181 286 2222	Notebook PCs/Printers/Peripherals/Consumables
Technomatic	0181 205 9558	PCs/Peripherals/Software/Components
Time Computer Systems	01282 777111	PCs
Tiny Computers	01293 821333	PCs
Viglen	0181 759 7000	PCs, Notebook PCs
Watford Electronics	01582 745555	PCs/Software/Peripherals/Components

UK general services

Data transfer, conversion, duplication

A. L. Downloading Services	0181 994 5471
Mapej	01691 778659

Data recovery (disk failure, corruption, viruses)

Authentic Data Recovery	0800 581263
Ontrack Data Recovery	0800 243996
Vogon International	01734 890042

PC Rental

MC Rentals	01952 604411
Micro-Rent	0171 700 4848
Skylake Rentals	0800 373118

PC security/anti-theft

Datamark Security	01494 434757
Secure PC	0171 610 3646

PC memory

AW Computer Memory Bargains	01382 643739
Click	0800 666500
Mem Com	0161 427 2222
Mr Memory	01483 799410
Offtek	0121 722 3993
Rightnight	0181 668 4199

Printer Consumables

Cartridge Express	01765 690790
Inkwell Direct	01344 843444
Jetica	0800 614153
Laser Printer Technologies	01482 656630
Mannink	01462 455651
Owl Associates	01543 250377
Squire International	0181 886 3078
Themis	01883 3330333
Vectorjet	01763 273115

Floppy disks

Owl Associates	01543 250377
Product Trade & Services	0800 136502
Squire International	0181 886 3078

Specialist suppliers

BBD Dust Covers (Computer dust covers)	01257 425839
C&T (Storage hardware)	0171 637 1767
Capital Litho (Personalized mouse mats)	01386 40321
Linefeed (CD writers and media)	0171 474 1765
MJ Communications (Modems)	07000 663367
Monitor Man (Monitors)	01453 885599
Semaphore Systems (Components)	0171 625 7744
The Keyboard Company (Keyboards)	07000 102105
The Monitor Shop (Monitors)	01159 110366

Shareware

AWH Computer Services	01563 850645
Demon Shareware	01325 301849
Ferrari Software	01843 865083
Hornesoft PD	01142 967825
Islander Software	0345 660429
MicroWorld	01425 610699
Telescan	01253 829292

Bulletin board services (premium rate charges apply)

BBS Elite	0891 518299
Café Net	0891 615010
Komputer Knowledge	0891 515066
Mainline BBS	0891 615795
MegaDownLoad	0891 516126
Microland Bulletin Board	0891 990505
Strangeways BBS	0891 408040

Index

Becoming a Prentice Hall Author

Getting published with Prentice Hall

1. Can I do it?

It is easy to think of the publishing process as a series of hurdles designed to weed out would-be authors. That may be true of some publishing houses, but not Prentice Hall.

- We do all we can to encourage new talent.
- We welcome unsolicited manuscripts.
- We carefully examine every proposal we receive, and we always write back to let the authors know what we think of it.

Although many of our authors have professional or educational experience, we look first for a passion for computing. Some of our most successful books are written by first-time authors. If you have built up expertise in any computing-related topic, please get in touch. You'll be surprised how easy it is to get through.

2. Is Prentice Hall a successful company?

Prentice Hall is a highly respected brand in technical and scientific publishing, a status reflected in our relationships with the book trade and various professional bodies. Our reputation has been made with classic computing titles such as Kernighan and Titchie's *The C Programming Language* (over two million copies sold) and Bertrand Meyer's ground-breaking *Object Oriented Software Construction.*

We're part of Simon & Schuster, a $2 billion dollar global publishing company. Simon & Schuster is host to Macmillan Computer Publishing, home of renowned computer imprints such as Sams, Que, Waite Group Press, Ziff-Davis Publishing, Hayden and New Riders Press (NRP). Simon & Schuster is itself owned by Viacom Inc, one of the world's largest entertainment and publishing companies. Viacom owns film and tv studios (Paramount Pictures), world-wide cable networks (MTV, Nickelodeon) and retail outlets (Blockbuster Video).

3. What sort of books does prentice Hall publish?

The computing revolution in the office and home has prompted a massive and diverse market for computer books. That diversity is reflected in our approach. We are happy to consider book proposals on absolutely any computing topic.

Essentially, Prentice Hall publishes books for anyone whose job or hobby connects them to a computer. We are already familiar with your intended readership, whether your book is written for professionals, students, enthusiasts or beginners. Our progressive editorial policy encourages new authors and gives us the flexibility required in a rapidly changing technological environment. However, we do have a 'books wanted' list – contact the editorial department for the latest copy.

4. What are the rewards of writing a book?

Prentice Hall royalty rates are among the most competitive in the industry, and many of our authors earn considerable sums through royalties. Payments are calculated along industry-standard guidelines, i.e., the author receives a percentage of the publisher's net sales revenue. We always offer preferential royalty rates for senior figures within the computing industry, or for books on hot topics written by experts. For the right book at the right time, the financial reward to the author can be extremely generous. This is especially true of books aimed at professional software developers.

If you are a computer professional or an academic, your livelihood depends upon your professional reputation. Successful Prentice Hall authors enjoy a constant stream of business and employment opportunities as a direct result of being published. A book works like a business card, advertising the author's talent across a vast newtork of potential contacts.

5. How do I know my ideas are good enough to publish?

In assessing the market-readiness of book proposals or finished manuscripts, Prentice Hall editors draw upon a high database of technical advisors. All of our reviewers are senior figures in modern computing, and their role is to offer free advice to potential authors, highlighting both the strengths and weaknesses of proposals and manuscripts. The aim of the review process is to add value to your ideas, rather than just approving or rejecting them.

We understand that errors are inevitable when writing books, but as a Prentice Hall author you need not worry about the quality of your finished work. Many of our authors have not written a book before, so we are there to help – scrutinise all our manuscripts for grammatical accuracy and style.

6. How much control would I have over my book?

We understand that a book is a highly personal statement from the author, so we invite your participation at all stages of the publishing process, from the cover design through to the final marketing plans. A Prentice Hall book is a co-operative venture between author and publisher.

7. Will I get any help with the technical aspects of book production?

Our highly professional staff will ensure that the book you envisaged is the book that makes it to the shelves. Once you hand over your manuscript to us, we will take care of all the technical details of printing and binding. Beyond the advice and guidance from your own editor, our 64-page *Author Guide* is there to help you shape your manuscript into a first-class book. Our large and efficient production department is among the quickest in the industry. We are experts at turning raw manuscripts into polished books, irrespective of the technical complexity of your work. Technical queries can be answered by your production contact, assigned, where relevant, to you at contract stage. Our production staff fully understand the individual requirements of every project, and will work with you to produce a manuscript format that best complements your skills – hard copy manuscripts, electronic files or camera-ready copy.

8. How quickly can you turn my manuscript into a book?

The production department at Prentice Hall is widely acknowledged to be among the quickest in the industry. Our turnaround times vary according to the nature of the manuscript supplied to us, but the average is about four months for camera-ready copy, five for electronic file manuscript. For time-sensitive topics, we can occasionally turn out books in under twelve weeks!

9. Where would my book be sold?

Prentice Hall has one of the largest sales forces of any technical publisher. Our highly experienced sales staff have developed firm business partnerships with all the major retail bookstores in Europe, America, Asia, the Middle East and South Africa, ensuring that your book receives maximum retail exposure. Prentice Hall's marketing department is responsible for ensuring the widest possible review coverage in magazines and journals – vital to the sales of computing books.

Our books are usually present at major trade shows and exhibitions, either on our own stands or those belonging to major retail bookshops. Our presence at trade shows ensures that your work can be inspected by the most senior figures within any given field of computing. We also have a very successful corporate and institutional sales team, dedicated to selling our books into large companies, user groups, book clubs, training seminars and professional bodies.

Local language translations can provide not only a significant boost to an author's royalty income, but also will alloy your research/findings to reach a wider audience, thus furthering your professional prespects. To maintain both the author's and Prentice Hall's reputation, we license foreign-language deals only with publishing houses of the highest repute.

10. I don't have time to write a book!

To enjoy all the advantages of being a published author, it is not always necessary for you to write an entire book. Prentice Hall welcomes books written my multiple authors. If you feel that your skills lie in a very specific area of computing, or that you do not have the time to write an entire book, please get in touch regardless. Prentice Hall may have a book in progress that would benefit from your ideas.

You may know individuals or teams in your field who could act as co-author(s). If not, Prentice Hall can probably put you in touch with the right people. Royalties for shared-author books are distributed according to respective participation.

11. Could my company benefit?

Many Prentice Hall authors use their book to lever their commercial interests, and we like to do all we can to help. If a well-written book is an excellent marketing tool for an author, then it can also be an excellent marketing tool for the author's company. A book is its own highly focused marketing channel, a respected medium that takes your company name to all the right people. Previous examples of marketing opportunities with our books include:

- free advertising in the back pages
- packaging in suitable corporate livery (book covers, flyers, etc.)
- mounting software demos in the back page on disk or CDROM.

Although Prentice Hall has to keep its publications free of undue corporate or institutional bias, in general the options for cross-marketing are varied and completely open to discussion.

12. I have an idea for a book. What next?

We invite you to submit a book proposal. We need proposals to be formatted in a specific way, so if you have not received our guidelines, please contact the Acquisition Editor at this address:

Jason Dunne
Professional and Consumer Computing
Prentice Hall
Campus 400, Maylands Avenue
Hemel Hempstead, Herts.
HP2 7EZ
England

Tel: +44 (0)1442 882246
Fax: +44 (0)1442 252544

e-mail: jason_dunne@prenhall.co.uk